THE PRAIRIE WEST TO 1905

A Canadian Sourcebook

THE PRAIRIE WEST TO 1905

A Canadian Sourcebook

General Editor
LEWIS G. THOMAS

Contributing Editors
DAVID H. BREEN
JOHN A. EAGLE
JOHN E. FOSTER
RODERICK C. MACLEOD
LEWIS H. THOMAS

647161

Toronto
OXFORD UNIVERSITY PRESS
1975

SETTLEMENT AND THE INDIAN

7. Testimony of the Rt Rev. David Anderson before the
British Parliamentary Select Committee on the Hudson's
Bay Company, 1857   30

*The Hudson's Bay Company's Officers and Servants during the
Period of Monopoly, 1820-70*   32

8. Testimony of Sir George Simpson before the British
Parliamentary Select Committee on the Hudson's Bay
Company, 1857   32
9. Testimony of Sir Edward Ellice before the British
Parliamentary Select Committee on the Hudson's Bay
Company, 1857   34
10. Excerpt from a letter from Rev. William Cockran to the
Secretaries of the Church Missionary Society, 1833   35

The Mixed-Bloods and the Red River Settlement   37

GENERAL STATEMENTS OF BRITISH OBSERVERS
11. Testimony of Dr John Rae before the British Parliamentary
Select Committee on the Hudson's Bay Company, 1857   38
12. Testimony of the Rt Rev. David Anderson before the
Parliamentary Select Committee on the Hudson's Bay
Company, 1857   38
13. Testimony of Lieut-Col. Caldwell before the British
Parliamentary Select Committee on the Hudson's Bay
Company, 1857   40
14. Testimony of Sir George Simpson before the British
Parliamentary Select Committee on the Hudson's Bay
Company, 1857   41
15. A Statistical Account of Red River Colony, 1856   43

THE MÉTIS IN RED RIVER: THEIR WAY OF LIFE
16. The Buffalo Hunt from Alexander Ross, *The Red River
Settlement*   47

A COUNTRY-BORN FAMILY
17. Excerpts from the correspondence of retired Chief Factor
James Sutherland   52

'WESTERN ALIENATION'?
18. Excerpt from a letter from Joseph Cook to the Lay Secretary
of the Church Missionary Society, 1846   54
19. Excerpt from a letter from Rev. W. Cockran to Rev. R.
Davies, C.M.S., 1847   56
20. Letter from James Sinclair *et al* to Alexander Christie, 1845   56
21. Letter from Alexander Christie to James Sinclair *et al*, 1845   58

22. Petition from the Inhabitants and Natives of the Red River
    Settlement to the Legislative Assembly of the Province of
    Canada   59

RIEL AND HIS SUPPORTERS; A VESTED-INTEREST GROUP OR
LEADERS OF A UNITED COMMUNITY?
23. Minutes of a Meeting of the Governor and Council of
    Assiniboia, 1869   62
24. Excerpt from a Report from Donald Smith to the Hon.
    Joseph Howe, 1870   64
25. The Bill of Rights, 1 December 1869 and the List of Rights,
    3 February 1870   66
GUIDE TO FURTHER READING   69

II Government and Politics in Manitoba and the North West Territories: LEWIS H. THOMAS

II *Government and Politics in Manitoba and the North
    West Territories:* LEWIS H. THOMAS   73

Introduction   73

*Inauguration of Government for the North West Territories and
Provincial Government for Manitoba, 1869-70*   74

26. The Temporary Government Act, 1869   76
27. The Manitoba Act, 1870   77
28. Extracts from the Parliamentary Debate on the Manitoba
    Act   79
29. Lieut.-Governor Archibald Reports to the Secretary of State
    for the Provinces, 1870   81
30. Lieut.- Governor's Speech from the Throne, 1871   81

Indian Affairs   83

31. Treaty Number One   83
32. The Indian Act, 1876   85
33. The Parliamentary Debate on the Indian Act, 1876   87

Federal Natural-Resources Legislation   88

34. The 'Dominion Lands' Act, 1872   89

The North West Territories Acts, 1875 and 1877   91

35. The North West Territories Act, 1875   91
36. Parliamentary Debate on the North West Territories Act,
    1875   93
37. The North West Territories Amendment Act, 1877   94
38. Senate Amendments Concurred In   94

Federal-Provincial Relations and the 'Better Terms' Agitation in Manitoba   95

39. Revision of the Provincial Subsidy, 1875   95
40. Manitoba and Northwest Farmers' Union Petition of Rights   96
41. Reforms Proposed by the Legislative Assembly   97
42. The Response of the Federal Government   98

The Saskatchewan Rebellion, 1885   100

43. The Deputy Minister of the Interior and Half-Breed Complaints   101
44. The North West Council and Half-Breed Complaints   101
45. Petition of Rights, 1884   102

The North West Council Challenges Federal Policies, 1885   103

46. Resolutions Passed in the 1885 Session   104

Constitutional Development in the North West Territories   107

47. Creation of the Legislative Assembly (Northwest Territories Amendment Act, 1888)   107
48. Debate on the Amendment   108
49. Responsible Government for the Territories (Northwest Territories Act, 1897)   109
50. Clifford Sifton on Responsible Government   109

Political Issues in Manitoba   110

51. The Burden of the National Policy as seen by the Manitoba Legislature   111
52. Abolition of French-language Rights in Manitoba, 1890   111
53. The Manitoba Schools Dispute: Debate on the Legislation, 1890   112
54. The Laurier-Greenway Compromise   114

Minority Rights in the North West Territories   115

55. Resolution of the Legislative Assembly, 1892   116
56. Debate on the Resolution   116
57. Haultain and Lacombe on Separate Schools   117
58. The School Ordinance of 1892   118
59. Debate on the School Ordinance Amendments   119

In Defence of the Grain Growers   120

60. The Patrons of Industry; Speech of the Rev. J. M. Douglas, Assiniboia, 1895   120
61. The Territorial Grain Growers' Association; Report of Deputy Commissioner   122

62. Formation of the Manitoba Grain Growers' Association   122

Sifton's Immigration Policy   123

63. East European Immigration   124

The Creation of Alberta and Saskatchewan   126

64. Haultain to Sifton, 1901   126
65. Haultain's Address to his Constituents, 1902   127
66. Laurier's Speech on the Autonomy Bills, 1905   128
67. The Alberta Act   129
GUIDE TO FURTHER READING   130

III   The Problem of Law and Order in the Canadian West, 1870-1905: RODERICK C. MACLEOD   132

Introduction   132

The Legislative Framework

68. The Canada Jurisdiction Act, 1803   139
69. Order in Council concerning the Administration of Justice in the North West Territories, 1870   141
70. Selections from the Report of Captain W. F. Butler, 1871   142
71. Selections from the Report of Lieut.-Col. P. Robertson-Ross, 1873   147
72. The Mounted Police Act, 1873   150
73. Amendments to the Mounted Police Act, 1874   157
74. Memorandum concerning the Transfer of Policing from the Federal Government to the North West Territories, 1901   159
75. Memorandum concerning the Agreements with the Provinces of Alberta and Saskatchewan for the Continued Services of the Mounted Police, 1906   161

The Judicial System in Action

76. The Queen vs. O'Kell, 1887   162
77. The Queen vs. Brown, 1893   164
78. The Queen vs. Brewster, 1896   168
79. The Queen vs. Charcoal, 1897   171
80. Some Typical Reports of Cases tried by Mounted Police Officers, 1894   175

The Control of Crime and Disorder

81. A Typical Mounted Police Weekly Report, Battleford, 1888   177
82. A Typical Mounted Police Monthly Report, Lethbridge, 1894   179

83. A Cattle-Rustling Case, Estevan, 1899 — 181
84. The Difficulties of Enforcing Prohibition, Prince Albert, 1887 — 185
85. A Mounted Police View on the Enforcement of Public Morality, Lethbridge, 1894 — 187
86. Murder, Edmonton, 1892 — 187
87. The Edmonton Land Office Disturbances, 1892 — 191

Special Problems: Native Peoples, Immigrants, and Labour

88. Keeping an Eye on the Indians, Battleford, 1888 — 195
89. Mounted Police Views on Indian Administration, 1889 — 196
90. Stamping out the Sun Dance, 1891 — 198
91. Welfare Work with Indians and Mixed-bloods, 1889 — 199
92. Protecting the Immigrant: German Settlers at Qu'Appelle, 1894 — 201
93. Protecting the Immigrant: Chinese at Calgary, 1892 — 202
94. Labour and the Police: Railway Construction, 1897 — 207
95. Labour and the Police: Coal Miners, 1905 — 212
GUIDE TO FURTHER READING — 215

IV *The Ranching Frontier in Canada, 1875-1905:*
DAVID H BREEN — 217

Introduction — 217

The Land

96. A Grazing Country *Par Excellence* — 228

The Cattle Industry

THE CATTLE COMPANIES AND THE 'BEEF BONANZA'
97. The Arithmetic of Vast Profit — 230
98. Senator Cochrane's Proposal — 234
99. The Frantic Rush for Grazing Leases — 235
100. Political Preferment an Asset — 236
101. The Environment of Urgency and Expectation — 237
THE STOCKMEN'S ASSOCIATIONS
102. A New Stock Association — 238
103. Constitution of the Canadian Northwest Territories Stock Association — 240
104. The Association as the Political Arm of the Cattlemen — 243
105. The Association as the Regional Administrator of the Cattle Industry — 244
PROBLEMS OF COLLECTIVE CONCERN
106. Encroachment of American Stockmen — 247

107. Mavericks   248
108. Sheepmen   249

The Range-Cattle Industry and the North West Mounted Police

109. Patrols and Outposts   251
110. Indians Killing Cattle   251
111. Cattle Theft   252
112. Prairie Fires   253
113. Boundary Patrol   254
114. A Testimonial from the Industry   256

Semi-Arid Lands: The Struggle for Control

THE CATTLEMEN
115. Harassment from Would-be Settlers   257
116. Squatters on the Leaseholds   258
117. The Threat of Violence   260
118. Range War Imminent   261

THE SETTLERS
119. Division in the Foothills   262
120. Meeting at John Glenn's   263
121. Confrontation in the Bow Valley   266
122. The Range Herd as a Protective Shield   267

THE GOVERNMENT
123. The Prime Minister's Irritation   269
124. An Influential Voice within the Department of the nterior   270
125. Parliamentary Debate, 1891   271
126. The Rule of Law   274
127. Guardians of the Peace   275

THE LEASE SYSTEM
128. Canada. Dominion Lands Legislation   276
129. The Original Lease Contract   276
130. Privy Council Report, 1892   278
131. Circular: Department of the Interior   279
132. Closed Leases Essential   280
133. Report on the Grazing Question, 1903   281
134. Leases to Curb Undesirable Settlement   283

STOCK-WATERING RESERVATIONS
135. Privy Council Report, 1886   284
136. Notice to Vacate   285
137. Stock-Watering and Shelter Reservations   286
138. An Opposing View   288
139. A Settler's Concern   291
140. The Stockmen's Association   292

A GRAZING OR A FARMING REGION
141. A Voice for Open and Unrestricted Settlement   294
142. A Cattleman's View   294
143. The Last Word   295

The Range-Cattle Industry in Decline

144. The Cattle Range Confined   296
145. Western Stock Growers' Association, Resolution, 1903   296
146. Progress of Southwestern Settlement during 1905:
      Immigration Officer's Report   297
147. Sale of the Cochrane Ranche, 1906   298

The Ranch Establishment and the Social Milieu

148. Caste and Class in the Foothills   298
149. The Hunt Club   300
150. A Lady's Life on a Ranche   301
151. A Visit to the Cochrane Ranche, 1902   303
A GUIDE TO FURTHER READING   305

V   *The Development of Transportation and
     Communications, 1870-1905:* JOHN A. EAGLE   308

Introduction   308

Transportation

152. York Boat   316
153. Red River Cart   317
154. Deficiencies of Prairie Trails   317
155. Steamboats on the Red River   319
156. The Start of Steamboat Navigation on the North
      Saskatchewan River   320
157. Steamboats on the North Saskatchewan River   321
158. The Pleasures of Steamboat Travel   321
159. A Government Report on the Dawson Route   322
160. A Contemporary Assessment of the Dawson Route   325
161. Diversion of Immigrants to the American West   326
162. Immigration via the Dawson Route   326
163. Manitoba's First Railway: the Pembina Branch   328
164. First Shipment of Wheat by Rail from Manitoba   329
165. A Manitoba Prediction on the Impact of Railways   329
166. Canadian Pacific Railway Charter   330
167. The Prime Minister Defends the CPR Charter   333
168. The Leader of the Opposition Condemns the CPR Charter   334
169. The CPR Adopts the Southern Route   336

170. The Effects of the Southern Route on Prairie Settlement   337
171. Manitoba asks Ottawa to Terminate the CPR Monopoly   338
172. Farmer Support for the Hudson Bay Railway Project   340
173. Federal Aid for the Calgary and Edmonton Railway   342
174. A Calgary View of the Calgary and Edmonton Railway   343
175. An Edmonton View of the Calgary and Edmonton Railway   343
176. A Prairie Liberal Criticizes the Crow's Nest Pass Agreement   344
177. The Early Development of the Canadian Northern Railway   346
178. The Canadian Northern Railway Reaches Edmonton   349
179. The Prime Minister Endorses the Grand Trunk Pacific
     Project   350
180. A Prairie Liberal Defends the Grand Trunk Pacific Project   351

Communications

181. Postal Service in Manitoba in 1870   352
182. Telegraph Connection Between Manitoba and Eastern
     Canada   354
183. Surveying the Route of the Dominion Telegraph   354
184. The Construction of the Dominion Telegraph   355
185. The Bell Telephone Company in Manitoba   358
GUIDE TO FURTHER READING   358

Maps

The Pattern of Land Settlement in the West   4
The Prairie West, 1835   18
The Red River Settlement in 1835   39
Manitoba and the Provisional Districts
     of the North West Territories, 1885   75
The Canadian Ranching Frontier, 1885   219
The Cattle Companies, 1884   233
Manitoba's Connections with Canada
     and the United States, 1872   327
The Prairie West, 1905   348

Preface

The process of settlement dominated the development of the Canadian prairie west in the half century that followed the entry of the region into confederation. By 1921 most of its land with any agricultural potential in terms of the available technology had been taken up. Much that has been written about the prairie west has a close relationship to the history of its settlement but access to the secondary literature, not to mention the source material, is not always easy. The purpose of this volume is to present material for an examination of five aspects of the settlement process, and thus to direct attention to the nature of prairie society as it existed at the time of confederation, to the kind of political institutions that were established in the region, to the conception of society embodied in the machinery set up for the maintenance of law and order, to one of the less understood attempts at a solution of the problem of land use, and to the fundamental rôle of communications, especially of railways. The documents themselves are all dated prior to 1905 but the introduction treats the period as far as 1921.

There are other important themes that are treated only incidentally, notably the rôle of the churches, of the educational institutions, and of the press. All played a vital part in the daily life of the settler. Relatively little is said of the ethnic and other groups whose distinctive flavour so enriched the pattern of the prairie mosaic. In terms of political development the prairie west is comparatively well served by the existing literature. The material here is particularly intended to document the part played by government and notably the federal government as the organizer of a society, or at least of a society's framework.

As the volume is primarily intended to serve as a resource for teachers and students, the contributors were not required to follow a set arrangement of the materials in the various sections. The intention is to permit the latter to reflect differences in teaching styles.

The assistance of the Public Archives of Canada, the Glenbow-Alberta Institute, and the Oxford University Press, and especially of Ms. Tilly Crawley, and of the never failing Mrs. Beryl Steel and her associates in the Department of History at the University of Alberta, is most warmly and gratefully acknowledged.

L.G.T.

Introduction

Lewis G. Thomas

The process of its settlement determined the shape of the development of Canada's prairie west. It also profoundly affected its relationship to the federal structure. What was done to what are now the three provinces of Manitoba, Saskatchewan, and Alberta was an integral part of national policy. The purpose of this policy was to create a new society between the Great Lakes and the Rockies that reflected and supported the values that central Canada believed itself to exemplify—the values of a peaceful, ordered, and law-abiding community based upon the controlled exploitation of the region's reputedly rich resources. Though this ideal society was visualized as primarily agricultural, the visionaries of Ottawa were by no means blind to the potentialities of mine and forest or even to the possibility of industrial development from the population base provided by agricultural settlement.

These values were seen as British values, values not transformed by their sea passage but rather given an opportunity to develop to a fuller and more perfect expression in the fertile and abundant lands of British North America. Though this conception might present difficulties to the province of Quebec, these were by no means insuperable. The same values were shared by the substantial English-speaking population of that province, as the interest of Montreal and the Eastern Townships in cattle ranching was soon to attest. Among the French-speaking there were those, from the officers recruited to the North West Mounted Police to Wilfrid Laurier, who held themselves attached to those values as firmly as anyone to whom English was the first language. Though the federal government was slow to grasp the significance of the fact that in the prairie region at the time of its transfer from the Hudson's Bay Company the majority of the population of European descent, and its most widely dispersed element, was French-speaking and Roman Catholic, the concessions of the Manitoba Act of 1870 and the North West Territories Acts of 1875 and 1877 recognized the possibility of a new Quebec in the west.

The determination that British and Canadian values should prevail in the new society was supported by what central Canada saw, or thought it saw, when it looked to the south, and even more when it looked to the southwest. To the influential majority the American tradition of violence seemed to move westward with the American frontier. Civil war, disorder, and disregard of law were its products. Canada's nervous preoccupation with the American threat was justified by evidence that the American frontier was thrusting northward and that the armies of the United States might follow Fenian agents, Fort Benton whiskey traders, and American Indians over the border into British territory. Settlers from the United States were not specifically discouraged, but Americans were viewed by the Mounted Police with the same suspicious eyes that John A. Macdonald's cabinets turned upon the intrusion of American capital into schemes for the Pacific railway. Though fashions were to change as the pace of settlement quickened, and a new emphasis was to be given to the community of the North American heritage and to the essential unity of the English-speaking peoples, there remained a deep unease at the evidence of the economic and cultural penetration of the prairie west by the dangerously attractive and highly persuasive values of the great republic to the south.

The first prerequisite for the kind of society envisioned for the prairie west by the early federal administration was the establishment of a machinery of local government and a means of enforcing law and order. This was the intention that lay behind the Manitoba Act of 1870, the North West Territories Act of 1875, and the Act of 1873 'Respecting the Administration of Justice, and for the Establishment of a Police Force in the North-West Territories'.[1] Perhaps provincial status for Manitoba was seen as premature, forced upon a reluctant government by the resistance that gathered around Louis Riel. In any case Manitoba's boundaries were rigorously constricted and control over its public lands and resources was withheld. The intention of central Canada may be even more clearly discerned in the act of 1869 for 'the temporary government of Rupert's Land and the North-Western Territory when united with Canada.[2] Though this measure was recognized as a stopgap and though Macdonald appreciated the ultimate inevitability of some form of representative government, the act provided only for an appointed lieutenant-governor and an appointed council with powers defined by the federal government. The relationship of the prairie west to the federal government was to be that of a colony.[3] Federal intentions were equally explicit in the act establishing the North West Mounted Police. This body shared with other colonial police forces a common inspiration in the Royal Irish Constabulary, which seemed to have dealt so effectively with problems of law and order in a troubled Ireland. Similarly the Department of the Interior, organized in 1873 and entrusted with the administration of the daily affairs of the North West Territories, was sufficiently imbued with the concepts of direct and centralized control to make inevitable the pre-Freudian Freudian slip of its first minister, who referred to his new position as that of 'Secretary for the Colonies'.[4]

The conception of the prairie west as a colony, to be administered directly by the central government in the interests of the dominion as a whole, interests that were often to be seen by the prairie west and other Canadian regions as synonymous with those of central Canada, is manifested throughout the relationship between the federal government and the governments of Manitoba and the Territories. It was by no means abandoned with the establishment of provincial autonomy for Saskatchewan and Alberta in 1905. It was indeed not thought necessary until 1930 that the new provinces, any more than their older sister, should control their public lands and resources and this second-class status generated the western resentment that found expression in 1911 in a book by A. Bramley-Moore, a member of the Alberta Legislature, *Canada and her colonies, or home rule for Alberta*.

The public lands and other natural resources safely secured to federal control, the Canadian government could turn to their disposition to intending settlers. The heritage was impressive, for the transfer of 1870 placed under direct federal administration, 'lands five times the area of the original Dominion'.[5] The necessary surveys had begun even before the transfer and were pressed forward with remarkable speed and efficiency so that by 1880 meridians had been established from Winnipeg to the Rockies and base lines from the international boundary to the North Saskatchewan. The principal meridian was established just west of Winnipeg and the boundary, the 49th parallel, provided the first base line. A system of numbered sections of six hundred and forty acres each, townships of thirty-six sections numbered north from the boundary, and ranges, thirty between each initial meridian, provided a simple method of land description. Thus North West Quarter, Section 22, Township 42, Range 3, West of the 3rd Meridian, gave a precise statement of exact location and bounds. The base lines running east and west were four townships, approximately twenty-four miles, apart. Between every two base lines correction lines were established to accommodate the curvature of the earth's surface. These lines jogged where the base lines intersected with the meridian lines on the west side of each block of four townships.

The system was based on practice established in the United States but the circumstances of the Canadian prairie west permitted it to be applied with a much greater degree of consistency. The major innovation, a departure from American practice, was in the establishment of road allowances one and a half chains (ninety-nine feet) wide between all sections. Exceptions were made to accommodate the river lots of the fur-trade period and the desire of mixed bloods to continue that system further west. Later exceptions met such demands as the need for irrigation, but the sectional system, as convenient as it was colourless, was imposed on almost all the surveyed land of the prairie west. Indeed it gave to the prairie landscape its distinctive checkerboard pattern and that predominance of straight lines that proclaims the determination of the prairie man to subdue the forces of nature. Insensitive as it was to natural features, including variations in fertility and local climate, it presented serious obstacles to future change, whether instigated by road engineers, agricultural experts, or urban planners. But through the period of settlement it provided an efficient means of identifying land and, with the Torrens system of land registration, eliminated endless disputes over land rights. The Torrens system, devised in Australia, was adopted in many British colonies and required by law that land titles, and transactions affecting them, should be recorded at a land-titles office. The system was adopted by Manitoba in 1885 and provided for in the Territories by federal legislation of 1886. It is perhaps worth noting

THE PATTERN OF LAND SETTLEMENT IN THE WEST

Township 41	Range 6	R. 5	R. 4	R. 3	R. 2	R. 1
Twp. 40		11th. Base Line				
Twp. 39						
Twp. 38		Correction Line				
Twp. 37						
Twp. 36						
		10th. Base Line				

Principal Meridian

Township 43 Range 4	Base Line					
	31	32	33	34	35	36
	30	29	28	27	26	25
Township 42 Range 4	19	20	21	22	23	24
	18	17	16	15	14	13
	7	8	9	10	11	12
	6	5	4	3	2	1
Township 41 Range 4	Township 41 Range 3					

that a similar system of numbered lots and streets was adopted in many prairie towns and cities.

The grid survey and the Torrens system were simply basic conveniences for the disposal of land to its ultimate owners. To attract settlers and to bring them to their destination was rather more important and much more difficult. From the beginning the Canadian government envisaged a system of free homesteads similar to that of the United States but also rooted in the experience of disposing of the unsettled lands of the older provinces. The Canadian attitude differed from that prevalent in the United States, a difference subtly expressed in the use of the term 'Crown land' rather than 'public land'. The idea of 'squatter sovereignty', of the moral right of the individual to appropriate public land to his own use, gained little support and certainly none among those who moulded the regulations of the Department of the Interior. The disposition of national resources, agricultural land included, was a matter with which authority felt itself properly concerned.

Provision was accordingly made for a variety of land grants, many of great extent. Railways and other transportation projects, settlement companies, and philanthropic organizations were all to be beneficiaries of the central authority's generosity. The most notable was the Canadian Pacific Railway, which received by its charter of 1881 the colossal grant of 25,000,000 acres, though this was a long way from the 50,000,000 provided in the Charter of 1871[7] or the 100,000,000 approved by parliament as late as 1880[8]. In all it is estimated that 32,000,000 acres of western Canadian land were alienated in railway land grants[9] compared with the estimated 150,000,000 acres in the United States.[10] The Hudson's Bay Company with its twentieth share of the land of the 'fertile belt' was estimated to have been allotted somewhere over 7,000,000 acres.[11]

Though the virtually free homestead was the foundation of the system of land use, policy developed under the pressure of interests more powerful than the individual settler. Regulations permitted a considerable variety in the amount of land allotted for agricultural purposes, from the quarter-section homestead to the grazing leases of southern Alberta and the large holdings made available in Manitoba and elsewhere for intending gentlemen farmers. Mineral and timber resources were not forgotten; it is significant that William Pearce, probably the most influential civil servant in the prairie west in the first quarter century of settlement, bore the title of Superintendent of Mines.

These provisions were backed up by a government effort, strongly supported by the press, to publicize the advantages of the prairie west for the prospective settler. Agencies were established in countries like the United Kingdom that were considered desirable sources of immigrants. The agent's major task was to ease the passage of the settler. A massive propaganda program, which extended from substantial books to flimsy leaflets, and which was directed through the press both in Canada and abroad, was supplemented by the encouragement of visits to the prairies by personages as distinguished as the Governor General, Queen Victoria's son-in-law, the Marquis of Athlone. No one was too inconspicuous to be ignored as a potential witness to the western future. A favourite device of land speculators and governments alike was to bring parties of farmers to see for themselves the possibilities of the prairies, in the hope that they would spread the good tidings to their fellows at home. The propaganda effort varied in intensity; it was noticeably stepped up in the period of the late nineties, after Laurier and the Liberals came into office and when the tide of immigration at last began to flow into 'the last best west'. The propaganda was highly effective but its inevitable misrepresentations gave rise to bitter disillusionment among settlers who found that the promised land did not always live up to the expectations its publicists aroused. (See, for example, James Minifie's account of his father's disillusionment.) A healthy skepticism about the promises of press and politicians, especially those of central Canada, quickly became one of the foundations of western xenophobia.

The pattern of prairie settlement was governed by the routes chosen by the railways, the pace of settlement by other factors, notably the supply of intending immigrants, itself the product of external social, political, and economic forces largely beyond the control not merely of the prairie west but of the dominion as a whole. The tide of agricultural settlement ebbed and flowed, but after 1870 it was consistently directed by the availability, or the prospect of availability, of railway services. (As far as there was settlement prior to the railway, it had followed the traditional water routes of fur-trading times.) Thus the decision of 1881 to move the route of the Canadian Pacific southward from that originally planned through the fertile lands of the North Saskatchewan and over the relatively low Yellowhead Pass was of singular importance in terms of prairie development as well as infinitely disappointing to those who had begun to establish themselves in advance of the anticipated railway.

The decision to change the route has never been satisfactorily explained or documented though it appears to have been affected largely by political considerations. The southern route blocked competition by United States railway interests and it asserted the Canadian presence in the prairie and mountain west in a way congenial to the policies of the Macdonald government. It could be justified partly on the ground that settlers were already moving directly west from southern Manitoba and partly by the evidence of John Macoun, a recognized agricultural expert, as to the agricultural possibilities of the southern region, which earlier surveys, such as those of Palliser and Henry Youle Hind, had dismissed as hopelessly arid for intensive cultivation. Time was to prove Macoun's optimism ill-founded, though not before many settlers had paid a high price in human misery for this misjudgement of the relationship between agricultural production, soil fertility, and climatic factors like precipitation cycles and the incidence of late and early frosts.

Settlement in the 1880s thus followed the Canadian Pacific's main line westward across the southern prairies. Regina, Moose Jaw, and Calgary became substantial communities while older settlements like Prince Albert and Edmonton languished. In southern Manitoba the beginnings were made on a network of branch lines acceptable to the farming interest, but not without a bitter struggle involving the province and a variety of railway interests on one side and the Canadian Pacific and the federal government on the other. By the early nineties Manitoba, with boundaries enlarged in 1881 (they were not extended to their present limits until 1912) was, as far as its most attractive agricultural lands were concerned, a settled province, assimilated, more than any other western province was to be, to the cultural image of nineteenth-century Ontario. Winnipeg, in 1891 by far the largest urban centre in the prairie west and very much the gateway of prairie settlement, was aspiring, not without success, to the metropolitan status of Toronto and Montreal.

By that time important branch lines were opening new lands in the Territories of Assiniboia and Alberta, the names given in 1882 to the southern part of the later provinces of Saskatchewan and Alberta. A line from Regina to Prince Albert was completed in 1890 and in the next year one from Calgary to Edmonton. The latter was extended south through the heartland of the southern Alberta ranching country where the prospering cattlemen looked askance at the homesteaders whose ploughs and fences threatened their open range. There the rancher had followed close behind the mounted policeman and, his herds protected by his close and friendly relationship with the force, had by the middle eighties made a successful and often highly profitable adjustment to the climate and soil conditions that made the region better grazing land than arable. Sustained by the substantial infusions of eastern and British capital that large-scale ranching demanded, and sharing eastern and British values that idealized the life of the large landowner of the United Kingdom, the rancher was well on his way to developing a style of living that bore little resemblance to the familiar stereotypes of the cattle country south of the border. In this process the police played a continuing part, for many of the early ranchers and some of the most enthusiastic publicists of the ranching industry were retired members of the force.

Other lines foreshadowed major developments though they did not always bring prospective sod-busters to adjacent lands. In 1885 the North-Western Coal and Navigation Company, incorporated in England but closely connected with the Galt family with its widespread interests in Canadian politics, international business, and the imperial relationship, built a narrow gauge line from Dunmore on the Canadian Pacific near Medicine Hat to Lethbridge, to exploit the coal mines the Galts were developing near the latter. This line was later extended by way of Coutts to Great Falls, Montana, where it made connection with J. J. Hill's Great Northern Railroad. The Canadian Pacific completed its line through the Crow's Nest Pass to Nelson in 1898 and to Golden, B.C., on its main line, by 1914. It also built lines in southeast Assiniboia, including an extension of an American line of which it had acquired control, the Minneapolis, St Paul and Sault Ste Marie. The latter was perhaps more useful in bringing settlers from the United States to the region between Calgary and Edmonton than in establishing viable farms in the arid lands through which it passed between the border and the main line at Moose Jaw, though there is better land along the 'Soo Line' than much of that along the CPR main line between Moose Jaw and Calgary.

Those lines, if they did not bring the immediate prosperity that had been expected, opened the southern prairie region to settlement and development. Though a succession of booms followed the path of construction, growth both in population and production was disappointingly slow in the last two decades of the nineteenth century. This was a period of beginnings, but for almost every advance there was a retreat. Many settlers arrived but many left, defeated by the harsh reality of the frontier. Nevertheless the outlines of a new society appeared as the survivors put flesh on the skeleton of the railway lines, a society that, tenuous and vulnerable though it was, reflected the values of the eastern provinces that had provided the dominant element in its population, orderly, exploitative, and little disposed fundamentally to question its relationships with its Canadian metropolis or its British cultural context.

Somewhere in the later nineties the tempo of prairie settlement began to change and the west, in common with Canada as a whole, moved into a phase of rapid development. Indeed a case might be made for the view that the development of the west, including British Columbia and perhaps the Yukon, provided the force behind the dynamic surge forward that led Sir Wilfrid Laurier to proclaim that as the nineteenth century had been the century of the United States, so the twentieth century would be the century of Canada. By 1905 the shape of the future seemed so plain that the creation of the two new provinces of Alberta and Saskatchewan was almost taken for granted by their people, preoccupied as they were by this astonishing growth.

A variety of explanations have been offered for this change of pace. Undoubtedly Canada, a country capable of a substantial contribution of primary products to a hungry world market, benefited from the general change for the better in the world trading climate as the industrialized countries moved out of the economic doldrums of the latter part of the nineteenth century. Both the United Kingdom and the European continent had long been the source of substantial numbers of immigrants but, until the mid-nineties, these had generally preferred the United States or even more salubrious climates elsewhere. Now the supply of free land south of the border was exhausted, that frontier was closed, and landseekers turned to the vacant lands and the apparently increasing opportunities of the Canadian west. Western Canada's railways made it, or parts of it, reasonably accessible, new railways could be provided and western Canada, though its progress for the quarter century since it entered confederation had failed to meet expectations, did offer the prospect of an orderly society with much of the institutional framework of those countries, especially the United Kingdom and the United States, that considered themselves the leaders of civilization.

This change in tempo happened to coincide with a change in régime at Ottawa. After Sir John A. Macdonald's death in 1891 the crumbling Conservative party fell apart and was replaced in office in 1896 by the Liberals under Laurier. Though the Liberal government's policies towards the west were not radically different from those of its predecessor, they were pressed forward with a vigour in tune with the new times and the freshness of outlook of a party long out of office. In Clifford Sifton, who had laid the foundations of his political career in Manitoba, the west felt it had an effective spokesman in the cabinet, and Sifton's name was identified with the more aggressive turn taken in settlement and development policies affecting the region. After his break with Laurier, ostensibly because of Laurier's policies towards separate schools in the new provinces of Alberta and Saskatchewan, his successor as Minister of the Interior was Frank Oliver, a pioneer journalist at Edmonton and an acid and persistent critic of Conservative permissiveness towards such interests as the Canadian Pacific, the settlement companies, and the southern Alberta ranchers. Though cabinet responsibility was to soften the cutting edge of Oliver's populist attitudes, he was far from disposed to put obstacles in the way of western development in the form of government controls over land use that would direct settlers away from unsuitable lands. Such controls, as Oliver saw them, would only frustrate the settler in the interests of eastern finance. In the Department of the Interior there had been at least some degree of skepticism about the wisdom of making every quarter section in the west a family farm. William Pearce, long the Department of the Interior's man in the west, and Oliver's particular target as the minion of the big interests, had harboured some imaginative views about the use of grazing lands, the control of water supplies, and the development of irrigation. In 1904 he left the government service for more congenial employment with the Canadian Pacific.

In terms of the west the most creative acts of the Laurier government were in the realm of railway policy. Before the century was many years old a new transcontinental, in its western guise the Grand Trunk Pacific, was cutting its way across the prairie region towards the Yellowhead Pass and a terminus at Prince Rupert. At the same time William Mackenzie and Donald Mann were putting together their Canadian Northern system, one which, though its primary base was in the prairie west, also had transcontinental ambitions. Mackenzie and Mann, shrewd and successful railway contractors, appreciated not only the possibilities of the lands lying along the route abandoned by the CPR in 1882 but also the advantages of the modest grades required by the Yellowhead. Thus west of Edmonton most of the way to the Rockies two lines were built almost parallel to one another through a terrain not likely to generate much agricultural traffic. The Laurier railway policy was thus laying the foundations for the future disasters that were to lead to the fusion of the Grand Trunk and the Canadian Northern into that obsessive burden of the Canadian taxpayer, the Canadian National Railway. The lines built through the prairies were however capable of profitable operation; it was elsewhere, in the mountains and in the inhospitable terrain of north central Canada, that the railway builders were to sink inextricably into a financial muskeg.

For the moment all seemed well. The Canadian Pacific was building branch lines to meet the threats posed by these aggressive competitors. Not only the federal government suffered from railway fever; provincial and municipal governments and the public at large were equally infected and even more delirious. Railway construction opened new areas to settlement and at the same time the expenditures for construction seeped into the western economy and attracted more money for other investments. The railways not only transported settlers but provided them with jobs that yielded the ready cash they needed to establish themselves. Railway building fed western development in the first decade of the twentieth century on such a nourishing diet that steady growth passed into the heady atmosphere of the boom.

The growth was real and affected the country at large, though nowhere else so markedly as in the west. Between the censuses of 1891 and 1911 the percentage of the national population resident there rose from a meagre 7.24 per cent to 24.09. The population of British Columbia nearly quadrupled, that of Manitoba more than tripled. The new province of Saskatchewan emerged as the third most populous province of the dominion, and Alberta's growth was equally impressive. The government of the latter was laying plans for railways into the promising Peace River country and reaching towards the Mackenzie valley. Although this dream of northern exploitation turned into a political nightmare, it did ultimately open the way to agricultural settlement and directed Alberta towards its role as a base and a point of departure for the penetration of the further north, still in 1914 the preserve of the Indian and the Eskimo, the fur trader and the missionary. By that date Edmonton, which had languished so long as a frontier outpost, could dispute with Calgary the claim to the largest population of any Alberta centre. In southern Alberta these were years not only of growth but of change as the rancher gave way before the farmer. For southern Saskatchewan this was a period of consolidation as it was for Manitoba and British Columbia. The two latter had frontier regions of their own that contributed to the prosperity of their metropolitan centres; Winnipeg and Vancouver were growing at a rate that many eastern cities envied.

The expansion of the settled area, the flood of immigrants, and the rapid growth of population in the prairie west in the generation following 1895 affected considerably the population mix. The period established that the characteristic pattern of the prairie west was to be the mosaic, the group settlement that maintained its ethnic or other particularity and had little more than an economic connection with its surrounding society. In the first generation after the west entered confederation the settlers came predominantly from the older provinces of Canada or from the United Kingdom. There were relatively few from the United States. In the ranching country of southern Alberta, though many of the techniques of the industry were acquired from American sources, most of the cowboys, not to mention the managers and the owners, were of British origin.

There were in this earlier period some important group settlements but many of these were attracted not by the fertility of the land or the joys of the northern climate but by the prospect of an easier maintenance of their identity in western Canada than in the less permissive republic. Fugitives from the Vietnam draft were by no means the first to take refuge in Canada from unacceptable responsibilities of American citizenship. In Manitoba as early as 1874 Mennonite colonies, accepting what they believed to be the Canadian government's assurances of immunity from military service, soon attained a modest prosperity and preserved much of their distinctive way of life. Further north on lands reserved in 1874 between lakes Manitoba and Winnipeg, the Icelanders established themselves at Gimli. Encouraged by no less a notable than the Governor General, Lord Dufferin, to retain their cultural heritage, the Icelanders, while they underwent severe hardships, were destined to make an impressive contribution to their adopted country. Hungarian, German, Scandinavian, and Rumanian groups settled in Manitoba and Assiniboia, but, though compatriots often joined them later, these 'New Canadians' did not settle in large blocks. They were somewhat less likely to withdraw from the land in the face of adversity than their English-speaking neighbours and by 1891 Assiniboia could be described as 'polyglot', whereas Manitoba, where settlement was earliest, was already, of all the western provinces, the one most reminiscent of Ontario. An exceptional group, whose pioneers arrived in southern Alberta in 1887, were the Mormons. Like the Mennonites they were in effect refugees from official persecution but they were predominantly English-speaking. They retained a close connection with the American centre of their church in Utah and were long disinclined to disperse through the west from their original base. They brought with them a working knowledge of irrigation and this was soon put into practice in an important modification of land use that fitted admirably into the region of comparatively low rainfall to which they came.

The prairie west was nevertheless until the early nineties overwhelmingly Anglo-Saxon. French-Canadian settlers, some repatriated from New England, were relatively few. The Métis were, and were to remain, largely in areas ill-served by the railways. The Indians, in the areas of actual and potential settlement largely confined to their reserves, were increasingly a forgotten people and declining in number as European predominance was ever more firmly established. The flood of immigrants that began to pour in even before the turn of the century was still predominantly English-speaking, but the increasing number of immigrants from continental Europe, who came either directly or after a sojourn in the United States, reinforced the concept of the prairie west as a mosaic rather than as a melting pot. There were pressures towards assimilation to some acceptable norm, but what that norm should be was difficult to establish. To a very large and influential element it was obvious that Ontario presented a suitable pattern but the numerous settlers from the United Kingdom had some difficulty in distinguishing the Ontario norm from that represented by the United States, hotly as the Ontario-born might protest their British loyalties. Though an American accent might be acceptable, attempts to assimilate newcomers from continental Europe to a Protestant and English-speaking culture were likely to give rise to difficulties over religion and language, difficulties of which both French and English Canadians had long and bitter experience and that it was of the essence of Canadianism to avoid. In the pioneer stage of economic and social development it was easier to accept difference than to seek to eliminate it. Though the individual consciousness of being a prairie westerner had not fully evolved by the nineties, a generation was growing to maturity that had little experience of life elsewhere. A growing sense of identity most often found its expression in the distinction between the old-timer and the newcomer, but within it were rooted possibilities both for the development of a positive and distinctive concept of Canadianism and for a dangerously negative western alienation.

Statistically the years of the greatest immigration into the prairie west, the years from 1895 to 1914 that determined its population base, present a puzzle as far as ethnic origin is concerned. Families who were linguistically and culturally German might come from Russia, Poles and Ukrainians from any one of the three great empires of central and eastern Europe before 1914. Many of the settlers of all backgrounds, and the vast majority of English-speaking settlers, came as individuals, though even among the English-speaking family and community ties were strong. Group settlements, from the gentry of Cannington Manor in Assiniboia in the early eighties, with their fine horses and their steeple-chases, to the less affluent but more durable Britannia settlers a generation later at Lloydminster—the Barr Colony—were part of the history of United Kingdom settlement in the prairie west. But neither the contemporary public nor later observers saw these colonies as typical of the English settler's experience in the west in the same way as the group settlement is seen as typical of the experience of the German, the Scandinavian, or the Ukrainian settler.

Much more intractable, from the point of view of those who thought in terms of assimilation to some undetermined but deeply felt norm, were groups like the Doukhobors and the Hutterites. The Doukhobors arrived in Saskatchewan from Russia after 1898 and their reluctance to conform to local requirements, such as those that they take an oath of allegiance to secure title to their land and that they educate their children, attracted much unfavourable attention, though the majority in due course adapted themselves to western conditions. Many, including most of the more radical, moved to British Columbia where the tactics of the Sons of Freedom, involving nude parades and arson, scandalized their neighbours. The Hutterites, ethnically and culturally German, pursued a more quietist resistance to the impact of western customs. Their communal farms prospered and, though their peculiarities alarmed some of their neighbours in the communities in which they bought land for expansion, western opinion was much divided about the adoption of repressive measures to restrict the expansion of their colonies.

The rapid growth of population in the prairie west and the hothouse development that accompanied it in the opening years of the twentieth century produced a highly vulnerable society. As early as 1912 the boom showed signs of giving way to recession. Homestead entries fell off in 1913, never to recover to anything like their earlier level.[12] Though this was in part the result of a diminishing supply of attractive land, it also reflected a slowing of the hectic pace of earlier years. The impact of the outbreak of world war in 1914 thus fell with particular violence upon a society that was still immature and already suffering from the strains of recession on an institutional and economic framework that under boom conditions was not much better than jerrybuilt.

Though agricultural prices recovered under the pressure of wartime demands, the same demands brought a serious shortage of agricultural labour. The level of enlistment in the armed forces was high, as was to be expected in newly settled areas where many of the men were of military age and many were British-born. The number of new settlers dwindled rapidly after trans-Atlantic sources were cut off. High prices for farm products and the economies of large-scale operation, in spite of labour shortages and the difficulty of obtaining appropriate machinery, tempted farmers into expanding their operations, often on land that was, under average conditions, only marginally or even less productive. Many assumed new burdens of debt that were to prove disastrously heavy when weather conditions were unfavourable or, as happened soon after the war ended, farm prices fell catastrophically.

By 1921 the dislocations of prewar recession, the war itself, and postwar depression in a society that had largely emerged out of a decade of frantic development, had brought the people of the prairies, and especially the farmers, to a mood of disillusion. This expressed itself in a rejection of the traditional parties of federal politics. Alberta, significantly the latest of the provinces to be developed, turned out its ageing Liberal régime in favour of the United Farmers of Alberta. Manitoba soon followed suit and in Saskatchewan the Liberal government survived only by bowing to the will of the organized agricultural interest. In the federal election of 1921 the west gave overwhelming support to the Progressives, who seemed less a new party than a movement that rejected altogether the concepts of traditional party politics. This verdict was an expression of western alienation as formidable as any in the history of the prairie region.

In 1921 the outlines of settlement in the prairie provinces were complete. Immigration was to resume, but not on the massive and creative scale of the early years of the century. The society that had emerged reflected in many of its dimensions the values of the founding fathers of the Canadian federation. It was by and large a peaceful and orderly society and, in spite of its political revolt, showed little disposition and less capacity to challenge effectively the subservient economic and social role in which it had been cast in relation to the central provinces. It was rather more American than John A. Macdonald and his supporters might have wished, though it had escaped the violence they deplored in the American west. It reflected the atmosphere of nineteenth-century England much less than those who had planned for large farms and ranches had hoped. Though large-scale cattle production survived as an important part of the western economy, the style of life the ranchers had cultivated had suffered a fatal blow in 1914 when so many of those who emulated it on smaller holdings went off to the war and those who remained faced the cold realities of wartime agriculture.

The prairie west was nevertheless still deeply attached to what were characterized as British values. These were enshrined in the curriculums of western school systems and in the teachings of its dominant religious bodies. They were implicit in the policies of its municipal and provincial governments and penetrated its civil services. The United Kingdom settlers, and many of those from the central and eastern provinces, were the most likely to take refuge in the towns and cities, impelled more by the rigours of rural life than by any sense of being swallowed up by encroaching hordes of non-English-speaking neighbours. From these urban bases, in but not entirely of their rural hinterlands, they maintained their cultural and economic predominance despite their diminishing voting strength. The English-speaking settlers and their descendants moved easily about the country as a whole, preserving personal ties with the United Kingdom and the easterly provinces and forming part of a network of individual communications that was characteristically Canadian and for at least a generation inhibited the expression of a self-consciously western position.

American settlers were by 1921 accepted almost without question. The extent of the influence of the immigrant from the United States in the prairie west is statistically even more confused than that of the former residents of the eastern and central European empires. Some were returning Canadians, some recent arrivals from the United Kingdom, some were part of the waves of immigrants from continental Europe who in the middle years of the nineteenth century had profoundly modified the ethnic mixture of the republic. Others were in one sense or another refugees from the pressure of what they saw as unacceptable American values. Especially after the pace of development in the western prairies began to quicken in the middle nineties, American settlers were welcome and there was no serious questioning of the assumption that they would conform to the Canadian system. Indeed many followed the example of the Mormons and proclaimed their desire to do so. But American settlers were under no greater pressure than any other group to assimilate to an established western Canadian norm and, even where they most ardently embraced what they thought of as Canadian values, the much-vaunted respect for law, for example, it may be questioned whether they did not insensibly modify them to fit an imported image of their own. It is perhaps excessive to suggest that the omnipresent American immigrant was the insidious forerunner of the ultimate impact upon the west and upon central Canada of a powerful and technologically advanced society and an agent of the homogenizing pressures emanating from a vital and aggressive society, whether those pressures were expressed in terms of breakfast foods, pop records, or the presidential system of government. Immigrants from the United States, like those from the older Canadian provinces and to a lesser extent those from the United Kingdom, certainly found it easier to maintain close ties with their former homes than the vast majority of the settlers whose place of origin was in continental Europe.

The prairie west in 1921 as it began to emerge from the shocks and dislocations of war and depression had no satisfactory image of itself. It still clung to a belief in its role as the source of energy for Canada's development but this scarcely corresponded to reality, well integrated though the region was into the wealth-producing activities that gave the Canadian federation such prosperity as it was to enjoy in the ensuing decade. Its people, and particularly its farmers, were far from satisfied with their share of the national income. The western farmer, in spite of the painful lessons of half a century's adaptation to the techniques of agriculture appropriate to a region of enormous disparities and variations in soil and climate, was still reluctant to abandon the fatal dream of a healthy society based on a farm family on every quarter section. He had paid, and was to pay, a high price for the uncontrolled and indiscriminate exploitation not only of the physical but also of the human resources of the prairie provinces.

NOTES

[1] 36 Vic. c. 35.

[2] 32-3 Vic. c. 3.

[3] Lewis H. Thomas, *The Struggle for Responsible Government in the North-West Territories, 1870-97* (Toronto, 1956), pp. 11, 16, and especially p. 14, n. 29, where reference is made to A. S. Morton's view of the Canadian authorities.

[4] *Ibid.*, p. 61.

[5] Chester Martin, *Dominion Lands Policy* (Toronto, 1938), p. 223.

[6] Don W. Thomson, *Men and Meridians* (Ottawa, 1968), vol. 2, p. 37.

[7] Martin, *op. cit.*, p. 45.

[8] *Ibid.*, p. 44.

[9] *Ibid.*, p. 29.

[10] *Ibid.*, p. 38

[11] *Ibid.*, p. 26

[12] Arthur S. Morton, *History of Prairie Settlement* (Toronto, 1938), Table xv.

GUIDE TO FURTHER READING

The settlement of the prairie west is such an important part of its historical experience, particularly prior to 1921, that little has been written on that period that does not bear, directly or implicitly, upon the topic. W. L. Morton's *Manitoba, a history* (Toronto, 1957), for example, describes and reflects upon the process of settlement in that province in a way unhappily not paralleled in the histories of other prairie provinces.

The first scholarly account of the settlement of the Canadian prairie provinces was Arthur S. Morton's *History of Prairie Settlement* (Toronto, Macmillan of Canada, 1938), published as part of Volume II of the Canadian Frontiers of Settlement series edited by W. A. Mackintosh and W. L. G. Joerg. It remains invaluable as an introduction to the topic. It has not yet been reprinted but its companion piece, Chester Martin's *'Dominion Lands' Policy*, is No. 69 in the Carleton Library Series (Toronto, McClelland and Stewart, 1973), edited and with an introduction by Lewis H. Thomas, and with helpful bibliographical notes. Other volumes in the Frontier of Settlement series that are particularly useful include. No. VI, C. A. Dawson and R. W. Murchie, *The Settlement of the Peace River Country: a Study of a Pioneer Area* (Toronto, 1934); No. VII, C. A. Dawson, *Group Settlement: Ethnic Communities in Western Canada* (Toronto, 1940); and No. VIII, C. A. Dawson, *Pioneering in the Prairie Provinces: The Social Side of the Settlement Process* (Toronto, 1940). Though these are dated, they are an interesting reflection of attitudes to settlement current among social scientists in the depression years.

For the student who is interested in early impressions of the suitability of the region for European settlement, John Warkentin, *The Western Interior of Canada: A Record of Geographical Discovery* (Carleton Library, No. 15, 1964) is helpful. Though its many excerpts (taken from what may be seen as primary sources for the historical geographer) are often brief, they, in conjunction with the bibliography, point the way to more extended accounts. Many other early works give accounts of the earliest settlements and some of these have been reprinted, like William Francis Butler, *The Great Lone Land* (Edmonton, M. G. Hurtig, 1968, with an introduction by Edward McCourt), first published in 1872; the Rev. George M. Grant, *Ocean to Ocean, Sandford Fleming's Expedition through Canada in 1872* (Edmonton, M. G. Hurtig, 1967, with an introduction by Lewis H. Thomas), first published in 1873; and the Earl of Southesk's amusing *Saskatchewan and the Rocky Mountains: a diary and narrative of travel, sport and adventure, during a journey through the Hudson's Bay Company's territories in 1859 and 1860* (Edmonton, M. G. Hurtig, 1969, with an introduction by L. G. Thomas), first published in 1875.

A valuable introduction to the historiography of the prairies is provided by T. D. Regehr's 'Historiography of the Canadian Plains after 1870' in *Canadian Plains Studies, I, A Region of the Mind*, edited by Richard Allen (Regina, 1973). The works listed in Bruce Braden Peel, *A Bibliography of the Prairie Provinces* (Toronto, University of Toronto Press, 1958, Supplement, 1963; revised edition, 1973), especially in Sections B, The People, and K, Settling the West, of the Subject Index, are representative of publications prior to 1953. Claude Thibault, *Bibliographia Canadiana* (Don Mills, Longmans, 1973) may also be helpful.

Much of the more recent scholarly work on settlement is available only in the form of theses presented for M.A. or Ph. D. degrees. Aspects of this research are sometimes reflected in articles published in journals like *The Beaver, Saskatchewan History, The Alberta Historical Review*, and *Transactions* of the Historical and Scientific Society of Manitoba. *The Canadian Historical Review* is particularly helpful in its book review section. New directions in research and interpretation are often indicated by papers delivered at conferences and subsequently printed in proceedings. *Historical Papers*, previously *Annual Report, Canadian Historical Association* appears yearly. Examples of printed proceedings that include relevant material are *A Region of the Mind: Canadian Plains Studies I*, Richard Allen, editor (Regina, 1973); *The twenties in western Canada (Papers of the Western Canadian Studies Conference, March 1972)*, Susan M. Trofimenkoff, editor (Ottawa, National Museum of Man, 1972); and *Men in Scarlet*, Hugh A. Dempsey, editor, papers presented at the Royal Canadian Mounted Police Conference at the University of Lethbridge, 1974 (Calgary, McClelland and Stewart West for the Historical Society of Alberta, 1974). Students should consult the *Register of Post-graduate Dissertations in Progress in History and Related Subjects*, compiled by the Public Archives of Canada and published by the *Canadian Historical Association.*

Since 1967 there has been a proliferation of local histories that, though of uneven quality, contain material on the development of smaller communities. A classic is *Third Crossing: A History of the First Quarter Century of the Town and District of Gladstone in the Province of Manitoba* by Margaret Fahrni and W. L. Morton (Winnipeg, 1946).

THE PRAIRIE WEST, 1835

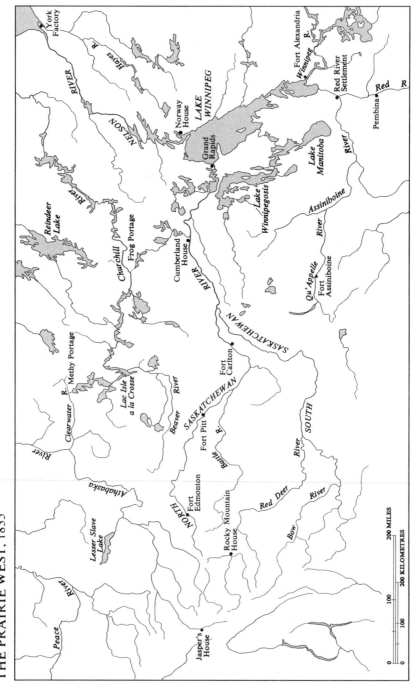

I Rupert's Land and the Red River Settlement, 1820-70

John E. Foster

INTRODUCTION

For two centuries, 1670 to 1870, the fur trade dominated the history of the region that was to become the Canadian west after 1870. The fur trade was the vehicle through which the North American Indian, whether he lived in the bush, in parkland, or on the prairie, tapped into European culture to take what he thought was valuable. Correspondingly European culture profited commercially and intellectually from its links with the Indian peoples. Each party to this meeting of different cultures influenced the other. Many aspects of Indian ways changed significantly with the development of the fur trade; yet such changes took place within an Indian context. The Indian remained Indian. Similarly British and French peoples reflected the experience of contact with Indian ways. It is in the trading post that the most dramatic developments took place. Homeguard Indians, those Indian bands in close association with the trading posts, interacted with Highland Scots, French Canadians, and Orkneymen. All had to adapt to the circumstances of their new environment. The extent and nature of this change is exemplified in a letter from a retired British officer:

> You are aware, Sirs, that by remaining in the Indian country such a length of time the Coustoms [sic] and habits we imbibe are so different to those of the Civilized World, add to which the attachment most people form to it, that it will be almost impossible for me to return to my native country.*

Such individual experiences marked the 200-year history of the fur trade before confederation. They played a major role in the historical process whereby not one but two distinct mixed-blood peoples emerged in what was to become the Canadian west. The two mixed-blood peoples were not only biologically but culturally distinct from both European and Indian peoples. The fur trade was the vehicle through which these two new distinct cultural traditions emerged.

---

*Hudson's Bay Company Archives, D.4/117, Henry Hallet to Gov. George Simpson and the Chief Factors, 25 June 1822.

How have historians viewed the fur trade? In the works of most historians who have dealt with what is today the Canadian west, the fur trade is central; yet, by virtue of the nature of the documents and their own cultural and scholarly biases, the fur trade is viewed from a single perspective. Intentionally or unintentionally, directly or indirectly, historians have perceived the fur trade in a metropolitan context. Briefly and somewhat simplistically stated, the metropolitan school views the fur trade as one aspect of the domination of European metropolitan centres over an ever-expanding and increasingly distant hinterland. The basis of the relationship between the metropolitan centre and its vast hinterland is economic. The metropolis exploits the staple products that the hinterland is capable of producing in surplus quantities by organizing capital and personnel, and locating and developing markets. This economic domination is the vehicle through which the metropolis extends its social, political, and cultural influence over the hinterland. The value of the metropolitan approach is indicated in the sound scholarship found in numerous works dealing with several aspects of the fur trade. Yet the results are curiously one-dimensional. Often we know more about the organizational structure that facilitated exchange and the furs and goods that were traded than we know about the men who traded them. The metropolitan approach has contributed much to the study of the west when 'fur was king'. But the historical understanding is incomplete.

While the fur trade was an aspect and an agent of the extension of metropolitan dominance, it was, at the same time, a socio-cultural complex in which Indians, mixed-bloods, and whites were intertwined. From this latter perspective new 'facts' and new questions emerge. From a socio-cultural context it is readily apparent that the fur trade was as much an Indian creation as it was European. It was the Indian who had the major say in determining what quantity and quality of goods would be traded. And it was the Indian who was the major determinant in assigning relative prices to European goods and western furs and provisions. Similar findings emerge as the drama of the fur trade unfolds. The Indian is no longer a largely inert environmental factor. His role in the way of life of the fur trade emerges with greater importance and clarity. His cultural ways take on much added significance in terms of trying to understand the historical experience encompassed in the fur trade. Similarly the mixed-bloods cease being biological and cultural curiosities of little significance, until the two Riel risings bring down the curtain on the fur-trade experience. And what of the whites in the fur trade, the Highland Scots officers, the French-Canadian voyageurs, and the Orkney tripmen; how were they marked by their years in the fur trade? Does the metropolitan perspective articulate with sufficient clarity the process whereby they imbibed 'Coustoms and habits... so different to those of the Civilized world'? Only when the fur trade is viewed as a socio-cultural whole, involving interaction among Indians, mixed-bloods, and whites, does an additional dimension to the fur-trade experience emerge.

If the foregoing discussion has validity, what are the implications for the scholar and the student? Perhaps the first implication of note is the tentative acceptance of the proposition that the two perspectives from which the fur trade can be viewed are not antagonistic; rather, they are complementary. It should be recognized that histories of the fur trade cannot be written without reference to the continuing influential input of metropolitan centres to the east. By the same token histories that ignore the fact that the fur trade was a socio-cultural complex of 200 years duration will no longer receive uncritical acclaim. In addition the complementary relationship between the two perspectives may serve to bridge the gap between scholarly writing in anthropology and ethnohistory on one hand and history on the other. Informally scholars have noted the fact that writings in each discipline, covering the same area and era, have little in common. They neither complement nor contradict each other. They seem to exist in orbits that rarely intersect. Possibly a socio-cultural view of the fur trade will offer a mechanism through which scholars of the separate disciplines may come to appreciate findings in different fields.

The most fundamental implication arising out of the acceptance of a complementary relationship between metropolitan and socio-cultural perspectives is the necessity of returning to the documents. Not only must new documents be sought out but documents that do not lend themselves to analysis from the traditional perspective must be utilized. Some examples of such documents are 'Lists of Officers and Servants', Wills, and in the later period, Census Reports, and Birth, Marriage, and Burial records. Finally documents previously used extensively in terms of the metropolitan perspective may provide new answers when fresh questions from a different perspective are asked.

The documents in this section have been selected with a view to providing basic insights into the world of the fur trade in Rupert's Land during the half century preceding confederation. The reader will note numerous extracts from the proceedings of the Parliamentary Select Committee on the Hudson's Bay Company, 1857. Circumstances in Great Britain in the middle of the eighteenth century make this document particularly valuable. In the minds of many Victorian Britons the Company was an 'unprogressive' monopoly that had survived beyond its time. Seizing upon the opportunity presented by the question of renewing the Company's license in territories beyond Rupert's Land, opponents sought its demise. For the student the nature of the Inquiry and the technique of question and answer lend themselves to profitable analysis. The other documents should provide insight into the ways of life of the different communities in Rupert's Land prior to 1870. For students of western Canadian history the documents provide interesting and startling answers to the nature of the ways of life that grew out of the fur trade. And perhaps more important they give rise to questions whose answers must be found elsewhere.

THE HUDSON'S BAY COMPANY AND THE INDIANS

The relationship between the Hudson's Bay Company and the Indians, with whom it had contact in the period 1820 to 1870, was the product of particular circumstances and the legacy of the previous 150 years of experience in the fur trade. What was the nature of the relationship between the Company and the missionaries on one hand and the Indian on the other? How did each party view and act towards the other? Men of one particular cultural origin found themselves in intimate contact with fellow human beings whose ways were always 'different'. How did they come to accept these differences in others and not view them as 'strange' and 'threatening'? The history of the Company's relations with the Indians during the period of monopoly is marked by co-operation and an absence of serious enduring conflict. Was this a product of the fur-trade 'system' or should we look to the individuals on both sides who functioned in the system? And lastly what was the legacy for the future derived from the Company's relationship with the Indian in this period?

THE FUR TRADE AND THE USE OF ALCOHOL

1.
'Indian Trade at York Factory 1769-1771' in Glyndwr Williams, ed., *Andrew Graham's Observations on Hudson's Bay 1767-1791* (London, Hudson's Bay Record Society, 1969), vol. xxvii, pp. 263, 265, 281. Reprinted by permission.

All gentlemen that are acquainted with the natives in Hudsons Bay know that it is not altogether by giving large presents to the leaders that will gain a trade, but by an affable, kind, easy behaviour to the whole body of natives; for as all natives are master over their own families they give no ear to the leader if they have any disgust to the fort. In short no leader has power to enforce what he would have put in execution. The trade will fluctuate a little let a person be never so careful, but when it gives way to a yearly decline it then plainly appears they don't love the usage.

    To prevent the natives from hurting themselves with brandy and strong waters, we at none of the settlements exchanges [sic] that commodity for any furs but the following viz. martens, cats, foxes coloured, wolves, and bears. This has been the case from the time the Company had the Charter and wisely done. If the natives were to receive brandy for whatever kind of furs etc. they bring down, they would trade little or nothing else, which would end in their ruin, and the Company's affairs. Please to observe keeping up spirituous liquors to the above value makes the natives trap valuable furs. In Europe the higher value that is set upon any commodity the greater the price he is given, so should spirituous liquors be highly valued in Hudson's Bay, and not be made a drug as it is now at York Fort.

I have heard great talking off and on concerning Hudson's Bay being laid open to all adventurers. The climate will not allow it; every necessary must be brought from England excepting fish, flesh and fowl, and that could not be got without the assistance of the natives who would enhance the price according to the demands. Each Factory at present are obliged to employ forty able hunters to bring in provisions, notwithstanding the supplies yearly sent out. There are not natives sufficient inhabiting between the Forts and the muscuty country, where the Archithinue [Blackfoot] and Aseenepoets [Assiniboine or Stonys] inhabits, to raise the fur trade above 20,000 skins more than is now sent home yearly from the Bay. And if the trading standard was enlarged in favour of the natives, would ruin it all; for I am certain if the natives were to get any more for their furs, they would catch fewer, which I shall make plainly appear viz. one canoe brings down yearly to the Fort one hundred made beaver in different kinds of furs, and trades with me seventy of the said beaver for real necessaries. The other thirty beaver shall so puzzle him to trade, that he often asks me what he shall buy, and when I make an answer, Trade some more powder, shot, tobacco and hatchets etc., his answer is, I have traded sufficient to serve me and my family until I see you again next summer; so he will drink one half, and trade the other with me for baubles.

2.

George Simpson, Governor of the Company's Territories in British North America, to Andrew Colvile, member of the Governing Committee in London, 20 May 1822, from Public Archives of Canada (hereafter PAC), Selkirk Papers, M.G. 19, EL (1), vol. 24.

It is not my province to go into this subject [use of alcohol in the fur trade] in a moral point of view and shall therefore confine my opinion thereon as to the effect such restriction might have on our Trade. If the quantity of Spirits given to Indians was calculated I am satisfied it would not amount to a pint p. man annually on an average, which may give some idea of the extent of Crime likely to result therefrom; and I'll venture to say there are not three murders committed annually on the average of the last Ten Years in the whole tract of Country occupied by the Hudson's Bay Coy. from ebriety. As an article of trade it is not generally used and I do not suppose we make Ten packs of Furs p. annum by it: it is, however, the grand Stimulus to call forth the exertions of the Indians and I have often heard them reason thus, "it is not for your Cloth and Blankets that we undergo all this labor and fatigue as in a short time we could reconcile ourselves to the use of Skins for Clothes as our forefathers did, but it is the prospect of a Drink in the Spring, to enable us to communicate freely and speak our minds to each other that carries us through the Winter and induces us to Work so hard." This I really believe to be the case, and that if Spirits were withheld it would materially discourage them and produce a lassitude which Weight of other property could not remove.—

In the Provision Countries it is, however, a very principal article of Trade and indispensibly necessary: the Plain Indians are a bold, independent race, Dress entirely in Skins and with them Tobacco and Spirits are the principal commodities, a Quart of Mixed Liquor will at times procure more Pounded Meat and Grease than a Bale of Cloth, indeed our whole profit in that Trade is upon those articles, and if Provisions were paid for in Dry Goods they would eat up all the gains of the Fur Trade. I therefore sincerely hope the [Governing] Committee will take due time to examine this subject and that they will not prematurely determine thereon as it might be very injurious to the interests of the Concern; . . .

3.
Testimony of Sir George Simpson before the Parliamentary Select Committee on the Hudson's Bay Company, 26 February and 2 March 1857.

1204. A witness informed us on the last day that, with regard to the barter between the trader or factor and the Indians, it was all done according to a tariff?—Yes, there is a tariff. . . .

1265. Is that tariff settled by the council, the governor, and factors, or is it settled in this country?—There is a tariff of very old standing; the Indian and the trader perfectly understand each other as regards the tariff.

1266. By whom was the tariff settled?—The tariff was settled originally by the original traders. It has been modified from time to time according to circumstances.

1267. The existing tariff in its modified form is ratified and carried out by the council?—Yes. It varies in different parts of the country.

1268. In the event of a variance of that tariff, who settles that variance?— The council do. . . .

1521. Can you give me any idea how that 60,000 £ worth of goods is distributed over that immense territory?—I think about two-thirds of that quantity of goods is given to the Indians; however, this is merely an approximation; I have no figures.

1522. What was the number of Indians which you just now stated?—On the east side of the Rocky Mountains, 55,000.

1523. I suppose that quantity is confined to the east side of the Rocky Mountains?—Yes.

1524. You distribute 40,000 £ worth of goods among 55,000 Indians?—I think that is about the estimate.

1525. What are those goods usually composed of?—British manufactures; the staple articles are blankets, cloths, arms, ammunition, iron works, axes and various things.

1526. I will direct your attention to arms; in what way are they sold; are they sold by barter or for money?—They are sold by barter.

1527. For so many skins?—For so many skins.

1528. When you sell a gun to an Indian, do you ever take inferior skins for that gun?—We outfit the Indian.

1529. Cannot you answer me that question?—We do not sell a gun for skins; we give the gun to the Indian, as everything else, on credit and he pays for those supplies in the spring of the year.

1530. Supposing a gun is sold to an Indian, would you take in payment an inferior kind of skins?—We take in payment whatever he can give us.

1531. If an Indian had nothing but musk rat skins, you would take those?— Yes.

1532. Do you mean to tell me that?—I mean to say that we would take from an Indian whatever he could give us. The Indian must have certain supplies.

1533. My question is a very plain one; would you take musk rat skins in payment for a gun from an Indian?—Certainly; we take whatever the Indian can give us.

1534. And you mean to state that to me, that guns are sold to Indians with the full understanding that they may pay you back in musk rat skins?—If an Indian has nothing but musk rat skins, we will take musk rat skins.

1535. Supposing that were to occur with an Indian once, would he be likely to get a second gun?—Yes, decidedly, if he required it.

1536. Do you know the relative proportions between musk rat skins and beavers?—We have a variety of tariffs; it depends upon the part of the country where the goods are traded; as, for instance, in Canada we pay in a great degree money for our furs. On the American frontier we pay frequently in money; in the interior it is principally a barter trade; and on the frontier we are regulated in our prices by the prices given by opposition.

1537. Are the prices rather higher upon the frontier than they are in the interior of the country?—Yes.

1538. Does not that arise from the competition?—Yes.

1539. So that the Indian, where there is competition, gets more than he does where there is none?—He does.

1540. Does not that rather improve the condition of the Indian?—No, certainly not.

1541. So that getting more does not improve him?—No, it does not improve his condition. I think that the condition of the Indian, in the absence of opposition, is better than where he is exposed to opposition.

1542. For what reasons?—The absence of spirituous liquors.

1543. First of all let us understand this: in the interior of the country you say you barter with the Indian?—Yes.

1544. And on the frontier you give him money?—That frequently happens in some parts of the country.

1545. On the frontier he gets a larger price for his goods than he does in the interior?—Yes.

1546. And you say that notwithstanding that, he is better off in the interior than he is on the frontier, because in the one case he gets spirituous liquors, and in the other case he does not?—And in other respects. The Indian in the interior depends upon us for all his supplies; whether he is able to pay for them or not, he gets them; he gets his blankets, he gets his gun, and he gets his ammunition. If from death in his family, or any other cause, he makes no hunt, it cannot be helped.

1547. I suppose you recollect that you distribute among the Indians less than 1 £ a head?—Very possibly we do.

HEALTH AND SOCIAL WELFARE

4.

Testimony of Dr. John Rae, Officer in the Company's service, before the Parliamentary Select Committee on the Hudson's Bay Company, 23 February 1857.

673. In a letter from Sir George Simpson, which is to be found in some papers laid before Parliament in 1842, he says: "Our different trading establishments are the resort or refuge of many of the natives who, from age, infirmity, or other causes, are unable to follow the chase; they have the benefit of the care and attention, free of expense, of our medical men, of whom about 12 are usually employed in the service; every trading establishment being in fact an Indian hospital." How far does your experience as a medical man in the service of the Company bear that out?—Wherever we act as medical men our services are given gratuitously. We go to a distance if an Indian is at a distance, and have him taken to a fort, and he is fed and clothed there. And it is no uncommon thing to hear the old Indians, when unfit for hunting, say, "We are unfit for work; we will go and reside at a fort." That is the ordinary feeling which prevailed in the country. Although there are no medical men up at the different posts (there may be the number Sir George has mentioned scattered over the country), yet medicines are sent up to all the posts in regular supplies.

674. If that attendance were asked it would always be afforded?—Yes.

675. Was it frequently afforded?—Frequently so; but those places on the coast are liable to much more disease than places inland.

676. Then, in short, you think that if a statement were made, that the Directors of the Hudson's Bay Company considered that it was their business to attend to the Company's own servants, but not to any other class of the population, it would be a false charge?—Perfectly erroneous; in fact the Indian is more readily attended to generally than the others.

677. And as a rule the medical men appointed by the Company would not consider it their sole duty to attend to the Company's servants?—Certainly

not; they are there for the Indians as much as for the Company's people.

678. How long did you say that you dwelt at Moose Factory?—Ten years.

679. During that time what was the average number of the worn-out hunters who lived there upon your charity?—I cannot exactly tell that. The population of the place was, I think, about 180 altogether; few Indians came there; but there were generally two or three or four old families, or six sometimes, pensioners at the place. They called at the Fort; they were there regularly every week; they had their encampment at the place, and they went and hunted at intervals as they were able, and if they were not able to get food enough, they had it given to them.

680. How many people would those families number?—Perhaps 12; perhaps 13 or 14 altogether.

681. Then I understand you that at the Moose Factory there was an average of about 12 old Indians?—Yes, women and men.

682. That was the sum of the great advantage that the Indians round about Moose Factory derived, namely, 10 or 12, or, say, 14 or 16?—The whole population there is about 180, and if any of them came in and were unfit to hunt, they were received at the Fort; we never forced them into the Fort; but if they came and asked assistance and wished to stay, they did so.

683. Mr. Labouchere [Chairman of the Committee] wishes to know whether anything is done with respect to vaccination?—Yes; vaccine matter is sent to all the posts. I may mention a curious fact, which is, that in the year 1835 the small-pox was brought up by a steamboat from the States. A gentleman at the Saskatchewan vaccinated all the Cree Indians that came in; and there was scarcely a single case occurred among the tribe; we supposed it was because they had all been vaccinated; whereas deaths took place amongst the more distant tribes, near the Missouri. The small-pox was brought by steamboat up the Missouri, and was brought over to the Saskatchewan by a quantity of horse stealers, who heard that the disease was at the Missouri, and went to steal horses there. They found the Indians dying by hundreds; they took the disease with them, and most of them died upon the road.

684. Taking you from Moose Factory to the mouth of the Mackenzie River, where you lived; how long did you live there?—About nine months at Fort Simpson, and two years at Bear Lake, which is in the Mackenzie district.

685. How many worn-out hunters lived there, deriving charity from you?—I do not remember; I think there were about two or three families whilst I was there; at the one post.

686. Say six people?—Yes, about that at that time; but it varies according to the privations which the Indians have suffered.

687. Did I understand you rightly, that in addition to the wornout hunters who were resident, there was also gratuitous medical advice given to the other Indians as they happened to require it?—To every one that came, or that we heard of. . . .

THE INDIAN AND THE MISSIONARY

5.

Testimony of the Right Rev. David Anderson, Bishop [Anglican] of Rupert's Land, before the Parliamentary Select Committee on the Hudson's Bay Company, 4 June 1857.

4296. I think you have travelled over a great extent of country. Have you found in the districts in which you have travelled, where missionaries have penetrated, any great improvement arising from the labours of those missionaries?—Very much so. Then it is controlled very much by the circumstances of the country. Of course it is very much more visible at the Red River Settlement and around it than it is in other spots. . . .

4262. What is the social state and prospects of that Christian village called the Indian Settlement, on the Red River?—The population there increases at the present moment.

4263. The purely Indian population increases?—Yes.

4264. Have you any statistical fact of that increase?—I have here the following, which is from the register of the settlement. The total number of baptisms administered in this parish (that is the Indian settlement parish) in 15 years is 545; total of deaths, 308; balance in favour of the increase, 237.

4265. That is a very large increase, is it not?—Yes; that is from the actual return on the spot, from the register.

4266. Would you gather from that fact, that if you were enabled to form other settlements of these Indians in a good climate, you have reason to suppose that the same results would occur?—I think so; I think when settled the Indians increase; up the country they would decrease, from want of food and want of clothing.

4267. Do the births among the settled Indians exceed the deaths generally? —Yes, wherever they are Christianised and settled.

4268. What is the state of the Christian Indians who are still leading the life of hunters; who are still following their old occupation?—I think many of them very exemplary, but chiefly around Moose Fort; that is our best exemplification of missionary work. There the Indians only come perhaps for a short time in the autumn, and a short time in the spring, and are away almost the whole of the winter. They come to the minister on the spot and get instruction. They are chiefly taught in this system (producing a paper), not in our own characters, but in what we call the syllabic character, a sort of system of short-hand.

4269. Is that found very effective?—On this plan they can learn in three days enough to puzzle out the system for themselves; but in a week they can learn sufficient to go away and read their little books for the winter.

4270. Have you found them bring back the same books, having improved between the periods of their hunting and returning?—Yes; they wear their books to the very last degree; and when away from the minister they have their own family worship night and morning, and have their worship on the Sunday when it comes round.

4271. What do you find is the capacity of the Indians for reading and writing their own language?—I think they are very quick. Since I have been in London I have received a letter from them written in this syllabic character, and they write one to another as freely as we should write letters. . . .

4273. Then you think that the Indians have responded to the benefits which they have had of the teaching to a much greater degree than you expected when you went out?—Very much more so. I am sure that a visit to Moose from any one would convince him of the fact. . . .

THE COMPANY'S POLITICAL RELATIONS WITH THE INDIANS

6.
Testimony of Sir George Simpson before the Parliamentary Select Committee on the Hudson's Bay Company, 26 February and 2 March 1857.

1747. What privileges or rights do the native Indians possess strictly applicable to themselves?—They are perfectly at liberty to do what they please; we never restrain Indians.

1748. Is there any difference between their position and that of the half-breeds?—None at all. They hunt and fish, and live as they please. They look to us for their supplies, and we study their comfort and convenience as much as possible; we assist each other.

1749. You exercise no authority whatever over the Indian tribes?—None at all.

1750. If any tribe were pleased now to live as the tribes did live before the country was opened up to Europeans; that is to say, not using any article of European manufacture or trade, it would be in their power to do so?—Perfectly so; we exercise no control over them.

1751. Do you mean that, possessing the right of soil over the whole of Rupert's Land, you do not consider that you possess any jurisdiction over the inhabitants of that soil?—No, I am not aware that we do. We exercise none, whatever right we possess under our charter.

1752. Then is it the case that you do not consider that the Indians are under your jurisdiction when any crimes are committed by the Indians upon the Whites?—They are under our jurisdiction when crimes are committed upon the Whites, but not when committed upon each other; we do not meddle with their wars.

1753. What law do you consider in force in the case of the Indians committing any crime upon the Whites; do you consider that the clause in your licence to trade, by which you are bound to transport criminals to Canada for trial, refers to the Indians, or solely to the Whites?—To the Whites, we conceive.

1754. Are the native Indians permitted to barter skins *inter se* from one tribe to another?—Yes.

1755. There is no restriction at all in that respect?—None at all.

1756. Is there any restriction with regard to the half-breeds in that respect?—None, as regard dealings among themselves. . . .

1060. I suppose this can hardly be considered as administration of justice: I find that in Mr. Alexander's Simpson's "Life of Mr. Thomas Simpson," at page 427, it is stated that the Company has the invariable rule of avenging the murder by Indians of any of its servants, by blood for blood, without trial of any kind. Is that the case?—We are obliged to punish Indians as a measure of self-preservation in some parts of the country.

1061. And without any form of trial?—We seldom get hold of them for the purpose of trial, and they are usually punished by their own tribe. I scarcely know a case, there may have been perhaps a few cases, in which our own servants have retaliated; but the Indians are usually punished by the tribe to which they belong.

SETTLEMENT AND THE INDIAN

7.

Testimony of the Right Rev. David Anderson, Bishop of Rupert's Land, before the Parliamentary Select Committee on the Hudson's Bay Company, 4 June 1857.

4392. Supposing colonization to be open to the white man, are you at all aware of the fact which has been proved by long history in America, that wherever colonization by the white man takes place the brown man disappears?—It has been so in the United States.

4393. Has not it been so in Canada?—It has been in a measure true in Canada.

4394. So that, in fact, in all parts of the territory of America in which the white man has appeared, the brown man has disappeared?—I am rather unwilling to believe it as regards one's own country, because I think that more of effort is made for the Indians. I am sure that the Indian effort is more successful in our country than in the States or in Canada.

4395. You are speaking of the Indian effort applying to 2,600 persons?—To the much larger number of 8,000 Indians, taking the whole territory.

4396. But that territory, I take it, has nothing to do with colonization?—No.

4397. As to that part which is affected at all by colonization, from the very imperfect colonization to which it has been subject hitherto, your experience goes in favour of the fact that the brown man can resist the encroachments of the white man?—It does, but of course I may be a partial judge in the matter.

4398. Have you at all contemplated the fact of the whole territory which is capable of colonization being thrown open to colonization; what would then be the effect upon the brown man of that altered circumstance?—I think of it almost daily. My hope is that the Indian may be raised in the interval before the civilization sweeps westward, as it must; and I always feel that my object is to raise a people as well as to give them Christianity. . . .

4402. Supposing that the policy of the Government were changed, and that the territory were opened to colonization, should you then consider it a matter of very great importance to maintain the Indian population there?—Very great.

4403. Why?—My own feeling is, that by opening the whole country to free competition the Indian would be sacrificed.

4404. He would disappear?—Yes; but I think that if we can keep the southern part as a colony or province, then the Indian may still be preserved.

4405. Why would he disappear; is it because a more energetic, a more civilized, and in fact, a more intellectual man would come in competition with him?—Because of the baits which would be held out; there would then be an abundance of spirituous liquor brought in.

4406. But spirituous liquor affects the health of the white man as it does that of the brown man, does it not?—But he falls more readily beneath the temptation.

4407. That is to say, he is less civilized?—Yes.

4408. The more civilized man conquers the less civilized man?—He does.

4409. Do you think it advisable to maintain the less civilized man in a community which will hold the more civilized man?—I should be very sorry to forfeit the Indians in the territory.

4410. That is not my question; the question is, do you think it would be advisable to keep the territory in such a condition as should maintain the existence of a less civilized population, when it would really maintain a more civilized population?—If I thought that the Indians were to be forfeited, I would rather keep back the more civilized.

4411. That is to say, you would prevent the colonization by the more civilized man, to maintain the existence of the less civilized man?—I think each might have his position in the country, the civilized in the south, and the Indian further north.

4412. Does not it come to the conclusion to which I have endeavoured to draw you?—I should be sorry to allow it, as regards the Indian.

4413. Though your sympathies may go thus, does not the reasoning lead you to the conclusion to which I wish to bring you?—I hope the experiment may yet save the Indian.

4414. Do you not think that the true policy would be to establish just and equitable laws, as between the brown and the white man, and to leave the rest to take its course?—My own feeling would be in favour of a settlement, a colony, or a province in the southern part of the territory, stretching from Lake Superior to the Rocky Mountains.

4415. Not asking whether a man was brown or white, provided he obeyed the laws and behaved well?—I think so, and I think the Indian might still be saved.

4416. From what you have seen of the half-breed race at the Red River, do you despair of their being useful and prosperous members of a civilized community, under proper laws?—I do not despair in the smallest degree of them. . . .

4419. Still I think you have expressed an opinion, that if there were free colonization the white man would overrun the brown man?—Yes, if it were free over the whole country.

4420. Therefore, if there were equal laws for the brown man and the white-man, the brown man would disappear?—Yes, unless it were controlled in some way.

THE HUDSON'S BAY COMPANY'S OFFICERS AND SERVANTS DURING THE PERIOD OF MONOPOLY 1820-70

No view of the fur trade would be complete without giving some attention to the men who staffed the trading posts, the officers, the servants, and seasonal labourers. Who were these men and why did they join the Company's service? What was life like in the Company's service? What became of these men, many of whom devoted their lives to the fur trade? How did they affect the land and the people to which they came, and how did the land and people affect them? The questions are simple. The answers are more complex.

8.
Testimony of Sir George Simpson before the Parliamentary Select Committee on the Hudson's Bay Company, 26 February 1857.

983. Will you state to us the system under which the country is managed, with regard to trade and government, with reference to the Indian population; in short, the machinery which is employed; how many officers and servants altogether are employed by you in the management of the territory of the Hudson's Bay Company?—There is the governor-in-chief, to begin with; there are 16 chief factors, who are the principal officers, members of our council; 29 chief traders, five surgeons, 87 clerks, and 67 postmasters; the last rank between the labouring man and the clerk.

984. How many are employed at your trading posts?—Those people are all employed at our trading posts.

985. How many other agents are there employed at your trading posts?— We have no other agents; we have servants.

986. How many servants have you?—There are about 1,200 permanent servants.

987. Does that include voyageurs and people of that sort?—No; there are about 500 voyageurs, and other temporary servants beside.

988. How many are employed besides those occasionally?—There are 150 officers and crews of vessels.

989. What number of persons do you think the Company gives employment to in the trading season?—Perhaps about 3,000.

990. Is that exclusive of Indians?—That is including Indian labourers.

991. Do you mean hunters?—After the hunting season is over the Indians are frequently employed as boatmen or canoemen; as temporary servants.

992. You do not include in that number, I presume, the Indian population employed by the people from whom you purchase furs?—No. . . .

1054. The greater portion of your European servants, I presume, come from England or Scotland; they are not born of white parents in the country? —The greater portion of our white servants are Orkney men; there are a few Highlanders, and a very few Shetlanders; a large proportion of our servants are half-breeds.

1055. With your Indian servants what sort of contract do you enter into; how long is their term of service?—Merely for the trip; merely for the summer. They are sometimes employed as express bearers going with letters, and they are frequently employed as boatmen, mixed with the Company's servants and with the half-breeds.

1056. Is there any provision made for your servants in case of sickness or old age?—There is no provision made for them. They are paid liberal wages, and our servants very frequently save large sums of money for their walk in life. They generally leave the country before extreme old age comes on.

1057. But there is no regular provision for a person who becomes disabled in your service?—There is no provision.

1058. That happens, I suppose, not unfrequently from accidents?—It does happen, and it frequently happens, that the Company, after their return to England, allow them a small pension.

1059. Have you ever known, in any case which was deserving, a small pension refused?—Never. . . .

1148. If any of your servants at the different posts wanted to place money at interest, you would allow them four per cent. upon it?—If they choose to leave their money in our hands they get four per cent. for it. . . .

1255. For what period of time do your servants that go from this country engage with you?—Generally five years.

1256. On the average do they return at the expiration of the five years?— No, I think they generally remain; I should say that six out of eight remain;

they renew their contract over and over again. There are many servants who have been in the service 25 or 30 years.

1257. As a general average, do they remain, say 20 years with you?—Perhaps barely 20 years at present.

1258. But they remain a long time?—Yes, many of our servants remain a long time. Many of our servants remain altogether in the country. They retire from the service, and become settlers at the Red River.

1259. What is the highest salary that the Company pay their servants?—The price of labour has increased very much. It was some years ago 17 £ sterling, and now it is increased to men coming direct from England on their first engagement to 20 £; and it is raised according to their position afterwards. A man from being a common labourer, takes either the stern or the head of a boat; being called the bowsman or the steersman; in that case, he is paid higher according to his capabilities as a boatman. Fishermen are paid higher; they are paid 30 £, 35 £ and 40 £, in many cases; tradesmen also are paid higher.

1260. The class that you describe as labourers are paid 20 £ to 30 £, and 35 £?—Yes.

1261. What may be the salary of the superior officers?—The factors and traders have an interest in the trade; they are partners.

1262. The 16 factors?—The 16 factors and the 29 traders.

1263. They are, to a certain extent, partners in the adventure?—Yes. . . .

1269. A question was put to you relative to any compensation or pension which might be given by the Company to old officers or servants, and those who might have received injuries in the service, and you stated that many of them were extremely comfortable?—Yes, many of them have retired with means saved in the country.

1270. Do you confine your answer to the superior officers, the factors, and traders, or do you extend it to the servants?—I speak of labourers. I have known labourers retire with from 200 £ to 300 £; Orkney labourers, who are extremely economical in their habits. I speak of those who have been in the country for a great length of time.

1271. They have saved that money out of the wages of from 20 £ to 30 £ a year, and the four per cent. which you allow them for money which they do not draw?—Yes. . . .

9.
Testimony of Edward Ellice, Member of Parliament and a member of the Company's Governing Committee, before the Parliamentary Select Committee on the Hudson's Bay Company, 23 June 1857.

5829. Are you careful in the selection of the young men [officers] whom you send out there?—I took great care in former times to send out the best men we could find, principally from the north of Scotland, sons of country gentlemen, clergymen, and of farmers, who had been educated in the schools and colleges of Scotland; they went out first as apprentices, then were made clerks, and then became gradually advanced to the higher positions in the service; some of these men have lived to become great benefactors to the country. You have heard of the donations of Mr. Leith and Mr. Black, two gentlemen whom my father sent from Aberdeen. Governor Simpson has taken very great interest in the matter for many years, but I think that lately it has been too much the habit to endeavour to supply the places of men who have retired by persons connected with the country, some of the half-breeds; and I doubt very much when we look to the future security of the country, whether that will be found to be good policy.

5830. Are the appointments made by individual directors?—No, four or five gentlemen sit round a table, and I believe if anybody recommends a competent young man, there is never any division of opinion as to appointing him to that office. My son recommended a boy, the son of our forester in Scotland, brought up at our own school, where he turned out a quick, clever boy; that boy had never seen a town, nor known anything of the vice and habits of towns; he has gone out as an apprentice, and will rise, if his merits justify the council in promoting him, to be one of our chief men.

5831. Is the conduct of these young men closely watched when they are out there?—It comes perpetually under the view first of the council and the Governor, and then under the view of the Government at home; and it is so much for the interest of all parties to have good, zealous, active men, in the management of affairs at such a distance from all human society, that that is the best security for good selections.

5832. From the nature of your trade, I suppose the moral conduct and good sense of your agents are quite indispensable?—Quite indispensable, and moreover, it is very essential to have men who can obtain influence over the Indians; if it is found that any man at a particular post gets indolent, inattentive, or has too intimate relations with particular Indians, or if his habits are supposed in any other way to interfere with his good administration of the post, he is instantly changed.

10.
Excerpt from a letter from Rev. W. Cockran, Anglican Missionary at Lower Church (Grand Rapids) Red River Setlement, to the Secretaries of the Church Missionary Society, 25 July 1833. PAC, Church Missionary Society Archives (microfilm), Incoming Correspondence.

(Private)
The Hon. Company's servants seldom continue more than 3 years at the same post, and often only one. In the summer the whole of their time is occupied in voyaging upon the rivers, carrying out the furs which they had traded in the winter from the Indians; and returning with a new outfit for the trade of the

ensuing year. During the summer there are plenty of opportunities for the young voyager to give vent to his licentious passions; at every post he will find women who will do anything for hire. He has no principles to contend with; he therefore finds it easy to do what is most pleasant to corrupt nature and most popular with his companions. When the young voyager comes to his winter quarters, he finds he wants many things to fit him for this new existence which he has entered upon. He wants his leather coat, trowsers, mittens, duffle socks and shoes, all then must be made and kept in repair. He has no time to do this himself; he applies to an Indian who has got some daughters, or two or three wives; here he is quickly served, he makes a present to the head of the family, they set to work, and make all ready for him, he comes at a certain time for his clothes, brings a little rum, and makes the principal persons of the family merry. He sleeps there, and out of gratitude and courtesy, the old woman puts her daughter to bed to him, or the Indian may give him one of his three wives, who lays under his displeasure; thus the unfortunate voyager forms his connexion with the natives, and raises an offspring. He may continue here two or three years, and enjoy the benefit of his helpmate. He goes off in the summer, returns in the autumn, and perhaps finds the same young woman given to another. This does not distract his mind, he forms another connexion as speedily as possible; by this time he believes that he cannot get on without a woman. The next time he leaves his winter quarters, he perhaps is sent to a post 600 or 1000 miles from all his former wives; he forgets them at once, and serves himself for the time being, with the first that comes to hand; he looks for neither beauty nor virtue; if she is a woman, that is sufficient. The same course is run until old age and grey hairs are upon him; his body emaciated with the fatigues of voyaging, and means too scanty to cast a robe once a year over all his adulterous progeny. His case being, desperate, he thinks of making an effort to remedy the errors of 30 or 40 years, by one mighty struggle. Out of his many connexions he finds some one that ranks above the rest. He selects her to be the companion of his old age; collects his multifarious progeny from the ends of the earth, (for he has been every where through all this Continent) and bends his course to Red River, with a worn out constitution, with small means, with a woman that knows none of the duties of civilized life, with a dispirited family who know nothing but what the heathen have taught them, who have no interest in each other's welfare, to begin life anew, to learn with his heathen family how to discharge his duty to God, his neighbour, and his own soul.

THE MIXED-BLOODS AND THE RED RIVER SETTLEMENT

With all deference to the labours of Lord Selkirk, the Red River Settlement was a creation of the fur trade. After competition had ceased between the North West Company and the Hudson's Bay Company, the reorganized and revitalized Hudson's Bay Company, for business and philanthropic reasons, took the infant Selkirk colony under its protection. Faced with the task of paring down the costs of labour and provisions in the fur trade, the Company encouraged older and less able officers and servants to retire and to migrate with their mixed-blood families to Red River where they would come under the influence of churches, schools, local government, and 'civilized' society. Red River was to develop in the image of a British agrarian community, but complementary to the interests of the fur trade. The predominant element in the migrations from the interior to Red River during the 1820s were the mixed-bloods. Eventually they numbered more than eighty per cent of the settlement's population.

The two mixed-blood communities in Red River were the product of two distinct cultural traditions in Rupert's Land. For their origins the Métis looked to the two-hundred-year historical experience of Indians and whites in the St Lawrence trading system. There the ways of the French-Canadian voyageur and the Highland-Scot bourgeois melded with those of the Saulteaux and Cree hunters, trappers, and traders. In the settlement the Métis came under the influence of French-speaking, Roman Catholic priests from Lower Canada who encouraged them to squat on river lots to the south and west of the junction of the Red and Assiniboine Rivers. Demonstrating little interest in agricultural pursuits, the Métis looked forward to the summer and autumn buffalo hunts. They were the principal suppliers of dried meat and pemmican to the fur trade. How would these semi-nomads function in a settlement predicated on the ideal of developing in the image of a British agrarian community? At what point and over what issues would their interests and those of the inhabitants of the British sector of the settlement diverge?

The second mixed-blood element in Red River, settled to the north of the Métis and further down the Red River, was the one we may call the country-born. Their historical antecedents lay in the posts of the Hudson Bay trading system. British, largely Orkney, and 'homeguard' Cree ways shaped their particular values and attitudes. Numbering thirty per cent of the settlement's population in comparison with the Métis who numbered fifty percent, the country-born were the largest community in the British sector of the Red River. They were the social and cultural foundation on which the Company and the Anglican missionaries rested their hopes and aspirations for Red River. More assiduous in attending their river-lot farms than the Métis, the country-born still took pleasure in the hunt. The greater part of their interest and enthusiasm, however, focused on the ways of the trading post. To this end they were the bulwark supporting the social and political order in Red River.

But in the 1840s a new generation questioned the achievements of their fathers. A few, in hesitant partnership with the Métis, attacked the 'tyranny' of the Company's monopoly and agitated for change. What would be the nature and direction of this change?

The first Riel rising in 1870 marked the end of the old order in Red River and Rupert's Land and the onslaught of new ways. Historians have examined exhaustively the role of Louis Riel and the Métis in national terms. But what of the regional stage, the Red River Settlement and the old North West— when placed in this perspective would the historical assessments of the actions of Riel and his supporters remain the same?

GENERAL STATEMENTS OF BRITISH OBSERVERS

11.

Testimony of Dr. John Rae before the Parliamentary Select Committee on the Hudson's Bay Company, 23 February 1857.

655. With regard to the half-breeds, do you consider them a material from which an agricultural population can be formed?—I believe that the English half-breeds may be so; they are a very excellent race generally, but careless and improvident.

656. Will they settle down and cultivate the ground?—There will be a difficulty about it, because they generally prefer the hunting.

657. Have they settled in any great numbers?—In the Red River to a considerable extent.

658. Have they given up hunting altogether?—Not so far as I know. They generally hunt as long as they are able; they go as voyageurs in the summer, and hunt in the autumn and winter.

659. And they do not really cultivate the ground much?—Many of them do, but the generality of them prefer the sort of wild life of hunting.

660. Are they troublesome people to govern?—Not so far as I am aware.

661. The Company has no difficulty in ruling them, and keeping them in order?—I think not; I speak particularly of the English half-breeds. I have generally had them with me on my expeditions, and found them good practicable men.

662. Is the number of the half-breeds much increasing?—I should think it is; where they are colonised, they are increasing largely.

12.

Testimony of the Right Rev. David Anderson before the Parliamentary Select Committee on the Hudson's Bay Company, 4 June 1857.

4383. In pursuance of those inquiries which I have made, I will ask you, with

THE RED RIVER SETTLEMENT IN 1835

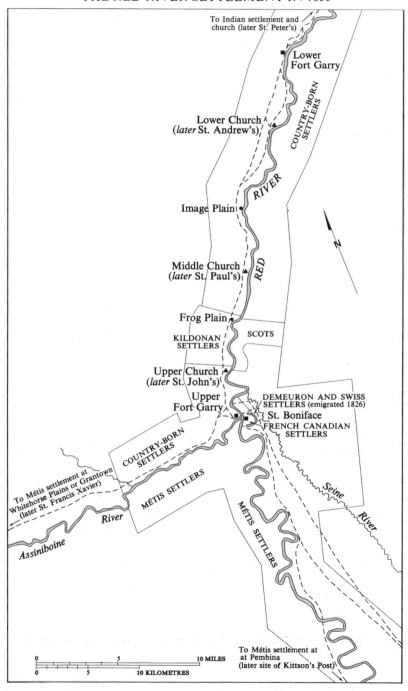

To Indian settlement and
church (later St. Peter's)

Lower
Fort Garry

COUNTRY-BORN SETTLERS

Lower Church
(*later* St. Andrew's)

RIVER

Image Plain

RED

Middle Church
(*later* St. Paul's)

Frog Plain

KILDONAN
SETTLERS

SCOTS

Upper Church
(*later* St. John's)

Upper
Fort Garry

DEMEURON AND SWISS
SETTLERS (emigrated 1826)

St. Boniface
FRENCH CANADIAN
SETTLERS

N

COUNTRY-BORN
SETTLERS

To Métis settlement at
Whitehorse Plains or Grantown
(later St. Francis Xavier)

MÉTIS SETTLERS

MÉTIS SETTLERS

Seine

River

River

Assiniboine

To Métis settlement at
at Pembina
(later site of Kittson's Post)

0   5   10 MILES

0   5   10 KILOMETRES

respect to the Red River, what is your opinion of the population there as regards their intelligence and their means of supporting themselves; that is to say, their knowledge of agriculture and their general information and intelligence?—We have very good schools, better than the average of parochial schools. They have very much of the comforts of life; more than the average of farm labourers at home; and I think every year there is a great measure of intellectual development going on among them.

4384. With regard to the half-caste population, will you have the kindness to tell the Committee your opinion in reference to that portion of the inhabitants of the Red River Settlement?—My own impression is favourable; that we must look to the half-caste population as the strength of the settlement of the country. The number of those of pure blood, the Scotch population, is comparatively only small, so that our dependence must be on the half-caste population in a great measure; and they are those more immediately connected with my own church. . . .

4421. With regard to this question, I think I asked you your opinion generally of the intelligence of the people who are resident in that colony of the Red River. May I specifically ask you what your opinion is with regard to the intelligence and thriftiness of the half-caste population at the Red River?—It is not equal to that of the European, but still I think that it is a matter of growth, and that there is no reason to despair regarding them.

4422. Are there not many very intellectual persons among the half-caste population at the Red River?—Very; some have been in my own service who have been very intelligent, and some have advanced in different ways in life.

4423. Are there many who are clergymen of the Church of England?—Yes, there is the one whom I called a country-born clergyman, though not a native Indian clergyman.

4424. But has he Indian blood in his veins?—He has.

4425. There are many of them possessing property?—Yes; all have their farms, and some have made a large amount of property. . . .

4427. Are there not numerous instances of alliances formed between the half-castes and the pure Europeans?—Very many.

4428. They are constantly going on?—Constantly.

4429. And alliances amongst those persons who are in the better class of society there?—Continually. . . .

13.

Testimony of Lieut-Col. W. Caldwell, formerly Governor of Assiniboia, before the Parliamentary Select Committee on the Hudson's Bay Company, 15 June 1857.

5573. Do the half-breeds associate on a footing of equality with the pure white men?—Some few do. The great majority of them are unlearned.

5574. You think that there is no prejudice of colour?—No, nothing of that kind; the only thing is their not having sufficient substance. There was a magistrate there, a Mr. Grant; he was one of the best there; he was a magistrate on the bench, and there is a Mr. Bunn, a medical man there; the only medical man they have there at present.

14.
Testimony of Sir George Simpson before the Parliamentary Select Committee on the Hudson's Bay Company, 2 March 1857.

1681. In that census which you have given in, is there an account of the numbers of the half-breeds in the Red River Settlement?—Yes; 8,000 is the whole population of Red River; that is the Indian and half-breed population.

1682. Can you give any notion of how many of those are half-breeds?—About 4,000, I think.

1683. Can you tell the Committee whether those half-breeds are improving in their intelligence?—I think they are.

1684. Have not the Company established schools there?—Yes, there are schools.

1685. Do not the half-breeds go to those schools?—Many of them do, especially the half-breeds of European parentage.

1686. Since they have gone to those schools have you found the half-breeds as submissive as they were before?—Yes, I think they are fully; more so.

1687. So that they do not give you any more trouble than they used to do?—We have little or no trouble with them.

1688. They do not demand free trade in furs; you never heard of such a thing?—They do not demand it, but they practise it; many of them do.

1689. Have you found the free trade increase since the instruction of the people increased?—No, I do not find that since the encouragement to trade has increased they have been extending their operations in that way.

1690. Do you mean to say that the free-trading has not increased of late years?—Not very materially; they have been in the habit of trading, more or less, for a great many years; perhaps there may be more engaged in it recently than there were a few years ago.

1691. So that the increase of education at the present moment has not at all increased the desire of the people to have communication with America?—No, I am not aware that it has; I am not aware that there is any particular desire to connect themselves with America.

1692. I mean to trade with America?—To trade in what?

1693. In all commodities?—I believe there is very little trade at present going across the frontier.

1694. Are you at all aware of any increased desire on the part of those people to carry on trade with the Americans?—No; I am not aware that there is any increased desire.

1695. So that we may take it as your statement that there is no increased desire on the part of that population in that respect?—They have more frequent communication with the United States than heretofore, inasmuch as they have larger dealings.

1696. That is not in furs?—Not in furs; principally in buffalo robes, and a very few furs.

1697. What do they give to the Americans?—They take cattle from Red River; buffalo robes, and a small quantity of tallow and horses; I think those are the principal articles. . . .

1814. Can you tell us at all, in round numbers, what proportion of the families who have settled at the Red River Settlement, have paid for land?—Nineteen twentieths have not paid.

1815. How do you reconcile the statements you have just made as to the mode of disposing of land with your answer to Question 1217, in which you said that land was granted at sums varying from 5 s. to 7 s. 6 d an acre, not in fee simple, but under leases of 999 years?—The parties frequently set themselves down on land without consulting us; we never disturb them.

1816. I asked you, in Question 1207, "If I wanted to buy land in the Red River Settlement, upon what terms could I buy it?" Your answer was, "Five shillings an acre?"—Yes.

1817. Am I to understand that if I applied for it for nothing I should get it, equally?—If you were to squat, we should not, in all probability, disturb you.

1818. You said that free grants were given to those who applied for them?—Yes.

1819. Squatters do not apply for free grants, do they?—We point out the situations where they may squat; we do not give them titles unless they make some arrangement for the payment.

1820. Are we to understand that squatters squat under terms of agreement with the Company?—Yes; very frequently.

1821. Then why are they called squatters?—A man without means, coming into the country says, "I should like to settle there, but I have not the means of paying;" we say, "There is no objection to your settling there."

1822. Are there settlers in the Red River Settlement who squat without any agreement with the Company?—Many. . . .

1825. Is it possible that a squatter should settle under distinct terms of understanding with the Company, even though he does not pay for his land?—Yes; very likely a man without means would say, "Where can I settle?" We should point out a certain district of country which we thought desirable, and the best situation for settlement.

1826. Are there many squatters in the Red River Settlement who had their location pointed out by the Company, and who paid nothing for their land?—Many.

15. A STATISTICAL ACCOUNT OF RED RIVER COLONY, taken on the 20th to the 24th of May 1856. Appendix to Report from the Select Committee on the Hudson's Bay Company.

Year	Number of Families	Average, 6³¹/₁₀₈₂ per Family	Ages.									Religion.			Country.						
			From 18 to 20.	From 20 to 30.	From 30 to 40.	From 40 to 50.	From 50 to 60.	From 60 to 70.	From 70 to 80.	From 80 to 90.	From 90 to 100.	Episcopalian.	Presbyterian.	Catholic.	England.	Ireland.	Scotland.	Canada.	Norway.	Rupert's Land.	Switzerland.
1856	1,082	6$\frac{31}{1082}$	5	243	276	220	153	85	58	15	4	488	60	534	40	13	116	92	1	816	2
1849	1,052		—	240	252	227	170	92	37	14	—	539	—	513	46	27	129	161	3	684	2
Increase—	30		—	3	24	—	—	—	21	1	4	—	60	21	—	—	—	—	—	132	—
Decrease—	—		5	—	—	7	17	7	—	—	—	51	—	—	6	14	13	69	2	—	—

Year	Men.		Women.		Sons.		Daughters.		Total.			Dwellings.		
	Married.	Un-married.	Married.	Un-married.	Above 16.	Under 16.	Above 15.	Under 15.	Male.	Female.	Total.			
1856	986	237	992	298	521	1,481	451	1,557	3,225	3,298	6,523	922	1,232	399
1849	873	145	877	135	382	1,314	373	1,292	2,714	2,577	5,291	745	1,066	335
Increase—	113	92	115	163	139	167	78	265	511	721	1,232	177	166	64
Decrease—	—	—	—	—	—	—	—	—	—	—	—	—	—	—

15. A STATISTICAL ACCOUNT OF RED RIVER COLONY taken on the 20th to the 24th of May 1856. Appendix to Report from the Select Committee on the Hudson's Bay Company.

Year.	Live Stock.								Implements.				
	Horses.	Mares.	Oxen.	Bulls.	Cows.	Calves.	Pigs.	Sheep.	Ploughs.	Harrows.	Carts.	Canoes.	Boats.
1856	1,503	1,296	2,726	290	3,593	2,644	4,674	2,429	585	730	2,045	522	55
1849	1,095	990	2,097	155	2,147	1,615	1,565	3,096	492	576	1,918	428	40
Increase	408	306	629	135	1,446	1,029	3,109	—	93	154	1,027	94	15
Decrease	—	—	—	—	—	—	—	667	—	—	—	—	—

Year.	Land.	Machinery.						Public Buildings.				Loss of Animals during Winter, 1855 and 1856.						
	Cultivated at Two Bushels Wheat per Acre.	Wind Mills.	Water Mills.	Threshing Mills.	Reaping Machines.	Winnowing Machines.	Carding Mill.	Churches.	Schools.	Shops: Merchants.	Gaol.	Horses.	Mares.	Oxen.	Cows.	Sheep.	Calves.	Pigs.
1856	*Acres.* 8,371	16	9	8	2	6	1	9	17	56	1	16	3	21	16	43	57	28
1849	6,392½	18	1	—	—	—	—	7	12	—	1	—	—	—	—	—	—	—
Increase	1,978½	—	8	8	2	6	1	2	5	56	—	—	—	—	—	—	—	—
Decrease	—	2	—	—	—	—	—	—	—	—	—	—	—	—	—	—	—	—

AVERAGE VALUE of the above Dwellings, Live Stock, Implements, and Machinery.

Houses.

	£ s. d.
25 Houses, at 300l. each.	7,500 – –
100 Houses, at 100l. each.	10,000 – –
200 Houses, at 50l. each.	10,000 – –
200 Houses, at 25l. each.	5,000 – –
397 Houses, at 12l. each.	4,764 – –

Stables.

	£ s. d.
616 Stables, at 8l. each.	4,928 – –
616 Stables, at 5l. each.	3,080 – –

Barns.

	£ s. d.
199 Barns, at 12l. each.	2,388 – –
200 Barns, at 8l. each.	1,600 – –

Live Stock.

	£ s. d.
2,799 Horses and Mares, at 8l. 10s. ea.	23,791 10 –
3,016 Oxen and Bulls, at 4l. 10s. ea.	13,572 – –
3,593 Cows, at 2l. 10s. ea.	8,982 10 –
2,644 Calves, at 1l. ea.	2,644 – –
4,674 Pigs, at 10s. 6d. ea.	2,453 17 –
2,429 Sheep, at 12s. ea.	1,457 8 –

Implements.

	£ s. d.
585 Ploughs, at 4l. 10s. ea	2,632 10 –
730 Harrows, at 5s. ea.	182 10 –
2,045 Carts, at 1l. ea.	2,045 – –
522 Canoes, at 12s. ea.	313 4 –
55 Boats, at 15l. ea.	825 – –

Machinery.

	£ s. d.
16 Mills, at 100l. each.	1,600 – –
9 Water-mills, at 150l. each.	1,350 – –
Threshing Mills, at 40l. each.	320 – –
2 Reaping Machines, at 30l. each.	60 – –
6 Winnowing Machines, at 2l. each.	12 – –
1 Carding Mill.	35 – –

Total Amount.

	£ s. d.
Dwellings.	49,260 – –
Live Stock.	52,901 5 –
Implements.	5,998 4 –
Machinery.	3,377 – –
GRAND TOTAL	111,536 9 –

COURTS

Quarterly General Courts, 1855-56.

August.	November.	February.	May.
No cases.	No cases.	One case.	No cases.

Petty Local Courts.

Petty Offences.

Number of Cases.	Cases of Damage Trespass. and Misdemeanor.	Hay Ground Privilege.	Assault and Battery.	Defamation of Character.	Total Number of Cases.
1	6	1	1	1	11

Petty Local Courts—continued.

Debt.

From 1/ to 5/	From 5/ to 10/	From 10/ to 20/	From 20/ to 30/	From 30/ to 40/	From 40/ to 50/	From 50/ to 60/	From 60/ to 70/	From 70/ to 80/	From 90/ to 100/	Total Number of Cases.
4	8	5	4	2	1	–	2	–	1	27

Total Amount of all the 38 Cases of Petty Courts for One Year.

£. s. d.
46 13 6

District of Assiniboia, 1 June 1856.

William R. Smith, Secretary.

T.G. Johnson, Governor of Assiniboia.

THE MÉTIS IN RED RIVER: THEIR WAY OF LIFE

16.
The Buffalo Hunt: excerpts from Alexander Ross, *The Red River Settlement* (London, Smith Elder & Co., 1856), pp. 245-73 *passim*.

From [Upper] Fort Garry the cavalcade and camp-followers went crowding on to the public road, and thence, stretching from point to point, till the third day in the evening, when they reached Pembina, the great rendez-vous on such occasions. . . . Here the roll was called, and general muster taken, when they numbered, on this occasion, 1,630 souls; and here the rules and regulations for the journey were finally settled. . . .

The camp occupied as much ground as a modern city, and was formed in a circle; all the carts were placed side by side, the trams outward. These are trifles, yet they are important to our subject. Within this line of circumvallation, the tents were placed in double, treble rows, at one end; the animals at the other in front of the tents. This is the order in all dangerous places; but where no danger is apprehended, the animals are kept on the outside. Thus the carts formed a strong barrier, not only for securing the people and their animals within, but as a place of shelter and defence against an attack of the enemy without. . . .

. . . The first step was to hold a council for the nomination of chiefs or officers, for conducting the expedition. Ten captains were named, the senior on this occasion being Jean Baptiste Wilkie, an English half-breed, brought up among the French; a man of good sound sense and long experience, and withal a fine bold-looking and discreet fellow; a second Nimrod in his way. Beside being captain, in common with the others, he was styled the great war chief or head of the camp; and on all public occasions he occupied the place of president. All articles of property found, without an owner, were carried to him, and he disposed of them by a crier, who went round the camp every evening, were it only an awl. Each captain had ten soldiers under his orders; in much the same way that policeman are subject to the magistrate. Ten guides were likewise appointed; . . . Their duties were to guide the camp, each in turn —that is day about—during the expedition. The camp flag belongs to the guide of the day; he is therefore standard-bearer in virtue of his office.

The hoisting of the flag every morning is the signal for raising camp. Half an hour is the full time allowed to prepare for the march; but if any one is sick, or their animals have strayed, notice is sent to the guide, who halts till all is made right. From the time the flag is hoisted, however, till the hour of camping arrives, it is never taken down. The flag taken down is the signal for encamping. While it is up, the guide is chief of the expedition. Captains are subject to him, and the soldiers of the day are his messengers: he commands all. The moment the flag is lowered, his functions cease, and the captains' and soldiers' duties commence. They point out the order of the camp, and every cart, as it arrives, moves to its appointed place. This business usually occupies about the same time as raising camp in the morning; for everything moves with the regularity of clock-work.

All being ready to leave Pembina, the captains and other chief men hold another council, and lay down the rules to be observed during the expedition. Those made on the present occasion were:—

1. No buffalo to be run on the Sabbath-day.

2. No party to fork off, lag behind, or go before, without permission.

3. No person or party to run buffalo before the general order.

4. Every captain with his men, in turn, to patrol the camp, and keep guard.

5. For the first trespass against these laws, the offender to have his saddle and bridle cut up.

6. For the second offence, the coat to be taken off the offender's back, and be cut up.

7. For the third offence, the offender to be flogged.

8. Any person convicted of theft, even to the value of a sinew, to be brought to the middle of the camp, and the crier to call out his or her name three times, adding the word "Thief", at each time. . . .

On the 21st, after the priest had performed mass (for we should have mentioned that a Roman Catholic priest generally accompanies these expeditions), the flag was unfurled, it being now six or seven o'clock in the morning. The picturesque line of march soon stretched on the length of some five or six miles, in the direction of south-west, towards Côte à Pique. At 2 P.M. the flag was struck, as a signal for resting the animals. After a short interval, it was hoisted again; and in a few minutes the whole line was in motion, and continued the route till five or six o'clock in the evening, when the flag was hauled down as a signal to encamp for the night. Distance travelled, twenty miles.

As a people whose policy it is to speak and act kindly towards each other, the writer was not a little surprised to see the captains and soldiers act with so much independence and decision, not to say roughness, in the performance of their camp duties. Did any person appear slow in placing his cart, or dissatisfied with the order of the camp, he was shoved on one side *sans ceremonie*, and his cart pushed forward or backward into line in the twinkling of an eye, without a murmur being heard. But mark: the disaffected persons are not coerced into order, and made to place their carts in line themselves—the soldiers do it for them, and thus betray their lack of authority; or rather it is their policy so to do, for it would be impossible, in such cases, to proceed to extremes, as in civilized life. The moment the flag was struck it was interesting to see the rear carts hasten to close up, the lagging owners being well aware that the last to arrive must take the ground as it happens, however inconvenient. In less than twenty minutes all was in order.

The camp being formed, all the leading men, officials and others, assembled, as the general custom is, on some little rising ground or eminence outside the ring, and there squatted themselves down, tailor-like, on the grass in a sort of council, each having his gun, his smoking-bag in his hand, and his pipe in his mouth. In this situation the occurrences of the day were discussed, and the line of march for the morrow agreed upon. This little meeting was full of interest; and the fact struck me very forcibly, that there is happiness and pleasure in the society of the most illiterate men, sympathetically if not intellectually, as well as among the learned: and I must say, I found less selfishness and more liberality among those ordinary men than I had been accustomed to find in higher circles. Their conversation was free, practical, and interesting; and the time passed on more agreeably than could be expected among such people, till we touched on politics.

Like the American peasantry, these people are all politicians, but of a peculiar creed, favouring a barbarous state of society and self-will; for they cordially detest all the laws and restraints of civilized life, believing all men were born to be free. In their own estimation they are all great men, and wonderfully wise; and so long as they wander about on these wild and lawless expeditions, they will never become a thoroughly civilized people, nor orderly subjects in a civilized community. Feeling their own strength, from being constantly armed, and free from control, they despise all others; but above all, they are marvellously tenacious of their own original habits. They cherish freedom as they cherish life. The writer in vain rebuked them for this state of things, and endeavoured to turn the current of their thoughts into a civilized channel. They are all republicans in principle, and a licentious freedom is their besetting sin.

. . . Having left my friends in council, I took a stroll through the camp; and was not long there among the tents and children, before I discovered that there was a dark side to this picture. Provisions were scarce; scarcely a child I met but was crying with hunger, scarcely a family but complained they had no food. How deceiving outward appearances are! Had I judged of things by the lively conversation and cheerful countenances I saw on the little council bluff, I had been greatly deceived indeed. The state of the families in the camp revealed to me the true state of things: the one half of them were literally starving! Some I did see with a little tea, and cups and saucers too—rather fragile ware, for such a mode of life—but with a few exceptions of this kind, the rest disclosed nothing but scenes of misery and want: some had a few pounds of flour; others, less fortunate, a little wheat or barley, which they singed, and were glad to eat in that state. Others, again, had no earthly thing but what chance put in their way—a pheasant, a crow, or a squirrel; and when that failed they had to go to bed supperless, or satisfy the pangs of hunger with a few wild roots, which I saw the children devour in a raw state! A plain hunter's life is truly a dog's life—a feast or a famine. . . . Their improvidence and want of forethought has become a proverb. They live by the chase, and at times wallow in abundance; but, like Indians, never provide against a bad day. Every year, every trip, sad experience teaches them this useful lesson, "In times of plenty provide against scarcity;" but yet, every year, every trip, finds them at this season in the same dilemma. Every summer they starve themselves over again going to the plains. Reason is thrown away on them. All that can be said on the subject is, that it is "their way", and it would be as easy to change their nature. . . .

. . . Our array in the field must have been a grand and imposing one to those who had never seen the like before. No less than 400 huntsmen, all mounted, and anxiously waiting for the word, "Start!" took up their position in a line at one end of the camp, while Captain Wilkie, with his spy-glass at his eye, surveyed the buffalo, examined the ground, and issued his orders. At 8 o'clock the whole cavalcade broke ground, and made for the buffalo; first at a slow trot, then at a gallop, and lastly at full speed. Their advance was over a dead level, the plain having no hollow or shelter of any kind to conceal their approach. We need not answer any queries as to the feeling and anxiety of the camp on such an occasion. When the horsemen started, the cattle might have been a mile and a half ahead; but they had approached to within four to five hundred yards before the bulls curved their tails or pawed the ground. In a moment more the herd took flight, and horse and rider are presently seen bursting in among them; shots are heard, and all is smoke, dust, and hurry. The fattest are first singled out for slaughter; and in less time than we have occupied with the description, a thousand carcasses strew the plain. . . .

. . . On this occasion the surface was rocky, and full of badger-holes. Twenty-three horses and riders were at one moment all sprawling on the ground; one horse, gored by a bull, was killed on the spot, two more disabled by the fall. One rider broke his shoulder-blade; another burst his gun, and lost three of his fingers by the accident; and a third was struck on the knee by an exhausted ball. These accidents will not be thought over numerous, considering the result; for in the evening no less than 1,375 tongues were brought into camp. . . .

We have stated, that when skinning the animals late, or at a distance, the hunters often run great risks. Many narrow escapes are reported on such occasions. It was while occupied on this duty, in an unfortunate moment, that Louison Vallé, as already noticed, lost his life by some lurking Sioux, who had concealed themselves among the long grass. Vallé had his son, a young boy, with him, who at the time happened to be on his father's horse keeping a look-out. At the critical moment, he had shifted his ground a few yards, and the enemy rushing in upon him suddenly, he had just time to call out to the boy, "Make for the camp, make for the camp!" and instantly fell under a shower of arrows. But the deed was not long unrevenged. The boy got to the camp, the alarm was given, and ten half-breeds, mounting their horses, overtook the murderers in less than an hour. The Sioux were twelve in number; four got into the bushes; but the other eight were overtaken and shot down like beasts of prey. One of the half-breeds had a narrow escape, an arrow passing between his shirt and skin; the others got off scot free, and all returned to the camp in safety. . . .

. . . There is no earthly consideration would make them relinquish the pursuit. They see the steady and industrious farmer indulge in every necessary and luxury of life, without risk, happy and contented; they may even envy his lot, and acknowledge their own poverty; and yet, so strong is their love for the uncertain pursuit of buffalo-hunting, that when the season arrives, they sacrifice every other consideration in order to indulge in this savage habit. Wedded to it from their infancy, they find no pleasure in anything else. . . .

Every movement, according to the existing system, is exceedingly well regulated; but the system is altogether a bad one, and far from producing that profitable result which a well-regulated business, under proper management, might do. How many of these people had a kettle to melt their fat in? For want of this simple and cheap article, much of it was lost. They had even to borrow axes, knives, and awls from each other for the duties of the camp. And after the first week, many of them had scarcely a ball to put in their guns, except what might be required for self-defence. There is a manifest conflict of want and waste in all their arrangements. As a proof of the most profligate waste of animals, after all their starving, we might mention, that during the first and second races, it was calculated that not less than 2,500 animals had been killed, and out of that number only 375 bags of pemmican and 240 bales of dried meat were made! Now, making all due allowance for waste, 750 animals would have been ample for such a result. What, then we might ask, became of the remaining 1,750? Surely the 1,630 mouths, starving as they had been for the month before (not forgetting a due allowance for the dogs), never consumed that quantity of beef in the short space of four or five days! The food, in short, was wasted; and this is only a fair example of the manner in which the plain business is carried on under the present system. Scarcely one-third in number of the animals killed is turned to account. . . .

While in this quarter, one of the Sioux chiefs, called the "Terre qui brule [sic]," or Burnt Earth, and his band, visited our camp. The affair of Vallé, and the eight Sioux who had been killed, was the subject of their mission. Among other things, the chief accused the half-breeds of wanton cruelty. "Only one of your friends fell," said he, "and for that one, you murdered eight of my countrymen." After some time, however, the affair was amicably settled. An Indian chief is always well received and kindly treated by the half-breeds. These people have a lively sympathy for the Indians, unless their half civilized, half barbarian blood is raised; and then they are worse than the worst of savages, for their cruelty and revenge have no bounds. A small collection was made and given to the chief, according to Indian custom, and we parted good friends, as far as outward appearances went. We, nevertheless, kept a strict watch day and night; and this was rendered the more necessary as we had noticed several suspicious parties on the distant hills. . . .

After a few more rambles and buffalo-hunts, we turned our backs to the south, and came gently down the smooth and undulating hills and dales, shrubless and bare, that lead to the north. The place being rather suspicious, scouts and armed parties were sent out to reconnoitre, and to occupy the heights; viewed from which, the line of carts, several miles in extent, presented an interesting and somewhat imposing aspect. Here Wilkie, with the officials grouped around him, stood viewing the different parties as they drew up to camp with as much dignity and self-satisfaction as Wellington could have marshalled his victorious army after the battle of Waterloo. . . .

The carts having now got back to the settlement, and the trip being a successful one, the returns on this occasion may be taken as a fair annual average. An approximation to the truth is all we can arrive at, however. Our estimate is 900 pounds weight of buffalo meat per cart, a thousand being considered the full load, which gives 1,089,000 pounds in all, or something more than 200 pounds weight for each individual, old and young, in the settlement. As soon as the expedition arrived, the Hudson's Bay Company, according to usual custom, issued a notice that it would take a certain specified quantity of provisions, not from each fellow that had been at the plains, but from each old and recognised hunter. The established price at this period for the three kinds over head, fat, pemmican, and dried meat, was 2d. per pound. This was then the Company's standard price; but there is generally a market for all the fat they bring. During the years 1839, 40, and 41, the Company expended 5,000£. on the purchases of plain provisions, of which the hunters got last year the sum of 1,200£., being rather more money than all the agricultural class obtained for their produce in the same year. The reader has already [been] advertised of the fact that the Company's demand affords the only regular market or outlet in the colony, and, as a matter of course, it is the first supplied.

A COUNTRY-BORN FAMILY

17.
Excerpts from letters written by Chief Factor James Sutherland, who retired to Red River with his mixed-blood family, to his brother in Scotland, John Sutherland; contained in the James Sutherland Correspondence, Glenbow-Alberta Institute, Calgary, Alberta.

Red River Settlement
August 10, 1828.
. . . In fact I do not see what I have to go in search of in another Country—here I have everything that man requires for the good of both soul and body. —Religion in its purity—the best of Climates, a soil that Produces all the Productions of the Earth in Perfection and with very little Labour, the society is not extensive but agreeable. My Children I can get them educated sufficient to enable them to serve their God, and enable them to Perform all the duties of Life, and if they are brought up to industry they will be as happy and independent as they can be in any other Country. . . .

August 8, 1831.
. . . I feel obliged for your kind offer towards your name son [sic] but I pre-

ceive [sic] that the children of this Country do the best that is brought up in this Country—all those that have been educated in Europe acquire a kind of Pride that unfits them for the customs and habits of this Country and the greater part of them turn out to be blackguards or unfit to do for themselves, I feel perfectly settled in mind that my family will get on in this place after I am no more as I now can leave them a Farm well stocked with Cattle, Horses, Pigs etc. and a Sufficiency of Ground in cultivation to support double their number and which can be increased to any extent as I now possess 800 Acres of the best of land. . . .

August 10, 1840.

. . . Your parental affection may induce you to keep them [your sons] about you, or more selfish motives in getting them to do the work of your farm but in either case you do not do yourself or them justice, you say you can do very little for them, they are born in a civilized country, has the wide world before them and ought to do for themselves as soon as they are of age; not so with my family, their lot to be born in this Country does not offer them any outlet for enterprise—to learn a trade here is mostly useless as every one is his own tradesmen, all is Carpenter, coopers, Ploughmakers, wheelwrights, Taylors and Shoemakers for themselves—The only lucrative trade here is a Blacksmith and it must be learned, and it is such a dirty slavish business that very few are inclined to follow it.

I have still three of my sons with me, that is, John, Roderick, and George, the first is a healthy robust chap, and can do several things in the carpentering line and is a tolerable farmer—, The second is a good scholar, has a better education than ever I had, but how can he apply it, I could get him in the Cos. service, but halfbreeds as they are called has no chance there nor are they respected whatever their abilities may be, by a parcel of upstart Scotchmen who now hold the power and Controle in the concern, This colony is not a place to acquire fortunes, but with moderate industry people can be comfortable, . . .

August 10, 1841.

I cannot muster resolution to separate myself from my Family; its true they are all grown up and ought to do for themselves, but it has been their lot to be born in a country where they have no chance of pushing through the world nor of making a livelihood by any other means than by the sweat of their Brow, it is true that the Country is a good Country, food can be procured for very little labour in comparison to most countries I know, but it is hard to get Money as their [sic] is no market for Produce at least no purchasers but the Company, and their wants are very limited and their Prices low for what they do take, and farming is the only desent [sic] way that a man can make a living here, no tradesman can get employment Except Blacksmiths and Taylors, and them only occasionally, it's true in the summer season young men make a few Pounds by Voyaging in Boats to York Factory, but the work is so laborious that some kill themselves by it, and many are sprung [i.e. ruptured] and so disabled that it makes old men of them before they come to the prime of life, another way of gaining a little is by hunting the Buffaloe in the summer time, but it is a blackguard kind of life and no one will follow it that has any regard to Character. Yet for all this, industrious People might be comfortable and happy here as the country is good, produces everything necessary for the Food of Man and now that sheep has become plentiful all will be able to make their own Clothing, some has done so for this 2 or three years Past, . . .

August 10, 1842.
. . . I thought that the interest of my money would have served me through life but I am now obliged to draw on the stocks—.We have now here some rich old fellows that has acquired large fortunes in the service, have got married to European females and cut a dash and have introduced a system of extravagance in the place that is, followed by all that can afford it, and I to keep up a little respectability have followed it in a small way, my housekeeping expences is double of what they were when I first came to Red River— . . .

'WESTERN ALIENATION?'

18.
Excerpt from a letter from Joseph Cook to the Lay Secretary, Church Missionary Society [Anglican], dated Red River Indian Settlement, 29 July 1846. Joseph Cook was a mixed-blood son of Chief Factor William Hemmings Cook. Joseph Cook was related to leading Country-born free traders: James Sinclair, brother-in-law, Peter Garrioch, nephew, and Henry Cook, son.

. . . Knowing well my deficiency to hold such office I could not make up my mind to remain as a School teacher, Clerk and Interpreter but here I am, and have been this long 15 years holding these offices for £50 when my predecessors had £100 for holding two offices, namely, School teachers and Clerks. It is only since Mr. Smithurst [Rev. John Smithurst, Anglican Missionary] arrived at this Indian Settlement I got £10 for my Interpreting, by asking for it, and during then the first 7 years when I held three distinct Offices I had £50. Now my dear Sir, I ask you the question, what would the C.M.S. think of us if we had acted so to them to make such a distinction between them and to our Countrymen? I may safely say they would think we was too partial and did not show that kindness and brotherly love as the Word of God required. About two or three years ago, the C.M.S. sent out a Catechist to Red River Settlement, of the name of J. Roberts, he lodged with Mr. Smithurst during the winter, eat [sic] and drank with Mr. Smithurst, and no doubt had his £100 a year, and was never once asked to assist me in the Sunday School during all the time he was here, when I had to attend the Sunday School by myself every other

Sunday when Mr. Smithurst had to go to preach at Mr. Cockran's Church, and I had to attend upwards of 160 Scholars. Now, my dear Sir, I ask the question again what right and reason has the C.M.S. to impose on me this part of duty to perform more than the European Catechists? I suppose they will say, because I am only half an Englishman, this is very true, but my good Sir, I can eat as good a plum pudding as any Englishman.

I shall only mention once more the distinction which has been made, which is not altogether agreeable; when I was so pressed and finding my salary so inadequate to supply the wants of my family (you must here Sir, remember I have faithfully complied with the Word of God to replenish the earth, for I am a man of 14 children) I mentioned to Mr. Smithurst a year or two ago, wishing to send to Europe for a little more goods than I required for my family and mentioned to him my reason, seeing I was failing very fast, and expecting to be obliged to leave my situation very soon I was very desirous to prepare some kind of dwelling place for my large family—to buy wood etc. for this purpose with the little goods which I might be able to spare, to enable me to accomplish this desirous object, but to my great surprise Mr. Smithurst told me, that it was the rule of the C.M.S. never to allow any of their servants to trade and if I did persist in it I would have to be discharged. I need not tell you Sir what I felt in consequence of this severity. I ask then the question do you think that the goods which are sent out to this place yearly, by the C.M.S., are all given away for nothing? . . .

. . . We must here plainly say we cannot submit to such severity; it would be well if the C.M.S. would send out a written agreement in what terms they wish us to engage and if it agrees with our wish we can enter to their employ—by this means it would avoid all ill feelings and disagreements, which will always take place beween the Missionaries and Native Catechists if they are treated and looked upon no better than a common labourer. . . . I can assure you, Sir, we are rather beginning to get disgusted with our situations and the treatment and the distinction which has been made between us and the European Catechists, and the too-much Lordship being exercised over us. I have indorsed [sic] these letters to you which I wish you to look over, and trust will convince you of the necessity of the C.M.S. coming to some understanding with the Native Catechists.[1] You must whoever [however?] do not think we wish to be kept as Lords and Govrs by no means, we are willing to be as useful as possible but we do not like to be looked on and treated as a labourers by your Missionaries. . . . You will excuse me my dear Sir for my bad English you well no [sic] I am poor, a half Englishman.

P.S. I have no doubt Mr. Cockran will be at London by the time you receive this note: you will please to ask him the truth of what I have said.

---

[1] Enclosed, three letters from James Settee, the native catechist at Cumberland House, to Joseph Cook detailing the poor relationship between the catechists, Settee and Henry Budd, and the missionary Rev. James Hunter.

19.

Excerpt from a letter from Rev. Wm. Cockran to the Rev. R. Davies, C.M.S., dated Indian Settlement, 5 August 1847.

. . . It would be well to give Mr. Hunter a hint to be more kind to his Schoolmasters. Budd and Settee are just on the point of leaving him. So they write to their friends and so they wrote to me in Canada. He ought to exact nothing from them except teaching the School and superintending the children in anything that they may have to do after School hours. He has been treating them as common labourers. This is never done by the Hudson's Bay Company to any of their Interpreters or Post Masters. And you may rest assured they have studied what is most politic. Mr. Hunter forgets there is no analogy between his position and theirs. If he toils to get himself a house he ought to remember that so has others done before him, and so has Mr. Budd and Settee. But they did not ask him to go and encamp out in the woods two months to saw the timber. The few luxuries which Budd and Settee have been able to command out of £50 per annum they have taken them the easiest way they could. They have never required Mr. Hunter to send a Canoe to any distance to furnish them. Now last summer when Settee returned from Rat River he took him all the way from the Pas to Norway House to steer his boat. Let Mr. Hunter study the golden rule better and he will never again make such demands on these for the future as he has done for the past. You will oblige by touching on this matter to Mr. Hunter in the gentlest way possible. The whole proceeds from an error of judgement and not studying the custom of the country in which he lives.

20.

Letter from James Sinclair et al. to Alex. Christie, Governor of Red River Settlement, dated 29 August 1845.

Sir,

Having at this present moment a strong belief, that we as natives of this Country, and as half-Breeds, have the rights, to hunt furs in the Hudson's Bay Company's Territories, wherever we think proper, and again, sell those furs to the highest bidder—likewise having a doubt, that, natives of this Country can be prevented from trading and trafficking with one another.—We would wish to have your opinion on the subject, lest we should commit ourselves by doing anything in opposition either to the Laws of England or The Hudson's Bay Company's privileges, and therefore lay before you, as Governor of Red River Settlement, a few queries which we beg you will answer in course, and address your answer to Mr. James Sinclair.—

No. 1st Has a Halfbreed, a Settler, the right to hunt furs in this Country?

2nd Has a native of this Country/not an Indian/a right to hunt furs?

3rd If a Halfbreed has the right to hunt furs, can he hire other half Breeds for the purpose of hunting furs?

4th Can a halfbreed sell his furs to any person he pleases?

5th Is a halfbreed obliged to sell his furs to the Hudson's Bay Company at whatever price the Company think proper to give him?

6th Can a Halfbreed receive any furs as a present; from an Indian, a relation of his?

7th Can a Halfbreed hire any of his Indian relations, to hunt furs for him?

8th Can one HalfBreed trade furs from another HalfBreed in, or out of the Settlement?

9th Can a halfBreed trade furs from an Indian in or out of the Settlement?

10th With regard to trading or hunting furs have the HalfBreeds, or natives of European origin, any rights or privileges over Europeans?

11th A Settler, having purchased Lands from Lord Selkirk, or even from the Hudson's Bay Company, without conditions attached to them, or without having signed any bond, deed or instrument whereby he might have willed away his right to trade furs, can he be prevented from trading furs in the Settlement with Settlers or even out of the Settlement?

12th Are the limits of the Settlement defined by the municipal law, Selkirk grant, or Indian Sale?

13th If a person cannot trade furs either in, or out of the Settlement, can he purchase them for his own or family use and in what quantity?

14th Having never seen any official statements nor known but one report that the Hudson's Bay Company has peculiar privileges over the British subjects, natives and HalfBreeds, resident in the Settlement, we would wish to know, what these privileges are and the penalties attached the infringement of the same?

We remain your most obedt Servants,
signed

James Sinclair	Peter Garriock
Bapti Larocque	Jack Spence
Thomas Logan	Alexis Goulait
Pierre Leverdure	Antoine Morin
Joseph Monkman	Willm McMillan
Bapti Wilkie	Louis LeTendre
Bapti Fanian	Robert Mountour
Edward Harmon	Jack Anderson
John Dease	James Monkman
Henry Cook	Antoine Desjarlois Lent
Willm Bird	Thomas McDermot
John Vincent	

21.

Letter from Alex. Christie, Governor of Assiniboia, to Messrs. James Sinclair, Bapti Larocque, Thomas Logan and others, dated Fort Garry, Red River, 5 September 1845.

Gentlemen,

I received your letter of 29th Ultimo on the evening of the 3rd instant; and I am sure that the solemn and important proceedings in which I was yesterday engaged, will form a sufficient apology for my having allowed a day to pass without noticing your communication.—

However unusual it may be for the rulers of any country to answer legal queries, in any other way than through the Judicial tribunals which alone can authoritatively decide any point of law, I shall on this particular occasion overlook all those considerations, which might otherwise prompt me to decline with all due courtesy the discussion of your letter; and I am rather induced to adopt this course by your avowal for which I am bound to give you full credit, that you are actuated by an unwillingness to do any thing in opposition either to the Laws of England, or to the Hudson's Bay Company's privileges.—

Your first nine queries as well as the body of your letter, are grounded on the supposition, that the HalfBreeds possess certain privileges over their fellow citizens, who have not been born in the country.—Now as British subjects, the halfbreeds have clearly the same rights in Scotland or in England as any person born in Great Britain; and your own sense of natural justice will at once see, how unreasonable it would be to wish to place Englishmen and Scotchmen on a less favorable footing in Rupert's Land than yourselves.—Your supposition further seems to draw a distinction between halfbreeds and persons born in the Country of European parentage; and to men of your intelligence I need not say that this distinction is still less reasonable than the other.—

Your tenth query is fully answered in these observations on your first nine queries.—

Your eleventh query, assumes that any purchaser of lands, would have the right to trade furs, if he had not "Willed" it away by assenting to any restrictive condition. Such an assumption, of course, is inadmissible in itself, and inconsistent, even with your own general views, the conditions of tenure, which, by the bye, have always been well understood to prohibit any infraction of the Company's privileges, are intended not to bind the individual, who is already bound by the fundamental law of the Country, but merely to secure his lands as a special guarantee for the due discharge of such his essential obligation.—

After what has just been said, your twelfth query becomes wholly unimportant.—

Your fourteenth query, which comprises your thirteenth, and, in fact, also all the queries that you either have or could have, proposed, requests me to enumerate the peculiar privileges of the Hudson's Bay Company, on the alleged ground that you know them only by report, considering that you have the means of seeing the charter, and the land-deed, and such enactments of the Council of Ruperts [sic] Land as concern your selves and your fellow citizens, and considering further that in point of fact, some of you have seen them, I cannot admit that you require information to the extent, which you profess and even if you did require it, I do not think that I could offer you anything more clear than the documents themselves are, on which any enumeration of the Company's rights must be based. If however any individual among you or among your fellow citizens should at any time feel himself embarrassed in any honest pursuit by legal doubt, I shall have much pleasure in affording him a personal interview.—

22.

Petition of Inhabitants and Natives of the Settlement situated on the Red River, in the Assiniboin Country, British North America. To the Honourable the Legislative Assembly of the Province of Canada in Parliament assembled, contained in the Appendix, no 15, to the Report of the Parliamentary Select Committee on the Hudson's Bay Company, 1857.

The Petition of the undersigned Inhabitants and Natives of the Settlement situated on the Red River, in the Assiniboin Country, British North America,
  Humbly showeth,
  That many years ago a body of British emigrants were induced to settle in this country under very flattering promises made to them by the late Earl of Selkirk, and under certain contracts.
  All those promises and contracts which had led them to hope that, protected by British laws, they would enjoy the fruits of their labour, have been evaded.
  On the coalition of the rival companies, many of us, Europeans and Canadians, settled with our families around this nucleus of civilisation in the wilderness, in full expectation that none would interrupt our enjoyment of those privileges which we believe to be ours by birthright, and which are secured to all Her Majesty's subjects in any other British colony.
  We have paid large sums of money to the Hudson's Bay Company for land, yet we cannot obtain deeds for the same. The Company's agents have made several attempts to force upon us deeds which would reduce ourselves and our posterity to the most abject slavery under that body. As evidence of this, we append a copy of such deeds as have been offered to us for signature.
  Under what we believe to be a fictitious charter, but which the Company's agents have maintained to be the fundamental law of "Rupert's Land," we have been prevented the receiving in exchange the peltries of our country for any of the products of our country or any of the products of our labour, and have been forbidden giving peltries in exchange for any of the imported necessaries of life, under the penalty of being imprisoned, and of having our prop-

erty confiscated; we have been forbidden to take peltries in exchange even for food supplied to famishing Indians.

The Hudson's Bay Company's clerks, with an armed police, have entered into settlers' houses in quest of furs, and confiscated all they found. One poor settler, after having his goods seized, had his house burnt to the ground, and afterwards was conveyed prisoner to York Factory.

The Company's first legal adviser in this colony has declared our navigating the lakes and rivers between this colony and Hudson's Bay with any articles of our produce to be illegal. The same authority has declared our selling of English goods in this colony to be illegal.

On our annual commercial journeys into Minnesota, we have been pursued like felons by armed constables, who searched our property, even by breaking open our trunks: all furs found were confiscated.

This interference with those of aboriginal descent had been carried to such extent as to endanger the peace of the settlement.

Thus we, the inhabitants of this land, have been and are constrained to behold the valuable commercial productions of our country exported for the exclusive profit of a company of traders who are strangers to ourselves and to our country.

We are by necessity compelled to use many articles of their importation, for which we pay from one hundred to four hundred per cent on prime cost, while we are prohibited exporting those productions of our own country and industry, which we could exchange for the necessaries of life.

This country is governed and legislated for by two distinct Legislative Councils, in constituting of which, we have no voice, the members of the highest holding their office of councillors by virtue of rank in the Company's service. This body passes laws affecting our interest; as, for instance, in 1845 it decreed that 20 per cent. duty would be levied on the imports of all who were suspected of trading in furs; this duty to be paid at York Factory. Again, in 1854, the same body passed a resolution imposing 12½ per cent. on all the goods landed for the colony at York Factory.

The local legislature consists of the Governor, who is also judge, and who holds his appointments from the Company: they are appointed by the same body, and are, with one or two exceptions, to a greater or less extent dependent on that body. This Council imposes taxes, creates offences, and punishes the same by fines and imprisonments, (i.e.) the Governor and Council make the laws, judge the laws, and execute their own sentence. We have no voice in their selection, neither have we any constitutional means of controlling their action.

Our lands are fertile, and easily cultivated, but the exclusive system of Hudson's Bay Company effectually prohibits the tiller of the soil, as well as the adventurer in any other industrial pursuit, from devoting his energies to those labours which, while producing to the individual prosperity and wealth, contribute to the general advantage of the settlement at large.

Under this system our energies are paralysed, and discontent is increasing to such a degree, that events fatal to British interest, and particularly to the interest of Canada, and even to civilisation and humanity, may soon take place.

Our country is bordering on Minnesota territory: a trade for some years has been carried on between us. We are there met by very high duties on all articles which we import into that territory, the benefits of the Reciprocity Treaty not being extended to us. Notwithstanding this, the trade has gone on increasing, and will continue to do so; we have already great cause to envy those laws and those commercial advantages which we see enjoyed by our neighbours, and which, wherever they exist, are productive of prosperity and wealth.

As British subjects, we desire that the same liberty and freedom of commerce, as well as security of property, may be granted to us as is enjoyed in all other possessions of the British Crown, which liberty is become essentially necessary to our prosperity, and to the tranquility of this colony.

We believe that the colony in which we live is a portion of that territory which became attached to the Crown of England by the Treaty of 1763, and that the dominion heretofore exercised by the Hudson's Bay Company is an usurpation antagonistic to civilisation and to the best interests of the Canadian people, whose laws being extended to us, will guarantee the enjoyment of those rights and liberties which would leave us nothing to envy in the institutions of the neighbouring territory.

When we contemplate the mighty tide of immigration which has flowed towards the north these six years past, and has already filled the valley of the Upper Mississippi with settlers, and which will this year flow over the height of land and fill up the valley of the Red River, is there no danger of being carried away by that flood, and that we may thereby lose our nationality? We love the British name! We are proud of that glorious fabric, the British Constitution, raised by the wisdom, cemented and hallowed by the blood of our forefathers.

We have represented our grievances to the Imperial Government, but through the chicanery of the Company and its false representations we have not been heard, and much less have our grievances been redressed. It would seem, therefore, that we have no other choice than the Canadian plough and printing press, or the American rifle and Fugitive Slave Law.

We, therefore, as dutiful and loyal subjects of the British Crown humbly pray that Your Honourable House will take into your immediate consideration the subject of this our petition, and that such measures may be devised and adopted as will extend to us the protection of the Canadian Government, laws and institutions, and make us equal participators in those rights and liberties enjoyed by British subjects in whatever part of the world they reside.

Wherefore, your petitioners will ever pray.

(signed) Roderick Kennedy,
and 574 others.

RIEL AND HIS SUPPORTERS: A VESTED-INTEREST GROUP OR LEADERS OF A UNITED COMMUNITY?

23.

Minutes of a Meeting of the Governor and Council of Assiniboia held 25 October 1869, contained in E. H. Oliver, ed., *The Canadian North West: Its Early Development and Legislative Records* (Ottawa, Government Printing Bureau, 1914), Vol. I, p. 615.

Present: John Black Esquire, President; The Right Revd. The Lord Bishop of Rupert's Land, Dr. Cowan, Dr. Bird, Messrs. Dease, Sutherland, McBeath, Fraser and Bannatyne, Esquires.

Mr. Black stated that, in consequence, as he very much regretted to say, of Govr. Mactavish's continued illness, he was again called upon to preside at the present meeting of the Council.

The Minutes of the last meeting having been read and approved, Mr. Black proceeded to say that, at their last meeting as the Council was aware, an address had been prepared, for the purpose of being presented to the Honble. William MacDougall on his arrival in the Settlement, an event which was expected to take place at some very early date; that the Council while preparing the address were impressed with the conviction that the feelings of welcome and loyalty therein expressed were concurred in by the Settlement generally, or at least were so far shared by the great majority of the people as to preclude all idea of open demonstrations of dissent, but he was very much concerned now to say, that unhappily such was not the case, and that a large party among the French population appeared to be animated by a very different spirit. It had become too evident that among them sentiments of a directly opposite nature prevailed with regard to the impending change in the Government of the Country, and prevailed so strongly, that, according to information lately received, and of the correctness of which there could be no doubt, they had organized themselves into armed bodies for the purpose of intercepting Govr. MacDougall on the road between this and Pembina with the openly avowed intention of preventing his entrance into the Settlement. It was to consider that serious state of matters that the Council had been assembled, and to see whether any and what measures could be adopted to prevent the threatened outrage.

The Council unanimously expressed their reprobation of the outrageous proceedings referred to by the President; but feeling strongly impressed with the idea that the parties concerned in them must be acting in utter forgetfulness or even perhaps ignorance of the highly criminal character of their actions, and of the very serious consequences they involved; it was thought that by calm reasoning and advice, they might be induced, to abandon their dangerous schemes, before they had irretrievably committed themselves. With this object in view, therefore, Mr. Riel and Mr. Bruce, who were known to hold leading positions in the party opposed to Mr. MacDougall, had been invited to be present at this Meeting of the Council; and on being questioned by the Council, as to the motives and intentions of the party they represented, Mr. Riel, who alone addressed the Council on the occasion, substantially said in the course of a long, and somewhat irregular discussion; that his party were perfectly satisfied with the present Government and wanted no other; that they objected to any Government coming from Canada without their being consulted in the matter; that they would never admit any Governor, no matter by whom he might be appointed, if not by the Hudson's Bay Company, unless Delegates were previously sent with whom they might negotiate as to the terms and conditions under which they would acknowledge him; that they were uneducated and only half civilized and felt that if a large immigration were to take place they would probably be crowded out of a country which they claimed as their own; that they knew they were in a sense poor and insignificant, but, that it was just because they were aware of this, that they had felt so much at being treated as if they were even more insignificant than they in reality were; that their existence, or, at least their wishes had been entirely ignored; that if Mr. MacDougall were once here most probably the English speaking population would allow him to be installed in office as Governor and then he would be our "Master or King as he says" and that therefore they intended to send him back; that they consider that they are acting not only for their own good, but for the good of the whole Settlement; that they did not feel that they were breaking any law, but, were simply acting in defence of their own liberty; that they did not anticipate any opposition from their English speaking fellow countrymen, and only wished them to join and aid in securing their common rights; that they might be opposed by some Canadian party in the Country, but for that they were quite prepared; and that they were determined to prevent Mr. MacDougall from coming into the Settlement at all hazards.

The Council endeavoured to convince Mr. Riel of the erroneous nature of the views held by himself and the party he represented, explained the highly criminal character of their proceedings, and pointed out the very disastrous consequences which might occur, not only to themselves, but, to the Settlement generally, if they persisted in their present course. He was earnestly advised to exercise his influence with the party in dissuading them from attempting to molest him (Mr. MacDougall) in any way and inducing them to return peacably to their homes; assuring him that sooner or later heavy retribution would fall upon them if they carried their plans into execution.

Mr. Riel, however, refused to adopt the views of the Council and persisted in expressing his determination to oppose Mr. MacDougall's entrance into the Settlement; declining even to press the reasoning and advice of the Council upon his party, although he reluctantly promised to repeat to them what he had just heard and to inform Govr. Mactavish of the result by Thursday at 11 o'clock.

Mr. Riel and Mr. Bruce having retired, the Council resumed the consideration of the subject before them, and the expediency of calling out an armed force to meet and protect Mr. MacDougall was suggested; but as it was seen that it would be from the English speaking part of the Community that such a force if forthcoming at all, would be chiefly drawn, the result would evidently be to bring into armed collision, sections of the people who—although they had hitherto lived together in comparative harmony, yet differed from each other so widely in point of race, of language and religion, as well as general habits, that the commencement of actual hostilities between them would probably involve not only themselves but the surrounding Indians in a sanguinary and protracted struggle; and the Council therefore felt, that without a regular military force to fall back upon they could hardly be held jusitifed, under almost any circumstances in resorting to an experiment so full of possible mischief to the whole country.

The Council at length, having learnt that a number of the more intelligent and influential among the French were not implicated in the hostile movement against Mr. MacDougall, adopted the following Resolution

That, Messrs. Dease and Goulet be appointed to collect immediately as many of the more respectable of the French community as they could and with them proceed to the camp of the party who intend to intercept Gov. Mac-Dougall and endeavour if possible to procure their peaceable dispersion and that Mr. Dease report to Gov. Mactavish on or before Thursday next as to their success or otherwise.

The Council then adjourned.

24.
Excerpt from a Report from Donald A. Smith, Canadian Government Emissary, to The Hon. Joseph Howe, Secretary of State for the Provinces, 12 April 1870, contained in E. H. Oliver, ed., *The Canadian North West: Its Early Development and Legislative Records* (Ottawa, Government Printing Bureau, 1914), vol. II, p. 934.

On reaching Red River in December last, I found the English-speaking portion of the inhabitants greatly divided in opinion as to the comparative advantages of union with Canada and the formation of a Crown colony, while a few, a very small number, favored annexation to the United States. The explanations offered on the part of Canada they received as satisfactory, and, with hardly a dissentient voice, they would now vote for the immediate transfer to the Dominion. They earnestly requested me to assure His Excellency the Governor General of their warm loyalty to the British Crown.

The case is different as regards the French half-breeds. A not inconsiderable number of them remained true to their allegiance during all the troubles through which they have had to pass, and with these will now be found associated many others whose minds had for a time been poisoned by gross misrepresentations made by designing men for their own selfish ends. A knowledge of the true state of the case and of the advantages they would derive from union with Canada, had been carefully kept from them, and they were told to judge of Canadians generally, by the acts and bearing of some of the less reflective immigrants, who had denounced them as "cumberers of the ground," who must speedily make way for the "superior race" about to pour in upon them.

It is also too true that in the unauthorised proceedings of some of the recent Canadian arrivals, some plausible ground had been given for the feeling of jealousy and alarm with which the contemplated change of Government was regarded by the native population. In various localities these adventurers had been industriously marking off for themselves considerable, and in some cases very extensive and exceptionally valuable tracts of land, thereby impressing the minds of the people with the belief that the time had come when, in their own country, they were to be entirely supplanted by the stranger, a belief, however, which I have no doubt, might have been completely precluded by the prevention of all such operations, until Canada had fully unfolded her policy and shown the goundlessness of these fears.

Let us further bear in mind that many of the Catholic clergy in the country are not French Canadians but Frenchmen, and consequently, it may be presumed, not very conversant with British laws and institutions and with the liberty and privileges enjoyed under them. Warmly attached to their flocks, they deemed it necessary to exact some guarantee that, in their new political condition, they would not be treated with injustice. It is unnecessary here to point out how the breach widened until at length it attained a magnitude and significance little dreamt of in the commencement, even by those who joined most heartily in the movement. It is far more pleasing to be able to state, which I do with much confidence, that a large majority of the French party have no misgivings as to union with Canada, and that joined by and under the guidance of His Lordship, Bishop Taché, and other members of the clergy who enjoy their confidence, they will very shortly prove themselves to be staunch supporters of the Dominion, firm in their allegiance to England.

In course of the insurrection one deplorable crime and many grossly illegal acts have unquestionably been committed, but it would be alike impolitic and unjust to charge them on the French population generally.

Much obloquy has been heaped on the Hudson's Bay Company and their Governor and officers in the North-west, which I consider it quite unnecessary at this moment, even to attempt to answer or refute, although, not doubting that both could be readily and satisfactorily done. Errors, many and grave, have, it cannot be denied, been committed on all sides, but wilful and intentional neglect of duty, cannot, I feel convinced, be laid to the charge, either of the Hudson's Bay Company, or their representatives in the Country. Personally, I have been entirely unconnected with the administration of affairs in that department.

I would respectfully submit, that is is of the utmost importance, there should be a strong military force in the North-west as early as practicable. The minds of the Indians, especially the tribes in the Saskatchewan Country have been so perplexed and confused, by the occurrences of the past six months, that it would be very unsafe to trust to their forbearance; and indeed, until the question of Indian claims has been finally settled, it would not, in my opinion, be prudent to leave the country unprotected by military. The adjustment of those claims will require early attention, and some memoranda and evidence in my hands on the subject, I shall, if desired, be prepared to lay before the Government.

25.
The Bill of Rights and the List of Rights as found in Alexander Begg, *The Creation of Manitoba* (Toronto, 1871), pp. 110, 255.

The Bill of Rights written by Riel's 'unofficial' Provisional Government, 1 December 1869.

1. The right to elect our own Legislature.

2. The Legislature to have power to pass all laws, local to the Territory, over the veto of the Executive, by a two-third vote.

3. No act of the Dominion Parliament (local to this Territory) to be binding on the people until sanctioned by their representatives.

4. All sheriffs, magistrates, constables, etc., etc., to be elected by the people —a free homestead pre-emption law.

5. A portion of the public lands to be appropriated to the benefit of schools, the building of roads, bridges and parish buildings.

6. A guarantee to connect Winnipeg by rail with the nearest line of railroad—the land grant for such road or roads to be subject to the Legislature of the Territory.

7. For 4 years the public expenses of the Territory, civil, military and municipal, to be paid out of the Dominion treasury.

8. The military to be composed of the people now existing in the Territory.

9. The French and English language to be common in the Legislature and Council, and all public documents and acts of Legislature to be published in both languages.

10. That the Judge of the Superior Court speak French and English.

11. Treaties to be concluded and ratified between the Government and several tribes of Indians of this Territory, calculated to insure peace in the future.

12. That all privileges, customs and usages existing at the time of the transfer be respected.

13. That these rights be guaranteed by Mr. McDougall before he be admitted into this Territory.

14. If he have not the power himself to grant them, he must get an act of Parliament passed expressly securing us these rights; and until such act be obtained, he must stay outside the Territory.

15. That we have a full and fair representation in the Dominion Parliament.

List of Rights adopted 3 February 1870 by the convention chosen by the people of the 'English' and 'French' Parishes after the meeting with Donald A. Smith.

1. That in view of the present exceptional position of the Northwest, duties upon goods imported into the country shall continue as at present (except in the case of spirituous liquors) for three years, and for such further time as may elapse, until there be uninterrupted railroad communication between Red River settlement and St. Paul, and also steam communication between Red River settlement and Lake Superior.

2. As long as this country remains a territory in the Dominion of Canada, there shall be no direct taxation, except such as may be imposed by the local legislature, for municipal or other local purposes.

3. That during the time this country shall remain in the position of a territory, in the Dominion of Canada, all military, civil and other public expenses, in connection with the general government of the country, or that have hitherto been borne by the public funds of the settlement, beyond the receipt of the above mentioned duties, shall be met by the Dominion of Canada.

4. That while the burden of public expense in this territory is borne by Canada, the country be governed by a Lieutenant-Governor from Canada, and a Legislature, three members of whom being heads of departments of the Government, shall be nominated by the Governor General of Canada.

5. That after the expiration of this exceptional period, the country shall be governed, as regards its local affairs, as the Provinces of Ontario and Quebec are now governed, by a Legislature by the people, and a Ministry responsible to it under a Lieutenant-Governor, appointed by the Governor General of Canada.

6. That there shall be no interference by the Dominion Parliament in the local affairs of this territory, other than is allowed in the provinces, and that this territory shall have and enjoy in all respects, the same privileges, advantages and aids in meeting the public expenses of this territory as the provinces have and enjoy.

7. That, while the Northwest remains a territory, the Legislature have a right to pass all laws local to the territory, over the veto of the Lieutenant-Governor by a two-third vote.

8. A homestead and pre-emption law.

9. That, while the Northwest remains a territory, the sum of $25,000 a year be appropriated for schools, roads and bridges.

10. That all the public buildings be at the expense of the Dominion treasury.

11. That there shall be guaranteed uninterrupted steam communication to Lake Superior, within five years; and also the establishment, by rail, of a

connection with the American railway as soon as it reaches the international line.

12. That the military force required in this country be composed of natives of the country during four years.

[Lost by a vote of 16 yeas to 23 nays, and consequently struck out of the list.]

13. That the English and French languages be common in the Legislature and Courts, and that all public documents and acts of the Legislature be published in both languages.

14. That the Judge of the Supreme Court speak the French and English languages.

15. That treaties be concluded between the Dominion and the several Indian tribes of the country as soon as possible.

16. That, until the population of the country entitles us to more, we have three representatives in the Canadian Parliament, one in the Senate, and two in the Legislative Assembly.

17. That all the properties, rights and privileges as hitherto enjoyed by us be respected, and that the recognition and arrangement of local customs, usages and privileges be made under the control of the Local Legislature.

18. That the Local Legislature of this territory have full control of all the lands inside a circumference having upper Fort Garry as a centre, and that the radius of this circumference be the number of miles that the American line is distant from Fort Garry.

19. That every man in the country (except uncivilized and unsettled Indians) who has attained the age of 21 years, and every British subject, a stranger to this country who has resided three years in this country and is a householder, shall have a right to vote at the election of a member to serve in the Legislature of the country, and in the Dominion Parliament; and every foreign subject, other than a British subject, who has resided the same length of time in the country, and is a householder, shall have the same right to vote on condition of his taking the oath of allegiance, it being understood that this article be subject to amendment exclusively by the Local Legislature.

20. That the Northwest territory shall never be held liable for any portion of the £300,000 paid to the Hudson's Bay Company or for any portion of the public debt of Canada, as it stands at the time of our entering the confederation; and if, thereafter, we be called upon to assume our share of said public debt, we consent only, on condition that we first be allowed the amount for which we shall be held liable.

GUIDE TO FURTHER READING

The student beginning to read in the history of the Canadian west in the half century preceding confederation should consult the pertinent chapters in the following standard works:

Begg, Alexander. *History of the North West* (Toronto, 1894), 3 vols.

Innis, H. A. *The Fur Trade in Canada* (Toronto, 1962), revised edition.

Morton, A. S. *A History of the Canadian West to 1870-71* (London, 1939). Encyclopedic in scope. For research purposes students should consult the second edition, edited by L. G. Thomas (Toronto, 1973).

Morton, W. L. *Manitoba: A History* (Toronto, 1967). The first six chapters constitute the best introductory survey of the fur trade in the west.

Rich, E. E. *The History of the Hudson's Bay Company, 1670-1870* (London, 1958). Two- and three-volume editions, an exhaustive treatment from a traditional perspective.

––––––. *The Fur Trade and the North West to 1857* (Toronto, 1967). A general survey of the fur-trade period.

Having familiarized him or herself with the major events and main developments in the period under study the student should consult B. B. Peel, *A Bibliography of the Prairie Provinces to 1953* (Toronto, 1956) and his *Supplement* (Toronto, 1963) for particular works on particular topics. Students can update Peel by referring to subsequent issues of the *Canadian Historical Review* under the heading 'Recent Publications Relating to Canada'. On reading Peel it will become apparent that many works, particularly those published in the last century, are relatively rare. For this reason students should familiarize themselves with such reprint series as *Coles Canadiana Collection*, Coles Publishers, Toronto; *The Canadiana Reprint Series*, Hurtig Publishers, Edmonton; and *Pioneer Books*, Macmillan Co., Toronto.

Quite quickly students will become aware of the importance of the Hudson Bay Record Society and The Champlain Society publications. The primary purpose of these series is to provide historians with ready access to documents that would otherwise be difficult to obtain. Equally important for students is the fact that these publications contain 'introductions' that constitute some of the best scholarly writing on the study of the west prior to confederation. In the *Hudson Bay Record Society* publications note particularly:

Fleming, R. H., ed. *Minutes of the Council, Northern Department of Rupert's Land, 1821-31* (London, 1940). Introduction by H. A. Innis.

Rich, E. E., ed. *Simpson's Athabaska Journal and Report, 1821-22* (London, 1938). Introduction by Chester Martin.

––––––. *Simpson's 1828 Journey to the Columbia* (London, 1947). Introduction by W. S. Wallace.

Williams, Glyndwr, ed. *Andrew Graham's Observations on Hudson's Bay, 1767-91* (London, 1969). Introduction by Richard Glover.

_____. *London Correspondence Inward from Sir George Simpson, 1841-42* (London, 1973). Introduction by J. S.Galbraith.

In The Champlain Society publications the editor is responsible for the introduction. Note the following works:

Glazebrook, G. P. de T., ed. *The James Hargrave Correspondence, 1821-43* (Toronto, 1938).

MacLeod, Margaret, ed. *The Letters of Letitia Hargrave* (Toronto, 1947).

Morton, W. L., ed. *Alexander Begg's Red River Journal and other Documents Relating to the Red River Resistance of 1869-70* (Toronto, 1956).

Spry, Irene, ed. *Papers of the Palliser Expedition, 1857-60* (Toronto, 1968).

Wallace, W. S., ed. *Notes of a Twenty-Five Years' Service in the Hudson's Bay Territories* (Toronto, 1932).

No discussion of published documents would be complete without reference to E. H. Oliver, ed. *The Canadian North-West, its Early Development and Legislative Records* (Ottawa, 1914), 2 vols. While somewhat dated as a result of more recent publications, many documents of much interest are contained within its covers.

Secondary materials covering the period under study are not extensive. Among the few leading works J. S. Galbraith, *The Hudson's Bay Company as an Imperial Factor, 1821-69* (Los Angeles, 1957), and A. S. Morton, *Sir George Simpson* (Toronto, 1944) are essential to an understanding of the times. In terms of the Company's last years as *the* political power in Red River and Rupert's Land, D. C. Tway, 'The Wintering Partners and the Hudson's Bay Company, 1863 to 1871' in *Canadian Historical Review*, 1952, is most pertinent.

The missionaries both as friend and foe of the fur trader have not been extensively served by the literature. T. C. B. Boon, *The Anglican Church from the Bay to the Rockies* (Toronto, 1962), and A. G. Morice, *History of the Catholic Church in Western Canada from Lake Superior to the Pacific, 1659-1895* (Toronto, 1910), 2 vols, are useful surveys. Other missionaries are to be found in biographies and monographs of varying scholarship as well as published journals. For a provocative study on the Protestant missions see Frits Pannekoek, 'Protestant Agricultural Zions for the Western Indian' in *Journal of the Canadian Church Historical Society*, 1972.

As yet a social history of the fur trade does not exist. Ample material for such a study exists in published and unpublished sources originating from the hands of fur traders, missionaries, and travellers. An amazingly successful work that introduces the student to this area is Eric Ross, *Beyond the River and the Bay* (Toronto, 1970). Also note Sylvia Van Kirk, 'Woman in the Fur Trade' in *The Beaver*, 1972.

Canadian historians have not served the Indian well. For a beginning students should consult Diamond Jenness, *The Indians of Canada* (Ottawa, 1967). While many historians would quarrel with many aspects of E. P. Patterson's *The Canadian Indian: A History Since 1500* (Don Mills, 1972), the book provides a different perspective from which the student can approach the Indian in Canadian history. Arthur J. Ray, *Indians in the Fur Trade, 1660-1870*, suggests an interesting typology of Indian history in the area that was to become Manitoba and Saskatchewan. While provoking much debate it should remain a significant authority for years. For specific groups of Indians anthropological and ethnohistorical studies such as David Mandlebaum, *The Plains Cree* (New York, 1940), and Harold Hickerson, *The Chippewa and their Neighbours: A study in Ethnohistory* (Toronto, 1970) are excellent. Topical studies such as G. T. Quimby, *Indian Culture and European Trade Goods* (Madison, 1966), and F. R. Secoy, *Changing Militiary Patterns of the Great Plains* (Locust Valley, N.Y., 1953) are most valuable. In addition students should note a highly controversial work, L. O. Saum, *The Fur Trader and the Indian* (Seattle, 1965). Some articles of interest to history students are:

Ewers, John. 'Influence of the Fur Trade on Indians of the Northern Plains', , in Malvina Bolus, ed., *People and Pelts* (Winnipeg, 1972).

Rich, E. E. 'Trade Habits and Economic Motivation Among the Indians of North America' in *Canadian Journal of Economics and Political Science*, 1960.

Rotstein, Abraham. 'Trade and Politics: An Institutional Approach' in *Western Canadian Journal of Anthropology*, 1972.

Stanley, G. F. G. 'The Indian Background of Canadian History' in *Canadian Historical Association*, Report, 1952.

In addition to particular chapters in general works, the history of the Red River Settlement is most adequately covered in:

Morton, W. L., ed. *Alexander Begg's Red River Journal and Other Documents Relating to the Red River Resistance of 1869-70* (Toronto, 1956).

Rich, E. E., ed. *Eden Colvile's Letters* (London, 1956). Introduction by W. L. Morton.

Ross, Alexander. *The Red River Settlement* (London, 1856; Minneapolis, 1957; Edmonton, 1972).

With respect to the mixed-bloods, the Métis in particular, two works are required reading:

Giraud, Marcel. *Le Métis Canadien* (Paris, 1945).

MacLeod, Margaret and W. L. Morton. *Cuthbert Grant of Grantown* (Toronto, 1963).

The first Riel rising has been examined in numerous works. In addition to W. L. Morton's edition of *Alexander Begg's Journal*, see:

Bowsfield, Hartwell, ed. *Louis Riel: Rebel of the Western Frontier or Victim of Politics and Prejudice?* (Toronto, 1969).

Stanley, G. F. G. *The Birth of Western Canada* (London, 1936; Toronto, 1966).

———. *Louis Riel* (Toronto, 1963).

Articles pertinent to the study of the Red River Settlement include:

Morton, A. S. 'The Place of the Red River Settlement in the Plans of the

Hudson's Bay Company, 1812-1825' in *Canadian Historical Association*, Report, 1929.

————. 'The New Nation, The Métis' in The Royal Society of Canada, *Transactions*, Series III, Section II, 1939.

Morton, W. L. 'Agriculture in the Red River Colony' in *Canadian Historical Review*, 1949.

II Government and Politics in Manitoba and the Northwest Territories

Lewis H. Thomas

INTRODUCTION

Although Manitoba and the North West Territories possessed two quite different forms of constitutional organization from 1870 to 1905, the overwhelming majority of their population occupied the same grassland country, commonly referred to as the prairie region. Consequently the same economic 'activity predominated in both Manitoba and the Territories, viz. agriculture, and more particularly grain growing. Of all the grain crops, wheat was the most rewarding, so that it can be said that from the beginning the material basis of prairie society was a one-crop economy. In no other province did this reliance on a single form for the production of wealth prevail, with the sole exception of the future province of Newfoundland, where the cod fish reigned supreme.

The prairie farmer was unique in that the cash return for his labours depended on the prices prevailing in the competitive international market, for he was soon producing more than Canada itself could consume. Irrespective of the price the farmer received, however, the Canadian Pacific Railway, the central Canadian manufacturer (protected from international competition by the tariff walls of the 'National Policy'), and the central Canadian banking and mortgage companies all enjoyed a handsome profit from the goods and services they contributed for the production of the wealth of the prairies.

Both Manitoba and the North West Territories were deprived of the control and disposal of their natural resources—another difference that set them apart from the provinces. This created a feeling of inferiority and alienation that continued until 1930, when the federal government surrendered its jurisdiction in this field.

It is not surprising, then, to observe the development of similar public opinion and political reactions in Manitoba and the Territories. These responses emerged first in Manitoba, for the obvious reason that it was the first part of the prairies to be settled. But these responses are echoed as the tide of settlement moved westwards into the Territories. The long and dramatic history of populist third parties dates from this period, as do other forms of prairie protest, including the Riel Rebellion. More constructive were the self-help organizations—the short-lived Farmers' Unions, and the immensely influential Grain Growers' Associations, which in due course were to be known as 'the farmers' parliaments', since their resolutions were quickly translated into provincial legislation.

There were, however, two minorities in Manitoba and the Territories that had no widespread public support and no one to plead their cause except for their own spokesmen. These were the Indians and the French-speaking minority. Despite solemn 'treaties' and, in the case of the French, constitutional guarantees, they became the forgotten men. 'Out of sight, out of mind' sums up the attitude of the westerner to the Indian; and the French-speaking westerner was unable to convert his English-speaking compatriot to the concept of a bi-cultural society. Most westerners rejected the idea that the bi-cultural pact upon which the nation was founded in 1867 extended to the west.

It would be misleading to represent federal western policy as entirely negative and restrictive. The federal government initiated legislation essential for local government, settlement of the country, agricultural development, and law and order. Despite its treatment of the west as a colonial dependency, on occasion its imperial rule was benevolent. On occasion, too, it responded to western political pressure.

But as the documents in the following section demonstrate, federal policy was always ambivalent.

INAUGURATION OF GOVERNMENT FOR THE NORTH WEST TERRITORIES, AND PROVINCIAL GOVERNMENT FOR MANITOBA, 1869-70

In 1869, in view of the impending acquisition of Ruperts' Land and the North Western Territory, it was necessary to provide a local government for the combined area. 'We are in utter darkness as to the state of affairs there', Prime Minister Macdonald wrote to an Ontario correspondent, 'what the wants and wishes of the people are—or, in fact, how the affairs are carried on at all.'* Hence a temporary local government of the territorial form was embodied in the Temporary Government Act of 1869. It owed nothing to the elaborate form of territorial government originally provided by the United States' Northwest Ordinance of 1787.

The Red River disturbances of 1869-70 made it necessary to provide a provincial rather than a territorial government for the Red River Settlement, but for the remainder of the Territories the Temporary Government remained untouched. It was a simple form of government with a Lieutenant-Governor who not only represented the Crown, but also was the chief local administra-

---

*See Lewis H. Thomas, *The Struggle for Responsible Government in the North West Territories, 1870-97* (Toronto, 1956), p. 15.

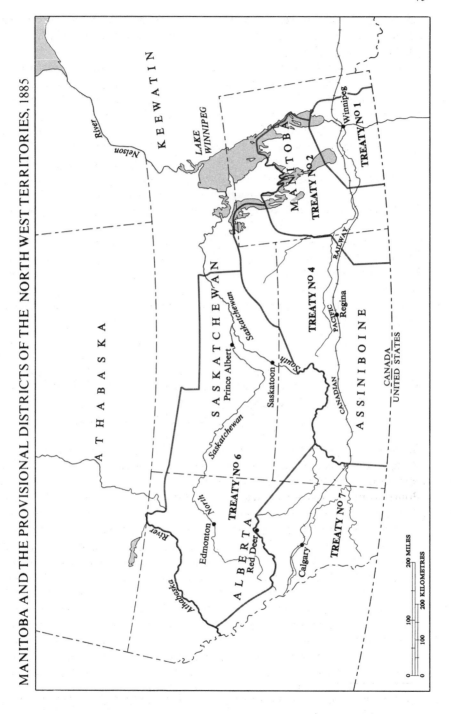

MANITOBA AND THE PROVISIONAL DISTRICTS OF THE NORTH WEST TERRITORIES, 1885

tor of the Territories. For reasons of economy the Lieutenant-Governor of Manitoba was also given a commission as Lieutenant-Governor of the Territories; this arrangement persisted to 1876. To aid the Governor in using his legislative and executive powers, councillors were to be appointed by the cabinet in Ottawa.

Louis Riel's demands in 1870, in addition to provincehood, included constitutional guarantees for denominational schools and the French language. The political influence of the old settlers would be guaranteed for a time by an appointed upper house of the legislature—the Legislative Council. The economic survival of the Métis was ensured by a large land reserve. These arrangements were explicit or implicit in Prime Minister Macdonald's speech. But the bill did not escape criticism by the leader of the Liberal opposition— Alexander Mackenzie. The new province was approximately 14,000 square miles in area, as compared with the estimated 2,550,000 square miles of the North West Territories.

Adams G. Archibald, a Nova Scotian Father of Confederation, was the first Lieutenant-Governor of Manitoba. He was responsible for the choice of the first cabinet and found it necessary during his brief term to be a quasi-Premier as well as a representative of the Crown. His speech from the throne, opening the first session of the Manitoba legislature, not only describes its responsibilities but forecasts the emergence of a new social order that would displace the fur-trade society of the west.

26. THE TEMPORARY GOVERNMENT ACT, 1869

Statutes of Canada, 32-3 Vic., Chap. 3 (1869).

. . . Her Majesty, by and with the advice and consent of the Senate and House of Commons of Canada, enacts as follows:

1. The said Territories when admitted as aforesaid, shall be styled and known as "The North West Territories."

2. It shall be lawful for the Governor, by any Order or Orders, to be by him from time to time made, with the advice of the Privy Council, (and subject to such conditions and restriction as to him shall seem meet) to authorize and empower such Officer as he may from time to time appoint as Lieutenant-Governor of the North West Territories, to make provision for the administration of Justice therein, and generally to make, ordain, and establish all such Laws, Institutions and Ordinances as may be necessary for the Peace, Order and good Government of Her Majesty's subjects and others therein; provided that all such Orders in Council, and all Laws and Ordinances, so to be made as aforesaid, shall be laid before both Houses of Parliament as soon as conveniently may be after the making and enactment thereof respectively.

3. The Lieutenant-Governor shall administer the Government under instructions from time to time given him by Order in Council.

4. The Governor may, with the advice of the Privy Council, constitute and appoint, by Warrant under his Sign Manual, a Council of not exceeding fifteen nor less than seven persons, to aid the Lieutenant-Governor in the administration of affairs, with such powers as may be from time to time conferred upon them by Order in Council.

5. All the Laws in force in Rupert's Land and the North-Western Territory, at the time of their admission into the Union, shall so far as they are consistent with "The British North America Act, 1867,"—with the terms and conditions of such admission approved of by the Queen under the 146th section thereof,—and with this Act,—remain in force until altered by the Parliament of Canada, or by the Lieutenant-Governor under the authority of this Act.

6. All Public Officers and Functionaries holding office in Rupert's Land and the North-Western Territory, at the time of their admission into the Union, excepting the Public Officer or Functionary at the head of the administration of affairs, shall continue to be Public Officers and Functionaries of the North-West Territories with the same duties and powers as before, until otherwise ordered by the Lieutenant-Governor, under the authority of this Act.

7. This Act shall continue in force until the end of the next Session of Parliament.

27. THE MANITOBA ACT, 1870

Statutes of Canada, 33 Vic., Chap. 3 (1870).

1. On, from and after the day upon which the Queen, by and with the advice and consent of Her Majesty's Most Honourable Privy Council, under the authority of the 146th Section of the British North America Act, 1867, shall, by Order in Council in that behalf, admit Rupert's Land and the North-Western Territory into the Union or Dominion of Canada, there shall be formed out of the same a Province, which shall be one of the Provinces of the Dominion of Canada, and which shall be called the Province of Manitoba, . . .

3. The said Province shall be represented in the Senate of Canada by two Members until it shall have, according to decennial census, a population of fifty thousand souls, and from thenceforth it shall be represented therein by three Members, until it shall have, according to decennial census, a population of seventy-five thousand souls, and from thenceforth it shall be represented therein by four Members.

4. The said Province shall be represented, in the first instance, in the House of Commons of Canada, by four Members, . . .

5. Until the Parliament of Canada otherwise provides, the qualification of voters at Elections of Members of the House of Commons shall be same as for the Legislative Assembly hereinafter mentioned: And no person shall be qualified to be elected, or to sit and vote as a Member for any Electoral District, unless he is a duly qualified voter within the said Province.

6. For the said Province there shall be an officer styled the Lieutenant-Governor, appointed by the Governor General in Council, by instrument under the Great Seal of Canada.

7. The Executive Council of the Province shall be composed of such persons, and under such designations, as the Lieutenant-Governor shall, from time to time, think fit; and, in the first instance, of not more than five persons.

8. Unless and until the Executive Government of the Province otherwise directs, the seat of Government of the same shall be at Fort Garry, or within one mile thereof.

8. There shall be a Legislature for the Province, consisting of the Lieutenant-Governor, and of two Houses styled respectively, the Legislative Council of Manitoba, and the Legislative Assembly of Manitoba.

10. The Legislative Council shall, in the first instance, be composed of seven Members, and after the expiration of four years from the time of the first appointment of such seven Members, may be increased to not more than twelve Members. Every Member of the Legislative Council shall be appointed by the Lieutenant-Governor in the Queen's name, by Instrument under the Great Seal of Manitoba, and shall hold office for the term of his life, unless and until the Legislature of Manitoba otherwise provides under the British North America Act, 1867. . . .

14. The Legislative Assembly shall be composed of twenty-four Members, to be elected to represent the Electoral Divisions into which the said Province may be divided by the Lieutenant-Governor, as hereinafter mentioned. . . .

17. Every male person shall be entitled to vote for a Member to serve in the Legislative Assembly for any Electoral Division, who is qualified as follows, that is to say, if he is:—

2. A subject of Her Majesty by birth or naturalization:

3. And a *bonâ fide* householder within the Electoral Division, at the date of the Writ of Election for the same, and has been a *bonâ fide* householder for one year next before the said date; or,

4. If, being of the full age of twenty-one years, and not subject to any legal incapacity, and a subject of Her Majesty by birth or naturalization, he was at any time within twelve months prior to the passing of this Act, and (though in the interim temporarily absent) is at the time of such election a *bonâ fide* householder, and was resident within the Electoral Division at the date of the Writ of Election for the same: . . .

22. In and for the Province, the said Legislature may exclusively make Laws in relation to Education, subject and according to the following provisions:—

(1). Nothing in any such Law shall prejudicially affect any right or privilege with respect to Denominational Schools which any class of persons have by Law or Practice in the Province at the Union:—

(2.) An appeal shall lie to the Governor General in Council from any Act or decision of the Legislature of the Province, or of any Provincial Authority, affecting any right or privilege of the Protestant or Roman Catholic minority of the Queen's subjects in relation to Education:

(3.) In case any such Provincial Law, as from time to time seems to the Governor General in Council requisite for the due execution of the provisions of this section, is not made, or in case any decision of the Governor General in Council on any appeal under this section is not duly executed by the proper Provisional Authority in that behalf, then, and in every such case, and as far only as the circumstances of each case require, the Parliament of Canada may make remedial Laws for the due execution of the provisions of this section, and of any decision of the Governor General in Council under this section.

23. Either the English or the French language may be used by any person in the debates of the Houses of the Legislature, and both these languages shall be used in the respective Records and Journals of those Houses; and either of those languages may be used by any person, or in any Pleading or Process, in or issuing from any Court of Canada established under the British North America Act, 1867, or in or from all or any of the Courts of the Province. The Acts of the Legislature shall be printed and published in both those languages. . . .

30. All ungranted or waste lands in the Province shall be, from and after the date of the said transfer, vested in the Crown, and administered by the Government of Canada for the purposes of the Dominion. . . .

31. And whereas, it is expedient, towards the extinguishment of the Indian Title to the lands in the Province, to appropriate a portion of such ungranted lands, to the extent of one million four hundred thousand acres thereof, for the benefit of the families of the half-breed residents, it is hereby enacted, that, under regulations to be from time to time made by the Governor General in Council, the Lieutenant-Governor shall select such lots or tracts in such parts of the Province as he may deem expedient, to the extent aforesaid, and divide the same among the children of the half-breed heads of families residing in the Province at the time of the said transfer to Canada. . . .

32. For the quieting of titles, and assuring to the settlers in the Province the peaceful possession of the lands now held by them, it is enacted as follows:—

1. All grants of land in freehold made by the Hudson's Bay Company up to the eighth day of March, in the year 1869, shall, if required by the owner, be confirmed by grant from the Crown.

28. EXTRACTS FROM THE PARLIAMENTARY DEBATE ON THE MANITOBA ACT

Parliamentary Debates (1870), 1287-96.

Hon. Sir JOHN A. MACDONALD. . . . It is a small Province as the House will observe, but yet it contains the prinipal part of the settlements which are ranged, as those who have studied the matter know, along the banks of Red River and the banks of Assiniboine from the point of their confluence at or near Fort Garry up westward towards Lake Manitoba. . . . With respect to the Legislative body, there was considerable difficulty and long discussion whether it should consist of one chamber or two; whether, if one chamber, it should be composed of the representatives of the people and of persons appointed by the Crown, or Local Government, or whether they should be severed and the two chambers constituted—all these questions were fully discussed. After mature consideration, it was agreed that there should be two chambers. . . . There are also provisions to satisfy the mixed population of the country inserted in the Bill for the same reason, although it will be quite in the power of the Local Legislature to deal with them. They provide that either the French or English language may be used in the proceedings of the Legislature, and that both of them shall be used in records and journals of both Chambers. That provision as far as the Province of Quebec is concerned, is contained in the Union Act. With respect to the lands that are included in the Province, the next clause provides that such of them as do not now belong to individuals, shall belong to the Dominion of Canada, the same being within boundaries already described. There shall, however, out of the lands there, be a reservation for the purpose of extinguishing the Indian title, of 1,400,000 acres. That land is to be appropriated as a reservation for the purpose of settlement by half-breeds and their children of whatever origin on very much the same principle as lands were appropriated to U.E. Loyalists for purposes of settlement by their children. . . .

This Bill contains very few provisions, but not too few for the object to be gained, which is the quiet and peaceable acceptance of the new state of things by the mass of the people there and the speedy settlement of the country by hardy emigrants from all parts of the civilized world. While, Sir, we believe that this measure will receive the acceptance of the people of the North West, that it will be hailed as a boon and convincing proof of the liberality of the people and the Legislature of the Dominion.

Mr. MACKENZIE said . . . With regard to the Government of the country . . . it did seem a little ludicrous to establish a little municipality in the North West of 10,000 square miles—about the size of two or three counties in Ontario—with a population of 15,000 people, having two Chambers, and a right to send two members to the Senate and four to the House here (laughter). The whole thing had such a ludicrous look that it only put one in mind of some of the incidents in Gulliver's Travels. It may be on more close investigation that more palliating circumstances might be brought to light for this extraordinary Constitution, but at the present moment he could only say that he looked upon it as one of the most preposterous schemes that was ever submitted to the Legislature. . . .

29. LIEUT.-GOVERNOR ARCHIBALD REPORTS TO THE SECRETARY OF STATE FOR THE PROVINCES, 17 SEPTEMBER 1870

Canada, *Sessional Papers* (1871), no. 20, 15-16.

There is very great uneasiness among the population. The French assert that they were promised an amnesty, and many of them declare there can be no solid peace till that promise is fulfilled.

The English party, many of whom were sufferers in the late troubles, declare that it is impossible peace can prevail, till the principal actors in the late troubles are arrested and punished, and they are very uneasy lest it should be the intention of Government to pass over all these matters and let the men from whom they have suffered go unpunished. . . .

Thinking it was now time to organize a Government, and that I had become sufficiently acquainted with the people to form some idea of the material out of which this could be formed, I have chosen a man representing each section of the population here, and appointed them Members of my Executive Council. Mr. Alfred Boyd is a merchant of good standing here. He is a man of fair abilities, of considerable means, and very popular among the English half-breeds. He was chosen by the Parish of St. Andrew's (the most populous parish in the settlement), as a delegate to the Convention last winter. While highly esteemed among the English party he is not obnoxious to the French. I have appointed him Provincial Secretary.

Mr. Marc Amable Girard is a French Canadian, from Varennes below Montreal, who has recently removed here. He is a notary by profession, has been Mayor of Varennes, and is a gentlemen of some property, and of good standing, and seems to be the nominee of the French party. I have appointed him Provincial Treasurer.

30. LIEUTENANT GOVERNOR'S SPEECH FROM THE THRONE, 15 MARCH 1871

Journals of the Legislative Assembly of Manitoba (1871), 18-20.

Honorable Gentlemen of the Legislative Council,
Gentlemen of the Legislative Assembly:
On this interesting occasion, when you meet for the first time under the new constitution which has been conferred upon you, I have much pleasure in welcoming you to the scene of your Legislative labors.

You are about to furnish a test, I trust I may say, you will furnish a vindication of the policy which has given you elective and representative institutions. These are seldom conferred on so small a population. Your case is almost, if not quite, exceptional. It will be your duty to show that the Legislature of the Dominion has not over-estimated your fitness for the discharge of the very grave duties imposed upon you by your new constitution.

The work before you is sufficient to task your utmost judgment and discretion. You have to construct your institutions from the foundation. The arrangements which have sufficed for the Government of this country in the past will no longer serve their purpose. Your isolation from the rest of the world, which deprived you of some advantages, protected you from many evils. That isolation is about to cease. A line of communication between Ontario and this Province will shortly be opened up by the lakes. Different lines of railroad are approaching your borders from the neighboring States, and within a year, there will be steam communication, partly by boat, and partly by rail, between this Province and the rest of the continent. Already a contract has been entered into, to construct a Line of Telegraph, which, before the snow falls again, will put you into instantaneous communication with all the world.

The arrangements recently made between the Governments of British Columbia and Canada, now requiring merely formal confirmation, have grouped into one country all that is British from the Atlantic to the Pacific in this Northern Continent.

As an incident of the arrangements so made, a railway will shortly be constructed through the heart of your country, traversing the rich valley of the Saskatchewan, and opening up to immigration vast tracts of the best unsettled country in the world.

In the new state of things which is at hand, you will find scope for the exercise of the best abilities and the purest patriotism. . . .

In conclusion, allow me to congratulate you upon the prospects now dawning on your country. I have been able for several months that I have been in the Province to maintain peace and order with scarce any of the institutions or aids of an organized society.

In my efforts to calm down the exasperations arising from the painful events of last winter, I have been seconded by the co-operation of the great body of the intelligent and respectable people of this country, irrespective of race or creed; and I owe it to you to say, that the manner in which the people generally have conducted themselves at the Polls, on their first essay under the new constitution, is such as would reflect no discredit upon people longer exercised in elective institutions.

I trust your deliberations will be marked by moderation, by good sense, by patriotism, and that when the labors of the Session shall have drawn to a close, you will leave behind you, in the work you shall have done, a lasting monument to the zeal, assiduity and success, with which you have applied yourselves to the task of laying the foundations of the institutions of a noble Province.

INDIAN AFFAIRS

The decade of the 1870s was the most important in western Canadian Indian history until a century later. This was the decade of the first seven Indian treaties, and of the federal legislation that governed both individuals and bands, much of which remains in force to the present day.

Treaty No. 1, negotiated in 1871, was a model for all subsequent Indian treaties, although the latter differed from each other in the obligations assumed by the Department of Indian Affairs. As the Indians learned from experience, they became more effective negotiators, although it must be kept in mind that the treaties were never between equal parties. The Indians never had any opportunity to dictate major concessions in return for the surrender of the vast areas that they had occupied. It was always a 'take it or leave it' proposition.

The Indian Act of 1876 and the policy statement of the Minister of Indian Affairs reveal the paternalistic attitude of the department, which was 'designed to lead the Indian people by degrees to mingle with the white race in the ordinary avocations of life'. (Canada *Sessional Papers*, 1871, no. 23, 4.) This assimilationist policy was in contradiction to the policy of segregation embodied in the reserve system.

31. TREATY NUMBER ONE

Alexander Morris, *The Treaties of Canada with the Indians of Manitoba and the North-West Territories* (Toronto, 1880), pp. 313-16.

ARTICLES OF A TREATY, made and concluded this third day of August, in the year of our Lord, one thousand eight hundred and seventy-one, between Her Most Gracious Majesty the Queen of Great Britain and Ireland, by Her Commissioner Wemyss M. Simpson, Esquire, of the one part, and the Chippewa and Swampy Cree Tribes of Indians, inhabitants of the country within the limits hereinafter defined and described by their Chiefs, chosen and named as hereinafter mentioned, of the other part:

Whereas, all the Indians inhabiting the said country have, pursuant to an appointment made by the said Commissioner, been convened at the Stone Fort, otherwise called Lower Fort Garry, to deliberate upon certain matters of interest to Her Most Gracious Majesty of the one part, and to the said Indians of the other; and whereas the said Indians have been notified and informed by Her Majesty's said Commissioner, that it is the desire of Her Majesty to open up to settlement and immigration a tract of country bounded and described as hereinafter mentioned, and to obtain the consent thereto of her Indian subjects inhabiting the said tract and to make a treaty and arrangements with them, so that there may be peace and good will between them and Her Majesty, and that they may know and be assured of what allowance they are to count upon and receive, year by year, from Her Majesty's bounty and benevolence.

And whereas the Indians of the said tract, duly convened in Council as aforesaid, and being requested by Her Majesty's said Commissioner to name certain Chiefs and head men, who should be authorized on their behalf to conduct such negotiations, and sign any treaty to be founded thereon, and to become responsible to Her Majesty for the faithful performance, by their respective bands, of such obligations as should be assumed by them the said Indians, have thereupon named the following persons for that purpose, that is to say: Mis-koo-kenew, or Red Eagle, (Henry Prince); Ka-ke-ka-penais, or Bird for ever; Na-sha-ke-penais, or Flying down Bird; Na-na-wa-nana, or Centre of Bird's Tail; Ke-we-tayash, or Flying round; Wa-ko-wush, or Whip-poor-Will; Oo-za-we-kwun, or Yellow Quill; . . .

The Chippewa and Swampy Cree Tribes of Indians, and all other the Indians inhabiting the district hereinafter described and defined, do hereby cede, release, surrender, and yield up to Her Majesty the Queen, and her successors for ever, all the lands included within the following limits, that is to say: [a semi-rectangular area of about 200 miles east and west and 100 miles north and south, between the international boundary and the south ends of Lakes Winnipeg and Manitoba, beginning east of the Lake of the Woods] to have and to hold the same to her said Majesty the Queen, and her successors for ever; and Her Majesty the Queen, hereby agrees and undertakes to lay aside and reserve for the sole and exclusive use of the Indians, the following tracts of land, that is to say: For the use of the Indians belonging to the band of which Henry Prince, otherwise called Mis-koo-ke-new, is the Chief, so much of land on both sides of the Red River, beginning at the south line of St. Peter's Parish, as will furnish one hundred and sixty acres for each family of five, or in that proportion for larger or smaller families; [here follow the same terms for three other bands] it being understood, however, that if at the date of the execution of this treaty, there are any settlers within the bounds of any lands reserved by any band, Her Majesty reserves the right to deal with such settlers as she shall deem just, so as not to diminish the extent of land allotted to the Indians.

And with a view to show the satisfaction of Her Majesty with the behaviour and good conduct of her Indians, parties to this treaty, she hereby, through her Commissioner, makes them a present of three dollars for each Indian man, woman and child belonging to the bands here represented.

And further, Her Majesty agrees to maintain a school on each reserve hereby made, whenever the Indians of the reserve should desire it.

Within the boundary of Indian Reserves, until otherwise enacted by the proper legislative authority, no intoxicating liquor shall be allowed to be introduced or sold, and all laws now in force or hereafter to be enacted to preserve Her Majesty's Indian subjects, inhabiting the reserves or living elsewhere, from the evil influence of the use of intoxicating liquors, shall be strictly enforced.

Her Majesty's Commissioner shall, as soon as possible after the execution of this treaty, cause to be taken an accurate census of all the Indians inhabiting the district above described, distributing them in families, and shall in every year ensuing the date hereof, at some period during the month of July in each year, to be duly notified to the Indians, and at or near the respective reserves, pay to each Indian family of five persons the sum of fifteen dollars Canadian currency, or in like proportion for a larger or smaller family, such payment to be made in such articles as the Indians shall require of blankets, clothing, prints (assorted colors), twine or traps, at the current cost price in Montreal, or otherwise, if Her Majesty shall deem the same desirable in the interests of Her Indian people, in cash.

And the undersigned Chiefs do hereby bind and pledge themselves and their people strictly to observe this treaty, and to maintain perpetual peace between themselves and Her Majesty's white subjects, and not to interfere with the property or in any way molest the persons of Her Majesty's white or other subjects.

In witness whereof Her Majesty's said Commissioner and the said Indian Chiefs have hereunto subscribed and set their hand and seal, at the Lower Fort Garry, this day and year herein first above mentioned.

32. THE INDIAN ACT, 1876

Statutes of Canada, 39 Vic., Chap. 18 (1876).

2. The Minister of the Interior shall be Superintendent-General of Indian Affairs, and shall be governed in the supervision of the said affairs, and in the control and management of the reserves, lands, moneys and property of Indians in Canada by the provisions of this Act.

3. The term "Indian" means

First. Any male person of Indian blood reputed to belong to a particular band;

Secondly. Any child of such person;

Thirdly. Any woman who is or was lawfully married to such person. . . .

Provided that any Indian woman marrying any other than an Indian or a non-treaty Indian shall cease to be an Indian in any respect within the meaning of this Act, except that she shall be entitled to share equally with the members of the band to which she formerly belonged, in the annual or semi-annual distribution of their annuities, interest moneys and rents; but this income may be commuted to her at any time at ten years' purchase with the consent of the band: . . .

5. The Superintendent-General may authorize surveys, plans and reports to be made of any reserve for Indians, shewing and distinguishing the improved lands, the forests and lands fit for settlement, and such other information as may be required; and may authorize that the whole or any portion of a reserve be subdivided into lots. . . .

11. No person, or Indian other than an Indian of the band, shall settle, reside or hunt upon, occupy or use any land or marsh, or shall settle, reside upon or occupy any road, or allowance for roads running through any reserve belonging to or occupied by such band; and all mortgages or hypothecs given or consented to by any Indian, and all leases, contracts and agreements made or purporting to be made by any Indian, whereby persons or Indians other than Indians of the band are permitted to reside or hunt upon such reserve, shall be absolutely void. . . .

59. The Governor in Council may, subject to the provisions of this Act, direct how, and in what manner, and by whom the moneys arising from sales of Indian lands, and from the property held or to be held in trust for the Indians, or from any timber on Indian lands or reserves, or from any other source for the benefit of Indians . . . shall be invested from time to time, and how the payments or assistance to which the Indians may be entitled shall be made or given, and may provide for the general management of such moneys, . . .

61. At the election of a chief or chiefs, or the granting of any ordinary consent required of a band of Indians under this Act, those entitled to vote at the council or meeting thereof shall be the male members of the band of the full age of twenty-one years; . . .

63. The chief or chiefs of any band in council may frame, subject to confirmation by the Governor in Council, rules and regulations for the following subjects, viz.:

1. The care of the public health;

2. The observance of order and decorum at assemblies of the Indians in general council, or on other occasions;

3. The repression of intemperance and profligacy;

4. The prevention of trespass by cattle;

5. The maintenance of roads, bridges, ditches and fences;

6. The construction and repair of school houses, council houses and other Indian public buildings;

7. The establishment of pounds and the appointment of pound-keepers;

8. The locating of the land in their reserves, and the establishment of a register of such locations. . . .

64. No Indian or non-treaty Indian shall be liable to be taxed for any real or personal property, unless he holds real estate under lease or in fee simple, or personal property, outside of the reserve or special reserve, in which case he shall be liable to be taxed for such real or personal property at the same rate as other persons in the locality in which it is situate. . . .

79. Whoever sells, exchanges with, barters, supplies or gives to any Indian, or non-treaty Indian in Canada, any kind of intoxicant, or causes or procures the same to be done, or connives or attemps thereat or opens or keeps, or causes to be opened or kept, on any reserve or special reserve, a tavern, house or building where any intoxicant is sold, bartered, exchanged or given, or is found in possession of any intoxicant in the house, tent, wigwam or place of abode of any Indian or non-treaty Indian, shall, on conviction thereof before any judge, stipendiary magistrate or two justices of the peace, upon the evidence of one credible witness other than the informer or prosecutor, be liable to imprisonment for a period not less than one month nor exceeding six months, with or without hard labor, and be fined not less than fifty nor more than three hundred dollars, with costs of prosecution, . . .

86. Whenever any Indian man, or unmarried woman, of the full age of twenty-one years, obtains the consent of the band of which he or she is a member to become enfranchised, and whenever such Indian has been assigned by the band a suitable allotment of land for that purpose, the local agent shall report such action of the band, and the name of the applicant to the Superintendent-General; whereupon the said Superintendent-General, if satisfied that the proposed allotment of land is equitable, shall authorize some competent person to report whether the applicant is an Indian who, from the degree of civilization to which he or she has attained, and the character for integrity, morality and sobriety which he or she bears, appears to be qualified to become a proprietor of land in fee simple; and upon the favorable report of such person, the Superintendent-General may grant such Indian a location ticket as a probationary Indian, for the land allotted to him or her by the band.

(1.) Any Indian who may be admitted to the degree of Doctor of Medicine, or to any other degree by any University of Learning, or who may be admitted in any Province of the Dominion to practice law either as an Advocate or as a Barrister or Counsellor or Solicitor or Attorney or to be a Notary Public, or who may enter Holy Orders or who may be licensed by any denomination of Christians as a Minister of the Gospel, shall *ipso facto* become and be enfranchised under this Act.

33. THE PARLIAMENTARY DEBATE ON THE INDIAN ACT, 1876

House of Commons *Debates* (1876), 342, 749-51.

Hon. Mr. LAIRD introduced a Bill entitled "An Act respecting the Indians of Canada." He said: The principal object of this Bill is to consolidate the several laws relating to Indians now on the statute books of the Dominion and the old Provinces of Upper and Lower Canada. We find that there are three different statutes on the Dominion law books, as well as portions of several Acts that were in operation under the laws of Old Canada, and which are still in operation. It is advisable to have these consolidated in the interests of the Indian population throughout the Dominion, and have it applied to all the Provinces. Several amendments of various kinds are introduced. The principal amendment relates to the enfranchisement of Indians. Under the present law an Indian who becomes enfranchised only obtains a life interest in the land set apart for him, and his children have no control over it after his death. The present Act proposes that his children can control the land after his death by will from him. The operation of this it is considered will be an inducement for the Indians to ask for enfranchisement. Hitherto the inducement has been so small that very few of the Indians have asked for the privilege. This Bill proposes to go further; any Indian who is sober and industrious can go to one of the agents appointed for the purpose, to see whether he is qualified for the franchise or not; if qualified he receives a ticket for land, and after three years he is entitled to receive a patent for it which will give him absolute control of the portion allotted to him for his own use during his lifetime, and after that it will be controlled by whoever it is willed to. It is thought that this will encourage them to improve their land, and have a tendency to train them for a more civilized life. It is also intended that after they have obtained the patent for their land, if they wish to go on further and get possession of their share of the invested funds of the band, they can make application accordingly, and after three years further they will be entitled to a distribution of the funds; thus after six years of good behaviour they will receive their land and their share of the moneys in the hands of the Government, and will cease in every respect to be Indians according to the acceptation of the laws of Canada relating to Indians. We will then have nothing more to do with their affairs, except as ordinary subjects of Her Majesty. . . .

. . . With regard to the enfranchisement of Indians, it has been deemed advisable to obtain the consent of the band, and unless this was done it was considered that there would be a great deal of trouble, and discontent would result. The consent of the band must be obtained for the distribution of the capital funds. This Bill would give the Indians some motive to be industrious and sober, and educate their children.

FEDERAL NATURAL-RESOURCES LEGISLATION

The legislation that guided the federal government in its administration of the natural resources of Manitoba and the North West Territories was embodied in the 'Dominion Lands' Act and in many subsequent revisions and amendments. A permanent feature was the survey system, which subdivided the land and provided for orderly settlement and the exploitation of the surface and sub-surface resources. The Act also arranged for the lands to which the Hudson's Bay Company was entitled by the agreement of 1869, for school lands, for the sale of government lands, for free homesteads, and for the acquisition of mining land.

34. THE 'DOMINION LANDS' ACT, 1872

Statutes of Canada, 35 Vic., Chap. 23.

1. This Act shall apply exclusively to the Lands included in Manitoba and the North-West Territories, which lands shall be styled and known as *Dominion Lands*; and this Act shall be known and may be cited as the *"Dominion Lands Act,"* . . .

SYSTEM OF SURVEY.

3. Subject always to the provisions hereinafter made with respect to special cases,—

1. The Dominion lands shall be laid off in quadrilateral Townships, containing thirty-six sections of one mile square in each, (except in the case of those sections rendered irregular by the convergence or divergence of meridians as hereinafter mentioned) together with road allowances of one chain and fifty links in width, between all townships and sections.

2. The sections shall be bounded and numbered as shewn by the following diagram:

N

31	32	33	34	35	36
30	29	28	27	26	25
19	20	21	22	23	24
18	17	16	15	14	13
7	8	9	10	11	12
6	5	4	3	2	1

W   E

S

4. The lines bounding townships on the east and west sides shall in all cases be true meridians, and those on the north and south sides shall be chords intersecting circles of latitude passing through the angles of the townships.

5. The townships shall be numbered in regular order northerly from the international boundary or forty-ninth parallel of latitude, and shall lie in ranges numbered, in Manitoba, east and west from a certain meridian line run in the year 1869, styled the "Principal Meridian," drawn northerly from the said forty-ninth parallel at a point ten miles or thereabouts westerly from Pembina. . . .

DISPOSAL OF THE DOMINION LANDS.
LANDS RESERVED BY THE HUDSON'S BAY COMPANY.

17. Whereas by article five of the terms and conditions in the deed of surrender from the Hudson's Bay Company to the Crown, the said Company is entitled to one-twentieth of the lands surveyed into townships in a certain portion of the territory surrendered, described and designated as the "Fertile Belt:"

And whereas by the terms of the said deed, the right to claim the said one-twentieth is extended over the period of fifty years, and it is provided that the lands comprising the same shall be determined by lot; and whereas the said Company and the Government of the Dominion have mutually agreed that with a view to an equitable distribution throughout the territory described, of the said one-twentieth of the lands, and in order further to simplify the setting apart thereof, certain sections or parts of sections, alike in numbers and position in each township throughout the said territory, shall, as the townships are surveyed, be set apart and designated to meet and cover such one-twentieth:

And whereas it is found by computation that the said one-twentieth will be exactly met, by allotting in every fifth township two whole sections of six hundred and forty acres each, and in all other townships one section and three quarters of a section each. . . .

EDUCATIONAL ENDOWMENT.

22. And whereas it is expedient to make provision in aid of education in Manitoba, and the North-West Territories, therefore sections eleven and twenty-nine in each and every surveyed township throughout the extent of the Dominion lands, shall be and are hereby set apart as an endowment for purposes of education. . . .

ORDINARY PURCHASE AND SALE OF LANDS.

29. Unappropriated Dominion lands, the surveys of which may have been duly made and confirmed, shall, except as otherwise hereinafter provided, be open for purchase at the rate of one dollar per acre; but no such purchase of more than a section, or six hundred and forty acres, shall be made by the same person; provided that whenever so ordered by the Secretary of State, such unoccupied lands as may be deemed by him expedient from time to time shall be put up at public sale (of which sale due and sufficient notice shall be given) at the upset price of one dollar per acre; and sold to the highest bidder. . . .

HOMESTEAD RIGHTS OR FREE GRANT LANDS.

33. Any person who is the head of a family, or has attained the age of twenty-one years, shall be entitled to be entered for one quarter section or a less quantity of unappropriated Dominion lands, for the purpose of securing a homestead right in respect thereof. (Form A.) . . .

THE NORTH WEST TERRITORIES ACTS, 1875 AND 1877

The North West Territories Act of 1875 (which came into force in 1876) improved the constitutional position of the Territories by providing it with its own Lieutenant-Governor, and a capital located within its boundaries (at Battleford, 1876 to 1882, and Regina 1882 and 1905). It also embodied the democratic principle of elected councillors, who would gain a majority as the number of constituencies increased. It provided that ordinances of the council, like the acts of a provincial assembly, were to come into force upon the assent of the Lieutenant-Governor, and not after approval by the federal cabinet. The provision governing the establishment of schools and permitting the creation of separate schools was to leave its imprint on the constitutions and school systems of Saskatchewan and Alberta.

The 1877 amendment to the Act recognized the bi-cultural character of the North West at this time by guaranteeing the right to use of the French language in the activities of the government and the court system.

35. THE NORTH WEST TERRITORIES ACT, 1875

Statutes of Canada, 38 Vic., Chap. 49 (1875).

1.(2). For the North-West Territories there shall be an officer styled the Lieutenant-Governor, appointed by the Governor General in Council, by instrument under the great seal of Canada, who shall hold office during the pleasure of the Governor General; and the Lieutenant-Governor shall administer the government under instructions from time to time given him by Order in Council, or by the Secretary of State of Canada. . . .

3. The Governor-General, with the advice of the Queen's Privy Council for Canada, by warrant under his privy seal, may constitute and appoint such and so many persons from time to time, not exceeding in the whole five persons,— of which number the Stipendiary Magistrates hereinafter mentioned shall be members *ex officio*,—to be a Council to aid the Lieutenant-Governor in the administration of the North-West Territories, with such powers, not inconsistent with this Act, as may be, from time to time, conferred upon them by the Governor General in Council; and a majority shall form a *quorum*. . . .

7. The Lieutenant-Governor, by and with the advice and consent of the Council of the North-West Territories, may make, ordain and establish ordinances as to matters coming within the classes of subjects next hereinafter enumerated, that is to say:—

(1.) Taxation for local and municipal purposes;

(2.) Property and civil rights in the Territories;

(3.) The administration of justice in the Territories, including maintenance and organization of courts, both of civil and criminal jurisdiction, and including procedure in civil matters in these courts, but the appointment of any judges of the said courts shall be made by the Governor General in Council;

(4.) Public health;

The licensing of inns and places of refreshment;

Landmarks and boundaries;

Cemeteries;

Cruelty to animals;

Game and wild animals and the care and protection thereof;

Injury to public morals;

Nuisances;

Police;

Roads, highways and bridges;

The protection of timber;

Gaols and lock-up houses;

(5.) Generally, all matters of a merely local or private nature;

(6.) The imposition of punishment, by fine or penalty or imprisonment, for enforcing any ordinance of the Territories made in relation to any matter coming within any classes of subjects herein enumerated;

(7.) Provided that no ordinance to be so made by the Lieutenant-Governor with the advice and consent of the Council of the said Territories, shall,—(1) be inconsistent with or alter or repeal any provisions of any Act of the Parliament of Canada . . . or, impose any fine or penalty exceeding one hundred dollars. . . .

11. When, and so soon as, any system of taxation shall be adopted in any district or portion of the North-West Territories, the Lieutenant-Governor, by and with the consent of the Council or Assembly, as the case may be, shall pass all necessary ordinances in respect to education; but it shall therein be always provided, that a majority of the ratepayers of any district or portion of the North-West Territories, or any lesser portion or sub-division thereof, by whatever name the same may be known, may establish such schools therein as they may think fit, and make the necessary assessment and collection of rates therefor; and further, that the minority of the rate-payers therein, whether Protestant or Roman Catholic, may establish separate schools therein, and that, in such latter case, the ratepayers establishing such Protestant or Roman Catholic separate schools shall be liable only to assessments of such rates as they may impose upon themselves in respect thereof. . . .

ELECTION OF MEMBERS OF COUNCIL OR ASSEMBLY.

13. When and so soon as the Lieutenant-Governor is satisfied by such proof as he may require, that any district or portion of the North-West Territories, not exceeding an area of one thousand square miles, contains a population of not less than one thousand inhabitants of adult age, exclusive of aliens or unenfranchised Indians, the Lieutenant-Governor shall, by proclamation, erect such district or portion into an electoral district, by a name and with boundaries to be respectively declared in the proclamation, and such electoral district

shall thenceforth be entitled to elect a member of the Council or of the Legislative Assembly, as the case may be. . . .

[3.] The persons qualified to vote at such election shall be the *bonâ fide* male residents and householders of adult age, not being aliens, or unenfranchised Indians, within the electoral district, and shall have respectively resided in such electoral district for at least twelve months immediately preceding the issue of the said writ.

[4.] Any person entitled to vote may be elected. . . .

[6.] When the number of elected members amounts to twenty-one, the Council hereinbefore appointed shall cease and be determined, and the members so elected shall be constituted and designated as the Legislative Assembly of the North-West Territories, and all the powers by this Act vested in the Council shall be thenceforth vested in and exercisable by the said Legislative Assembly.

[7.] The number of members so to be elected, as hereinbefore mentioned, shall not exceed twenty-one, at which number the representation shall remain; the members so elected shall hold their seats for a period not exceeding two years. . . .

36. PARLIAMENTARY DEBATE ON THE NORTH WEST TERRITORIES ACT, 1875

House of Commons *Debates* (1875), 657, 659.

Hon. Mr. MACKENZIE.

. . . It seemed to be exceedingly desirable, at the earliest point of time, that there should be a firm Government established within the territories and that the Governor should reside several hundred miles west of the present point of authority, in order to exercise a proper influence for the maintenance of peace, or overlooking Indian affairs, and generally helping the Government to establish law and order throughout the territories. The Government had ascertained, from the most authentic source, that within the last eighteen months there were very nearly 150 murders committed in the North-West Territories, and no person had been brought to trial. No doubt those were mostly slain in Indian fights with traders from Missouri and Montana, of a most reckless character, who introduced the vilest passions of human nature into the territories and slaughtered the poor people with their improved fire-arms and dealing death and destruction by their vile intoxicating liquors. It seemed very clear that there was an absolute necessity for the establishment of a firm Government within the boundaries of the territories, and that provisions should be made for a popular Government, for the establishment of schools and of some municipal system which would enable the people to maintain roads, bridges, and other local works. That cannot be done under the old laws, for although they were suitable for a short period of time, it was now evident that the country required an improved system. The Government were, therefore, quite justified in submitting this measure to Parliament, and no doubt whenever the Bill went into operation it would immensely promote the settlement of the country, for nothing was so essential to the settlement of the country as the maintenance of law and order within its bounds. . . .

Practically the legislation of the territory would be in the hands of the Government here at Ottawa. The Lieutenant Governor in Council would have power to make only such laws and ordinances as the Bill provided for, and it would be for Parliament, when the population had increased sufficiently, to confer upon them more extensive powers than it was proposed to give them under the present measure. As to the subject of public instruction, it did not in the first place attract his attention, but when he came to the subject of local taxation he was reminded of it. Not having had time before to insert a clause on the subject, he proposed to do so when the Bill was in committee. The clause provided that the Lieutenant Governor, by and with the consent of his Council or Assembly, as the case might be, should pass all necessary ordinances in respect of education, but it would be specially provided that the majority of the rate-payers might establish such schools and impose such necessary assessment as they might think fit; and that the minority of the rate-payers, whether Protestant or Roman Catholic, might establish separate schools; and such rate-payers would be liable only to such educational assessments as they might impose upon themselves.

37. THE NORTH WEST TERRITORIES AMENDMENT ACT, 1877

Statutes of Canada, 40 Vic., Chap. 7 (1877).

11. Either the English or the French language may be used by any person in the debates of the said Council, and in the proceedings before the Courts, and both those languages shall be used in the records and journals of the said Council, and the ordinances of the said Council shall be printed in both those languages.

38. SENATE AMENDMENTS CONCURRED IN

House of Commons *Debates* (1877, 1872).

Mr. MILLS moved that the amendments made by the Senate to the Bill relating to the North-West Territories be read the first time. One of them, he stated, provided for the publication of the proceedings of the North-West Council in English and French, and for the use of both languages in the Courts. They had thought that this was a matter which had better be left to the Council in question. He regretted that the amendment had been made, but it would be impossible to get the measure through at this late period in the Session, unless the amendments were accepted. The action taken by the Senate would add very considerably to the expense. Almost every one in that part of the country spoke Cree, though some spoke, in addition, English or French, and, if the proceedings were to be published in the most prevalent language, Cree should be chosen for the purpose.

Amendments *read the first and second times* and *concurred in.*

FEDERAL-PROVINCIAL RELATIONS AND THE 'BETTER TERMS' AGITATION IN MANITOBA

The political history of Manitoba during the 1870s and 1880s was dominated by quarrels with the federal government over the effects of national policies on the province, and over the amount of the provincial subsidy. Manitoba, even after the extension of its boundaries in 1882, was too small to support the institutions and services of a province. The federal government had improved the subsidy in 1875 on the condition that Manitoba economize by abolishing the upper house of its legislature, but these 'better terms' did not prove to be sufficient. However the most acrimonious quarrel between Winnipeg and Ottawa concerned railway services, which was only resolved in 1888 when the CPR agreed to abandon the monopoly clause of its charter.

The Macdonald administration adopted a firm stand in response to the Manitoba agitation, illustrated by its policy statement of 1884 dealing with the natural-resources question, the railway question, the protective tariff, and the extension of the provincial boundaries.

39. REVISION OF THE PROVINCIAL SUBSIDY, 1875

Canada, *Sessional Papers* (1876), no. 36, 2-3.

Copy of a Report of a Committee of the Honorable the Privy Council, approved by His Excellency the Governor General in Council, on the 26th October 1875.

The Committee of the Privy Council have had under consideration the Memorandum hereunto annexed prepared by the Honorable the Minister of Justice on behalf of the Sub-Committee of Council appointed to confer with the Hon. Mr. Davis the first Minister and Treasurer, and the Hon. Mr. Royal, the Minister of Public Works of the Province of Manitoba, on the subject of the financial position of that Province, and they respectfully report their concurrence in the views expressed by the Sub-Committee. . . .

It is the opinion of the Sub-Committee that the expenses of carrying on the machinery of Government as proposed in the estimate are disproportionately large, and that no satisfactory results can be anticipated unless a simpler and less expensive system be adopted and greater economy be exhibited. . . .

. . . Even if no more radical change be made it appears to the Sub-Committee that the present form of Government should be simplified and cheapened by the abolition of the second Chamber and the material reduction of the other expenses of Government and legislation, and that (in case it is proposed to expend a sum larger than that which may be available from the Dominion) provision should be made for supplementing the revenue from local resources to the necessary extent so as to avoid deficits.

The Sub-Committee are of opinion that having regard to the whole circumstances of the case, it would be proper, provided the Local Government and Legislature should make such changes in their system as would (without diminishing the total aggregate amount to be devoted to the great objects of education, agriculture, public works, charity and administration of Justice) bring down the total expenditure to a sum not exceeding (independent of the amount of local revenues) $90,000; it would be proper to charge as an advance on the debt account the balance due the Dominion, and to invite Parliament to make an additional annual grant to the Province of $26,746.96, being the amount necessary in order to raise its revenue derivable from the Dominion to $90,000; such grant to commence from the 1st day of July, 1875, and to continue until 1881, when the Province will become entitled to the increased population allowance, based upon the Census to be taken in that year.

40. MANITOBA AND NORTHWEST FARMERS' UNION PETITION OF RIGHTS

Manitoba *Daily Free Press*, December 20, 1883.

(Adopted by the Manitoba and Northwest Farmers' Convention, met in the city of Winnipeg on the 19th day of December, 1883.)

Whereas, in view of the present depression in agricultural and commercial industries, in the Province of Manitoba, the farmers of the Province have assembled for the purpose of expressing their views upon the causes of the said depression and the means of removing the same.

And whereas the present and future prosperity of this Province depends both commercially and otherwise upon the successful prosecution of agriculture.

And whereas numerous and embarrassing restrictions are placed upon the effort made by the settlers to extend their operations and improve their conditions.

And whereas such restrictions are unjust and unnecessary and have been inaugurated and continued in defiance of the just rights of Manitoba.

And whereas some of the said restrictions consist of the oppressive duty upon agricultural implements, the monopoly of the carrying trade now enjoyed by the Canadian Pacific Railway Company and the improper and vexatious methods employed in the administration of the public lands in Manitoba.

And whereas the inhabitants of Manitoba are British subjects and have made their homes here upon the representation that they would be allowed all the privileges which, as such subjects, they would elsewhere in Canada be entitled to, and it appears that by the terms of the admission of Manitoba into Confederation they should be allowed such rights and privileges.

And whereas they are denied such rights, and they find that the representative system of the Province is such that they are practically denied the privilege of securing the redress of their grievances through their representatives in the Provincial and Dominion Parliaments.

Resolved 1. that this Province insists on the right of the Local Government to charter railways anywhere in Manitoba free from any interference.

2. The absolute control of her public lands (including school lands) by the Legislature of the Province, and compensation for lands sold and used for Federal purposes.

3. That the duty on agricultural implements and building materials be removed, and the customs tariff on articles entering into daily consumption be greatly modified in the interests of the people of this Province and Northwest.

4. That it is the duty of the Provincial Government to make such amendments to the Municipal Act as shall empower Municipal Councils to build or assist in building elevators, grain warehouses and mills, within the limits of such municipalities.

5. That it is the duty of the Provincial Government to appoint grain inspectors, whose duty it shall be to grade all grain brought into the market at central points.

6. That this convention is unanimously of opinion that the Hudson Bay Railroad should be constructed with the least possible delay.

41. REFORMS PROPOSED BY THE LEGISLATIVE ASSEMBLY

Journals of the Legislative Assembly of Manitoba (April 22, 1884), 98.

On motion of Hon. Mr. *Norquay*, second by Hon. Mr. *LaRiviere*.

Resolved, That the following instructions be given by this House to the delegates appointed to confer with the Committee of the Privy Council at *Ottawa*.

(1.) To urge the right of the Province to the control, management and sale of the Public Lands within the limits for the public uses thereof and of the mines, minerals, wood and timber thereon or an equivalent therefor and to receive from the Dominion Government payment for the lands already disposed of by them within the Province less cost of surveys and management.

(2.) The management of the lands set apart for education in the Province ...

(3.) The adjustment of the capital account of the Province decinally according to population of the same ...

(4.) The Right of the Province to charter lines of railway from any one point to another within the Province, except so far as the same has been limited by its Legislature in the Extension Act of 1881.

(5.) That the grant of 80 cents a head be not limited to a population of four hundred thousand souls (400,000), ...

(6.) The granting policy to the Province extended railway facilities notably the energetic prosecution of the *Manitoba* Southwestern, the *Souris* and *Rocky Mountain* and the *Manitoba* and Northwestern Railways.

(7.) To call the attention of the Government to the prejudical affect of the tariff on the Province of *Manitoba*.

(8.) Extension of Boundaries.

42. THE RESPONSE OF THE FEDERAL GOVERNMENT

Canada, *Sessional Papers* (1885), no. 61, 2ff.

CERTIFIED COPY *of a Report of a Committee of the Honorable the Privy Council, approved by His Excellency the Governor General in Council on the 30th May, 1884.*
The Committee of the Privy Council have named a Sub-Committee to confer with Hon. Messrs. Murray, Norquay and Miller, duly accredited delegates from the Legislature of Manitoba, upon the subject embraced in the memorandum of instructions given by the said Legislature of Manitoba to the delegates, as well as many other matters affecting the Province.

The Sub-Committee, after having very fully discussed with the delegates all the points embraced in the said memorandum, and the other matters referred to, report as follows:— ...

The lands of Manitoba hold a very different position, in relation to the Dominion Government, from the lands of the other provinces. Shortly after the union of the old provinces, the Government formed from that union, purchased at a large price in cash, all the rights, title and interest of the Hudson's Bay Company, in and to the territory out of which the Province of Manitoba has been formed; it incurred, further, a very large expenditure to obtain and hold this territory in peaceable possession, and at a still further cost which is continuous and perpetual in extinguishing Indian titles and maintaining the Indians, so that the Dominion Government has a very large pecuniary interest in the soil, which does not exist in respect to any other of the confederated provinces.

The purpose expressed in the memorandum of instructions for which the lands are sought "is that they may be applied to the public uses of Manitoba."

This purpose seems to be most fully met by the Federal Government already, viz., in providing railway communication to and through Manitoba in aiding the settlement of vacant lands, and in public works of utility to the Province.

It was urged by the delegates that the Canadian Pacific Railway is being constructed in fulfilment of the terms of union with British Columbia, and not in the interests of Manitoba and the North-West. The sub-committee, however, maintain that, desirable as it may be to have railway connection with the Province, Parliament would not have gone beyond the original proposition of a waggon road had not the Dominion Government been the owner, by purchase, of a large territory, which would be made accessible and valuable by railway, and largely contributary to the cost of so great an undertaking. Accompanying the proposition to construct a railway was the declaration that the lands of the North-West would bear a considerable proportion of the cost; and from time to time large subsidies in land were offered to any company that would undertake the work. In 1880 Parliament solemnly set aside one hundred million acres of those lands towards meeting the cost of the work; and in 1881 contracted with the Canadian Pacific Railway Company to hand over certain portions of constructed road, together with twenty-five millions of dollars in cash, and grant twenty-five million acres of land for the completion of the line. . . .

The Dominion Government had also set apart, at greatly reduced prices, lands to aid the construction of other roads in Manitoba and the Territories, and given free of cost a large acreage in aid of a line to Hudson Bay, so that the Dominion Government is as stated using the "public lands of Manitoba for the benefit thereof." Moreover, it should not be forgotten that it has provided, in the Act of 1881, for an annual cash payment of $45,000, which was then accepted in lieu of public lands. Other considerations of vital import to the Province of Manitoba have much weight with your Sub-Committee. The success of all the undertakings by the Dominion Government, in and for the North-West, depends largely upon the settlement of the lands. Combined with a great expenditure in organizing and maintaining an immigration service abroad and at home, Parliament pledged its faith to the world that a large portion of those lands should be set apart for free homesteads to all coming settlers, and another portion to be held in trust for the education of their children. No transfer could therefore be made without exacting from the Province the most ample securities that this pledged policy shall be maintained; hence, in so far as the free lands extend, there would be no monetary advantage to the Province, whilst a transfer would most assuredly seriously embarrass all the costly immigration operations which the Dominion Government is making, mainly in behalf of Manitoba and the Territories. . . .

7th. "To call the attention of the Government to the prejudicial effects of the tariff on the Province of Manitoba."

In the discussion on this point, the Sub-Committee is of opinion that it was not shown that the effect of the Tariff is prejudicial to the Province, or that it operates exceptionally, unless perhaps in some few cases, which it is believed will be remedied, as means of transport from the other Provinces improves, or which if not so remedied, may be adjusted on the recommendation of the Ministers of Finance and Customs.

8th. "Extension of boundaries."

The Sub-Committee having given to this proposal, and the arguments advanced by the delegates, the most careful consideration, cannot recommend any change or modification of the views entertained by Council, as set forth in the Order in Council of date of 1st April last. . . .

The boundaries of Manitoba were originally fixed at the instance of the delegates from that Province, who came to Ottawa in the year 1870, to adjust with the Government of Canada the terms upon which Manitoba was to enter the Confederation of Her Majesty's North American Provinces.

The limits then agreed to embraced an area of about 9,500,000 acres. In the year 1881 these limits were enlarged, and territory added to the west and north, making the total area of the Province 96,000,000 acres, or 150,000 square miles.

In the same year the true western boundary of Ontario was fixed as the eastern limit of Manitoba, which may add largely to the area of the Province. . . .

The further enlargement now asked for by Manitoba would add about 180,000 square miles to the already large area of the Province, and would be viewed with disfavor as well by the old Provinces as by the new Districts of Assiniboia, Saskatchewan, Alberta and Athabasca, which have been created in the North West Territories and which will ultimately become Provinces of the Dominion. It would largely add to the expenses of the Government without increasing the resources of Manitoba, already pronounced by the Government of the Province to be insufficient to meet its normal and necessary expenditure.

The Committee, under these circumstances, humbly submit to Your Excellency that it is inexpedient to alter the boundaries of the Province as prayed for.

THE SASKATCHEWAN REBELLION, 1885

The origins of the Saskatchewan Rebellion of 1885 can be traced to the complaints of the white pioneer settlers and the half-breeds regarding federal policies and administrative activity, or inactivity, in the west. The half-breed complaints were of particular importance, as the territorial council recognized, because their claims arose from their position as a distinct ethnic group that had played an exceptional part in the history of the west. The Petition of Rights of

December 1884 was endorsed by both whites and half-breeds (the majority being Métis), and clearly reveals the complaints and aspirations of the people residing in the District of Saskatchewan, as well as in other parts of the Territories.

43. THE DEPUTY MINISTER OF THE INTERIOR AND HALF-BREED COMPLAINTS

Manitoba *Daily Free Press,* July 17, 1884.

Mr. Burgess thought the half-breed trouble at St. Laurent and Prince Albert would not amount to much. He thought the majority of half-breeds were content to be treated the same as white men. They were entitled to free homesteads the same as white men, but nothing further. Some of them could probably accept treaty as Indians and place themselves under the tutelage of the Government. He thought they made a mistake in calling Louis Riel to their assistance. Riel's day was done and he could no longer have any power or influence in this country. The Red River half-breeds when the country was taken over by Canada were afraid that in the march of civilization they would be trampled under foot and they therefore asked and received a grant of 1,400,000 acres of land for their sole use and benefit. He thought the half-breeds had not received much benefit from their grants. The lands fell into the hands of speculators at ridiculously low prices, and were locked up from settlement to the detriment of the whole country. He thought it would be a mistake to extend such a system to the Territories.

44. THE NORTH WEST COUNCIL AND HALF-BREED COMPLAINTS

Journals of the Council of the North-West Territories (1884), 39.

On motion of Mr. *Macdowall,* seconded by Mr. *Jackson,*

 Resolved, That this Council regret the expressions attributed to the Deputy Minister of the Interior, in an interview with a reporter of the Manitoba Free Press, published on July 17th, respecting Half-breed rights;

 In the absence of more definite information this Council desires to record its sense of the justice of the demand of the Half-breeds of these Territories for concessions in the matter of Land-grants;

 That the question of the claims of the Half-breeds in these Territories be referred to the Executive Council to be dealt with.

45. PETITION OF RIGHTS, 1884

Department of the Interior, Dominion Lands Branch, File No. 83808.

To His Excellency the Governor General of Canada, in Council.

We, the undersigned, your humble petitioners, would respectfully submit to Your Excellency in Council, the following as our grievances:

1. that the Indians are so reduced that the settlers in many localities are compelled to furnish them with food, partly to prevent them from dying at their door, partly to preserve the peace of the Territory;

2. that the Half-breeds of the Territory have not received 240 acres of land, each, as did the Manitoba Half-breeds;

3. that the Half-breeds who are in possession of tracts of land have not received patents therefor;

4. that the old settlers of the N.W.T. have not received the same treatment as the old settlers of Manitoba;

5. that the claims of settlers on odd numbers, prior to survey, and on reserves, prior to the proclamation of such reserves, are not recognized;

6. that settlers on cancelled claims are limited to eighty acres Homestead and eighty acres of pre-emption;

7. that settlers are charged more than one dollar per acre for their pre-emptions;

8. that settlers are charged dues on timber, rails and firewood required for home use;

9. that customs duties are levied on the necessaries of life;

10. that settlers are not allowed to perform the required amount of breaking and cropping on their pre-emption, in lieu of their Homestead, when, as frequently happens in the vicinity of wooded streams, it is convenient to have farm buildings and grain fields on separate quarter sections;

11. that purchasers of claims from bona fide settlers who have not completed the required time of actual residence, do not get credit for the term of actual residence, by sellers;

12. that contracts for public works and supplies are not let in such a manner as to confer upon North West producers as large a benefit as they might derive therefrom, consistent with efficiency;

13. that public buildings are often erected on sites little conducive to the economical transactions of public business;

14. that no effective measures have yet been taken to put the people of the North West in direct communication with the European Markets, via Hudson's Bay;

15. that settlers are exposed to coercion at elections, owing to the fact that votes are not taken by ballot;

16. that while your petitioners wish to give the eastern government every credit for the excellent liquor regulations which obtain in the N.W.T. yet they must express their anxiety, lest those beneficial restrictions should be loosed,

more especially as the country is sparsely settled and the Indians numerous and dissatisfied; . . .

17. (g) that although, by the last clause of the "Manitoba act" Rupert's Land and the North West Territories were to have been under temporary government until the 1st of January 71 and until the end of the session then next succeeding, those Territories are nevertheless, today, under a government, which has remained temporary for fifteen years and which, by the nature of its constitution is destined to remain temporary for an indefinite period;

(h) that the N.W.T. although having a population of 60,000, are not yet granted responsible government, as was Manitoba, when she had less than 12,000 of a population;

(i) that the N.W.T. and its Premier Province [the District of Saskatchewan] are not yet represented in the Cabinet, as are the Eastern Provinces;

(j) that the North West is not allowed the administration of its resources [sic.] as are the eastern Provinces and British Columbia.

In submitting this as a fundamental grievance, your petitioners would disclaim any intention of defrauding the Federal Government of the Monies which they may have contributed to the improvement of the N.W.

In Conclusion, your petitioners would respectfully state that they are treated neither according to their privileges as British subjects nor according to the rights of people and that consequently as long as they are retained in those circumstances, they can be neither prosperous nor happy;

Your humble petitioners are of opinion that the shortest and most effectual methods of remedying these grievances would be to grant the N.W.T. responsible government with control of its own resources and just representation in the Federal Parliament and Cabinet.

Wherefor your petitioners humbly pray that your excellency in Council would be pleased to cause the introduction, at the coming session of Parliament, for a measure providing for the complete organization of the District of Saskatchewn as a province, and that they be allowed as in/70, to send Delegates to Ottawa with their Bill of rights; whereby an understanding may be arrived at as to their entry into confederation, with the constitution of a free province, And your humble Petitioners will not cease to pray.

THE NORTH WEST COUNCIL CHALLENGES FEDERAL POLICIES, 1885

Because the North West Territories lacked representation in the House of Commons until 1887, the North West Council assumed the role that members of Parliament would have been expected to play in articulating the ideas and attitudes of their constituents. In other words, the North West Council did not confine itself to matters over which it possessed jurisdiction. It felt a compulsion to comment on federal policies and activities because these were so important in shaping western development and in affecting the economic interests of residents of the Territories. The Council resolutions of 1885 clearly reveal the scope and character of the political concerns of these practical-minded Canadians.

46. RESOLUTIONS PASSED IN THE 1885 SESSION

Journals of the Council of the North-West Territories (1885), 65-72.

The Council according to Order resolved itself into a Committee of the Whole on the Report of the Special Committee to memorialize the Dominion Government on certain matters; and after some time spent therein, His Honor resumed the Chair; and Mr. *Macleod* reported, That the Committee had come to certain Resolutions. . . .

1. That power should be given to the North-West Council to incorporate Companies having purely Territorial objects;

2. That all old established Trails should be at once surveyed by the Government, and afterwards vested in the North-West Council.

3. That this Council is informed that there are yet many old settlers claims unsettled, principally in the *Prince Albert* and *Edmonton* Districts and urgently recommended that immediate steps be taken to determine such matters, and that in the settlement of claims the possessory rights of squatters to land as regards extent of claims as recognized by the custom of the country prior to the passing of the Dominion Lands Act of 1879, and the right to transfer such claims, should be recognized.

4. That notwithstanding the repeated assertions to the contrary the freight rates imposed by the Canadian Pacific Railway are yet found to be a severe tax on the products of the North-West. This Council therefore respectfully suggests that the influence of the Government should be used to induce the Canadian Pacific Railway Company to reduce their rates, so as to compare favorably with rates in other Provinces of the Dominion, who have the advantage of railway competition, also that exceptionally favorable rates should be given on lumber coming into the Territories from *British Columbia.*

5. That no charge be made for any wood used for fuel purposes by *bona fide* settlers and not cut for sale, and that each homesteader be allowed 4000 Lineal feet of building timber on free permit.

6. That the improvement heretofore suggested by the North-West Council, of the navigation of the *North Saskatchewan River*, should receive the further and favorable consideration of the Government . . .

7. That the rights of *Habeas Corpus* be granted to the *North-West Territories.*

8. That all lands cancelled for any cause, should be thrown open for free

homesteading on ordinary homestead conditions and not held for purposes of sale.

9. That owing to the great expense now attending appeals to the Court of Queen's Bench of *Manitoba*, and the rapid settlement of the country and increase of litigation in the Territories, this Council recommends the establishment of a Territorial Court of Appeals for the *North-West Territories*.

10. That this Council recommends to the favorable consideration of the Government a certain Petition, a copy of which is hereto annexed, adopted at a public meeting at *Edmonton*, June 30th, 1884, asking that a Trail be constructed from that point into the *Peace River* Country.

[No resolution numbered 11]

12. This Council respectfully submits that it is in the interests of *Canada*, as a whole, as well as the *North-West Territories*, that the people of the Territories should be represented in the Senate and House of Commons of *Canada*, and in the sub-division of the Country, for representative purposes, that reference should be had as well to Territorial area as to population.

13. That the *Torrens* System introduced into Parliament last Session, should be made applicable to the *North-West Territories* at once. And so soon as the system becomes law, all titles to land should come under its operation at the same time.

14. That settlers who have entered for a homestead and pre-emption, and who are now, or may hereafter be, entitled to a patent for their homestead quarter-section be allowed to enter their pre-emption as a second homestead on condition of an additional three years homestead duties on their former homestead quarter-section and cultivation duties on present pre-emption or homestead as circumstances will permit. . . .

16. That the Dominion Government should encourage the building of branch lines of railways, particularly those running north and south through the Territories. Such lines would not only enable those settlements, now far removed from the Canadian Pacific Railway, to reap the advantages hoped to be derived from the completion of that national work, but would as well, open for settlement some of the finest areas of land in the Territories. That such encouragement, if at all practicable, should be by cash subsidy or guarantee by the Government of the bonds of companies constructing such lines, thus preserving the public lands for purposes of settlement.

17. That the benefits derived from the National Policy to the older provinces of the Dominion do not apply to the *North-West Territories*, as regards agricultural implements and lumber, and it being necessary to the future development of the country that every encouragement should be extended to the agricultural interests of the North-West; this Council recommends that a rebate should be given equal to the duty now imposed on agricultural implements and lumber.

18. That the fact of the odd numbered sections of land being principally held by companies and individuals for speculative purposes, and in most instances such lands, particularly in the Canadian Pacific Railway Belt, being

exempt from taxation, is a bar to settlement and progress; this Council recommends that immediate steps should be taken by the Dominion Government towards acquiring the odd numbered sections and opening them for homesteading purposes.

19. That moneys voted by Parliament for expenses of Government in the *North-West Territories*, including printing, roads, bridges, ferries, aid to schools, etc., should be vested in the North-West Council as representatives of the people.

20. That it is of the utmost importance to the *North-West Territories* that the *Hudson's Bay* Railway be constructed as rapidly as possible, if the scheme is found practicable. That the success of the North-West very largely depends on the agricultural industries of the country and the cost of transport is now, and as must be, we fear in the future, a very severe tax on the industries of the North-West in consequence of its great distance from European market. This Council is of the opinion that the most liberal encouragement should be extended the scheme by the Government of *Canada*.

21. That notwithstanding the settlement of a very large number of claims amongst the Half-breeds, and the very satisfactory manner in which the Commission appointed for that purpose performed their work, so far as the time occupied by them would permit, there yet remains a very large number of Half-breeds who are entitled to a recognition of their claims we cannot impress too strongly upon the Dominion Government the desirability of settling all Half-breeds claims without delay, and would strongly urge the immediate appointment of a Commission to continue its work until thoroughly completed. . . .

23. That where stock is kept by a homesteader some rule should be adopted and made a part of the Land Regulations, so that the stock of a homesteader over a fixed number might be allowed to count as cultivation duties, in whole or in part, and that encouragement should be given to tree planting in prairie sections of the country, and to count also as cultivation duty.

24. That this Council respectfully intimates that in their opinion it would be most satisfactory to the people of these Territories, were the Government in future to fill appointments to positions of trust and emolument from amongst the residents of these Territories. . . .

26. That the position of several townsites in the Territories, in which the Crown is interested, proves from year to year more unsatisfactory owing to the impossibility of collecting taxes from unsold lots therein, which are increased in value owing to the expenditure of taxes paid by the residents of such towns, the Crown thereby being benefitted without sharing any of the burdens of taxation; And as great difficulties are met with in establishing and sustaining Schools and Municipal organization in such townsites, in the opinion of this Council, it is advisable that the Government should at once dispose of their interests in such townsites so that the same may be made available for taxation.

27. Whereas representations have been made to this Council by the elected

Members of *Prince Albert, Saint Albert* and *Edmonton*, that certain Colonization Companies in and near their Electoral Districts, viz., The *Prince Albert* Colonization Company and The *Edmonton* and *Saskatchewan* Land and Colonization Company, have not complied with their agreements, the effect of which is that large blocks of land are locked up from settlement and the progress of these Districts materially retarded; therefore this Council requests that immediate steps be taken to have these Companies inspected and if it is found that such representations are correct, to insist upon such Companies carrying out the agreements entered into with the Government, or the cancellation of their grants.

The said Resolutions were read a second time and agreed to.

CONSTITUTIONAL DEVELOPMENT IN THE NORTH WEST TERRITORIES

By 1888 the number of elected councillors was approaching twenty-one, at which point, under the North West Territories Act of 1875, the council was to be replaced by a legislative assembly (see above). That act was silent on the question of whether the creation of an assembly involved the creation of an executive council (cabinet) responsible to the majority of the assembly. The North West Territories Amendment Act of 1888 formally brought the assembly into existence, but with twenty-two members rather than twenty-one, to provide increased representation. Instead of creating an executive council, it established 'an advisory council in matters of finance' chaired by the Lieutenant-Governor. This was one of many examples of the treatment of the Territories as a colonial dependency of Ottawa, since the Lieutenant-Governor was responsible to Ottawa, not to his local advisers. David Mills, one of the authors of the act of 1875 and now a leading member of the Liberal opposition, unsuccessfully attempted to force the Prime Minister to concede responsible government to the Territories.

Following the legislation of 1888 there was nearly a decade of agitation in the Assembly, led by F.W.G. Haultain, for the creation of an executive council to replace the advisory council. The objective was achieved in 1897 when the Laurier ministry implemented this reform.

47. CREATION OF THE LEGISLATIVE ASSEMBLY (NORTH WEST TERRITORIES AMENDMENT ACT, 1888)

Statutes of Canada, 51 Vic., Chap. 19 (1888).

Whereas it is expedient to amend "*The North-West Territories Act*" as hereinafter provided: Therefore Her Majesty, by and with the advice and consent of the Senate and House of Commons of Canada, enacts as follows:— . . .

2. There shall be a Legislative Assembly for the North-West Territories which shall have the powers and shall perform the duties heretofore vested in and performed by the Council of the North-West Territories, and shall be composed of twenty-two members elected to represent the electoral districts set forth in the schedule to this Act, and of legal experts, not exceeding three in number, appointed by the Governor in Council: . . .

7. The persons qualified to vote at an election for the Legislative Assembly, shall be the male British subjects, by birth or naturalization (other than unenfranchised Indians), who have attained the full age of twenty-one years, who have resided in the North-West Territories for at least the twelve months, and in the electoral district for at least the three months, respectively, immediately preceding the time of voting.

8. Any British subject by birth or naturalization shall be eligible for nomination and election. . . .

13. The Lieutenant Governor shall select from among the elected members of the Legislative Assembly four persons to act as an advisory council on matters of finance, who shall severally hold office during pleasure; and the Lieutenant Governor shall preside at all sittings of such advisory council and have a right to vote as a member thereof, and shall also have a casting vote in case of a tie.

48. DEBATE ON THE AMENDMENT

House of Commons *Debates* (1888), 454-5.

Sir JOHN A. MACDONALD moved for leave to introduce Bill (No. 76) to amend the Revised Statutes of Canada, chapter 50, respecting the North-West Territories. He said . . . The Lieutenant Governor shall no longer sit with the council or assembly, but shall, as in the Provinces, be a separate estate, and the assembly will be presided over as this assembly is, by a Speaker. There is an extension of the powers of the assembly which I need not trouble the House with now, but the subject will be fully entered into when the Bill is under discussion.

Mr. MILLS (Bothwell). What about executive councillors.

Sir JOHN A. MACDONALD. We do not propose to have executive councillors. There is a proposition of that kind in one of the petitions of the North-West Council which is before the House, but after consideration those gentlemen are opposed to it themselves. . . .

MR. MILLS (Bothwell). I am sure the House will be glad if the hon. gentleman would afford us some further information on this important Bill. The people in that country have made considerable progress in number and in the development of the country, and a government a little more approaching that of a Province than that which at present exists there is no doubt required; but in all our Provinces we have parliamentary responsible government, and I do not understand from the hon. gentleman's observations how he proposes that the executive government shall be carried on. The proposition he has made relates purely to matters of legislation. . . . Does he propose that the Lieutenant Governor of the Territories shall have an executive council to advise him with regard to the administration of the affairs of the Territories? For you will observe that the powers possessed by the Governor in Council there, now are not purely legislative powers, but administrative and executive powers as well. How are those administrative and executive powers to be exercised? Are they to be exercised by the Executive of the Territories, acting under the advice and approval of the majority of those whom the people have elected to represent them? Does the hon. gentleman propose they shall act on the advice which they may, from time to time, receive from the Government here? Now, I say that these are matters of the very first importance, and that before we are asked to take any step in advance in the legislative and governmental development of that country, we should note precisely what we are called upon to do; for it does seem to me to be rather extraordinary to admit that the people of the Territory are so far advanced, by way of organisation, into a political and social community, as to make it necessary that they should have what may be considered a mature system devised for the purposes of legislation, and yet that the legislative and administrative affairs of the country should be in the hands of an irresponsible body. . . .

49. RESPONSIBLE GOVERNMENT FOR THE TERRITORIES (NORTH WEST TERRITORIES ACT, 1897)

Statutes of Canada, 60-1 Vic., Chap. 28.

"17. There shall be a Council to aid and advise in the government of the Territories, to be styled the Executive Council of the Territories; and the persons who are to be members of the Council shall be, from time to time, chosen and summoned by the Lieutenant-Governor and sworn in; and members thereof may be, from time to time, removed by the Lieutenant-Governor.

50. CLIFFORD SIFTON ON RESPONSIBLE GOVERNMENT

House of Commons *Debates* (1897), 2797, 4115.

The MINISTER OF THE INTERIOR (Mr. Sifton) moved for leave to introduce Bill (No. 114) to amend the North-West Territories Act. He said: . . . the main provision of the Bill is to change the constitution of the government of the North-West Territories in this respect, that whereas they have what is called an executive committee, a committee that was entirely a statutory body —and I fancy without precedents in our constitutional system—under the proposed Bill they will have an executive council which will, to the extent of the statutory powers conferred upon the Government of the North-West Territories by the Act, exercise such powers in the same way as the executive council of a province. The effect will be rather as to the methods in which the Government is carried on than as to any extension of the powers of the Government itself. The natural effect of this provision will be that the system of responsible government in the North-West Territories will be more clearly defined and established than it has been heretofore. . . .

The Bill will give the people of the Territories a government which shall not have the full powers of a provincial government, but in so far as they have power to deal with subjects, they shall do it in the same way as the other provinces. They will have Ministers who are responsible to the legislature, and the rules and precedents that apply to the provincial governments will apply to the government of the Territories.

POLITICAL ISSUES IN MANITOBA

The prairie farmers' resentment of the protective-tariff system introduced by the federal government in 1879, which has already been noted, was reiterated in 1893 in a resolution of the Manitoba legislature. This complaint was so persistent in later years that it became a notable feature of the western political tradition.

In 1888 the Liberal party under the leadership of Thomas Greenway gained power in Manitoba. In 1890 the Attorney General, Joseph Martin, sponsored legislation eliminating the official use of French and abolishing separate schools—thus at one stroke eliminating the guarantees that Louis Riel had secured by the provisions of the Manitoba Act. The spokesman for the French minority, J. E. Prendergast, thereupon resigned from the cabinet. But the influx of Protestant Ontarians provided fertile ground for the francophobe ideas of the Torontonian M.P., D'Alton McCarthy, who campaigned against Roman Catholic and French political influence in Manitoba and the Territories. The 'Manitoba Schools Question' became a national political controversy since the provision of the British North America Act assigning education to the provinces (section 93) permitted the federal government to intervene in provincial affairs where separate schools were involved. The long-drawn-out and complex dispute was finally resolved by 'the Laurier-Greenway compromise' of 1897.

51. THE BURDEN OF THE NATIONAL POLICY AS SEEN BY THE MANITOBA LEGISLATURE

Journals of the Legislative Assembly of Manitoba (1893), 111.

Moved by the Hon. Mr. Watson
Seconded by the Hon. Mr. Greenway,
Whereas the protective policy of the present Dominion Government has been in force in Canada for a period sufficiently long to enable the people of Manitoba to fairly judge of its effect upon the trade and progress of this Province;

And Whereas such a policy presses severely upon the people of Manitoba, particularly the agricultural and working classes, by maintaining extravagantly high prices on many articles required for every day use, without the Province or the Dominion as a whole receiving a corresponding benefit from such a policy;

And Whereas a policy of protection is unfair and unequal in its operation upon the various classes of the people, and the continuance of the same will be provocative of great discontent as well as continuing to hamper the natural development of this Province;

And Whereas this House is fully aware of the facts connected with the matters herein recited, and it is the duty of this House to consider the welfare of the Province and place itself on record as entirely disapproving of a policy which has retarded the progress of the country;

Therefore this House hereby declares its strong disapproval of the protective policy in regard to trade, and is of opinion that the same should speedily be abolished and a tariff imposed for the purposes of revenue only.

52. ABOLITION OF FRENCH-LANGUAGE RIGHTS IN MANITOBA, 1890

Journals of the Legislative Assembly of Manitoba (March 20, 1890).

The Hon. Mr. Martin brought up the dual language question again by moving the second reading of bill 61, providing that English shall be the official language of the Province of Manitoba. This bill was to give effect to the general policy of the House with respect to the use of one language. It provides that the English language shall be the only one that of right can be used in the House, or in the courts of this country. It was expressly stated that this shall only apply so far as the jurisdiction of the Province enables them to enact.

Mr. Campbell (South Winnipeg) asked whether this law would prevent counsel pleading in French in the courts.

Hon. Mr. Martin said he thought that would be the effect of the bill. The idea was that only English should be spoken.

Mr. Prendergast ridiculed the provision that the act only applied within the jurisdiction of the court as absurd. . . . The pretence in abolishing the use of French in the House had been that it was a matter of expediency; that it was useless to spend money in printing documents in French for a few Frenchmen who could all read English. But they were growing bolder. Now they abolished their right of speaking French in the courts, and their action in this respect could not be dictated by motives of economy, because it cost nothing. It was becoming more and more a matter of persecution. . . .

Hon. Mr. Martin said that a judge could listen to counsel in any language he pleased, but as a matter of right no man will be entitled to insist on speaking any language other than English. The intention of the bill was to place the French language in this province on exactly the same footing as any other foreign language. They were entitled to no special privileges. . . .

[Mr. Prendergast said] they had made no threats; but if the French majority in Quebec treated the English minority there as the English majority in Manitoba treated the French minority, there would be such a storm as Canada had not yet seen; there would be a cry of war. But apparently what is right in the province of Quebec is wrong in Manitoba. But they were only a minority and had to submit. If the idea of the Attorney-General was to make this a homogeneous people, this legislation would not do much towards attaining this object. . . .

Mr. Wood characterised the manner in which this agitation had arisen and been conducted, as culminating in persecution of the Roman Catholic minority; a persecution based on the contemptible motive of political expediency. He anticipated a general election in the near future, the government regarding such as absolutely necessary to distract attention from certain past records.

53. THE MANITOBA SCHOOLS DISPUTE: DEBATE ON THE LEGISLATION, 1890

Winnipeg *Free Press*, March 5, 1890.

Hon. Mr. [Joseph] Martin. . . . The first feature of the measure that he proposed to touch upon, and perhaps the most important change in his opinion was, that hereafter the schools will be under the direct control of the Government. . . . The House understood the present system of education in this province. There is a Board of Education, consisting of 21 members divided into a Protestant board of 12 members and a Catholic board of 9. One member of each section is appointed as superintendent of Education of his section. This is the system which has been in existence since 1871; there is not proposed a radical change and to place the schools in the hands of a responsible Minister of the Crown. Among the provinces of the Dominion there is only one which has a Minister of Education—the Province of Ontario. . . . There is no subject dealt with in the legislative assemblies of greater importance to the people than the subject of education. . . . This being so, should it be taken from direct control of the people's representatives? (In many American states education was controlled by a board composed of elected politicians). . . .

. . . It was proposed here to imitate the example [of New Brunswick] and do away with the monstrous evil of separate schools. He anticipated that having once dealt with this evil, the House would never be troubled with it again. They would have in the province no special rights for any denomination, for any race; they would be able to say to people of all nationalities and all religions. "If you want a home in which religious liberty is recognized in the fullest sense of the word, come to Manitoba." . . .

. . . The government had overcome his scruples in laying before the House the compromise contained in the act. . . . [T]hey had agreed there should be no sectarian teaching in the schools. So far as religious exercises were concerned . . . it was left entirely optional with the trustees whether they would or would not accept the programme of religious exercises laid down by the advisory board. . . .

Mr. Roblin [said] It is the duty of a government to provide a system of education, and an administration that would be satisfactory to the people. He contended the bill before the House was not of that nature; but was calculated to disturb and disarrange the harmony that had existed in the educational affairs of the province, and produces at least equivocal results. . . .

Mr. Prendergast . . . reviewed the history of education in the province. . . . The practice of this country prior to the union was that the Anglican, Presbyterian and Catholic denominations had their own school, under the charge of their clergy; the members of each denomination supported their own school and no other. . . . [The Hudson's Bay Company] had been in the practice of making a yearly grant of £100 to the Catholic schools. That was not law, of course; but it showed the practice of the time. . . . There could be no doubt of the "practice" of the country prior to union; and this act would be a flagrant violation of all those practices. . . .

The essential thing is the religious instruction. He had the honor to share the views of the [Anglican] Bishop of Rupert's Land on this point. His Lordship had said that he did not desire the Scriptures simply to be read in school, or learned by heart, but taught. . . . They claimed that no Catholic should be called upon to pay for Protestant schools; that no Protestant shall be called upon to pay for a Catholic school. . . . He asked the same treatment as was accorded in England. The Government of that country practically say . . . "Build up your schools; do a good work in education and when you come to us and show us the results we will recognize you by giving you your just share of the public moneys."

54. THE LAURIER-GREENWAY COMPROMISE

Canada, *Sessional Papers* (1897), no. 35, 1-2.

TERMS OF AGREEMENT BETWEEN THE GOVERNMENT OF CANADA AND THE GOVERNMENT OF MANITOBA FOR THE SETTLEMENT OF THE SCHOOL QUESTION, NOVEMBER 16, 1896.

1. Legislation shall be introduced and passed at the next regular session of the Legislature of Manitoba embodying the provisions hereinafter set forth in amendment to the "Public Schools Act," for the purpose of settling the educational questions that have been in dispute in that province.

2. Religious teaching to be conducted as hereinafter provided:—

(1.) If authorized by a resolution passed by a majority of the school trustees, or,

(2.) If a petition be presented to the board of school trustees asking for religious teaching and signed by the parents or guardians of at least ten children attending the school in the case of a rural district, or by the parents or guardians of at least twenty-five children attending the school in a city, town or village.

(3.) Such religious teaching to take place between the hours of 3.30 and 4 o'clock in the afternoon, and to be conducted by any Christian clergyman whose charge includes any portion of the school district, or by a person duly authorized by such clergyman, or by a teacher when so authorized.

(4.) Where so specified in such resolution of the trustees, or where so required by the petition of the parents or guardians, religious teaching during the prescribed period may take place only on certain specified days of the week instead of on every teaching day.

(5.) In any school in towns and cities where the average attendance of Roman Catholic children is forty or upwards, and in villages and rural districts where the average attendance of such children is twenty-five or upwards, the trustees shall, if required by the petition of the parents or guardians of such number of Roman Catholic children respectively, employ at least one duly certificated Roman Catholic teacher in such school.

In any school in towns and cities where the average attendance of non-Roman Catholic children is forty or upwards, and in villages and rural districts where the average attendance of such children is twenty-five or upwards, the trustees shall, if required by the petition of the parents or guardians of such children, employ at least one duly certificated non-Roman Catholic teacher.

(6.) Where religious teaching is required to be carried on in any school in pursuance of the foregoing provisions, and there are Roman Catholic children and non-Roman Catholic children attending such school, and the school-room accommodation does not permit of the pupils being placed in separate rooms for the purpose of religious teaching, provisions shall be made by regulations of the Department of Education (which regulations the Board of school trustees shall observe) whereby the time allotted for religious teaching shall be divided in such a way that religious teaching of the Roman Catholic children shall be carried on during the prescribed period on one-half of the teaching days in each month, and the religious teaching of the non-Roman Catholic children may be carried on during the prescribed period on one-half of the teaching days in each month.

(7.) The Department of Education shall have the power to make regulations not inconsistent with the principles of this Act for the carrying into effect the provisions of this Act.

(8.) No separation of the pupils by religious denominations shall take place during the secular school work.

(9.) Where the school-room accommodation at the disposal of the trustees permits, instead of alloting [sic] different days of the week to the different denominations for the purpose of religious teaching, the pupils may be separated when the hour for religious teaching arrives, and placed in separate rooms.

(10.) Where ten of the pupils in any school speak the French language (or any language other than English) as their native language, the teaching of such pupils shall be conducted in French (or such other language), and English upon the bilingual system.

(11.) No pupils to be permitted to be present at any religious teaching unless the parents or guardians of such pupils desire it. In case the parents or guardians do not desire the attendance of the pupils at such religious teaching, then the pupils shall be dismissed before the exercises, or shall remain in another room.

MINORITY RIGHTS IN THE NORTH WEST TERRITORIES

During the session of 1891-2 the Legislative Assembly of the Territories, with the consent of the federal government, repealed the guarantee of the official use of French. As in Manitoba, the majority of the population were so francophobe that they were unwilling to recognize the existence and the aspirations of this cultural minority and their 'right to be different'.

Although the existence of separate schools in some form was guaranteed by the North West Territories Act of 1875, the majority of the territorial politicians in the 1890s favoured the modification of the school law to reduce to the minimum the privileges of a religious minority. Since F.W.G. Haultain was the dominant figure in the Assembly from 1888 to 1905 his attitude is of particular importance. The school law of 1892, although not abolishing separate schools, greatly reduced Roman Catholic educational influence.

55. RESOLUTION OF THE LEGISLATIVE ASSEMBLY, 1892

Journals of the Legislative Assembly of the North-West Territories (1891-2), 110.

Moved by Mr. HAULTAIN, seconded by Mr. TWEED,

That it is desirable that the proceedings of the Legislative Assembly shall be recorded and published hereafter in the English Language only,

And the Question being proposed, it was moved in amendment by Mr. PRINCE, seconded by Mr. MITCHELL,

That, whereas in the electoral districts of North Qu'Appelle, South Qu'Appelle, Moose Jaw, Red Deer, Edmonton, St. Albert, Battleford, Prince Albert, Cumberland, Mitchell and Batoche, there is a large population of French speaking Canadians;

And whereas the French Language has been recognised as an official language in the North-West Territories in consideration of the services rendered to this Country by the first Canadian voyageurs and missionaries who evangelised, civilized and settled there, at the cost of many lives;

And whereas the French speaking population is increasing every day and, in the interests of the cause of immigration in the North West Territories, no act should be done tending to make it appear that the people of the North West Territories are lacking in justice, liberality or political tact in regard to the national interest of every Canadian;

Therefore, be it resolved that it is not in the public interests that any change be made in the system of public printing in the North-West Territories as far as the use of the French Language as an official language is concerned.

[Amendment defeated by a vote of 20 to 4, and motion passed]

56. DEBATE ON THE RESOLUTION

Leader (Regina), January 26, 1892.

He [*Mr. Haultain*] believed that two or three numbers of the Journals had been printed in French and had not been distributed at all. . . . He brought up the question simply as one affecting expenditure and he commended the motion to them as reasonable from the point of view of economy, convenience and necessity. (Hear, hear). . . .

Mr. Nolin said he must claim the privilege of speaking in his own language. (Hear, hear). He then addressed the House in French and spoke about twenty minutes. He said the French Canadian people of these Territories were not asking any favour. The right for which they now contended had been recognized since 1763, and every Act passed since that time by the Imperial and Canadian Parliaments had always recognized that right. Could this Assembly claim that it would act wiser than the statesmen of England and Canada? It might be said that the Germans and Swedes had the right possessed by the French Canadian people, but he said no; we were here before anybody else. We are Canadians and British subjects and what we ask for is in our capacity as Canadians. The part of the population that he represented could claim some consideration from this Assembly, because if it had not been for the fact that the Halfbreeds had been here for the last 100 years there would be no Assembly today.

57. HAULTAIN AND LACOMBE ON SEPARATE SCHOOLS

Macleod Gazette, February 12, 1891.

Haultain's Address to Pincher Creek constituents.
There was one matter that he could not expect to be in accord with the whole of the district, and that was the school question. There was no use shirking responsibility on that question. . . . We now have two systems. Under our present constitution a Protestant or Roman Catholic minority have the right to establish separate schools. He (Haultain) was thoroughly opposed to such a system. He did not wish to interfere with religious belief, but religious training was not necessary in the schools. . . . His position with regard to the separate school question was that he would work and vote against it as hard as he could (Loud applause). He believed that a large majority of the people felt that the children should be educated together without regard to religious belief at all. The fact of two schools tended to divide boys. . . . Don't have them think that there is something alien between them. . . .

REV. A. LACOMBE'S LETTER TO THE EDITOR

Ibid., February 21, 1891.
. . . I don't want to mix myself with political discussions, but here, today, I have to answer the challenge of my friend and opponent on what I consider a religious question. . . . As a Christian priest and a defender of principles, I believe and consider sacred and necessary that no compromise on my part can be offered. . . . Yes, sir, to the last we will fight for our religious system and privileges in our schools. We may be overwhelmed, but will never surrender. Yes, Mr. Haultain, your affirmation is false, when you say it is enough to teach children religion at home, and during Sunday school at church. Can you point out, even in this country, to many instances where children are receiving proper religious instruction at home? About Sunday schools in the populous centre, in the large cities, you know very well that many children never, or very seldom go to Sunday school; they grow up as pagans, in a complete ignorance of Christianity, their moral duties towards God, their fellow-men and themselves. . . .

... It has been said very properly: "A school without religious teaching is like a body without a soul."

58. THE SCHOOL ORDINANCE OF 1892

Ordinances of the North-West Territories (1892), no. 22.

COUNCIL OF PUBLIC INSTRUCTION

5. The members of the Executive Committee, and four persons, two of whom shall be Protestants and two Roman Catholics, appointed by the Lieutenant-Governor-in-Council, shall constitute a Council of Public Instruction, and one of the said Executive Committee, to be nominated by the Lieutenant-Governor-in-Council, shall be Chairman of the said Council of Public Instruction. The appointed members shall have no vote, and shall receive such remuneration as the Lieutenant-Governor-in-Council shall provide.

(1) The Executive Committee, or any sub-Committee thereof appointed for that purpose, shall constitute a quorum of the Council of Public Instruction.

6. It shall be lawful for the Lieutenant-Governor-in-Council to appoint a Superintendent of Education for the Territories, who shall also be Secretary of the Council of Public Instruction.

7. It shall be lawful for the Council of Public Instruction from time to time

(a) To appoint two or more Examiners at such remuneration as shall be thought proper, and who shall constitute a Board of Examiners to examine teachers and grant certificates of qualification.

(b) To make and establish rules and regulations for the conduct of Schools and Institutes and to prescribe the duties of teachers and their classification.

(c) To determine the subjects and percentages required for all classes and grades of certificates of teachers as well as to make and prescribe rules for the guidance of candidates for certificates of qualification as teachers.

(d) To select, adopt and prescribe the text-books to be used in the Public and Separate Schools of the Territories.

(e) To arrange for the proper training, examination, grading and licensing of teachers, and the granting of certificates. ...

(f) To determine all cases of appeal, disputes and complaints, arising from decisions of Trustees or Inspectors, and to make such orders thereon as may be required.

(g) To make any provisions, not inconsistent with this Ordinance, that may be necessary to meet exigencies occurring under its operation.

(h) To make and establish rules and regulations for the guidance of Inspectors.

8. The Council of Public Instruction shall report annually to the Lieutenant-Governor upon all the Schools and Institutes herein mentioned, with such statements and suggestions for promoting education generally as they may deem useful and expedient.

59. DEBATE ON THE SCHOOL ORDINANCE AMENDMENTS

Leader (Regina), August 18, 1892.

Mr. Mowat said in rising to move the second reading of this bill he had last winter expressed himself very fully, and would merely reiterate what he had said then. The first argument was that this House had now assumed the functions and responsibility of Government. He proposed to throw the duties which had been in the past largely entrusted to the Board of Education on the shoulders of the Executive who were responsible to the House. . . . The provinces of Ontario, Manitoba, New Brunswick, and British Columbia, were running their schools on the principles laid down in this bill. The bill was mainly founded on the British Columbia School system. . . . In doing away with the Board of Education no doubt some members would claim that the members of the Executive were not specialists on education. He would say that while one gentleman, the chairman of the present Board had had a great deal of experience, with regard to the Board as a whole, there were quite as capable men among the members of the present Executive. The hon. gentleman claimed that the bill did not interfere with separate schools. . . .

One of the changes is section 39 which provides that no clergymen of any denomination shall be eligible for the position of Superintendent, Inspector or Trustee. He was one of those who do not favor clergymen of any denomination holding positions of this sort. . . . Section 79 provides that all schools shall be taught in the English language. There are a great many people of different nationalities, Germans, Swedes, Polish, etc., coming into the country, and it is most important that the rising generation should be taught English. . . . Mr. Mowat considered that we would never have true patriotic feeling in the country until there was one language. . . .

Mr. Prince rose to oppose the bill. There were many reasons why the House should not accept the second reading. It was a radical change from the old system. He could not see how the Executive could fulfill the duties, and did not think they would accept the work. He could not agree with the hon. member for South Regina with regard to abolishing the Board. As to expense he did not consider there would be any saving, they would have to appoint a superintendent of education whose salary could not be less than $2000 per year, which would cost more than the Board and there was nothing to gain. The bill did away with the liberty of Roman Catholics to control their schools. With regard to the hon. gentleman's statement about nationalities, it was our duty to encourage immigration, the French Canadians formed 40 per cent. of the population, and it would not encourage them to enter the Territories if they took away the control of their schools. With regard to clause 79 he didn't think it would tend to increase patriotic feeling. He himself was a French Canadian and he hoped his children would talk the French language. . . .

Mr. Haultain could not allow the motion to be put without a few remarks. The bill was a good one and should be considered in committee. There were some points he could not agree to, which he would mention. He could not agree to the clause making uniform text books compulsory, it was contrary to the constitution. With regard to the clause debarring clergymen from holding office, it was almost he might say 17th century. No one was better fitted from education and training to guide educational matters than clergymen. . . .

IN DEFENCE OF THE GRAIN GROWERS

The first 'third party' formed to challenge the Liberals and Conservatives and to articulate western grievances was the Patrons of Industry, which gained some influence in Manitoba and the eastern part of the Territories (the District of Assiniboia) in the 1890s. This populist party was critical of the political influence of central Canada on the federal government. The Patron candidate in the constituency of Assiniboia East in the general election of 1896 reveals the political philosophy of the discontented westerner at this time.

The Territorial Grain Growers' Association, founded in 1902, was a voluntary self-help organization designed to defend the interests of the western farmer. It gained prestige and influence in 1902, after it induced the warehouse commissioner (the federal government officer responsible for regulating the grain trade) to sue the CPR under the provisions of the Manitoba Grain Act. The Railway was found guilty of violating one of the provisions of the Act. The chief strength of the Association was in what is now the province of Saskatchewan, although a few locals were also established in Alberta.

In 1903 the Manitoba Grain Growers' Association was formed, inspired by the success of the Territorial Association.

60. THE PATRONS OF INDUSTRY; SPEECH OF THE REV. J.M. DOUGLAS AT SALTCOATS, ASSINIBOIA, FEBRUARY, 1895

The Patrons Advocate , February 13, 1895.

. . . Some objected to a minister, said that he should be dead to the world and not interfere with politics. With this he did not agree, he had been a pastor for twenty-one years and had found he had to labor, not only for the spiritual, but the temporal and even the physical welfare of his people. Since 1883 he had known this country, and how the farmer was bled and fleeced until he was very dry about the pocket. He had taken no part in politics, had read both sides, as a minister had both Grits and Tories in his congregations and now the time had come for a change, and though in spite of all that was said against him he was a minister in full standing in the Presbyterian church to-day. . . .

Some say that Patronism is no good; and at Ottawa they have said that the farmers are satisfied and all is well, for they are quiet, no sound is heard. Now, the fact is, it is pressure that makes the Patrons. There are some toys that when you press them on the stomach they cry out, and this is like the farmers, they have been pinched until they have become Patrons, for it seems impossible to get along, and each year things become worse. . . .

This is altogether an agricultural country; by agriculture, not by manufactures, this great Northwest will rise or fall, and at present we have not the fair conditions of success. You all know the story of the National Policy and high protection, said Mr. Douglas, how fifteen years ago Alexander Mackenzie refused to be put in power by the great manufacturers at the price of high tariff, and how the late Sir John A. Macdonald agreed to the terms and instituted his National Policy, which no doubt has done great things for Ontario and Quebec, but only has produced evil for us. At the time it may have been wise, but now, at any rate, its work is done, it has grown old, corrupt, dead, and should be buried out of sight. Wheat has so far been the farmer's hope, and to Great Britain he has looked for his market. . . . About free trade with the States I am not certain, it is a question on which I am not quite clear, but with all my heart I cry for free trade with Great Britain, our natural market.

The cry, of course is 'protect our infant industries', but these infants have been too long at the breast. Shame on them, children fifteen years old, and unable yet to stand alone. They have had their chance at our expense, and now it is our turn. . . . *As a friend remarked, when we first came to this country, we lived on faith, that failed, and we lived on hope, hope even is deserting us, and almost it seems as though at last, we should live on charity.*

With regard to reform of the tariff much has been promised, little performed, more, perhaps, from want of power than want of will, for the manufacturers seem all powerful at Ottawa—the manufacturers and the C.P.R. . . .

Then, our freight rates are oppressive. Don't mistake me. I have a great admiration for the C.P.R.; as a nation we are proud of that railway but it has had great privileges and it is not treating us fairly. They say, the directors, that one part of the line must pay for another, but we do not forget that the government granted special aid for those parts of the line which are not so profitable, for the track round Lake Superior and the run through the mountains, while, in addition, the line is free from taxation with its millions of acres of land. Perhaps the freight rates commission will elicit some information, *will tell us why we are punished for living west of Winnipeg,* and why in some cases it will pay better to ship from points in Ontario to Vancouver than from Brandon. . . .

61. THE TERRITORIAL GRAIN GROWERS' ASSOCIATION: REPORT OF C. W. PETERSON, DEPUTY COMMISSIONER, NORTH WEST TERRITORIES DEPARTMENT OF AGRICULTURE

Department of Agriculture, North West Territories, *Annual Report* (1901), 38-9.

Although the wheat blockade has had a most unfortunate effect on business in the Territories it has had at least one good result, namely, in apparently arousing our farmers to the fact that combination and cooperation are necessary if any headway is to be made against the various grievances by which they are each year harassed in the disposal of their produce, and this feeling has been given tangible expression to by the formation of The Territorial Grain Growers' Association. The initial meeting in connection with this association was held at Indian Head on January 7, 1902. . . .

The object of the organisation is put forth in Section 2 of the constitution as follows:

(a) To forward the interests of the grain growers in every honourable and legitimate way.

(b) To watch legislation relating to the grain growers' interest, particularly that affecting the marketing of their grain.

(c) To suggest from time to time, as it is found necessary through duly appointed delegates, the passing of any new legislation to meet changing conditions and requirements.

62. FORMATION OF THE MANITOBA GRAIN GROWERS' ASSOCIATION

Winnipeg *Free Press*, March 4, 1903.

Brandon, Man., March 3—An exceedingly large number of representative farmers from all parts of Manitoba and the Northwest Territories met this afternoon in the city hall to organize a Provincial Grain Growers' association.

Mr. J. W. Scallion, of Virden, opened the meeting by remarking that he wished the movement to extend all over the west. He believed that the farmers had been "done" and the reason for this organization was to maintain the rights of the farmers. Forty thousand farmers had produced 60,000,000 bushels of wheat, and they should all be wealthy, but where was the wealth they had produced? Certainly not in the farmers' hands, but in the homes of the manufacturer, the railway promoter and grain dealer. He wished for unanimity of action. The action of the Virden association, in calling this convention was then unanimously endorsed by the meeting. . . .

Mr. W. R. Motherwell, president of the Territorial Grain Growers' association, was appointed a full delegate to the convention and spoke briefly upon the objects of the Grain Growers' association and at what stage of development they had arrived. In the Territories great suffering had been experienced by the utterly inadequate transportation facilities afforded by the railway companies and the farmers had been forced to action by necessity. The main object of organizing was to ask the government to amend the Grain Act with particular reference to the distribution of cars. The act provided that each applicant should have one car, but in the Territories the C.P.R. company has bunched numbers of farmers together and regarded them as only one applicant.

To illustrate the disgraceful and impotent state of transportation the speaker said that 67 cars arrived at Sintaluta during the first two months of the opening of the market. Of these the farmers got seven. Complaints were lodged before the warehouse commissioner for violations of the Grain Act and he immediately visited Sintaluta and investigated the charges with the result that he satisfied himself that there had been gross violation of the Grain Act by the C.P.R. and he at once instituted an action against them, which met with great success. The association wished the C.P.R. and all other railways to recognize and obey the law in spite of the different interpretations put upon it by the contending counsels. Thousands and thousands of bushels of grain in the Territories were still unmarketed, simply for lack of transportation facilities. . . .

After the prosecution and conviction at Sintaluta [1902] the attitude of the C.P.R. changed and during the last three weeks ninety cars had arrived at Sintaluta for farmers. (Cheers). It was the intention of the association at the coming session of parliament to see that the amendments to the Grain Act were enforced and they were resolved to prosecute to the uttermost the railway companies for each and every infringment of the act. (Applause)

This evening was taken up by the convention of Grain Growers with the discussion of the constitution for the association. The constitution was modelled upon that of the Territorial Grain Growers' association with a few slight alterations. . . .

SIFTON'S IMMIGRATION POLICY

Clifford Sifton, Minister of the Interior from 1896 to 1905 and a member of Parliament from Manitoba, was an influential member of the Laurier cabinet. He reorganized the department on more efficient lines, but his chief claim to fame was the success of his immigration policy. Assisted by a combination of circumstances, including the occupancy of the last good lands in the American west, lower ocean freight rates, and more general prosperity, settlers from the

United States, Great Britain, and western and eastern Europe flowed into the prairies in unprecedented numbers. The European migration aroused political controversy, despite the fact that the Conservatives while in office had encouraged immigration from much the same area. But Anglo-Saxon nativists both in and outside Parliament were critical, particularly of eastern European Slavic immigrants who, it was claimed, could not be assimilated. These criticisms did not deter Sifton, as will be seen from the following extract from a speech in the House of Commons in 1901.

63. EAST EUROPEAN IMMIGRATION

House of Commons *Debates* (1901), 2072ff.

The MINISTER OF THE INTERIOR. The Mennonites were sent to Manitoba as part of a policy which involved a loan which was arranged by the government of the late Hon. Alexander Mackenzie. . . .

Mr. WALLACE. They were in the country long before that, and the hon. gentleman (Hon. Mr. Sifton) cannot deny it.

The MINISTER OF THE INTERIOR. This policy of settling these people there was met with abuse of the Hon. Mr. Mackenzie for bringing them in, precisely as we are being abused now for bringing in the Doukhobors. We have been carrying out a policy of immigration which to-night for the first time has been denounced by a man sitting on the front bench of the Conservative party. . . . And, as I have shown, the hon. gentleman (Mr. Wallace) has spoken in total ignorance of the record of his own party on that question. . . . You would have thought from the hon. gentleman's remarks that the York Farmers' Colonization Company had peopled that country with those of British lineage and that the miserable Doukhobors and Galicians of that locality were a detriment, and prevented him from getting settlers for his lands. I can tell the hon. gentleman that the year before the Galicians went there, I drove over the York Farmers' Colonization tract, and I saw the abandoned mill, the stones of which had been taken out, and the walls of which stood tenantless, while the thousands of acres of the tract were unoccupied. . . . The hon. gentleman sought to leave upon the public mind the impression that these people were of criminal tendency, that they were not of good character morally. I make the statement here that there is not an equal number of people in the Dominion of Canada among whom, for an equal length of time, there has been a lower record of crime than among these people. There is my challenge; let the hon. gentleman take it up. He has no right to stand up, in this House, and seek to give the people of this country the impression that any class of people in Canada are of criminal tendency or have a criminal record when such is not the case. He said that it had been necessary to hang one of the Galicians. Well, it has been necessary to hang Canadians before this. But I say that the record of these people in connection with crime is not less favourable than that of the best class nationally speaking that can be found in Canada. . . .

I will say one or two words about the general effect of the immigration policy of the government. One would think from the statements which have been made . . . that the whole question of immigration as we have dealt with it in the last four years was a question of Doukhobors and Galicians. . . . [The] Doukhobors and Galicians are comparatively a small proportion of the people that have been brought in there. This talk about the Doukhobors and Galicians has arisen almost entirely from the fact that our friends on the other side, having had for some years past the painful experience of failure in their immigration policy, think there is an opportunity of raising national prejudice against the policy of this government by attacking us upon that question. Forgetful of the record of their own party, careless of consistency so far as that is concerned, they endeavour to attack us particularly upon these two points, and they have endeavoured to lead the public mind to the supposition that we were bringing only these two classes into the country. The very first year after our taking office, something like 700 or 800 people came from the United States into Manitoba and the North-West Territories; last year, Mr. Speaker, as a result of the organization which we have perfected in the western states, we brought no less than 15,000 settlers from the United States into Manitoba and the North-West Territories. This year our friends from the North-west who are familiar with what is going on at the present time, tell me, and the officers of my department tell me, there will be a considerably larger number. Sir, if the whole of the nearly half million dollars which we have expended had no other result in those three years than to bring those 20,000 people from the western states into this country, it would be one of the best expenditures the Dominion of Canada ever made.

Hon. gentlemen, I presume, were not serious when they said: We will wait, wait, we won't develop the country by bringing in population, but we will wait until the sons and daughters of Canadians spread themselves over the western prairies and become tillers of the soil. My hon. friends do not take the trouble to think what they are talking about. We get a few people in the shape of farmers from the older provinces, but don't my hon. friends know that the average young Canadian to-day does not want to go out on a western farm and grub there as his forefathers grubbed in the wilderness of eastern Canada? The great majority of these young men desire a different kind of life, and they won't go there, and if you get them to go in the first place you cannot get them to stay. That has been to a large extent the experience that we have had in that western country. But, Mr. Speaker, what we should be able to do as a result of populating that country is this, we should be able to furnish those young men with profitable occupations of all kinds in the cities and towns of the west which will be built up upon the prairies, and in the cities and towns of British Columbia. . . .

THE CREATION OF ALBERTA AND SASKATCHEWAN

In 1905 an area that included the chief settled portion of the North West Territories was established as two provinces of approximately equal size south of the sixtieth parallel. The initiative in this matter was taken by the Territorial premier, F.W.G. Haultain, in 1901. In a letter to the Minister of the Interior he advanced the practical arguments for provincial autonomy. These centred on the need for larger public revenues to cover the costs of services that the pioneers demanded. Implicit in this presentation was the argument that there should be one province between Manitoba and the Rockies—an argument that was made explicit in Haultain's address to his constituents during the election campaign of 1902.

The failure of the Liberal ministry at Ottawa to respond promptly to the Territorial government's request resulted in the 1902 Territorial election being fought on the issue. Haultain won, but Ottawa still procrastinated, arguing that there was a difference of opinion in the Territories on the one-province question. Finally in the autumn of 1904 Laurier promised Haultain that should his party win the impending general election, an autonomy measure would be introduced at the next parliamentary session. The extract from Laurier's speech deals with some of the features of the two autonomy bills, and the extract from the Alberta bill includes the more salient features of the two provincial constitutions.

64. HAULTAIN TO SIFTON, 30 JANUARY 1901

E. H. Oliver, ed., *The Canadian North-West, Its Early Development and Legislative Records* (Ottawa, 1915), vol. II, pp. 1158-9.

SIR,—Following up the discussion between you, Mr. Ross and myself, on the subject of the North-West Assembly Memorial of the Second of May last, I now beg, agreeably to your request, to make a further statement in writing. The Memorial, while leading to definite constitutional changes, approaches the subject from the financial point of view and points out how, in the opinion of the Legislature, our legislative jurisdiction and administrative responsibilities have been enlarged and increased out of all proportion to the means placed at our disposal. I need not enlarge on this side of the question, as it has already been placed very fully before you in the financial statements furnished to you for the past two years by my colleague Mr. Ross. While financial embarrassments rather than constitutional aspirations have led the North-West Government and Legislature to discuss the provincial status I think that sufficient practical reasons can be given for the early establishment of provincial institutions in the West. . . .

. . . For nearly thirteen years the North-West Legislative Assembly has been occupied with founding local institutions and a body of laws suitable to the condition and circumstances of the country. Our parliamentary vote is apparently incapable of expansion at all in proportion to the needs of a rapidly developing country and our powers circumscribed as they are by the necessities of our present anomalous constitutional position, falls short just at the point where further progress demands their exercise.

The Territories have arrived at a point, where, by reason of their population and material development, the larger powers and larger income of a Province have become necessary. I have already in former communications pointed out to you how our limited powers are still more limited by the reservation of subjects such as the Land Titles law, the administration of the Criminal law and the control of the public domain. It is undoubtedly in the interest of any Province or Provinces hereafter to be established, that the important questions surrounding the subject of the public domain should be settled at once, and before any more of the public lands of the Territories are alienated from the Crown.

65. HAULTAIN'S ADDRESS TO HIS CONSTITUENTS, 1902

Macleod Gazette, May 16, 1902.

The Government has presented to the Federal authorities the claims of the people of the Territories in a document which has been published and is being widely distributed. In that document the Territorial Government has expressed its opinion in favour of the organization of one Province only. Action upon the whole question has been postponed by the Dominion Government, principally upon the ground that there is a "divergence of opinion respecting the question whether there should be one Province only or more than one Province"—a question which in the last resort is one for the Dominion Government to settle. The opinion of the Territorial Government is based upon the fact that in the past one Government and one Legislature have found no difficulty in conducting the affairs of the country other than such as arose from the inadequacy of the revenue, and it is not anticipated that any difficulty which cannot be met will arise in the future. There is a widespread and well founded opinion existing throughout Canada against what has been called "over-Government" or "multiplicity of Governments", and there appears to be no substantial reason for the formation of more than one Province in the Territories at the present time. Much less is there any reason for considering that other proposition which has been made on the part of the Province of Manitoba, namely, the division of the people of the Territories by including within the limits of that Province a considerable portion of the present district of Assiniboia, for the whole sentiment of the people concerned is against that proposal. Upon this phase of the question, at least, there is no divergence of opinion. . . .

66. LAURIER'S SPEECH ON THE AUTONOMY BILLS, 1905

House of Commons *Debates* (February 21, 1905).

Mr. Speaker, the Bill which I have now the honour to present is for the admission of another member into the Canadian family of provinces. As the House, no doubt, has noticed, this Bill is to be followed immediately by another for the same purpose, in relation to the province of Saskatchewan. These two Bills are intimately connected; they form part of the same subject; and, by your leave, Sir, the explanations which I shall have the honour to give to the House, will apply to both. . . .

It has been observed on the floor of this House, as well as outside of this House, that as the nineteenth century had been the century of the United States, so the twentieth century would be the century of Canada. This opinion has not been deemed extravagant. On this continent and across the waters, it has been accepted as the statement of a truth, beyond controversy. The wonderful development of the United States during the space of scarcely more than one hundred years may well be an incitement to our efforts and our ambition. Yet to the emulation of such an example there may well be some exception taken; for if it be true that settlement of the western portion of the American union has been marked by almost phenomenal rapidity, it is also true that every other consideration seems to have been sacrificed to this one consideration of rapid growth. Little attention was given, up to the last few years, to the materials which were introduced into the republic; little regard was paid among the new settlers to the observance of the law; and it is not a slander upon our neighbours—for, indeed, the fact is admitted in their current literature—that frontier civilization was with them a byword for lawlessness. We have proceeded upon different methods. We have been satisfied with slower progress. . . .

The time has arrived when we are all agreed, I believe, nay, I feel sure, upon both sides of the House, that another step, and the last, can now be taken to complete the passage of the Northwest Territories from what was once necessary tutelage, into the fullness of the rights which, under our constitution, appertain to provinces. . . .

. . . Up to the year 1875 the Northwest Territories had been administered under no special form of government. But in 1875 Mr. Mackenzie, being then Prime Minister of Canada, introduced into this House and carried unanimously a measure, a very important measure, the object of which, as he said himself, was to give to the Northwest Territories an 'entirely independent government.' This measure has been the charter under which the Northwest Territories have come to their present state of manhood. It has never been repealed. Additions have been made to it from time to time, but it has remained and is to this day the rock upon which has been reared the structure, which we are about to crown with complete and absolute autonomy. . . .

When we came to consider the problem before us it became very soon apparent to me, at all events, that there were four subjects which dominated all the others; that the others were of comparatively minor importance, but that there were four which I was sure the parliament of Canada and the Canadian people at large might be expected to take a deep interest in. The first was: How many provinces should be admitted into the confederation coming from the Northwest Territories—one, or two or more? The next question was: In whom should be vested the ownership of the public lands? The third question was: What should be the financial terms to be granted to these new provinces? And the fourth and not the least important by any means was the question of the school system which would be introduced—not introduced because it was introduced long ago, but should be continued in the Territories. . . .

. . . We propose to give autonomy, not to the whole of the Territories, but to that section which extends from the American boundary up to the boundary line between the provisional district of Mackenzie and the provisional district of Athabaska, that is the 60th parallel of north latitude. . . .

. . . By dividing it into two you have two provinces of 275,000 square miles in round numbers, each about the size of the province of Ontario. . . .

67. THE ALBERTA ACT

Statutes of Canada, 4 & 5 Edward VII, Chap. 3.

3. The provisions of *The British North America Acts*, 1867 to 1886, shall apply to the province of Alberta in the same way and to the like extent as they apply to the provinces heretofore comprised in the Dominion, as if the said province of Alberta had been one of the provinces originally united, except in so far as varied by this Act . . .

4. The said province shall be represented in the Senate of Canada by four members: Provided that such representation may, after the completion of the next decennial census, be from time to time increased to six by the Parliament of Canada.

5. The said province and the province of Saskatchewan shall, until the termination of the Parliament of Canada existing at the time of the first readjustment hereinafter provided for, continue to be represented in the House of Commons as provided by chapter 60 of the statutes of 1903, . . .

8. The Executive Council of the said province shall be composed of such persons, under such designations, as the Lieutenant Governor from time to time thinks fit.

9. Unless and until the Lieutenant Governor in Council of the said province otherwise directs, by proclamation under the Great Seal, the seat of government of the said province shall be at Edmonton. . . .

13. Until the said Legislature otherwise provides, the Legislative Assembly shall be composed of twenty-five members, to be elected to represent the electoral divisions defined in the schedule to this Act.

14. Until the said Legislature otherwise determines, all the provisions of the law with regard to the constitution of the Legislative Assembly of the North-West Territories and the elections of members thereof shall apply, *mutatis mutandis*, to the Legislative Assembly of the said province and the elections of members thereof respectively. . . .

17. Section 93 of *The British North America Act*, 1867, shall apply to the said province, with the substitution for paragraph (1) of the said section 93, of the following paragraph:—

"1. Nothing in any such law shall prejudicially affect any right or privilege with respect to separate schools which any class of persons have at the date of the passing of this Act, under the terms of chapters 29 and 30 of the Ordinances of the North-west Territories, passed in the year 1901, or with respect to religious instruction in any public or separate school as provided for in the said ordinances."

2. In the appropriation by the Legislature or distribution by the Government of the Province of any moneys for the support of schools organized and carried on in accordance with the said chapter 29 or any Act passed in amendment thereof, or in substitution therefor, there shall be no discrimination against schools of any class described in the said chapter 29.

3. Where the expression "by law" is employed in paragraph 3 of the said section 93, it shall be held to mean the law as set out in the said chapters 29 and 30, and where the expression "at the Union" is employed, in the said paragraph 3, it shall be held to mean the date at which this Act comes into force. . . .

20. Inasmuch as the said province will not have the public land as a source of revenue, there shall be paid by Canada to the province by halfyearly payments, in advance, an annual sum based upon the population of the province as from time to time ascertained by the quinquennial census thereof, . . .

21. All Crown lands, mines and minerals and royalties incident thereto, and the interest of the Crown in the waters within the province under *The North-west Irrigation Act*, 1898, shall continue to be vested in the Crown and administered by the Government of Canada for the purposes of Canada, . . .

25. This Act shall come into force on the first day of September, one thousand nine hundred and five.

GUIDE TO FURTHER READING

GOVERNMENT AND POLITICS IN MANITOBA AND THE NORTH WEST TERRITORIES

Clark, L., ed. *The Manitoba School Question: Majority Rule or Minority Rights* (Toronto, 1968). Reproduces with a commentary the chief primary sources and selections from historians' treatment of this predominant political issue in Manitoba in the 1890s.

Lingard, C. C. *Territorial Government in Canada. The Autonomy Question in the Old North-West Territories* (Toronto, 1946). A account of the movement that led to the establishment of the provinces of Alberta and Saskatchewan.

Martin, C. '*Dominion Lands Policy* (Toronto, 1938, 1972). A discussion of the legislation and regulations governing the administration of federal lands (natural resources) from 1870 to 1930.

Morton, A. S. *History of Prairie Settlement* (Toronto, 1938). The standard account of the settlement of the prairies and the influences involved from 1870 to 1925.

Morton, W.L. *Manitoba: A History* (Toronto, 1957, 2nd ed., 1967). The standard treatment of the political, social, and economic history of Manitoba.

Patterson, E.P., ii, *The Canadian Indian. A History Since 1500* (Don Mills, 1972). Contains a discussion of the treaties with the Indians of Manitoba and the North West Territories and subsequent federal Indian policy.

Patton, H.S. *Grain Growers' Cooperation in Western Canada* (Cambridge, 1928). The early chapters contain a description of the grievances of the grain growers of the prairie region, collaborative action, and the federal government's response.

Stanley, G. F. G. *The Birth of Western Canada. A History of the Riel Rebellions* (London, 1936; Toronto, 1960). An impartial, and still the best account of the movements led by Louis Riel, and of the position of the Indians of the North West during the period.

_____. *Louis Riel* (Toronto, 1963). The most complete and thorough biography of Riel.

Thomas, L. H. *The Struggle for Responsible Government in the North-West Territories, 1870-1897* (Toronto, 1956). An account of constitutional and political developments in the Territories.

Wood, L. A. *A History of Farmers' Movements in Canada* (Toronto, 1924, 1974). Includes an account of the evolution of farmers' movements having political and economic objectives in Manitoba and the Territories prior to 1905.

III The Problem of Law and Order in the Canadian West, 1870-1905

Roderick C. Macleod

INTRODUCTION

Any consideration of the question of law and order in the Canadian west tends to be dominated by the North West Mounted Police. This is inevitable and, to a degree, desirable since the Mounted Police were by far the most original, creative, and successful of the instruments by which the Canadian government attempted to shape the development of the region. But while the creation of the Mounted Police was an innovation of the utmost importance for the character of the Canadian west, it was neither entirely new nor was it the only significant element in the system of criminal justice. Much of the machinery of justice, including the courts and their officials, procedures, and the law itself, was transferred to the west without significant change. The NWMP itself grew directly out of the experience of the Hudson's Bay Company in trying to establish and maintain order in Rupert's Land; the Force was a new response to a problem that had existed for seventy years. The fact that the problem was of long standing did not make it any less pressing. If anything, the failure of the Company to find an adequate solution to the problem of exerting effective political control over its vast territories made the situation more urgent for the Canadian government when it stepped in in 1870.

The charter of the Hudson's Bay Company gave it political and legal authority in the territories covered by its monopoly. Until the nineteenth century, however, these clauses of the charter had greater commercial than legal or political significance. The powers granted by the charter were intended primarily to allow the Company to control its employees and protect its monopoly by excluding rival traders. The Company had neither the desire nor the resources to apply British law to the native inhabitants. To the extent that relations with the Indians went beyond the commercial, they were quasi-diplomatic, dealing with groups rather than individuals. Internal disputes between the Company's servants were handled by the Governor in an informal but generally satisfactory fashion.

In the period of bitter competition with the North West Company in the early years of the nineteenth century, a new element was added to the situation. Incidents, up to and including murder, occurred that involved Europeans outside the employ of the Company. The North West Company was understandably reluctant to submit to its rival's jurisdiction in such matters and in 1803 the British government attempted to resolve this explosive situation by passing the Canada Jurisdiction Act. The Act gave the courts of Lower Canada the authority to try criminal offences committed north and west of the Great Lakes. A further act of 1821 attempted to make the system more workable by giving Upper Canadian courts greater jurisdiction. Both Acts provided that the Governor General of Canada could establish courts in the North West but this was never done, largely because the merger of the two companies in 1821 removed most of the difficulties. The final challenge to the Company's political authority came instead from within.

As the tiny settlement at Red River grew, so did the necessity for a more sophisticated legal system. As part of a general reorganization carried out by Governor George Simpson in 1835, four judicial districts (later reduced to three) were created, each with its own magistrate. These courts dealt with minor civil and criminal matters. More serious cases and appeals went to a General Quarterly Court consisting of the Governor, the Council of Assiniboia, and all the magistrates. All these officials were legal amateurs to begin with, but by 1839 it became apparent that professional advice was needed. In that year the first full-time, legally trained judge was appointed to the General Quarterly Court. This official, known as the Recorder of Rupert's Land, was the most influential in the legal system until 1870. The Recorders (Adam Thom 1839-51, Francis G. Johnson 1854-8, Dr John Bunn 1861, John Black 1862-70) succeeded in introducing a number of important reforms, notably the codifying of the laws of Rupert's Land and the updating of the British law that applied to the region from 1670 to 1837. They also began the process of incorporating the native peoples into the legal system.

As it turned out, it was one thing to establish courts but quite another to enforce the decisions of those courts if they did not meet with the approval of any substantial part of the population. The court system was adequate for the needs of the community but the Company was never able to devise a complementary police system that could ensure that the decisions of the courts were obeyed. In contrast to the achievements of the courts, the history of the Company's efforts at enforcement is a catalogue of failures. In the period of intercompany rivalry prior to 1821, sheriffs were appointed but their effectiveness as officers of the law was virtually nil. All the Selkirk settlers were required as part of their agreements with the Company to assist in maintaining order. The authorities expected the ex-soldiers of the de Meuron regiment to be particularly useful but in fact they caused more trouble than they prevented. (The de Meuron regiment were mercenaries, mainly Swiss, who fought for the British in the War of 1812. They took their discharges in Canada, and in 1817 Lord Selkirk hired them to protect the Red River Settlement.) In 1822, with the North West Company safely out of the way, the Hudson's Bay Company attempted to improve the system. Governor Bulger was authorized to appoint constables and two were chosen in 1823. Later in the same year, the new governor, Roberty Pelly, went much further, establishing a force of twenty paid, part-time constables supplemented by a force of fifty volunteers.

Pelly's organization seems to have existed largely on paper. In the general reorganization of the mid-1830s it was eliminated and replaced by a new Volunteer Corps, which had a quasi-military character—a sure sign that discipline had been a major problem in its predecessor. The new body had, in addition to its commanding officer, Sheriff Alexander Ross, a sergeant-major, four sergeants, and fifty-four privates who could be called upon to serve up to four weeks in a year. At first the new force worked well enough but within a decade it had begun to disintegrate and had to be disbanded in 1845.

The single exception to the otherwise fruitless search for an effective law-enforcement body came from outside the community and, for that matter, outside the resources of the Company. In the years 1846-8 a regiment of British troops was stationed at Red River as a result of the Oregon crisis with the United States. As long as the magistrates could call upon this disciplined and disinterested group of soldiers, the settlement enjoyed its most tranquil period. When they left a force of fifty-six retired soldiers from the British army was imported to replace them. These pensioners proved quite unable to do the job; a fact that was dramatically demonstrated in 1849 with the famous Sayer trial.

With transportation routes opening up to the American territories to the south, the Company could no longer count on its control of trade routes to preserve its monopoly. Many of the mixed-bloods at Red River took advantage of the opportunity to become free traders in violation of the Company's monopoly. In May of 1849 Pierre Guilleaum Sayer and several others were brought to trial on a charge of violating the monopoly. The evidence was clear and a verdict of guilty was reached, but the presence of an armed and angry mob of Métis ensured that there would be no effort to take action against any of the convicted. From this point on the Company did not even go through the motions of prosecuting the free traders. After the Sayer trial the legal authority of the Company and its courts was rapidly eroded. Other groups, particularly the Canadians who began to appear in the 1850s, found they could defy the courts with impunity.

By the time the Canadian government began negotiations for the acquisition of Rupert's Land a tradition of lawlessness had been established. Effective control of the region lay in the hands of the group that could muster the largest number of armed men. The uprising led by Louis Riel in 1869-70 was, in this sense, merely a continuation on a larger scale of the series of incidents begun twenty years earlier. The factor that upset the balance and turned it into a major political crisis was the decision of the Canadian group led by John Christian Schultz to challenge the supremacy of the Métis. This confrontation resulted in the execution of Scott and the political repercussions that followed in Ontario and Quebec.

The Riel rising brought the situation in the North West forcibly to the attention of Sir John A. Macdonald, who rapidly assimilated the lessons of fifty years of Hudson's Bay rule. The most important lesson was that the traditional institutions of law and order as found in Britain and Canada, of which those in Rupert's Land were a rough copy, would not work when they were needed most. Life might proceed peacefully for years but a handful of individuals could bring chaos in short order. The lack of effective law enforcement was a standing invitation to violence even among the relatively settled Métis of Red River. Farther west there would be contacts between settlers and Indians, some of whom had not had even the experience of the fur trade to prepare them. To allow mob law in such circumstances was to risk the kind of Indian wars the United States government was waging to the south. Such wars were enormously expensive; even a small one would bring the country close to bankruptcy. The indirect costs would be even greater since conflict would delay settlement and the projected Canadian Pacific Railway. A new solution would have to be found.

That solution was, of course, the North West Mounted Police. But before the Mounted Police could come into existence a number of obstacles had to be surmounted. One of these was a constitutional barrier. The BNA Act clearly stated that law enforcement was a provincial responsibility. Plans had existed for the establishment of a federal police force in the North West prior to 1870 but the Riel affair, by forcing the immediate creation of the province of Manitoba, had disrupted those plans. A police force that could not operate in the only settled part of the prairies was of doubtful value and the plans were shelved temporarily while Ottawa awaited developments. Perhaps the difficulties at Red River had been an aberration. Perhaps the militia stationed there would be sufficient to maintain order, making an expensive police force unnecessary.

These hopes soon proved illusory. Winnipeg, as Red River was now called, remained turbulent and tensions increased as settlers from Ontario began to arrive. Farther west there was little change, the vast reaches undisturbed by events on the Red. Two reports commissioned by the government, however, emphasized the fragility of this peace. Captain W. F. Butler of the British Army toured what he christened the 'Great Lone Land' in 1870. Lieutenant-Colonel Patrick Robertson-Ross of the Canadian Militia followed in 1873. Both reported the complete absence of law and recommended the establishment of a police force to work closely with magistrates in the area.

Probably even more important than the constitutional problems or the large sums of money the police would cost was a psychological barrier. The NWMP represented a distinct departure from the British tradition of local control of law enforcement, and Macdonald, a Conservative by instinct as well as party label, was deeply suspicious of innovation. It was only with the greatest reluctance that he could bring himself to establish the Mounted Police in 1873 and he did so only when all other alternatives had been exhausted. He appeased his conscience by maintaining that the new police force was modelled on the Royal Irish Constabulary and on British experience in India. There is also no doubt that Macdonald regarded the Mounted Police for many years as a temporary expedient. They were essential to smooth the early stages of settlement but once the frontier period had passed, law enforcement would revert to the old pattern.

The uprising of 1869-70 and the creation of Manitoba with the accompanying postponement of the formation of the police was thus greeted by Macdonald with something approaching relief. The court system would have to be established in Manitoba in any case and it might prove adequate by itself to keep matters under control. Alexander Morris, a trusted associate of Macdonald's, was despatched to the new province to organize the courts and attempt to bring the fractious population of Winnipeg under control. Morris lost no time in establishing the Manitoba Court of Queen's Bench, but discovered that without an effective enforcement agency the courts were powerless to suppress the endemic violence of the community. When urged by Macdonald to use the Militia to back up the courts, Morris pointed out that the soldiers were parties to much of the unrest and therefore useless. Even had the Militia been neutral and disciplined, they were too clumsy an instrument for the purpose.

In the fall of 1872 Macdonald gave in and agreed to set up the Mounted Police. The Act that was passed the following spring clearly reflected the experience gained in Manitoba in the three years since 1870. The police were to be very closely integrated with the court system so that disputes could be settled at once, before they developed into unmanageable conflicts. Justice was to be swift and efficient above all. The Act provided for the appointment of stipendiary magistrates for the North West Territories and, in addition, all officers of the Mounted Police were to be *ex officio* justices of the peace. The judicial powers of the Force were strengthened by an amendment to the Act in 1874 that gave the Commissioner the powers of a stipendiary magistrate.

Much of the early success of the Mounted Police was due to the fact that it could handle the great majority of cases entirely without reference to outside authority. Punishments were consistent, swift, and certain. The most basic principle of criminology is that certainty of punishment is the key factor in deterrence. The judicial powers given to the Mounted Police made possible a degree of certainty of punishment unique in Canadian history. The reputation of the Mounted Police rested fundamentally on thousands of cases of assault, drunk and disorderly, or petty theft, rapidly despatched, rather than on dramatic pursuits of murderers in the wilderness.

The quest for a simplified and efficient system of criminal justice for the Territories went beyond the courts and the Mounted Police. The grand jury, a prominent feature of the legal system in Ontario and Manitoba, was eliminated in the North West. The petit jury was reduced in number from the traditional twelve men to six. At first, serious cases were sent to Manitoba for trial, but transportation difficulties proved so great that the powers of magistrates in the Territories were rapidly expanded. By 1877 a stipendiary magistrate sitting with two justices of the peace could try capital offences, although such cases were subject to review by Ottawa. The functions of two important court officers, sheriff and coroner, were absorbed by the Mounted Police until the 1880s.

This tendency to reduce the system to its barest essentials persisted throughout the territorial period, even after the judicial system reached its fullest development with the formation of the Supreme Court of the North West Territories in 1886. There was a general overhaul of the legal machinery in that year that, in addition to the creation of the supreme court, increased the number of sheriffs and coroners and made the law of England as of 1870 applicable (Canadian criminal law had been extended to the region in 1873).

Since 1875 the Lieutenant-Governor in Council had had the power to appoint justices of the peace. As the population of the Territories increased, more and more civilian JPs were sworn in, especially in the larger towns. Until 1905 and after, however, the majority of all criminal cases continued to be tried by Mounted Police officers. In isolated areas the Force remained the entire criminal-justice system. This was not a situation that the police particularly relished. Judicial duties were time-consuming and involved inordinate quantitities of paper work. But as long as the numbers of civilian JPs were insufficient, the police had no choice.

The Mounted Police were organized into Divisions (called troops for the first few years) of fifty to a hundred officers and men. Divisions were under the command of a superintendent who was normally assisted by two inspectors. Depending upon its size, the division would have ten to twenty non-commissioned officers (staff-sergeants, sergeants, and corporals). The rest of the strength was made up of constables. Scouts, interpreters, and special constables were recruited from the native population as needed.

During the first decade of the existence of the Force divisions and parts of divisions were frequently shifted from place to place to meet changing conditions. By the mid-1880s population trends were stable enough for the divisions to acquire permanent headquarters and territories for which they were responsible. These divisional territories changed little over the next twenty years, although the numbers of men in each fluctuated according to need. The distribution of the Force in 1889, reproduced below, is typical of the period. Numbers in brackets indicate strengths.

    'A' Division—Maple Creek (100)
    'B' Division—Regina (74)
    'C' Division—Battleford (89)
    'D' Division—Ft Macleod (96)
    'E' Division—Calgary (111)
    'F' Division—Prince Albert (86)
    'G' Division—Fort Saskatchewan (78)
    'H' Division—Fort Macleod (80)
    'K' Division—Lethbridge (102)
    Depot Division—Regina (222)

Depot Division trained new recruits and carried out all headquarters administrative work.

Within each division half to three-quarters of the men were stationed at headquarters with the rest scattered throughout the area in small detachments. Roughly half of those at headquarters were assigned to patrol duty. Patrols were of two kinds; regular and flying patrols. The former followed a fixed route at regular intervals. Constables on regular patrols carried a book that was signed by all settlers on their route and in which any complaints were recorded. Flying patrols were random in their timing and did not follow fixed routes. They were intended to plug gaps in the coverage and prevent lawbreakers from taking advantage of the predictability of the regular patrols. The rest of the men stationed at divisional headquarters were fully occupied acting as jailers, attending court sessions, and looking after routine housekeeping chores as well as any special assignments that came along. For those in the outlying detachments, the greatest problem was tedium, since most crimes were committed in the towns.

Divisional headquarters compiled all the information gathered by the patrols and in the weekly reports from detachments into a monthly summary that went to the Commissioner in Regina. This efficient communications system gave the police an accurate and up-to-date picture of conditions everywhere in the Territories. Much of the content of the reports had no direct connection with criminal activities. The reports noted the state of crops and livestock, weather conditions, cases of poverty and destitution, movements in and out of the area; in short, the general social and economic condition of the district. The format of the reports was a matter of deliberate policy since the police were at least as concerned with preventing crime as with apprehending offenders. Families in need of relief could be given a little money to tide them over or temporary work around the police barracks. Neighbourhood quarrels could be settled before they escalated into violence. New settlers could be given advice on local conditions, and dangerous rumours could be nipped in the bud.

The NWMP was able to develop rapidly into a flexible and efficient force, almost ideally suited to the peculiar conditions of the North West Territories, largely because of the independence it enjoyed both from control by local elites and from the dead hand of Ottawa bureaucracy. The federal government was too far away to exercise effective control over anything except budgetary matters and patronage. As long as the Force remained relatively inexpensive, accepted the nominees of the political party in power as recruits, and got results, it was allowed to go its own way. Perhaps for this reason residents of the Territories came to think of the Mounted Police as belonging to them; a unique and essential part of their way of life.

The Mounted Police were not the only law-enforcement officers on the prairies at this time. Several of the towns had their own police forces and Manitoba had a provincial police force that predated the NWMP by several years. Unfortunately so little is known of these forces that comparisons are impossible. It would be safe to say, however, that the Mounted Police dominated the criminal-justice system to such a degree that they set the tone for the entire region.

THE LEGISLATIVE FRAMEWORK

68. THE CANADA JURISDICTION ACT, 1803

E. H. Oliver, *The Canadian North-West: It's Early Development and Legislative Records*, vol. II (Ottawa, 1915).

Whereas crimes and offences have been committed in the Indian Territories and other parts of America not within the limits of the Provinces of Upper or Lower Canada, or either of them, or of the jurisdiction of any of the Courts established in those provinces or within the limits of any civil government of the United States of America, and are therefore not cognizable by any jurisdiction whatever, and by reason thereof great crimes and offences have gone, and may hereafter go unpunished, and greatly increase—for remedy whereof, *May it please your Majesty* that it may be enacted, and be it enacted by the *King's Most Excellent Majesty* by and with the consent and advice of the Lords Spiritual and Temporal and Commons in this present Parliament assembled, and by the authority of the same, THAT, from and after the passing of this Act, all offences committed within any of the Indian Territories or parts of America, not within the limits of either of the said Provinces of Upper or Lower Canada, or of any civil government of the United States of America, shall be, and be deemed to be, offences of the same nature and shall be tried in the same manner and subject to the same punishment as if the same had been committed within the Province of Lower or Upper Canada.

2. *And be it further Enacted*, that it shall be lawful for the Governor or Lieutenant Governor, or person administering the Government for the time being of the Province of Lower Canada by Commission under his hand and seal, to authorise and empower any person or persons whomsoever resident or being at the time, to act as Civil Magistrates and Justices of the Peace for any of the Indian Territories or parts of America not within the limits of either of the said provinces or of any civil government of the United States of America, as well as within the limits of either of the said Provinces, either upon informations taken or given within the said Provinces of Lower or Upper Canada, or out of the said Provinces in any part of the Indian Territories or parts of America aforesaid, for the purpose only of hearing crimes and offenses to safe custody in order to his or their being conveyed to the said Province of Lower Canada to be dealt with according to law, and it shall be lawful for any person or persons whatsoever to apprehend and take before any person so commis-

sioned as aforesaid, or to apprehend and convey or cause to be safely conveyed with all convenient speed to the Province of Lower Canada any person or persons whomsoever resident or being at the time, to act as Civil Magistrates and Justices of the Peace for any of the Indian Territories or parts of America not within the limits of either of the said provinces or of any civil government of the United States of America, as well as within the limits of *either of the said Provinces, either upon informations taken or given within* the said Provinces of Lower or Upper Canada, or out of the said Provinces in any part of the Indian Territories or parts of America aforesaid, for the purpose only of hearing crimes and offenses to safe custody in order to his or their being conveyed to the said Province of Lower Canada to be dealt with according to law, and it shall be lawful for any person or persons whatsoever to apprehend and take before any person so commissioned as aforesaid, or to apprehend and convey or cause to be safely conveyed with all convenient speed to the Province of Lower Canada any person or persons guilty of any crime or offence there to be delivered into safe custody for the purpose of being dealt with according to law.

3rd. *And be it further Enacted*, that every such offender may and shall be prosecuted and tried in the Courts of the Province of Lower Canada (or if the Governor, or Lieutenant Governor, or person administering the government for the time being, shall from any of the circumstances of the crime or offence, or the local situation of any of the witnesses for the prosecution or defence think justice may be more conveniently administered in relation to such crime or offence in the Province of Upper Canada and shall by any instrument under the great seal of the Province of Lower Canada, declare the same, then that every such offender may and shall be prosecuted and tried in the Court of the Province of Upper Canada) in which crimes or offences of the like nature are usually tried, and where the same would have been tried, if such crime or offence had been committed within the limits of the Province where the same shall be tried under this Act; and every offender tried and convicted under this Act shall be liable and subject to such punishment as may by any law in force in the Province where he or she shall be tried be inflicted for such crime or offence, and such crime or offence may and shall be laid and charged to have been committed within the jurisdiction of such Court, and such Court may and shall proceed therein to trial, judgment and execution or other punishment for such crime or offence in the same manner and in every respect as if such crime or offence had really been committed within the jurisdiction of such Court, and shall also be lawful for the Judges and other officers the said Courts to issue subpoenas and other processes for enforcing the attendance of witnesses on any such trial, and such subpoenas and other processes shall be as valid and effectual and be in full force, and put in execution in any parts of the Indian Territories or other parts of America out of and not within the limits of the civil government of the United States of America as well as within the limits of either of the said Provinces of Upper or Lower Canada in relation to the trial of any crimes or offences by this Act made cognizable in such Court, or to the more speedy and effectually bringing any offender or offenders to justice under this Act as fully and simply as any subpoenas or other processes are within the limits of the jurisdiction of this Court, from which any such subpoenas or processes shall have issued as aforesaid; any Act or Acts, law or laws, custom, usage, matter or thing to the contrary notwithstanding.

4th. *Provided always, and be it further enacted*, that if any crime or offence charged and prosecuted under this act shall be proved to have been committed by any person or persons not being a subject or subjects of His Majesty and also within the limits of any Colony, Settlement or Territory, belonging to any European States, the Court before which such prosecution shall be had, shall forthwith acquit such person or persons, not being such subject or subjects as aforesaid, of such charge.

5th. *Provided nevertheless*, that it shall and may be lawful for such Court to proceed in the trial of any other person being a subject or subjects of His Majesty, who shall be charged with the same or any other offence, notwithstanding such offence shall appear to have been committed within the limits of any Colony, Settlement or Territory, belonging to any European State as aforesaid.

69. ORDER IN COUNCIL CONCERNING THE ADMINISTRATION OF JUSTICE IN THE NORTH WEST TERRITORIES, 1870

Canada, *Sessional Papers* (1871).

Government House,
Ottawa, 13th September, 1870.

Present:—His Excellency the Governor General in Council.

On the recommendation of the Hon. Sir George Et. Cartier, acting in the absence of the Hon. the Minister of Justice, and under the provisions of the 2nd Section of the Act 32 and 33 Vic. ch. 3, His Excellency in Council has been pleased to order, and it is hereby ordered that the Hon. Adams George Archibald, Lieutenant-Governor of the North West Territories, or the Lieutenant-Governor of the North West Territories for the time being, be, and it is hereby authorized and empowered to make provision for the administration of justice within such North West Territories, and to make, constitute and appoint the Hon. Francis Godschall Johnson, one of the Judges of the Superior Court for Lower Canada, Recorder of such portion of the North West Territories as heretofore, and before the admission into Canada of Rupert's Land and the North West Territory was known as the Territory of Rupert's Land, and of all such other places wherein trade was heretofore, and is authorized to be carried on by the Hudson's Bay Company, under the charter given thereto by King Charles the Second, under the Great Seal of England, and dated 2nd May, in the 22nd year of his Reign, together with the powers and duties which may be by law exercised and performed by Recorders.

And it is hereby further ordered that subject to the laws now in force in the North West Territories like authority be, and the same is hereby given to the Lieutenant Governor for the time being to appoint Justices of the Peace for the portion of the North West Territories hereinbefore mentioned.

And it is further ordered that subject as aforesaid, like authority be and the same is hereby given to the Lieutenant-Governor for the time being to appoint Justices of the Peace for the portion of the North West Territories wherein no jurisdiction was formerly exercised by the Hudson's Bay Company.

Certified.

70. SELECTIONS FROM THE REPORT OF CAPTAIN W. F. BUTLER, 1871

W. F. Butler, *The Great Lone Land: A Narrative of Travel and Adventure in the North-West of America* (London, 1873).

Having in the foregoing pages briefly alluded to the time occupied in travel, to the route followed, and to the general circumstances attending my journey, I now propose entering upon the subjects contained in the written instructions under which I acted, and in the first instance to lay before you the views which I have formed upon the important question of the existing state of affairs in the Saskatchewan.

The institutions of Law and Order, as understood in civilized communities, are wholly unknown in the regions of the Saskatchewan, and destitute of any means to enforce the authority of the law.

I do not mean to assert that crime and outrage are of habitual occurrence among the people of this territory, or that a state of anarchy exists in any particular portion of it, but it is an undoubted fact that crimes of the most serious nature have bee committed, in various places, by persons of mixed and native blood, without any vindication of the law being possible, and that the position of affairs rests at the present moment not on the just power of an executive authority to enforce obedience, but rather upon the passive acquiescence of the majority of a scant population who hitherto have lived in ignorance of those conflicting interests which, in more populous and civilized communities, tend to anarchy and disorder.

But the question may be asked, if the Hudson Bay Company represent the centres round which the half-breed settlers have gathered, how then does it occur that that body should be destitute of governing power, and unable to repress crime and outrage? To the question I would reply that the Hudson Bay Company, being a commercial corporation dependent for its profits on the suffrages of the people, is of necessity cautious in the exercise of repressive powers; that, also, it is exposed in the Saskatchewan to the evil influence which free trade has ever developed among the native races; that, furthermore, it is brought in contact with tribes long remarkable for their lawlessness and ferocity; and that, lastly, the elements of disorder in the whole territory of Saskatchewan are for many causes, yearly on the increase. But before entering upon the subject into which this last consideration would lead me, it will be advisable to glance at the various elements which comprise the population of this Western region. In point of numbers, and in the power which they possess of committing depredations, the aboriginal races claim the foremost place among the inhabitants of the Saskatchewan. These tribes, like the Indians of other portions of Rupert's Land and the North-West, carry on the pursuits of hunting, bringing the produce of their hunts to barter for the goods of the Hudson Bay Company; but, unlike the Indians of more northern regions, they subsist almost entirely upon the buffalo, and they carry on among themselves an unceasing warfare which has long become traditional. Accustomed to regard murder as honourable war, robbery and pillage as the traits most ennobling to manhood, free from all restraint, these warring tribes of Crees, Assineboines, and Blackfeet form some of the most savage among even the wild races of Western America.

Hitherto it may be said that the Crees have looked upon the white man as their friend, but latterly indications have not been wanting to foreshadow a change in this respect—a change which I have found many causes to account for, and which, if the Saskatchewan remains in its present condition, must, I fear, deepen into more positive enmity. The buffalo, the red man's sole means of subsistence, is rapidly disappearing; year by year the prairies, which once shook beneath the tread of countless herds of bisons, are becoming denuded of animal life, and year by year the affliction of starvation comes with an ever-increasing intensity upon the land. There are men still living who remember to have hunted buffalo on the shores of Lake Manitoba. It is scarcely twelve years since Fort Ellice, on the Assineboine River, formed one of the principal posts of supply for the Hudson Bay Company; and the vast prairies which flank the southern and western spurs of the Touchwood Hills, now utterly silent and deserted, are still white with the bones of the migratory herds which, until lately, roamed over their surface. Nor is this absence of animal life confined to the plains of the Qu'Appelle and of the Upper Assineboine—all along the line of the North Saskatchewan, from Carlton to Edmonton House, the same scarcity prevails; and if further illustration of this decrease of buffalo be wanting, I would state that, during the present winter, I have traversed the plains from the Red River to the Rocky Mountains without seeing even one solitary animal upon 1200 miles of prairie. The Indian is not slow to attribute this lessening of his principal food to the presence of the white and half-breed settlers, whose active competition for pemmican (valuable as supplying the transport service of the Hudson Bay Company) has led to this all but total extinction of the bison.

Nor does he fail to trace other grievances—some real, some imaginary—to the same cause. Wherever the half-breed settler or hunter has established himself he has resorted to the use of poison as a means of destroying the wolves and foxes which were numerous on the prairies. This most pernicious practice has had the effect of greatly embittering the Indians against the settler, for not only have large numbers of animals been uselessly destroyed, inasmuch as fully one-half the animals thus killed are lost to the trapper, but also the poison is frequently communicated to the Indian dogs, and thus a very important mode of winter transport is lost to the red man. It is asserted, too, that horses are sometimes poisoned by eating grasses which have become tainted by the presence of strychnine; and although this latter assertion may not be true, yet its effects are the same, as the Indian fully believes it. In consequence of these losses a threat has been made, very generally, by the natives against the half-breeds, to the effect that if the use of poison was persisted in, the horses belonging to the settlers would be shot. . . .

Passing west from Edmonton, we enter the country of the Rocky Mountain Stonies, a small tribe of Thickwood Indians dwelling along the source of the North Saskatchewan and in the outer ranges of the Rocky Mountains,—a fragment, no doubt, from the once powerful Assineboine nation which has found a refuge amidst the forests and mountains of the West. This tribe is noted as possessing hunters and mountain guides of great energy and skill. Although at war with the Blackfeet, collisions are not frequent between them, as the Assineboines never go upon war-parties; and the Blackfeet rarely venture into the wooded country.

Having spoken in detail of the Indian tribes inhabiting the line of *fertile country* lying between Red River and the Rocky Mountains, it only remains for me to allude to the Blackfeet with the confederate tribes of Blood, Lurcees and Peagins. These tribes inhabit the great plains lying between the Red Deer River and the Missouri, a vast tract of country which, with few exceptions, is arid, treeless and sandy,—a portion of the true American desert, which extends from the fertile belt of the Saskatchewan to the borders of Texas. With the exception of the Lurcees, the other confederate tribes speak the same language—the Lurcees being a branch of the Chipwayans of the North, speak a language peculiar to themselves, while at the same time understanding and speaking the Blackfeet tongue. At war with their hereditary enemies, the Crees, upon their northern and eastern boundaries—at war with Kootanais and Flathead tribes on south and west—at war with Assineboines on southeast and north-west—carrying on predator excursions against the Americans on the Missouri, this Blackfeet nation forms a people of whom it may truly be said that they are against every man, and that every man is against them. Essentially a wild, lawless, erring race, whose natures have received the stamps of the region in which they dwell; whose knowledge is read from the great book which Day, Night, and the Desert unfold to them; and who yet possess a rude eloquence, a savage pride, and a wild love of freedom of their own. Nor are there other indications wanting to lend to the hope that this tribe may yet be found to be capable of yielding to influences to which they have heretofore been strangers, namely, Justice and Kindness.

Inhabiting, as the Blackfeet do, a large extent of country which from the arid nature of its soil must eer prove useless for purposes of settlement and colonization, I do not apprehend that much difficulty will arise between them and the whites, provided always that measures are taken to guard against certain possibilities of danger, and that the Crees are made to understand that the forts and settlements along the Upper Saskatchewan must be considered as neutral ground upon which hostilities cannot be waged against the Blackfeet. As matters at present stand, whenever the Blackfeet venture in upon a trading expedition to the forts of the Hudson Bay Company they are generally assaulted by the Crees, and savagely murdered. Père Lacombe estimates the number of Blackfeet killed in and around Edmonton alone during his residence in the West, at over forty men, and he has assured me that to his knowledge the Blackfeet have never killed a Cree at that place, except in self-defence. Mr. W. J. Christie, chief factor at Edmonton House, confirms this statement. He says, "The Blackfeet respect the whites more than the Crees do, that is, a Blackfoot will never attempt the life of a Cree at our forts, and bands of them are more easily controlled in an excitement than Crees. It would be easier for one of us to save the life of a Cree among a band of Blackfeet than it would be to save a Blackfoot in a band of Crees." In consequence of these repeated assaults in the vicinity of the forts, the Blackfeet can with difficulty be persuaded that the whites are not in active alliance with the Crees. Any person who studies the geographical position of the posts of the Hudson Bay Company cannot fail to notice the immense extent of country intervening between the North Saskatchewan and the American boundary-line in which there exists no fort or trading post of the Company. This blank speace upon the maps is the country of the Blackfeet. Many years ago a post was established upon the Bow River, in the heart of the Blackfeet country, but at that time they were even more lawless than at present, and the position had to be abandoned on account of the expenses necessary to keep up a large garrison of servants. Since that time (nearly forty years ago) the Blackfeet have only had the Rocky Mountain House to depend on for supplies, and as it is situated far from the centre of their country it only receives a portion of their trade. Thus we find a very active business carried on by the Americans upon the Upper Missouri, and there can be little doubt that the greater portion of robes, buffalo leather, &c., traded by the Blackfeet finds its way down the waters of the Missouri. There is also another point connected with American trade amongst the Blackfeet to which I desire to draw special attention. Indians visiting the Rocky Mountain House during the fall of 1870 have spoken of the existence of a trading post of Americans from Fort Benton, upon the Belly River, sixty miles within the British boundary-line. They have asserted that two American traders, well-known on the Missouri, named Culverston and Healy, have established themselves at this post for the purpose of trading alcohol, whiskey, and arms and ammunition of the most improved description, with the Blackfeet Indians, and that an active trade is being carried on in all these articles, which, it is said, are constantly smuggled across the boundary-line by people from Fort Benton. This story is apparently confirmed by the absence of the Blackfeet from the Rocky Mountain House this season, and also from the fact of the arms in question (repeating rifles) being found in possession of these Indians. The town of Benton on the Missouri River has long been noted for supplying the Indians with arms and ammunition; to such an extent has this trade been carried on, that miners in Montana, who have suffered from Indian attack, have threatened on some occasions to burn the stores belonging to the traders, if the practice was continued. I have already spoken of the great extent of the Blackfeet country; some idea of the roamings of these Indians may be gathered from a circumstance connected with the trade of the Rocky Mountain House. During the spring and summer raids which the Blackfeet make upon the Crees of the Middle Saskatchewan, a number of horses belonging to the Hudson Bay Company and to settlers are yearly carried away. It is a general practice for persons whose horses have been stolen to send during the fall to the Rocky Mountain House for the missing animals, although that station is 300 to 600 miles distant from the places where the thefts have been committed. If the horse has not perished from the ill treatment to which he has been subjected by his captors, he is usually found at the above-named station, to which he has been brought for barter in a terribly worn-out condition. In the Appendix marked B will be found information regarding the localities occupied by the Indian tribes, the names of the principal chiefs, estimate of numbers in each tribe, and other information connected with the aboriginal inhabitants, which for sake of clearness I have arranged in a tabular form.

It now only remains for me to refer to the last clause in the instructions under which I acted, before entering into an expression of the views which I have formed upon the subject of what appears necessary to be done in the interests of peace and order in the Saskatchewan. The fur trade of the Saskatchewan District has long been in a declining state, great scarcity of the richer descriptions of furs, competition of free traders, and the very heavy expenses incurred in the maintenance of large establishments, have combined to render the district a source of loss to the Hudson Bay Company. This loss has, I believe, varied annually from 2000l. to 6000l., but heretofore it has been somewhat counter-balanced by the fact that the Inland Transport Line of the Company was dependent for its supply of provisions upon the buffalo meat, which of late years has only been procurable in the Saskatchewan. Now, however, that buffalo can no longer be procured in numbers, the Upper Saskatchewan becomes more than ever a burden to the Hudson Bay Company; still the abandonment of it by the Company might be attended by more serious loss to the trade than that which is incurred in its retention. Undoubtedly the Saskatchewan, if abandoned by the Hudson Bay Company, would be speedily occupied by traders from the Missouri, who would also tap the trade of the richer fur-producing districts of Lesser Slave Lake and the North. The products of the Saskatchewan proper principally consists of provisions, including pemmican and dry meat, buffalo robes and leather, linx, cat, and wolf skins. The richer furs, such as otters, minks, beavers, martins, &c., are chiefly procured in the Lesser Slave Lake Division of the Saskatchewan District. With regard to the subject of Free Trade in the Saskatchewan, it is at present conducted upon principles quite different from those existing in Manitoba. The free men or "winterers" are, strictly speaking, free traders, but they dispose of the greater portion of their furs, robes &c., to the Company. Some, it is true, carry the produce of their trade or hunt (for they are both hunters and traders) to Red River, disposing of it to the merchants in Winnipeg, but I do not imagine that more than one-third of their trade thus finds its way into the market. These free men are nearly all French half-breeds, and are mostly outfitted by the Company. It has frequently occurred that a very considerable trade has been carried on with alcohol, brought by free men from the Settlement of Red River, and distributed to Indians and others in the Upper Saskatchewan. This trade has been productive of the very worst consequences, but the law prohibiting the sale or possession of liquor is now widely known throughout the Western territory, and its beneficial effects have already been experienced.

I feel convinced that if the proper means are taken the suppression of the liquor traffic of the West can be easily accomplished.

71. SELECTIONS FROM THE REPORT OF LIEUTENANT-COLONEL PATRICK ROBERTSON-ROSS, 1873

Canada, *Sessional Papers* (1873).

With regard to the measures which should be adopted for the settlement of the country, I feel satisfied that the introduction of a civil police force unsupported by any Military into the Saskatchewan Territory would be a mistake, and that no time should be lost in establishing a chain of military posts from Manitoba to the Rocky Mountains. The appointment of a Stipendiary Magistrate for the Saskatchewan, to reside at Edmonton, and act as the Indian Commissioner, is also a matter of the first importance. The individual to fill this important post, should be one, if possible, already known to, and in whom the Indians have confidence. I consider that it is very necessary to invite the co-operation of the Hudson's Bay Company in the adoption of any steps towards establishing law and order in the Saskatchewan for the first few years, and no Indian Commissioner should proceed unaccompanied by a military force.

A large military force is not required, but the presence of a certain force, I believe, will be found to be indispensible for the security of the country, to prevent bloodshed and preserve peace.

The number of the Indians dwelling in the extensive country which lies between the Red River and the Rocky Mountains on Dominion Territory, has been much exaggerated. It is very difficult to arrive at any accurate Indian census, but having made every enquiry during last summer on this point, whilst travelling through the country, from those most competent to judge, I doubt if there are more than four thousand Prairie Indians capable of bearing arms in the Dominion Territory, between Fort Garry and the Rocky Mountains, south of the Sub-Arctic Forest, and north of the International Boundary Line,—the total Prairie Indian population amounting, perhaps, to 14,000 or 15,000.

These Indians are scattered over such an immense extent of country, that anything like a formidable combination is impossible; most of the tribes, moreover, have been hostile to one another from time immemorial.

It is believed that the Blackfeet and the Plain Crees, the two strongest tribes of prairie Indians, may have respectively about one thousand fighting men, but it is doubtful if either tribe could ever concentrate such a number, or if concentrated, that they could long remain so from the difficulty of obtaining subsistence.

Although many of the Blackfeet have breech-loading rifles, the Indians generally are poorly armed and badly mounted.

Under these circumstances, it will be readily understood, that comparatively small bodies of well armed and disciplined men judiciously posted throughout the country, could easily maintain military supremacy. A body of fifty mounted riflemen, armed with breech-loading rifles, is a formidable power on the Prairies.

One regiment of mounted riflemen, 550 strong, including non-commissioned officers, divided into companies of fifty, would be a sufficient force to support Government in establishing law and order in the Saskatchewan, preserving the peace of the North West Territory, and affording protection to the Surveyors, Contractors, and Railway Labourers about to undertake the great work of constructing the Dominion Pacific Railway.

Although the proposed military strength, and consequent expense, may appear somewhat considerable, I have been guided by every consideration of economy in recommending the above number.

It is wiser policy and better economy to have one hundred soldiers too many, than one man too few; the great extent of the country, and detached nature of the service must also be taken into account, and it should be borne in mind what the majority of Indians really respect, and will bow to, is actual power.

It should be borne in mind too, that in addition to the Indian element, there is a half-breed population of about 2,000 souls in the Saskatchewan, unaccustomed to the restraint of any government, mainly depending as yet upon the chase for subsistence, and requiring to be controled [sic] nearly as much as the Indians.

If it be in harmony, therefore, with the policy of the Government to do so, I would recommend the establishment of Military Posts at the following places, strength as below:

1. At Portage de la Prairie	. . . .	50 Mounted Riflemen
2. At Fort Ellice	. . . .	50 Mounted Riflemen

3. At Fort Carlton . . . . 50 Mounted Riflemen
4. At Fort Pitt . . . . 50 Mounted Riflemen
5. At Fort Victoria . . . . 50 Mounted Riflemen
6. At Fort Edmonton . . . . . . 100 Mounted Riflemen
7. At Fort Porcupine Hill . . . . 150 Mounted Riflemen
Total 500

With a proportion of officers and non-commissioned officers.

If no permanent Custom House and Military Post is established at the Porcupine Hills, then the strength of the force at Edmonton should be 250, of which 150 men should be encamped during the summer months at the Porcupine Hills, or at the junction of the Bow and Belly Rivers, returning to Edmonton for the winter; but the establishment of a Custom House and Military Post at Porcupine Hills, is of far more importance and would have a much better general effect towards securing the peaceful settlement of the country than at any other places named. During the summer months a detachment of 50 men from this Post might with advantage be employed in improving the communication across the mountains with the Kootenay District of British Columbia.

It would be necessary that each of the companies of mounted riflemen should be made as far as possible self supporting communities, provided with a few carts, intrenching tools, agricultural implements, seed for raising corn, and some cattle. These military posts would partake of the character of military settlements, in the vicinity of which many settlers would ere long establish themselves.

It would be very desirable moreover that a medical officer should be appointed to each military post, and his duties not confined to the medical charge of the military only, but extended to all the Indians in the vicinity.

Past experience has proved that no measure is better calculated to secure the confidence and attachment of the Indian tribes than by attending to their wants in time of sickness, and supplying medical aid.

The men to compose the corps should be enlisted to serve for three years, receiving on the termination of the engagement, (provided they have performed their duties in a satisfactory manner,) the same amount of land as is granted on discharge to the men of the militia in Manitoba; I would recommend that the corps be raised by volunteers out of the active militia. It would be desirable to attach to the military force at each post three or four half-breeds, or Indians, as scouts, who could serve as interpreters and usually carry the mail.

At the places indicated for military posts no great difficulty would be experienced, or expense incurred in hutting the men, they themselves performing the work, or an arrangement might be more easily made with the Hudson's Bay Company to provide barrack accommodation and rations at the different posts for the number of men required.

In the event of this proposed arrangement meeting with the views of Government, I have the honour to state the probable expense that would be incurred for the establishment and maintenance of the militia force proposed, would be about $300,000 annually.

I would further beg to suggest, if it be decided to establish any chain of military posts, that for the first year the soldiers be employed in laying down a telegraphic work from Manitoba towards British Columbia, if not required to hut themselves.

From my own knowledge and observation of the country, I think that if proper energy be used, the very desirable work of establishing telegraphic communication from Fort Garry through Dominion Territory, with British Columbia, could be carried out by the soldiers in one or two seasons. I would further observe that no time should be lost in making the preliminary arrangements. The men and horses should, if possible, be concentrated at Fort Garry in the month of May or June, their equipment forwarded sooner and the companies despatched without delay.

An easy and agreeable march of a few weeks duration would suffice to establish them in the respective posts of occupation.

72. THE MOUNTED POLICE ACT, 1873

Statutes of Canada (1873).

An Act respecting the Administration of Justice, and for the establishment of a Police Force in the North West Territories.

Assented to 23rd May, 1873.

HER MAJESTY, by and with the advice and consent of the Senate and House of Commons of Canada, enacts as follows:—

1. The Governor may from time to time appoint, by commission under the Great Seal, one or more fit and proper person or persons to be and act as a Stipendiary Magistrate or Stipendiary Magistrates within the North West Territories, who shall reside at such place or places as may be ordered by the Governor in Council; and the Governor in Council shall assign to any such Stipendiary Magistrate a yearly salary not exceeding three thousand dollars, together with his actual travelling expenses.

2. Every Stipendiary Magistrate shall hold office during pleasure; and shall exercise within the North West Territories, or within such limited portion of the same as may be prescribed by the Governor in Council, the magisterial, judicial and other functions appertaining to any Justice of the Peace, or any two Justices of the Peace, under any laws or Ordinances which may from time to time be in force in the North West Territories.

3. Any Stipendiary Magistrate shall further have power to hear and determine, in a summary way and without the intervention of a jury, any charge against any person or persons for any of the following offences alleged to have been committed within the North West Territories, as follows:—

1. Simple larceny, larceny from the person, embezzlement, or obtaining money or property by false pretences, or feloniously receiving stolen property, in any case in which the value of the whole property alleged to have been stolen, embezzled, obtained or received, does not, in the judgment of such Stipendiary Magistrate, exceed one hundred dollars; or

2. Having attempted to commit larceny from the person or simple larceny; or

3. With having committed an aggravated assault, by unlawfully and maliciously inflicting upon any other person, either with or without a weapon or instrument, any grievous bodily harm, or by unlawfully and maliciously cutting, stabbing or wounding any other person; or

4. With having committed an assault upon any female whatever, or upon any male child whose age does not, in the opinion of the magistrate, exceed fourteen years, such assault, if upon a female, not amounting, in his opinion, to an assault with intent to commit a rape; or

5. Having assaulted, obstructed, molested or hindered any Stipendiary Magistrate, Justice of the Peace, Commissioner or Superintendent of Police, a policeman, constable or bailiff, or Officer of Customs or Excise, or other officer, in the lawful performance of his duty, or with intent to prevent the performance thereof;

And upon any conviction by such Stipendiary Magistrate, the person so convicted may be sentenced to such punishment as he thinks fit, by imprisonment for any period less than two years in any gaol or place of confinement, with or without hard labour, and with or without solitary confinement, or by fine, or by such imprisonment and fine.

4. The Chief Justice or any Judge of the Court of Queen's Bench of the Province of Manitoba, or any two Stipendiary Magistrates sitting together as a Court, shall have power and authority to hear and determine within the North West Territories, in a summary way and without the intervention of any Grand or Petty Jury, any charge against any person or persons for offences alleged to have been committed within the North West Territories, and the maximum punishment for which does not exceed seven years imprisonment; and such Court shall be a Court of record; and if imprisonment in a penitentiary be awarded in any such case, the Court may cause the convict to be conveyed to the penitentiary in the Province of Manitoba; and he shall undergo such punishment therein as if convicted in the Province of Manitoba.

5. Any Justice of the Peace, or any Stipendiary Magistrate or any Judge of the Court of Queen's Bench of the Province of Manitoba, shall have power and authority to commit and cause to be conveyed to gaol in the Province of Manitoba, for trial by the said Court of Queen's Bench according to the laws of criminal procedure in force in the said Province, any person or persons at any time charged with the commission of any offence against any of the laws or Ordinances in force in the North West Territories, punishable by death or imprisonment in the penitentiary: and the Court of Queen's Bench and any Judge thereof, shall have power and authority to try any person arraigned before the said Court on any such charge; and the jury laws and laws of criminal procedure of the said Province shall apply to any such trial; except that the punishment to be awarded, upon conviction of any such person, shall be according to the laws in force in the North West Territories: and the sentence may be carried into effect in a penitentiary or other place of confinement in the said Province, as if the same were in the North West Territories.

6. Whenever, under either of the two next preceding sections, any convict or accused person is ordered to be conveyed to gaol or to the penitentiary in Manitoba, any constable or other person in whose charge he is to be so conveyed, shall have the same power to hold and convey him, or to re-take him in case of an escape, and the gaoler or warden of the penitentiary in Manitoba shall have the same power to detain and deal with him, in the said Province, as if it were within the North West Territories, or as if the said convict or accused person had been ordered to be conveyed to such gaol or penitentiary by some competent Court or authority in the said Province.

7. Where it is impossible or inconvenient, in the absence or remoteness of any gaol or other place of confinement, to carry out any sentence of imprisonment, any Justice of the Peace or Stipendiary Magistrate, or any two Stipendiary Magistrates sitting together as aforesaid, or any Judge of the Court of Queen's Bench of Manitoba, may, according to their several powers and jurisdictions hereinbefore given, sentence such person so convicted before him or them, and sentenced, as aforesaid, to such imprisonment, to be placed and kept in the custody of the Police of the North West Territories, with or without hard labour,—the nature and extent of which shall be determined by the Justice of the Peace or Stipendiary Magistrate or Stipendiary Magistrates, or Judge, by or before whom such person was convicted.

8. The Governor in Council may cause to be erected in any part or parts of the North West Territories any building or buildings, or enclosure or enclosures, for the purposes of the gaol or lock-up, for the confinement of prisoners charged with the commission of any offence, or sentenced to any punishment therein; and confinement or imprisonment therein shall be held lawful and valid.

9. Whenever in any Act of the Parliament of Canada in force in the North West Territories, any officer is designated for carrying on any duty therein mentioned, and there shall be no such officer in the North West Territories, the Lieutenant Governor in Council may order by what other person or officer such duty shall be performed; and anything done by such person or officer, under such order, shall be valid and legal in the premises: or if it be in any such Act ordered that any document or thing shall be transmitted to any officer, Court, territorial division or place, and there shall be in the said North West Territories no such officer, Court or territorial division or place, then the Lieutenant Governor in Council may order to what officer, Court or place such transmission shall be made, or may dispense with the transmission thereof.

MOUNTED POLICE FORCE

10. The Governor in Council may constitute a Police Force in and for the North West Territories, and the Governor may from time to time, as may be found necessary, appoint by commission, a Commissioner of Police, and one or more Superintendents of Police, together with a Paymaster, Surgeon and Veterinary Surgeon, each of whom shall hold office during pleasure.

11. The Commissioner of Police shall perform such duties and be subject to the control, orders and authority of such person or persons, as may, from time to time, be named by the Governor in Council for that purpose.

12. The Governor in Council may, from time to time, authorize the Commissioner of Police to appoint, by warrant under his hand, such number of Constables and Sub-Constables as he may think proper, not exceeding in the whole three hundred men; and such number thereof shall be mounted as the Governor in Council may at any time direct.

13. No person shall be appointed to the Police Force unless he be of a sound constitution, able to ride, active and able-bodied, of good character, and between the ages of eighteen and forty years; nor unless he be able to read and write either the English or French language.

14. No person shall exercise any office in the said Force until he shall have taken the oath of allegiance and the following oath of office: "I, A.B., solemnly swear that I will faithfully, diligently and impartially execute and perform the duties and office of   in the Police Force of the North West Territories, and will well and truly obey and perform all lawful orders or instructions which I shall receive as such, without fear, favor or affection of or towards any person or party whomsoever. So help me God:" and such oath may be taken by the Commissioner of Police before any Judge, Stipendiary Magistrate, or Justice of the Peace having jurisdiction in the North West Territories, and by any other member of the Police Force before the Commissioner of Police, or any person having such jurisdiction as aforesaid; and such oaths shall be retained by the Commissioner as part of the records of his office.

15. The Commissioner and every Superintendent of Police shall be *ex-officio* a Justice of the Peace; and every constable and sub-constable of the Force shall be a constable in and for the whole of the North West Territories; and may execute the office in any part thereof, and in Manitoba in the cases hereinbefore mentioned and provided for.

16. Every constable and sub-constable shall, upon appointment to the said Force, sign articles of engagement; and any penalty which may be therein assigned may be enforced; and one condition in the said articles shall always be that he shall serve for the period of three years, and shall not leave the force or withdraw from his duties, unless he be dismissed or discharged therefrom, or shall have previously given six months notice in writing, to the Commissioner. The engagement shall be contracted to the Commissioner, and may be enforced by the Commissioner for the time being.

17. The Governor in Council may, from and out of any of the lands of the

Dominion in the Province of Manitoba or in the North West Territories, make a free grant not exceeding one hundred and sixty acres, to any constable or sub-constable of the said force, who, at the expiration of three years of continuous service in the said Force, shall be certified by the Commissioner of Police to have conducted himself satisfactorily, and to have efficiently and ably performed the duties of his office during the said term of three years.

18. The Governor in Council shall appoint the place at which the Head Quarters of the Force shall from time to time be kept, and the office of the Commissioner shall be kept there, and the same may be at any place in the North West Territories or the Province of Manitoba.

19. It shall be the duty of the Force—

1. To perform all duties which now are or shall be hereafter assigned to constables in relation to the preservation of the peace, the prevention of crime, and of offences against the laws and Ordinances in force in the North West Territories, and the apprehension of criminals and offenders, and others who may be lawfully taken into custody;

2. To attend upon any Judge, Stipendiary Magistrate or Justice of the Peace, when thereunto specially required, and, subject to the orders of the Commissioner or Superintendent, to execute all warrants and perform all duties and services in relation thereto, which may, under this Act or the laws and Ordinances in force in the North West Territories, lawfully be performed by constables;

3. To perform all duties which may be lawfully performed by constables in relation to the escort and conveyance of convicts and other prisoners or lunatics, to or from any Courts, places of punishment or confinement, asylums or other places,—

And for these purposes, and in the performance of all the duties assigned to them by or under the authority of this Act, they shall have all the powers, authority, protection and privileges which any constable now has or shall hereafter by law have.

20. The Governor in Council may, from time to time, make rules and regulations for any of the following purposes, viz:—To regulate the number of the Force, not exceeding in the whole the number of three hundred men as hereinbefore provided; to prescribe the number of men who shall be mounted on horseback; to regulate and prescribe the clothing, arms, training and discipline of the Police Force; to regulate and prescribe the duties and authorities of the Commissioner and Superintendents of the Force, and the several places at or near which the same, or the Force or any portions thereof may from time to time be stationed; and generally all and every such matters and things for the good government, discipline and guidance of the Force as are not inconsistent with this Act: and such rules and regulations may impose penalties, not exceeding in any case thirty days' pay of the offenders, for any contravention thereof, and may direct that such penalty when incurred may be deducted from the offender's pay: they may determine what officer shall have power to declare such penalty incurred, and to impose the same; and they shall have force as if enacted by law.

21. All pecuniary penalties so imposed shall form a fund to be managed by the Commissioner with the approval of the Governor in Council; and be applicable to the payment of such rewards for good conduct or meritorious services as may be established by the Commissioner.

22. Any member of the Force may be suspended from his charge or dismissed by the Commissioner or by any Superintendent to whom the Commissioner shall have delegated the power to do so; and any Superintendent may be suspended from office by the Commissioner until the pleasure of the Governor in Council shall be known; and every such suspension or dismissal shall take effect from the time it shall be made known either orally or in writing to the party suspended or dismissed.

23. Any Superintendent or any member of the Force suspended or dismissed shall forthwith deliver up to the Commissioner or to a Superintendent or to any constable authorized to receive the same, his clothing, arms, accoutrements and all property of the Crown in his possession as a member of the Force or used for police purposes; or in case of his refusing or neglecting so to do, shall incur a penalty of fifty dollars.

24. Whenever the Commissioner shall deem it advisable to make or cause to be made any special enquiry into the conduct of any Superintendent or of any member of the Police Force, or into any complaint against any of them, he, or the Superintendent whom he may appoint for that purpose, may examine any person on oath or affirmation on any matters relative to such enquiry, and may administer such oath or affirmation.

25. If any person shall unlawfully dispose of, receive, buy or sell or have in his possession without lawful cause, or shall refuse to deliver up when thereunto lawfully required, any horse, vehicle, harness, arms, accoutrements, clothing or other thing used for police purposes, such person shall thereby incur a penalty not exceeding double the value thereof, in the discretion of the Magistrate before whom he is convicted.

26. It shall be lawful for the Governor in Council, from time to time, to fix the sums to be annually paid to the Commissioner, Superintendents and other Officers of the said Force, regard being had to the number of Constables and Sub-Constables, from time to time, actually organized and enrolled, and the consequent responsibility attaching to their offices aforesaid, respectively, and to the nature of the duty or service and amount of labor devolved upon them, but such sums shall not be less than or exceed the amounts following, that is to say:—

Commissioner of Police, not exceeding		$2,600
And not less than	$2,000	
Each Superintendent, not exceeding		1,400
And not less than	1,000	

Paymaster, not exceeding		900
Quarter Master, not exceeding		500
Paymaster, if acting also as Quarter Master		1,400
Surgeon, not exceeding		1,400
And not less than	1,000	
Veterinary Surgeon, not exceeding		600
And not less than	400	

And each Constable shall be paid not exceeding the sum of one dollar per day; and each Sub-Constable shall be paid not exceeding the sum of seventy-five cents per day.

27. The Governor in Council may in lieu of the appointment of a Surgeon or of a Veterinary Surgeon, authorize arrangements to be made with any person or Veterinary Surgeon to perform the duties of Surgeon or Veterinary Surgeon for the said Force as to any portions or detachments thereof, and may pay reasonable and proper remuneration for any services so rendered.

28. The Governor in Council may also from time to time regulate and prescribe the amounts to be paid, for the purchase of horses, vehicles, harness, saddlery, clothing, arms and accoutrements, or articles necessary for the said Force: and also the expenses of travelling, and of rations or of boarding or billeting the force and of forage for the horses.

29. The Governor in Council may make regulations for the quartering, billeting and cantoning of the Force, or any portions or detachments thereof; and for the furnishing of boats, carriages, vehicles of transport, horses and other conveyances for their transport and use, and for giving adequate compensation therefor; and may, by such regulations, impose fines not exceeding two hundred dollars for breach of any regulation aforesaid, or for refusing to billet any of the said Force, or to furnish transport as herein mentioned. But no such regulations shall authorize the quartering or billeting of any of the Force in any nunnery or convent of any Religious Order of females.

30. All sums of money required to defray any expense authorized by this Act may be paid out of the Consolidated Revenue Fund of Canada.

31. A separate account shall be kept of all moneys expended under this Act, and a detailed statement thereof shall be laid before Parliament at each session thereof.

32. All regulations or Orders in Council made under this Act shall be published in the *Canada Gazette*, and shall, thereupon have the force of law from the date of their publication, or from such later date as may be therein appointed for their coming into force; and a copy of any such regulations purporting to be printed by the Queen's Printer shall be *prima facie* evidence thereof.

33. The Department of Justice shall have the control and management of the Police Force and of all matters connected therewith; but the Governor in Council may, at any time order that the same shall be transferred to any other Department of the Civil Service of Canada, and the same shall accordingly, by such order, be so transferred to and be under the control and management of such other Department.

34. The Commissioner and every Superintendent of Police, shall be *ex-officio* a Justice of the Peace, within the Province of Manitoba; and the constables and sub-constables of the Police Force shall also have and exercise within the Province of Manitoba, all the powers and authority, rights and privileges by law appertaining to constables under the laws of the Dominion, for the purpose of carrying the same into effect.

35. The Governor in Council may from time to time enter into arrangements with the Government of the Province of Manitoba for the use or employment of the Police Force, in aiding the administration of justice in that Province and in carrying into effect the laws of the Legislature thereof; and may, in any such arrangement, agree and determine the amount of money which shall be paid by the Province of Manitoba in respect of any such services of the said Police Force.

73. AMENDMENTS TO THE MOUNTED POLICE ACT, 1874

Statutes of Canada (1874).

An Act to amend *"An Act respecting the administration of Justice and for the establishment of a Police Force in the North-West Territories."*
Assented to 26th May, 1874.

15. The Commissioner shall have all the powers of a Stipendiary Magistrate under this or any other Act in force in the North-West Territories. The Assistant Commissioner and Inspectors, and such other officers as the Governor in Council may approve, shall be *ex-officio* Justices of the Peace; and every constable and sub-constable of the force shall be a constable in and for the whole of the North-West Territories, for carrying out any laws or ordinances in force therein, and also in every Province in the Dominion for the purpose of carrying out the criminal and other laws of the Dominion. . . .

22. Any member of the force who shall be found guilty of disobedience of the lawful commands of his superior, or who shall strike his superior, or who shall be guilty of any oppressive or tyrannical conduct towards an inferior, or shall be convicted of intoxication, however slight, or who shall directly or indirectly receive any gratuity without the Commissioner's sanction, or any bribe, or who shall embezzle or misapply any public moneys, arms, ammunition, clothing, appointments or public property or stores, or who shall take and convert to his own use any of the necessaries belonging to any comrade, without his consent, or who shall wear any party emblem, or shall otherwise manifest political partizanship, or shall wear any medal (not granted by the sovereign) or any badge whatsoever, without authority from the Commissioner, or who shall make use of any mutinous words, or shall overhold any complaint or be guilty of any mutinous or insubordinate conduct, or who shall knowingly make any false return or statement, or sign any false certificate or be privy thereto, or who shall make any alteration or erasure (for the purpose of fraud or deceit) in any public documents, or shall forge the name of any person on any warrant, summons, or other public document, or who shall make any false entry in any official book, or diary, or who shall wilfully omit to make an entry therein as to the performance of any duty, matter or thing which ought to be so entered, or who shall by any concealment or wilful omission attempt to evade the true spirit and meaning of this Act, or of the rules, orders or regulations respecting the force, or who shall refuse or omit to make a true and faithful return of all fines received by him, or to which he may be entitled upon any conviction in which he shall have been a prosecutor or witness, or who shall be convicted of any offence by a court of justice, or who shall unduly overhold any allowances or any other public money entrusted to him, or who shall be guilty of gambling, or who shall misapply any money or goods levied under any warrant or taken from any prisoner, or who shall give notice or otherwise cause to be intimated, either directly or indirectly, to any person against whom there shall be a warrant or order, notice thereof, with a view to the evasion of such warrant or order, or who shall divulge any matter or thing which it may be his duty to keep secret, or who shall make any anonymous complaint to the Government or the Commissioner, or who shall communicate without the Commissioner's authority, either directly or indirectly, to the public press, any matter or thing touching the force, or who, knowing where any offender shall be residing or concealed, shall not immediately inform his superior of the same, or shall not take due and prompt measures for the arrest of such person, or who shall wilfully or through negligence or connivance allow any person to escape, or who shall use any cruel, harsh or unnecessary violence towards any prisoner or other person, or who shall leave any post on which he has been placed as a sentry or on other duty, or who shall absent himself from his duties or quarters without leave, or who shall be guilty of any prevarication before any court, or upon any enquiry, or who shall behave in a scandalous or infamous manner, or shall be guilty of disgraceful conduct, or who shall be seen in any public house when not necessarily there on duty or by the permission of a superior officer, or who shall be guilty of profane or grossly immoral conduct, or who shall directly or indirectly borrow money from or through any other member of the force of inferior rank for his own private use or benefit, or who shall violate any standing order, rule or regulation, or any order, rule or regulation hereafter to be made, or who shall be guilty of any disorder or neglect to the prejudice of morality or discipline, though not specified in this Act or in any lawful rules or regulations, shall be held to have committed a breach of discipline, and, if a commissioned officer, shall be dismissed the service, or if a chief, staff or other constable shall, in the discretion of the Commissioner, be dismissed the service and thereby forfeit any benefit arising from his past service, or shall suffer suspension or loss of rank, or be liable to a fine not exceeding one month's pay, to be deducted in one sum or by monthly instalments from any pay accrued or accruing to the offender, or in failure thereof, to be levied by warrant under the hand of the Commissioner or Assistant Commissioner, or an Inspector, or any Justice of the Peace, from the goods and chattels of the offender, in addition to and besides any punishment to which the offender may be liable under any law in force in the North-West Territories, or in any Province in which the offence may be committed in respect thereof.

74. MEMORANDUM CONCERNING THE TRANSFER OF POLICING FROM THE FEDERAL GOVERNMENT TO THE NORTH WEST TERRITORIES, 1901

PAC, RCMP Records, Section A-1, vol. 528, no. 108.

Ottawa, 2nd November 1901

Memorandum: —

In compliance with the instructions of Sir Wilfrid Laurier, the undersigned begs to submit the following remarks respecting the N.W.M. Police: —

The Force was organized in 1873-4 for the establishment and preservation of law and order; to administer justice in a rough sort of way; and to assist in gradually bringing the Indians, with whom no Treaties had then been made west of Winnipeg, under civilization.

So long as the strictly legal element remained out of the Territories, the Police experienced little difficulty, with the exception of occasional friction with the Indians, in convincing them that the white man's method of administering justice must prevail.

By degrees Treaties were made with the Indians, the white man commenced to penetrate the Indian territory, the legal fraternity established themselves, and the Police had to contend with legal technicalities instead of simple adjudication based on the principles of right and wrong.

In those early days it was necessary to give the white settler or white pioneer Police protection sufficient to assure him against fear of injury to himself, or his family, by Indians. This led to the establishment of small detachments of Police throughout the Territories, and, I am afraid, to the fostering of unreasonable dependence on the Police, and the discouragement of that self-reliance for protection of the person and personal property which has generally prevailed in new and sparsely settled countries.

Rapid development of the lines of self government has been made in the North West, but as yet there is no provision for the assumption by the Regina Executive of much work which in the older Provinces would be under the control of the Attorney General or Municipal authorities.

Demands are constantly being made for the extension of Police jurisdiction north of the Saskatchewan River, which, until recently, was considered the northerly limit of ordinary Police supervision. These demands are certain to increase; in the Edmonton District alone we now have five detachments extending 800 miles north from that place. The construction of the Canadian Northern Railway, which enters the Territories at the north-west corner of the Province of Manitoba, will within the next few years create new settlements similar to those along the main line of the C.P. Railway—with the advantage of greater facilities for mixed farming—which will call for Police supervision.

Efforts to reduce, or close up, Police detachments in the more settled portions of the Territories have been unsuccessful; nor is it likely that much can be done in that direction until legislative authority is obtained for some other system to take the place of the Police. On the other hand, if reductions cannot be made in the older sections of the Territories, increased expenditure will be necessary to provide the required supervision in the north and west.

I would respectfully suggest that the conferences which it is understood are now being held between the Government here and representatives of the N. W. Executive might, with advantage, include consideration of legislation which would permit the gradual absorption, by the Executive of the Northwest, of the administration of justice and other duties performed by the Mounted Police—different sections of the Territories being brought under the operation of the Statute from time to time by Proclamation of the Governor General.

The first effort in this direction might be made to cover the larger portion of the Electoral District of Eastern Assiniboia, which must be in as good a position for local administration as the westerly portion of Manitoba, where there are no Mounted Police.

The Indians in Eastern Assiniboia are all settled on Reserves, and so devoted to Agricultural pursuits that they capture many prizes at the Agricultural Fairs.

The patrolling of the U.S. frontier might possibly be continued by the Police for a few years.

A commencement has been made in the direction of extending Militia organization to the Territories. The withdrawal of the Police from any section would probably give greater impetus to this movement; and if Militia organization is adapted to the conditions of the country—that is to say, on the lines of an irregular but yet serviceable Force, without too much gold lace, there can be no doubt that it would be taken up heartily by the settlers.

Mounted Police jurisdiction should continue to expand north—local administration of justice and local Militia filling the blank created by the receding of the Police westward and northward.

Respectfully submitted.

(signed)

Fred White

Comptroller.

75. MEMORANDUM CONCERNING THE AGREEMENTS WITH THE PROVINCES OF ALBERTA AND SASKATCHEWAN FOR THE CONTINUED SERVICES OF THE MOUNTED POLICE, 1906

PAC, RCMP Records, Section A-1, vol. 528, no. 108.

Ottawa, 24th April, 1906

Memo: for the Minister,—

I have had very pleasant interviews with the local Governments of Saskatchewan and Alberta respecting the Mounted Police, and, with your consent, they are prepared to agree to an arrangement as outlined in the annexed memorandum.

Briefly stated, it means that everything will go on as at present, with the exception of (1) substituting the Attorney General of each Province for the Minister of Justice in matters requiring legal advice and direction, (2) each Province, after the 1st July next, contributing $75,000.00 per annum to the Dominion Treasury towards the expenses of maintenance of the Police Force —total from the two Provinces $150,000.00 per annum.

The question of the period during which this arrangement is to continue in force was discussed. I suggested three or five years, as you might decide. The Alberta Government would like ten years, and Mr. Scott, of Saskatchewan, expressed his desire to have it made as long as possible, so as to be assured of permanency.

From a Police point of view, a fixed period would be an advantage, because our men are engaged for a total of five years, and it would be inconvenient to have the arrangement abrogated on very short notice.

Another important point with us is the question of Barracks. We have spent very little during the last few years, in anticipation of changes, but many of our buildings are absolutely beyond further repair, to say nothing of the enormous cost of fuel and stoves to keep them warm—and if the life of the Force is to be prolonged some new buildings will be necessary.

Respectfully submitted for Sir Wilfrid's consideration.

(signed)

Fred White
Comptroller.

THE JUDICIAL SYSTEM IN ACTION

76. THE QUEEN VS. O'KELL, 1887

North-West Territories Law Reports (1887).

[Court in banc, June 11th, 1887]

T. C. Johnstone, on the 9th June, 1887, moved on notice for a rule calling on Justices of the Peace to shew cause why a writ of *certiorari* should not issue for the return of a certain conviction.

D. L. Scott, Q.C., appeared *contra*, and the matter was argued on the motion for the rule.

The facts with the grounds upon which the motion was made and the points raised in argument appear in the judgement.

[June 11th, 1887]

ROULEAU, J., not having been present at the argument, took no part in the judgment. The judgment of the remainder of the Court (RICHARDSON, MACLEOD, WETMORE, and McGUIRE, J. J.) was delivered by

ay 29th, 1887, whereby the defendant was convicted for that he, the said Arthur O'Kell, within the space of twelve months last past, to wit, on the 23rd May, 1887, at the house known as the "Canteen," near the North-West Mounted Police Barracks, near Regina, had in his possession a quantity of intoxicating liquor, without the special permission in writing of the Lieutenant-Governor of the North-West Territories contrary to the form of the statute in such case made and provided, in order that the same be quashed upon the grounds:—

(1) That there was no evidence that the liquor found in his possession was intoxicating within the meaning of the statute;

(2) That if the said liquor was in fact intoxicating, there was no evidence that the applicant knew it; but on the contrary, there was evidence that he did not know it.

As to the first ground, we are of opinion after hearing counsel for O'Kell, and for the convicting Justices, and reading the depositions, that there was evidence that the liquors in question were intoxicating. The testimony of Dr. Jukes was that they contained from 3.9 to 8.1 per cent. of proof spirit or about one-half these quantities of pure alcohol, and that ordinary fermented malt liquor beer usually contains only from 4 to 6 per cent. of proof spirits. He also said that the liquors tested by him were all intoxicating, if taken in sufficient quantities, a qualifying remark that applies to all intoxicants.

There was also the evidence of Constable Frederick Smith, that one of the three kinds of liquor found in the applicant's possession, had, in fact, intoxicated him.

There was therefore, not only some, but also substantial, evidence before the Justices on which to base the conclusion they arrived at. Whether that conclusion was right or not is not a matter which, on this application we can review, the law is clear that where the charge is one that if true is within the Magistrate's jurisdiction, the finding of the facts by him is conclusive and is not open to review here. *Barber v. Nottingham & Grantham Ry. Co., Reg. v. Grant.* We are not, however, to be understood as suggesting that even if we were trying the case on the merits we would feel bound to arrive at the same conclusion the Magistrate did, or that in any case where there may be any, even slight, evidence of the presence of alcohol, a conviction should be sustained.

As to the second ground relied on by the applicant, two questions arise. Is ignorance of fact a defence in a case of this kind? and, if it is: is there evidence on which the magistrates could come to the conclusion that the facts did not support the applicant's contention?

The section under which the applicant is charged, does not require that the offender shall "knowingly" have intoxicating liquor in his possession, and it is not, therefore, necessary for the prosecution to allege or prove a scienter. (See Bishop on Statutory Crimes, s. 1022.) Neither was it sufficient for the applicant to prove that he had no knowledge of the intoxicating quality of the liquors in question. He should have gone further and shown that he was misled, without fault or carelessness on his part. (See Bishop on Statutory Crimes, s. 1022. Bishop on Criminal Law, ss. 301-310, *Lavett's Case*, Cro. Car. 538; 1 Hale 42-43.) A party must not shut his eyes to the character of the liquor he is selling; he must exercise a reasonable degree of care in ascertaining whether the liquor is intoxicating or not. Moreover the onus is upon him to show that after careful investigation and inquiry, he honestly believed that the liquors in question were not intoxicating. Did defendant O'Kell produce such testimony, and if so was the evidence on this point all one way? If the evidence was conflicting, or if it did not satisfy the magistrates, we are not here to review the decision arrived at. The magistrates were the judges on that point. They had before them the evidence of Constable Smith that on the 21st, 22nd, and 23rd of May, he had been served by the applicant, in person, with liquor similar to some tested by Dr. Jukes, and subsequently found in applicant's possession, and that the liquor so served intoxicated him. Was the applicant unaware that this man was being intoxicated by the liquor so given him and drunk in the applicant's presence and on his premises? If he was, can it be said that he could not by reasonable investigation have ascertained what effect it produced on Smith? It was also in evidence that the liquor in applicant's possession had nearly if not quite as much alcohol in it as in ordinary beer. Ought not the applicant, a dealer in such things, to have been able, had he exercised that care required of him, to ascertain whether the liquor so sold by him was in fact intoxicating or not? All this was evidence for the magistrate in arriving at a conclusion as to whether the applicant had established his innocence. It was for the magistrate to be satisfied on this point, and if the evidence as a whole did not convince him that the defence of innocence had been established, this Court does not feel justified in reversing their finding.

The Court is against the applicant upon both grounds, and therefore refuses his application.

Motion dismissed.

77. THE QUEEN VS. BROWN, 1893

North-West Territories Law Reports (1893).

This was a Crown case reserved by WETMORE, J., for the opinion of the Court *in banc.*

The case stated by the learned Judge was as follows:

The prisoner Brown was charged before me at the last sitting of the Supreme Court, Judicial District of Eastern Assiniboia, held at Grenfell, in March last, with manslaughter of one William White. The prisoner elected to be tried by me in a summary way and without the intervention of a jury, and was accordingly so tried. I convicted the prisoner.

But questions of law having arisen in such trial, I reserved the same for the consideration of the Justices of the Court for Crown Cases reserved, and thereupon postponed judgment upon such conviction until such questions have been considered and decided; and admitted the prisoner to bail with two sureties, to appear at such time and place as may be appointed, of which the prisoner is to have notice, to receive judgment upon the said conviction in case the same be affirmed.

I found that the deceased William White entered the employment of the prisoner as a servant on the 13th May, 1892, and that he was obtained as such servant from the Reverend Mr. Leslie, an agent stationed at Winnipeg, Manitoba, for a society in England called the Children's Aid Society, which sends young lads to this country. The only consideration which the deceased was to receive for his services was his board and clothing.

The deceased was about fifteen years of age when he died, which was on the 14th day of February last. Death was caused by the gangrenous condition of the body resulting from frost bites. The post-mortem examination disclosed that the toes, the soles of the feet, extending up to the ankle joints behind the heels, the penis, the left ear, the fingers and thumbs to be gangrenous from this cause. Some two or three months before the death the deceased commenced to wet his bed, and in consequence of that and of the smell arising therefrom becoming disagreeable, the prisoner put him to sleep in his stable, and kept him sleeping there until the 10th February.

During the latter period of that time, either from infirmity of the urinary organs, or from inability to unbutton his clothes, caused by the state in which his fingers were from the frost bites, the deceased wet his clothing also. From the 1st of February to the 10th, both inclusive, the weather was excessively cold, the thermometer ranging from thirty to forty-five degrees below zero. The evidence does not establish when, or under what circumstances, the frost bites which occasioned the gangrenous condition of the penis, the ear and the fingers occurred. But I found that the fingers were badly frozen at least three weeks before the lad's death, and that the prisoner then knew it. The evidence did not satisfy me that the mere fact that the prisoner sent the deceased to the stable to sleep was a culpable act, nor did the evidence satisfy me that the prisoner was alive to the serious condition the deceased's hands were in, but I did find that from the knowledge he had he ought to have been alive to it, and that if he had exercised ordinary care and showed the reasonable interest in the boy's welfare which he ought to have done, he would have been alive to it. No care or attention whatever was paid to the deceased in respect to this condition of his hands up to the 10th of February.

During the night of the 9th and the morning of the 10th February, while sleeping in this stable, the deceased's feet became frozen solid up to the ankles, and he was so discovered by the prisoner early in the morning of the 10th, and was then carried by him to the house. I found that the deceased's feet became so frozen by reason of the state his system was in as the result of the other frost bites before mentioned, rendering him unable properly to look after and attend to himself, and being left in that condition unattended to in the stable during the excessive cold weather beginning on the 1st February, and possibly his urinating in his clothes to some extent contributed towards it. The prisoner after he carried the deceased to the house took his clothes off, bathed him and put him to bed, he asked a neighbor for a remedy for frost bites, and he saw Dr. Hutchinson, told him the deceased's feet were frozen, asked him for something for them, and obtained a prescription from him; but he did not tell the doctor how badly the feet were frozen, or the condition of the lad in respect to the other parts of his body, although he knew that the feet were badly frozen, that the fingers were frozen at least three weeks before, and that they had been getting worse, and with ordinary attention he must have observed the condition the deceased's body was in generally when he bathed him. The evidence did not satisfy me that even then the prisoner was alive to the serious condition the deceased was in; but, as before, I found that from the knowledge he had, he ought to have been alive to it, and that if he had exercised ordinary care and showed the reasonable interest in the deceased's welfare which he ought to have shown, he would have been alive to it. Up to the 10th February, the deceased was physically able to withdraw himself from the prisoner's control and service, but owing to want of means he was unable to do so; and owing to the state he was in from the time his hands became frozen, coupled with the infirmity respecting his urinary organs, no one in the neighborhood knowing these facts would be at all likely to receive him. Upon and after the 10th of February he was helpless and unable to take care of himself. The prisoner had means to procure medical attendance. Under these findings, I held that in view of the age of the deceased, and the circumstances of the country, there being no provision for maintaining poor people, that it was the duty of the prisoner from a period beginning three weeks before the lad's death, to have either removed him from the stable, and brought him into the house, and there taken care of him, or to have sent him back to Mr. Leslie to have him cared for; or to have cared for him in some other way, and not to have left him entirely unattended to in the manner he was left in the stable, especially during the excessive cold weather, commencing at least on the 1st February; and that in omitting to do this, the prisoner was guilty of gross negligence amounting to indifference. I also held that from and after the 10th February, he was guilty of gross negligence amounting to indifference, in not acquainting the doctor with the actual condition of the deceased. I found that by reason of such gross neglect in keeping the deceased in the stable the feet became frozen, and that from such neglect, and the other negligence stated, the condition of the feet and the other frost bites became aggravated and gangrenous, and that the death was attributable to such negligence, and I therefore convicted the prisoner.

The questions for the consideration of the Court are:—

First—Whether the findings and circumstances stated warranted the holdings.

Second—Whether under the findings and holdings stated the prisoner ought to have been convicted.

Third—As the learned counsel for the prisoner urged, that the evidence would not support the findings of fact, I also reserve that question for the consideration of the Court, and attach hereto a copy of the evidence.

Dated this 19th day of May, A.D. 1893.

(Sgd.) E. L. WETMORE, J. S. C.

[*June 12th, 1893.*]

The judgment of the Court (RICHARDSON, MACLEOD, ROULEAU, WETMORE and MCGUIRE, J. J.) was delivered by

RICHARDSON, J.—James Wheelton Brown was tried and convicted before Mr. Justice WETMORE, of manslaughter, but consequent upon objections raised by accused's counsel at the trial, the learned Judge reserved for the consideration of this Court the following questions:—

1. Whether the findings and circumstances stated warranted the holdings.

2. Whether under the findings and holdings stated, the prisoner ought to have been convicted.

3. Whether the evidence given at the trial was sufficient to support the findings of fact.

From the evidence as stated by the learned trial Judge the following facts appear:—

1. That the lad, William White, whose death formed the subject of the prosecution, entered the prisoner's (a farmer) service on or about 13th May, 1892.

2. That White was then about 14 years of age.

3. That in return for faithful services rendered White was to have "a good

home," including clothing, board, and lodging, but no money wages.

4. Thus at least the relation of master and servant was then established between White and the prisoner.

5. That some time early in January, 1893, about a month before his death, the lad's hands were badly frost-bitten, and from inattention his fingers became raw and sloughing, consequent upon which state he was unable to use his fingers for the ordinary purposes of nature.

6. That this condition was openly in view of the prisoner, who paid no attention, so far as shown, whatever to the lad until the morning of the 10th February, 1893, when the prisoner found the lad utterly helpless, and on examining him discovered his feet and lower legs up to above the ankles frozen solid and the inside of his upper legs raw, etc.

7. Instead of communicating the true state of affairs outside his own house during the 10th February, the prisoner, on the following day, the weather very severe, left the lad alone, helpless, so far as appears, and drove into Grenfell, sixteen miles distant, where he called on Dr. Hutchinson, whom he asked for medicine for frost bites, then informing the doctor that the lad was *slightly* frost-bitten, which to his knowledge was an untrue statement, since by his own evidence before the coroner he admitted that for a period of a month previous the lad's hands had been frozen and kept getting worse, and he had told the witness, Harry Read, on 11th February that he found him badly frozen on the 10th. What the prisoner did for the lad after calling on the doctor does not appear. The lad died on the 14th February, and death was shown to have been caused or accelerated by gangrene following severe frost-bites.

The question for this Court in effect is,—

Was there a common law duty devolving upon the prisoner to do more than he did, knowing the condition of the lad from the time he was frozen three weeks or a month prior to his death?

It will be recollected that the prisoner undertook to provide a good home, which would certainly mean taking much better care than there is shown to have been given to an utterly helpless lad after being, as he was, severely frost-bitten, and as it must be assumed that the case was so serious as to require the prisoner to consult a medical man, it was surely his duty to explain to the doctor the condition the lad was discovered in on the 10th, which he certainly did not do, representing him as being "slightly frozen."

The learned trial Judge has found from the facts disclosed on the trial, that the prisoner was guilty of negligence "that by reason of gross neglect in keeping the deceased in the stable the feet became frozen, and that from such neglect and other negligence stated, the condition of the feet and the other frost-bites became aggravated, and that the death was attributable to such negligence."

This Court is of opinion that the evidence warranted the learned trial Judge so finding, that at common law the prisoner was bound to supply care and attention reasonably suited to the lad's condition, in which he failed, and for want of which death was accelerated, and that upon the authority of *Regina v.*

Marrioll, Regina v. Finney, Regina v. Nicholls, and *Regina v. Instan,* the conviction of the said James Wheelton Brown by Mr. Justice WETMORE should be affirmed.

Conviction affirmed.

78. THE QUEEN VS. BREWSTER, 1896

North-West Territories Law Reports (1896).

The prisoner, on trial before ROULEAU, J., and a jury, was convicted of theft. Leave to appeal was granted on the ground that the verdict was against the weight of evidence.

The appeal was argued before the Court *in banc* at Regina on 2nd June, 1896.

J. A. Lougheed, Q.C., for the prisoner.

C. C. McCaul, Q.C., for the Crown.

[*June 5th, 1896.*]

WETMORE, J.—The defendant was convicted before my brother ROULEAU and a jury, of the offence of stealing a number of cattle from one Page, and by leave of the learned Judge has appealed to this Court, on the ground that the verdict is against the weight of evidence.

The evidence establishes beyond all question that a number of cattle which were once owned by Page, were found in the possession of the defendant with the brand which was on them when so in Page's possession, changed and disfigured.

The defendant accounts for these cattle getting into his possession as follows:—That Page was indebted to him in $300 for money loaned, that pressing him for this money Page agreed to sell him about 38 head of cattle at $20 a head, and that the defendant thereupon paid Page $450. These cattle were to be delivered to the defendant, and Page employed one Bowers to drive them over to the defendant's place at a place called Lone Pine, and on the 10th September met the defendant at Innisfail and told him that the cattle were on the way to Lone Pine. That Page and the defendant proceeded in the direction of Lone Pine, when they met Bowers with 38 head of young cattle and 12 calves, and Page helped the defendant and Bowers to drive these cattle some seven miles farther on to a place called Sproat's Creek, when he (Page) left them and went home. The defendant and Bowers proceeded the next morning with the cattle to John Brewster's, where the defendant proposed to winter them. That after Page and the defendant met the cattle and before Page went home, the defendant paid him $10 to make up the price of the 38 head at $20 a head, and the calves were thrown in. In short, the defendant sets up that Page sold him these cattle for $760. Bowers corroborated the defendant, and swore that Page employed him to drive these cattle and deliver them to the defendant. Page swore that he never sold the cattle to the defendant, that he never authorized Bowers to drive or deliver them as above stated, that at the time of the alleged agreement for the sale of the cattle he did not owe the defendant $300 or any other sum, that the defendant did not pay him $450, and that he never informed him that the cattle were on the way to Lone Pine, or helped to drive them.

If the testimony given by Page is true, the evidence for the prosecution establishes a clear case of theft. If the evidence on the part of the defendant is true he is not guilty. The evidence given by Page was in some respects of such a character that the jury would have been warranted in discrediting it altogether.

He certainly with respect to some important matters showed that his memory must have been very bad or he was untruthful. At the same time I cannot say that the jury would for these reasons be bound to wholly discredit him. It was just a case where the credit to be given was entirely for the jury, and there was other evidence that the jury might consider corroborative of Page. There was also testimony which the jury might consider corroborative of the defendant's testimony. He was corroborated by Bowers as before stated, and also by the fact that Page and the defendant met him with the cattle and helped him drive them to Sproat's Creek. Other witnesses were called who testified that they saw Page and the defendant and Bowers together driving the cattle; other witnesses testified that they saw the defendant and Bowers with cattle over the route they stated they drove them, and at or about the time stated. A witness testified he met Page and the defendant riding together on the 10th September between Innisfail and where the defendant says he met the cattle. Another witness swore that he heard the bargain between Page and the defendant for the sale of the cattle, as stated by the defendant. But while there was this testimony, the credit to be given to the witnesses was entirely for the jury. On behalf of the Crown there was the testimony of Page, to which I have referred; there was the fact that the brands which were on the cattle when they were in Page's possession were altered and disfigured by the defendant. A very important question upon which the parties contradicted each other was, whether Page was indebted to the defendant in $300 or any other sum when the alleged agreement for the sale of the cattle was made in the latter part of July. Because if he was so indebted the defendant's story would be quite probable; but if he was not so indebted the defendant's story must be a fabrication. The defendant swore that this indebtedness of $300 was made up of a sum of $200 loaned by him to Page on October 17th, 1893, and a sum of $100 loaned to him before that date. Page, although at the first trial of this case (for it was tried twice) he denied borrowing the $200, eventually admitted it, and the cheque for that amount signed by the defendant was produced. But he swore that on the 5th February, 1894, he and the defendant had a settlement of their affairs, and everything was then adjusted between them, and he produced a receipt of that date signed by Brewster, which acknowledged payment of all accounts in full up to that date.

The defendant swore that the $300 was not included in settlement, that the settlement was money of a partnership between him and Page, and that the $300 was left out because Page did not want his wife to know about the $200 loan. There however is the receipt, and that on its face corroborates Page; and moreover Mrs. Page corroborates her husband that all accounts were settled on the 5th February, and she swore that at that time she was aware of the $200 indebtedness to the defendant. The testimony for the defendant was to the effect that the place where they camped with the cattle at Sproat's Creek on the 10th of September was at the bridge. The evidence shows that this bridge was in sight of Sproat's house and that the country is open; while Sproat will not swear that there was a band of cattle there that evening, he swears that he was home, and that he neither saw the defendant or Bowers or a band of cattle that evening or the next morning. Several witnesses were called who were in a position to see a bunch of cattle such as the defendant alleged he was driving if they passed along the road at the time specified, yet while they will not swear such a bunch did not pass, they swear they did not see them.

While this testimony was possibly of a slight character, still it was a circumstance for the jury to consider. It is, I think, significant and worthy to be marked, although possibly not of very great weight, that when the cattle broke loose the night they were taken to John Brewster's, they wandered back in a direct line between that place and Page's ranche, instead of going by the very circuitous route which they had been driven to John Brewster's. It is also significant that two witnesses swore that they saw the defendant and Bowers down at James Brewster's, which is close to Page's ranche, before the snow storm, and one of these witnesses swore that they were then looking for cattle.

Then it is stated that this drive of over seventy miles in three days was a very long drive, and one that it is very unlikely that a person would force his own cattle at that time of the year. The jurors would be quite familiar with that question. According to Bowers' own statement, some of the calves were about played out when they got to Lone Pine at noon on the 10th, yet they drove them on that day to Sproat's Creek, and drove them 30 miles next day. The probability of this was a question entirely for the jury. The defendant's case attempted to set up that Page put a new brand on the cattle, or altered the brand before the delivery, because the defendant did not want any cattle with another brand on the E brand. There was some evidence on the part of the Crown other than that of Page, to show that after the alleged contract of sale and before the alleged delivery, no cattle were branded at Page's ranche, and that there were no cattle in the corrals at Page's on the 9th September for Bowers to drive away. The jury might also have considered it out of the usual course for the defendant to have returned the receipt of $750 when the cattle were delivered. The learned trial Judge has informed the members of this Court that he is dissatisfied with the verdict and thinks that the defendant ought to have been acquitted, and that while he left the question of fact to the jury, and under the evidence he could not do otherwise, yet on commenting on the facts he charged in honour of the defendant.

I am free to confess that looking at the evidence as it appears on paper, I think if I had been trying the case without the intervention of a jury I would have acquitted the defendant. I have not, however, had the opportunity of observing the demeanour of the witnesses, the jury have, and they are, when there is a jury, the constituted judges of the facts. It has been urged that when an appeal has been brought on the ground that the verdict is against the weight of evidence, the Court will as a matter of course order a new trial if the trial judge expresses himself dissatisfied with the verdict. That, however, is not the law as established by the later authorities. The law as so laid down, is that in deciding whether there should be a new trial, the question is whether the verdict is one that the jury as reasonable men would properly find: *Solomon* v. *Bitton, Webster* v. *Fried-berg*, and see the *Metropolitan Railway Company* v. *Wright, Commissioners of Railways* v. *Brown*, and *Phillips* v. *Marlin*. No doubt in deciding the question as to the reasonableness of the verdict the opinion of the trial Judge is entitled to and ought to receive great weight. But it is not conclusive.

I am unable to bring my mind to the conclusion that the verdict in this case was one that the jury as reasonable men ought not to have come to. I moreover think that it is worthy of consideration that the defendant, although he has had two trials, was unable to satisfy either jury that Page's testimony was fabrication, the first jury having disagreed.

I think the new trial should be refused.

79. THE QUEEN VS. CHARCOAL

North-West Territories Law Reports (1897).

Crown case reserved by SCOTT, J.

Reginald Rimmer, for the accused, instructed by the Department of Indian Affairs.

T. C. Johnstone, for Attorney-General of Canada.

[March 5th, 1897.]

WETMORE, J.—The prisoner was convicted before my brother SCOTT and a jury of the murder of another Indian called Medicine-Pipe-Stem-Crane-Turning. The murdered man was found in a house on the Blood Reserve on the Belly River near Fort Macleod. He evidently had been murdered by some person. The only evidence connecting the prisoner with the murder was an admission made by him to Robert N. Wilson, who at the time was acting as interpreter to James Wilson, the Indian Agent on the Blood Reserve, to which the prisoner belonged. After the prisoner was arrested on the barge and while he was a prisoner he was interviewed by Wilson, the Indian Agent, through Robert N. Wilson, the interpreter, and made the following statement: "I killed the policeman and killed him well. I also killed a boy up the river, but I did not shoot the policeman at Lees Creek. Those who accuse me of that crime lie about me. What I have done I do not deny, I do not hide. I do not like people to accuse me of crimes I did not commit." Wilson, the Indian Agent, then asked the prisoner, "Where did you kill the boy, inside the house or out," to which the prisoner replied "outside." He was then told that the body was found inside and was asked if he did not kill him inside, to which he replied, "No. I killed him outside." Mr. Wilson then asked him, "Where did you kill the man, near the house or below the house or where?" Prisoner replied "Beyond the house." Prisoner was then told that the body was found inside the house and that it was believed that the young man was killed there, and he was to recollect where the killing took place, to which he finally replied, "Ask my wife, she knows all about it and can tell it all to you, my memory is not clear." The part of this admission which it is claimed admitted the murder of the Indian man "Medicine-Pipe-Stem" by the prisoner was, "I also killed a boy up the river." The murdered man was about 25 years old; the prisoner is a much older man, and the only evidence which pointed to the fact that the prisoner had reference to the murdered man was the fact that the man was found murdered at the place I have stated, and the following facts testified to by Robert N. Wilson, namely, that Indians of the prisoner's tribe are from superstitious notions not in the habit of mentioning the names of deceased personal acquaintances in ordinary conversation, if they can avoid it; that middle-aged and elderly Indians are in the habit of speaking of any young man whom they have known from boyhood as a boy, and that the prisoner and the interpreter both reside on a point on the Belly River below the scene of the murdered man's death. The evidence of Robert N. Wilson as to the admission in question was objected to. Before it was received Robert N. Wilson, the only witness who gave evidence of the admission, testified as follows: "Neither during the conversation nor at any other time before, did I, to my knowledge, nor did any one else, make any threat or hold out any inducement to him to procure him to make a statement in regard to the killing." On cross-examination he testified as follows: "At the interview I was acting as interpreter to Mr. Wilson, the Indian Agent. In the first instance the interview was between Mr. Wilson and the prisoner through me as interpreter. I do not remember the opening of the conversation. I did not ask him about the shooting. I do not remember telling him that he need not be afraid, as we were not policemen. As far as I can remember any statement he made was entirely voluntary." The learned Judge then put the following question: "Assuming that prisoner did make any implicating statements, can you state from what occurred why he should have made such a statement?" Answer: "I think it was because he was in the boasting mood at the time." The learned Judge then put the following question: "From your knowledge of Indian character can you state whether they are in the habit of boasting of acts which were never committed by them?" Answer: "I would say they are not." The evidence was then admitted subject to objection, by which I mean the counsel for the prisoner still pressing his objection.

After the evidence was admitted, Robert N. Wilson in cross-examination testified as follows: "I was rather surprised when he started on the subject of his crime, as they had no connection with the previous subjects. If Mr. Wilson had said anything to him to induce him to speak about his crimes I would have remembered it. I do not remember whether he stated why he had killed the Indian, but I would not swear that he did not make any statement as to his motives." After the admission was received, James Wilson, the Indian Agent, was called and examined by the Crown, and testified as to what occurred at the interview in question as follows: "I am instructed to act as legal adviser to Indians under my jurisdiction. As a rule I always tell them that I am here as their adviser to help them. I remember being in the guard room and having a conversation with prisoner through Mr. Robert Wilson as my interpreter. I heard his evidence with reference to that conversation and what took place there. I believe that he faithfully interpreted between us. I am not prepared to say I did not hold out any threats or inducements to get the prisoner to make a statement. I am not prepared to contradict him when he says that no threat or inducement was held out, and the prisoner's statement as to killing was a voluntary one." On cross-examination he stated: "I as a rule always look after the defence of Indians of my reserve who are charged with offences. They all understand that I do that. They have been repeatedly told so. When necessary to retain advocates to conduct such defences I have always assisted them in the defence and in procuring evidence. I always interview the accused before the trial if possible. I make a rule to tell Indians so charged that what they tell is to their benefit to assist in their defence. I do not remember whether I told prisoner that at the time of the inverview at which Robert N. Wilson acted as interpreter. I procured the interview for the purpose of assisting him in his defence."

At the close of the case the counsel for the prisoner applied to have the evidence of Robert N. Wilson as to the admission struck out, which the learned Judge refused. The learned Judge reserved three questions for the consideration of this Court:

1st. Whether the admission was properly received?

2nd. If properly received whether from what subsequently appeared it should have been struck out?

3rd. Whether the evidence is sufficient to support the conviction?

I am of opinion that the evidence should have been struck out. The authorities are abundantly clear that an admission of guilt made by a party charged with an offence to a person in authority under the inducement of a promise of favour or by menaces or under terror, is inadmissible. This is so clear that it does not require authority to be cited in support of it. Whether if the promise or threat is made by a person not in authority that is sufficient to reject the admission it is not now necessary to decide, because I am of opinion that James Wilson, the Indian Agent, was quoad the Indians on his reserve a person in authority. In the first place he is appointed by the Governor in Council to carry out The Indian Act (R.S.C. c. 43) and the Orders in Council made under it (see s. 8. s.-s. 3 of that Act), and in the second place he is *ex officio* a justice of the peace: see Vic. 1900 c. 29, s. 9.

Assuming the rule which provides that such admissions to persons in authority should not be admissible if made under the inducements mentioned to be sound in principle (and the contrary cannot be now held). I cannot conceive of a case where it ought to be more strictly insisted on than as between an Indian and the Agent of his reserve. These Indians are, for the most part, as we who reside in the Territories know, unacquainted with the English language, or but imperfectly acquainted with it. The rules and principles of British law, or upon which it is administered, are not familiar to them, and when a serious matter arises such as has arisen in this case, they must be largely dependent upon the Indian Agent who is over them for assistance and guidance. So we find it stated in evidence in this case by James Wilson, the Indian Agent, that he is instructed to act as legal adviser to Indians under his jurisdiction, and that he always interviews the accused before the trial if possible. I do not wish to be understood as holding that communications made by an Indian to the Agent under such circumstances are privileged. It is not necessary to hold that for the purposes of this case, and I therefore express no opinion on that question. But I do most unhesitantly hold that a confession made to such an Agent under the inducement of a promise or of a threat or menace is not admissible. The character of the inducement to render the admission inadmissible may be of a very slight character. An admission obtained under the following inducement, "You had better tell the truth, it may be better for you," was held inadmissible: *Reg. v. Fennell.*

It was urged, however, that in this case no positive evidence that an inducement was offered was proved. This is true. But while I do not rule that if an admission of the accused is admitted in evidence without the question being raised whether it was made under some inducement or threat, I do hold that if that question is raised, the burden of proving that it was not made under an inducement or threat is on the Crown and not on the prisoner. This question was discussed in a very recent case in England, decided in 1893, *Reg. v. Thompson*, in which CAVE, J., giving the judgment of the Court, lays it down that it is the duty of the prosecution to prove "in case of doubt that the prisoner's statement was free and voluntary," and in concluding his judgment, referring to the evidence on which it was sought to put in the admission, he says: "In this particular case there is no reason to suppose that Crewden's evidence was not perfectly true and accurate, but on the board, plain ground that it was not proved satisfactorily that the confession was free and voluntary, I think it ought not to have been received."

So that in this case I say that in view of the testimony given by James Wilson it was not proved satisfactorily by the testimony of Robert N. Wilson that the confession was free and voluntary, and therefore the admission ought to have been struck out. I will not repeat the evidence which I have quoted beyond this, that James Wilson swore that he made it a rule to tell Indians so charged that what they tell is to their benefit to assist in their defence, and that he is there as their adviser to help them. Now, while there is no positive evidence that this or anything to that effect was stated to the prisoner in this case, it is not to my mind satisfactorily established that it was not, and the onus of establishing this is on the Crown.

Robert N. Wilson swearing that he does not remember this and he does not recollect that, is not sufficient. In my opinion Robert N. Wilson's testimony on cross-examination that if the Indian Agent had said anything to the prisoner to induce him to speak about his crimes he would have remembered it, will not help the Crown for two reasons. First, because his previous evidence shows that his memory as to what took place is not very accurate or reliable, and in the second place, what would in law be an inducement might not strike the Wilsons as such. I do not wish to be understood as drawing too close lines around the question of the admissibility of such admissions beyond what is laid down in *Reg. v. Thompson*. But in this case, in view of Mr. James Wilson's evidence as to his usual course in such cases and Mr. Robert Wilson's want of memory or rather want of positiveness, I am of opinion that the Crown failed to establish satisfactorily what was necessary to allow the evidence of the admission to remain on the Judge's notes.

As without this admission there was no evidence to connect the prisoner with the murder, the conviction must be quashed. It is not therefore necessary to express any opinion as to the other questions reserved by the learned Judge.

RICHARDSON, ROULEAU, and McGUIRE, J. J., concurred.

80. SOME TYPICAL REPORTS OF CASES TRIED BY MOUNTED POLICE OFFICERS ACTING AS MAGISTRATES, LETHBRIDGE, 1894

PAC, RCMP Records, Section A-1, vol. 91, no. 148.

Lethbridge,
31st December, 1894

The Commissioner,
N.W.M. Police,
Regina.
Sir,

I have the honour to render my report for the past month.

On the 1st Inst Joseph McKay, charged with robbery, as previously reported, was brought up and discharged as the evidence was insufficient to convict.

A Prize fight took place here on the 3rd. Inst. Our old friend James Pearce backed one James Carr against one W. B. Faulkner; the stakes were $100.00 a side; 5 oz gloves. The fight took place in a stable near No. 3 shaft. The referee being a Mr. Jackson of Calgary, erstwhile of Fort Qu'Appelle. At the outset the referee announced that it was a scientific contest "for points". In the course of the 2nd round Faulkner could not come to time. The referee declared a "Knock out" and there was the end of it for that evening. Carr and his backer Pearce, went to the stakeholder, O. Burge (who was not present) and claimed the stakes which were handed over to Pearce. Pearce then deposited the $200.00 on Carr for another bout, which was arranged to take place next morning. In the second round of that affair, Carr was "knocked out" and Faulkner got the stakes from the stakeholder. Pearce consoled himself by getting drunk and being robbed of his gold watch, which he is not at all likely ever to see again. I tried the two pugilists for prize fighting and in a lengthy written judgment after looking up all the authorities I could find, convicted them. Carr obtained bail prior to appealing but Faulkner has begun his 3 months labour. Pearce has been keeping out of the way, but I intend to try him on a charge of promoting a prize fight.

Lethbridge, 30th November 1894.

The Commissioner
N.W.M.P.
Regina
Sir:

I have the honor to forward my report for the past month.

On Saturday night the 3rd instant, a Rancher known as "Scotty" Ross, complained that two neighbors named Arnold, father, and son, had stolen from him a cow, and calf valued at $50. Earlier in the day the Arnold's had been to me about laying an information against Ross for stealing a calf. The facts are that a young calf about a fortnight old was claimed by two cows, one belonging to the Arnold's and one to Ross. I committed the Arnold's for trial, and admitted them to bail on their own recognizances, but it is doubtful if the Crown Prosecutor will follow the case up. The expert testimony was very amusing, a selection of dairy men, stockmen agreed that a certain cow with a broken horn was the mother of the calf, and was clearly the cow which had calved last. For my own satisfaction I asked Vet'y Sur: Evans to give an opinion. He gave it as his opinion that the other cow had calved last and pointed to a discharge resulting from the cow not having been properly cleaned. One of the Stockmen retorted that he had noticed the discharge himself, but it was not due to the after birth discharge, but was the sign the cow was bulling. Asked whether he could distinguish between the character of an after birth discharge, and that of a "bulling" cow, he replied that he could not, all of which was very satisfactory from a Judicial point of view. The Arnold's were apparently determined to give Ross some trouble, so they went off to Stand Off, and there laid an information charging Ross with having stolen the identical calf. This complaint was heard at Macleod, and was I believe dismissed.

On the 6th instant Thomas Elliott was committed for trial on a charge of unlawful wounding. On the Sunday previous he had gone home drunk, and beaten his wife to such an extent that she was not out of bed for some time and wound on the head caused by a pitchfork, is the cause of the charge of wounding being laid. This man habitually supplies liquor to Indians. Sergt. Ware found and destroyed a decoction of tea, and whiskey, which he had brewed for the Indian trade, and I thought it as well to keep him locked up instead of allowing him out on bail.

A wholesale liquor dealer named Roy, was on the 8th instant convicted by me of allowing liquor to be sold in his store to a person under the age of 18. Sergt Ware, watched a young Selevich boy aged 11, and in course of time took from him two bottles of whiskey which the boy had bought for an Indian. The Indian gave him $2. to buy the whiskey, and 50 cents for himself, and the boy told me that he had altogether $7.50 worth of whiskey, and earned $1.75 for himself thereby. The penalty for a first conviction is $25, and I inflicted that amount. The license inspector here is worse than useless. This man Roy, it is well known, does retail business in his wholesale store and the fact could be easily proved if the machinery of the liquor license law were in proper working order.

After the years of abuse that the Police underwent in connection with the old prohibition law, I do not feel called upon to go myself, or to order one of my men to go into Roy's store and buy one or two drinks, and then lay an information. There is a particular grade of odium attached to that kind of proceeding, and when there are duly appointed officials whose special business it is to look after the liquor law I think at least they should make an attempt in the proper direction.

THE CONTROL OF CRIME AND DISORDER

81. A TYPICAL MOUNTED POLICE WEEKLY REPORT, BATTLEFORD, 1888

PAC, RCMP Records, Section A-1, vol. 17, no. 192.

N.W.M.P.
Battleford
Jany. 21st 1888

Sir:

In furnishing you with my report on matters affecting this District for the week ending this day.

I have the honor to state for your information that the Indians and half breeds in this neighbourhood still continue to follow their customary peaceful avocations. I had the Bresoylor settlement patrolled during the week and all is reported quiet at that place.

The at one time notorious Cree Indian chief the Big Bear—died at Pound-maker's Reserve on Tuesday last, the 17th instant.

Owing to the violence of the storm which raged throughout this district on Wednesday and Thursday of last week, the incoming mail was delayed for twenty four hours. On its arrival the teamster reported that he had found the body of one Thomas Mitchell lying beside a surveyor's mound on The Swift Current trail. Mitchell kept a "stopping place" about twenty miles south, and his dead body was found a mile south of his own house. George Smith—the mail driver—put the corpse in his sleigh and locked it up in Mitchell's house. At the coroner's request I had the body brought in to Battleford and, after the inquest, buried. The coroner's jury brought in the simple verdict of "found frozen to death."

Inspector Starnes and party returned from Onion Lake on the 17th instant. In his report to me upon his inspection of that outpost, Inspector Starnes says "I inspected the mens kits and found them complete and in good order. The arms and accoutrements are very clean and in good order.

The men's quarters are clean and comfortable. I found the saddles and harness in good order. I inspected the stables which I found very clean and well kept. The horses are fat, and in good condition. One had an old sore on the shoulder and I led it into Battleford leaving another in its place.

"A small stone house has been partitioned off in the stable where oats and other stores are kept under lock and key. It was in good order.

The hay is being cut out of the stack and is keeping very well; Sergt. Hall seems to think there will not be enough to last until the new grass comes out. In that case there is only one lot at Onion Lake of 8 or 10 tons. The owner would sell it for $8.00 per ton.

"The Indians on the reserve are very quiet, a good many of them are working for The Indian Department.

"The Indian Agent says we have not enough men at Onion Lake, and he does not seem to feel quite safe. I do not see the use of any more men, but I think it would be a measure of safety if there was a telegraph office at Onion Lake. There is one at Fort Pitt, but the distance is 12 miles, and a messenger would have to pass through the reserve to go to Fort Pitt, which might be dangerous work in case of trouble.

"The men are all in good health, and well satisfied.

"This Detachment does much credit to Sergt. Hall who is in charge."

I have the honor to be,

Sir,
Your Obedt. Servant
(sgd) John Cotton Supt. Commanding

The Commissioner
N.W.MP
Regina.

82. A TYPICAL MOUNTED POLICE MONTHLY REPORT, LETHBRIDGE, 1894

PAC, RCMP Records, Section A-1, vol. 91, no. 148.

Lethbridge,
28th February, 1894.

The Commissioner,
N.W.M. Police,
Regina.
Sir,

I have the honour to render my report for the past month.

On the 1st Inst. Edward Holmes was fined $10 for cruelty to the mule previously mentioned in last month's report, half of the fine going to the Corporation and half to the informer.

On the 6th Inst. Vet. Surg. Wroughton began an inspection of the horses of the Division, proceeding to Coutts by rail on the 7th. Inst. His report has been forwarded.

A man named Schoonover alias Hill was brought up on the 6th. charged with having stolen a shawl from the Hudson's Bay Company. He was awarded one months imprisonment H. L. under the summary Trials act. He began his term by persuading another prisoner to join him in refusing to work. They were therefore kept locked up and dieted accordingly, so that they very soon came to reason and asked to be allowed to go out & work.

The Supreme Court sat here on the 13th. Inst and the case of the two Sclavs charged with rescuing a prisoner from the Police as detailed in my report for January was first proceeded with. They were found guilty and sentenced to 4 months Imp. H.L.

The case of Purcel—charge murder, began on the 14th. Inst, and the Court sat until 10.30 p.m. in the hope of arriving at a speedy conclusion, but so much time was taken up in cross examining witnesses, that the Jury did not render their verdict until 2 a.m. on Sunday the 18th. Inst. their dictum being "manslaughter, with a very strong recommendation to mercy on account of the prisoner's age", viz; 64. The Judge gave effect to this by imposing a penalty of 3 years in the Penitentiary. I have rendered full special reports upon this trial so that it is unnecessary to repeat the same here.

On the 19th ex-Const. Potter was found guilty of arson. Mr. Wrigley, however, succeeded in persuading the Judge to suspend the sentence of 3 months imprisonment, which he proposed to inflict and to admit the prisoner to bail, to admit of some points of law being decided by the full Bench at Regina in June next.

On the 15th. Inst. the mines were closed here and all the men discharged, the Company giving notice that they would in future require fewer men and that wages would be reduced. They gave the men until the 22nd. Inst. to subscribe to their terms.

On the 16th. Inst. at Mr. Galt's request, I furnished 4 men for duty at Shafts No's 1 & 3 during the night, but when they went to Mr. Barclay to report for duty they were told they were not wanted.

On the 22nd Inst. Mr. Galt showed me a threatening anonymous letter which had been mailed to Mr. Simpson, the new Superintendent of Mines, who has certainly incurred the dislike of the men, who blame him for the reduction in wages.

The Company lay to their souls the flattering unction that they have managed this "Lock-out" very well, but "the proof of the pudding is the eating". For myself I question the expediency of throwing a large number of men out of employment without warning. A total number of 580 men connected with the mines have been paid off. (In my weekly report I said 480, but Mr. Galt made a mistake in giving me the figures. I also reported that 179 had left town; these were actually counted by Sergt. Hare but I found subsequently on comparing notes with Mr. Barclay, that some of the men so counted were labourers going out to work on the sections and were not discharged miners at all.) Of these 580 men, rather less than 150 have actually left the neighbourhood, and of the remaining 430, Mr. Galt informed the men yesterday that the Company require to re-engage only about 130. All of those must be good miners, whose names must be approved by himself, who must be married men having interests in the town, and who must sign a contract to work at a certain wage. The preferred wage is a reduction of 17% on the prices formerly paid and the men will not consider it. They say there is no living to be obtained from the money and a man may as well starve while walking about, as starve while working.

The situation to-day is this:—There are 300 men in town who have no hope of work; there are 130 men who dare not if they would, accept the Company's terms; one man has been already beaten in the mine and others have been threatened. The Company are full of "tall" talk and the men are full of irritation, complaining of the many highly paid officials in & the mismanagement of their little concern.

At my prolonged and earnest remonstrance, Mr. Galt published on Monday last, 26th., a notice offering free passes to Great Falls for batches of not less than 50 men who may wish to go there; this offer to hold good for one week, and further offering to carry married men and their families to the same destination free during the month of March. So far no advantage has been taken of these offers. After many years' example of indecision on the part of the Company's management many of the men even now think that this is simply a "bluff" on the part of the Company, and that if they wait long enough they will be re-engaged at the old prices. The question is what will happen when they eventually find that it is no bluff, but an act imperatively necessary for self preservation. It goes without saying that there is something wrong somewhere. Other mines can be run at a profit, why not these? The miners have a good deal to say about it. I mix freely with them and they will talk to me as to one of themselves, in fact the only reliable information that

Mr. Galt gets is from me. It is not always palatable, but I cannot help that.

I think myself that if during the past few months a given number of men had been gradually paid off, told that there was no more work for them, and offered free passes to Great Falls, a great deal of the present difficulty would have been overcome. The men say they have been treated meanly and resent it accordingly. It was at first given out that no free passes would be given at all, though happily that has been set aside. The Company are under the impression that starvation will drive the men to accept their terms, that would be all very well if they could offer them all work, but when there are 300 men to be provided for for whom no work can be obtained, the situation is likely to become strained, unless they can be persuaded to leave the neighbourhood. I have 3 Constables and 2 horses at No. 3 shaft, two of the men for night duty, and 3 constables similarly employed at No. 1 shaft, looking after the engine house etc. Const. Tryhaft understands Sclavish and moves about amongst those miners to hear what they have to say. They do not know that he understands them. I have also 4 constables on town duty in addition.

If any trouble should ensue, it will take from 20 to 25 men at a time to watch the Company's property, but at present I cannot express an opinion as to what is likely to happen.

Extension to the cell accommodation in the Guard room is urgently required here. We have now 7 prisoners undergoing sentence besides the convict Purcel, who will not, I believe, leave for the Penitentiary before the 3rd. prox. To accommodate these we have only 6 cells.

6 P.M. I have just returned from a tour in town. Mr. Galt has made out a list of 130 miners whom he proposes to re-engage at his own terms, which are to be subsequently discussed. This list will be published at 10 a.m. to-morrow and it remains to be seen what the other men say to the selection. Mr. Galt is more confident of a mutually satisfactory settlement than I am, but I hope he may be right.

I have etc., etc.,
(Sgd.) R. Burton Deane, Sup.

83. A CATTLE-RUSTLING CASE, ESTEVAN, 1899

PAC, RCMP Records, Section A-1, vol. 168, no. 241.

To,   N.W.M. Police,
Officer Commanding,   Estevan Detachment,
N.W.M. Police,   March 25th, 1899.
Regina.
Sir:—

I have the honour to make the following report re my trip to Culbertson, Mont., re the Anderson case.

On receiving your telegram on the 7th inst saying you had expressed $50.00 and ordering me to leave at once. As I had sufficient ready money on hand and know how precious time was, I did not wait for your letter but left by the 10.17 train that night. I arrived at Minot at 2.43 next morning and took the first train, the local, for Culbertson that afternoon. I arrived at Culbertson at 11.10 P.M. same date. At Williston, 56 miles this side, I met Sam McMurtry and he came on to Culbertson and gave me what information and facts he could. He told me that Frank Jones had been trying to repossess the cattle and that James Jones in order to prevent this had wired to Harry Lund the Government Stock Inspector to come and take the cattle in charge. Lund arrived a few days before I did, seized the cattle, placed them in charge of a rancher named John Murray, living on the Muddy River, some 25 miles north from Culbertson and then returned to Fort Benton.

McMurtry warned me not to confide in anybody in Culbertson not even the Deputy Sheriff, as they were all either owned by the gang or afraid of them. Harry Lund, he said, was allright, so I wrote him a letter telling him who I was and what my business was and asking him to come to Culbertson. In the meantime I represented myself as an Estevan Merchant saying that Anderson owed me money and that I was there to represent him and my own interests at the same time. I had to account for my presence in Culbertson somehow and I thought this was the best plan. I wanted to locate Frank Jones and Frank Webber before the gang began to suspect who I was, for I knew that they kept a couple of good horses saddled day and night ready to send men riding any distance to give the alarm if they once thought I was a police officer. I then saw James Jones and learned that he had purchased 11 head of cattle from Frank Jones and Frank Webber about the end of July last year, for which he had paid the equivalent $220.00 ($37 cash and two mares). Two head were branded "P" on right shoulder, the balance unbranded.

It naturally transpired that I was unable to identify Anderson's cattle, so I wired to Const McElroy to send him on at once. He arrived at 11.10 P.M. 10th inst. On the following day I hired a team and together with Jones and Anderson went to Murray's ranch where Anderson saw his cattle and recognized them easily. I returned to Culbertson following day. Harry Lund arrived about 4 P.M. and gave an order for cattle to be handed over to Anderson. In the meantime I had learned the whereabouts of both Frank Jones and Webber. The former was in hiding at the house of one Cristy about 50 miles north. The latter was down among the Bear Paw Mtns about 40 miles south of Big Landg. This was 350 miles from Culbertson. I held an interview with Harry Lund and the Deputy Sheriff and we decided on the following programme:—I spread a report that I had got track of the balance of cattle near Glasgow. Myself and Lund left on next train in search of them. After we got well away and the gang was lulled into security, the Deputy Sheriff would start after dark, travel all night and make a raid on Cristy's place. Lund was to go after Webber and I to get off at Glasgow and stay there until I heard from them. I reached

Glasgow on the morning of the 14th inst and got the Sheriff to write to the Fort Benton Sheriff asking him to send his Deputy after Webber also.

For a couple of days I made inquiries about Glasgow re the balance of Anderson's cattle and learned that a short time before the Stock Association had a case against the Williston butcher for having 13 unbranded skins in his possession. The butcher proved that he had purchased the cattle from the Bell Bros, near Williston. Ten of the cow skins answered the description of Anderson's missing 10. They say if a man has a maverick that he has rustled, the Bell Bros will always take it off his hands.

On the 16th a case of small-pox broke out in the hotel at Glasgow and I had the good fortune to be outside when the Doctor quarantined the building. On the 17th there was talk of quarantining the town so I took the first train back to Culbertson. On the 18th the Sheriff wired saying Webber was arrested at Fort Benton and asked if he would bring him on, so I wired back "Better hold until your Deputy returns. Expected tomorrow". I then wired you the fact that Webber had been arrested. I next got James Jones to make a sworn statement before a Notary Public in case he went back on us, or in case he got murdered before the trial comes off which is very probable. I then had a fear that the Sheriff might not hold prisoner very long if there was any money in sight. A chance excuse for letting him go, so I wired again asking him to bring prisoner on, or if he preferred I would take witnesses and go on to Glasgow. The Sheriff reached Culbertson with prisoner at 4 P.M. 20th, but by that time the only J. P. in the vicinity was quarantined on the Indian Reservation at Poplar. The Sheriff then decided to return to Glasgow and bring the prisoner before a Magistrate there and to also consult the State Attorney. We reached Glasgow at 4 A.M., 21st and found the State Attorney absent on a shooting expedition. The Sheriff then consulted the Ex or late State Attorney. This gentleman turned up and read books for about 3 hours and then told the Sheriff that the arrest of prisoner was illegal and that he had no right to hold him any longer. As the American laws seem to be made very much in favor of the prisoner and an Officer is liable for Civil Action unless he proves his case, the Sheriff got anxious and was going to let the prisoner go. The lawyer read an extract from a Treaty between Great Britain and the United States dated 1842, which said that before a refugee could be molested or arrested, or even a warrant issued, the foreign country had to make application to the President and have authority granted. This we had neglected to do. In the meantime Webber had decided to waive extradition papers, but the Country Attorney would not advise the Sheriff to furnish me with an escort to the Boundary Line, stating that since the prisoner was willing to return all they had to do was turn him loose and let me bring him back. Of course I knew that as soon as Webber got out of reach of the American Authorities he would walk away and leave me and if I used force he would come back at me for kidnapping. I finally got Geo. H. Dunnell late Stock Inspector to try and reason with them but he could not do anything. They would not even hold the prisoner until next day. Dunnell then explained about all the assistance we had rendered him in a like case when he came across the line and finally said that rather than see me stuck, if the Sheriff would make him Deputy for the occasion he would see me safely across the Line. The Sheriff agreed so we left on the flyer at 4 P.M. Dunnell paid the prisoner's and his own expenses and said he would take chances on the Board of Commissioners paying it back. In case they do fail to pay he will come back on this Government. Dunnell has a pass on the Great Northern so there will be only prisoner's fare from Glasgow to Minot ($12.75) and 2 fares from Minot to Portal ($6.00) and board about $2.50. Of course I paid my own expenses. The train was late reaching Minot so we had to wait for a freight next P.M. The engine broke down and we took 17 hours to reach here. I had practically been up 5 nights so I answered your telegram which came a few minutes after my arrival, and went to bed. The telegram I sent you from Williston was when I passed through that town en route home.

Webber does not deny taking the 11 head of cattle that were seized. James Jones will swear that he paid Webber part of the money and that he took part in the deal. John Anderson will swear that Webber is one of the two men that came to his place at Wood End just before the cattle disappeared, so there will be no difficulty in proving the case.

The Deputy Sheriff returned to Culbertson on the evening I started for home and reported his failure to capture Frank Jones. They were after him for 8 days. He fired on them twice. He is known as the best shot, best horseman and owner of the best horse in the State of Montana. They have been trying to catch him for 18 years but without success. I have the names of the Sheriffs near all his old haunts and shall write to them.

Anderson sold his 11 head of cattle for $253.00, the purchaser to pay duty 27 and one half % A.V.

Your letter of the 17th containing express order for $50.00 had not reached me before I left for home so I told Geo. H. Dunnell to have it forwarded here.

I received a letter from you this morning asking why I had not wired or written to you more frequently. I wrote a letter to you from Culbertson on the 12th and this was as soon as I had anything definite to report. The next day a man who is a friend of the gang asked me if I was acquainted in Regina and if I knew any of the Police Officers there. This same man left Regina 12 years ago to escape being arrested, and was tried for murdering and robbing the night operator of Culbertson last year. I was continually watched and I knew that if they once found out that I was connected with the law I would never catch either Jones or Webber. I fully realized that you would naturally want to know how I was doing etc., but I felt sure also, that you would want me above all things to succeed in my undertaking. I trusted to be able to make you realize how important it was for me to conceal my identity, but it is not nearly so easy now as I imagined when I was right in the thick of the gang. For the last four days I was at Culbertson they tried hard to get me where they could have a shot at me, or smash my head with a colt revolver. Of course they would not dare to attack me in cold blood before witnesses but the only stopping place in the town is run by the head of the gang and they can generally work a man into a room with two double beds. The whole town came down to the local train last Tuesday night with the expressed intention of having a shot at me but I suspected something like this and took the flyer, or fast train, which only stops every 200 miles or at Divisional points. In order to understand the predicament I was in you would have to visit the country and see the state of society. Nobody can be trusted. The Post-Master, Station Agent and Sheriff are all alike. At Glasgow the Deputy Sheriff and Sheriff take turns as Bartender in a saloon. If you want the Sheriff you can generally find him in the saloon shooting craps or playing poker for money. I wired to you at once when Webber was arrested and again when I started for home. Letters cannot be put on train in Montana the same as here. They must be put in the post-office and then unless you have sealing wax the Postmaster knows your business and I had no sealing wax handy.

Your letter of the 17th had not arrived when I started home so I asked Dunnell to forward it on here. I will send my accounts in on Form 93 as soon as I can get them ready. I think the total will come under $70.00.

Both James Jones and Harry Lund will come here as witnesses if subpoenaed. Lund will not be required. I fully expected Insp Macdonell down last night as he told me when here that if we get the men he would come and hold the preliminary.

> I have the honour to be, Sir,
> Your obedient servant,
> (signed) G. W. Byrne Sgt.

84. THE DIFFICULTIES OF ENFORCING PROHIBITION, PRINCE ALBERT, 1887

PAC, RCMP Section A-1, vol. 1.17, no. 63.

EXTRACT FROM REPORT BY SUPT. PERRY,
DATED 6TH DECEMBER, 1887.

On Friday night Const. Leslie was sent into town by my direct order to watch the Queen's Hotel and search if necessary.

There was a ball that night, he was in full uniform with side arms on, about 12 P.M. the Town Constable arrested him on the direction of Mr. Oram, later on a warrant was obtained, and Leslie brought up to the Guard room here. The case was adjourned from Saturday, on our request, but costs reserved against us.

On Monday it was tried and today judgment given. The result of which I have telegraphed you. A fine of $25.00 and costs was imposed.

The Department of Justice
Ottawa 20th April 1888

Sir,

I have the honour to acknowledge the receipt of your three communications of the 12th April instant, enclosing papers relative to the following prosecutions before Justices of the Peace at Prince Albert, N.W.T. viz;—

Queen vs Leslie a Provincial Policeman
   do vs Leslie and a Provincial Policeman
   do vs Sutherland, a Provincial Policeman

which papers were sent to me for the information of the Minister of Justice. These papers have received the Minister's careful consideration, and, in his opinion, call for the following observations;—

The two cases against Leslie and especially the vagrancy case, disclose on the part of the prosecutors and convicting Magistrate an evident intention to hinder and defeat the enforcement of the Statute in relation to intoxicating liquors and to throw discredit upon the Mounted Police in their honest efforts to administer the Law. For this purpose Col. Sproat, a Magistrate of mature years and long experience, has not hesitated to prostitute the forms of Law and he has, without evidence, and in spite of the clearest proof of innocence, convicted and imprisoned a Police Constable for doing simply his duty, and for doing what Colonel Sproat must have known to have been his duty. Inasmuch, however, as, upon appeal, this conviction was reversed, by Mr. Justice McGuire, no further action appears necessary, except that all the papers should be transmitted to the Lieutenant Governor of the North West Territories, in order that he may consider the advisability, in view of the facts, of relieving Colonel Sproat from the performance of further magisterial duties.

The Minister of Justice thinks that His Honour's serious consideration should be given to this question, notwithstanding the statement made, by Mr. Justice McGuire when he was giving judgments.

The conduct of Mr. W. M. Maclise, the Crown Prosecuter, as detailed in the evidence, has not escaped the attention of the Minister of Justice. Papers returned.

I have the honour to be
Sir
Your obedient servant
sgd Robt Sedgewick
D.M.J.

85. A MOUNTED POLICE VIEW ON THE ENFORCEMENT OF PUBLIC MORALITY, LETHBRIDGE, 1894

PAC, RCMP Records, Section A-1, vol. 91, no. 148. Lethbridge Monthly Report for July 1894.

Within the last few days two complaints have been made to me of girls in town getting into trouble. In one case, that of a french miner named Brucher who was in great distress about his 2nd daughter who was enamoured of an Italian (married man) miner. I believe and hope the difficulty is settled the man went east by train last night, and the girl assures me that there is nothing wrong with her. The other case is hopeless and a baby will appear on the scene ere long. I told her mother the other day that, had she appealed to me when the circumstances first came to her knowledge some months ago, I might have been able to do something but now I cannot do anything. The Presbyterian and Methodist ministers have been of late making a great deal of talk about prostitutes being allowed in town. If they would turn their attention to the juvenile depravity and promiscuous fornication that is going on under their own eyes and in their own congregations, they would be kept so busy that they would have no time to think of the professional ladies, who at all events are orderly, clean, and on the whole not bad looking. The Methodist congregation is exercised because its pastor is wicked enough to play cricket, which he does well. Not long ago the two ministers above mentioned formed themselves into a delegation and interviewed the Town Council in public sessions convened and talked about the "soiled doves" &c. The whole town was there to see and hear. The "doves" had a lawyer present to watch the case for them and I was told that the whole business was great fun. The Reverend gentlemen got no satisfaction from the Council and retired covered with ridicule. The Church of England parson had declined to join in the agitation at all. He said he would go with the other ministers to try and reform the ladies of easy virtue, but he did not believe in the step the ministers were about to take, they did not accept his invitation.

86. MURDER, EDMONTON, 1892

PAC, RCMP Records, Section A-1, vol. 47, no. 63.

MURDER

$200. Reward, for information that will lead to the arrest of Ole Mickleson, Late of Crookston, Minnesota. About 5 feet 6 inches high, slim built, 25 years old, shaven face, except small dark mustache, nose slightly hooked, a Swede. When last seen wore long dark overcoat, rubbers or overshoes, either low black felt hat or imitation fur cap with peak.

Arrived in Edmonton on train of Thursday, November 10th. Last seen near South Edmonton Station between nine and ten o'clock on Friday, November 11th, 1892.

(Sgd) A. H. Griesbach,
Supt. Com. G. Division, NWMP

13th December 1892

Memorandum to:—
Superintendent Griesbach,
Fort Saskatchewan.

After carefully reading the correspondence in connection with the recent murder at Edmonton I can only come to the conclusion that there was a great want of judgement and energy displayed by Inspector Piercy in the pursuit; this opinion is based on the following facts:—

At 9.45 A.M. on November 11th, it was reported to Inspector Piercy at North Edmonton that a man had been murdered at S. Edmonton, and that Officer crossed the river with the Coroner, but neglected before starting to order a party over to take up pursuit. Nor did he at once wire the Conductor of the train, or the Mounted Police along R.R although he was aware that a train had started South that A.M. and there was nothing to show that the murder had not been committed before departure of train; again, Inspector Piercy neglected to wire his C.O. until about six hours after he himself was apprised of the murder. On the victim being washed and identified at 4.00 P.M., and the conclusion come to that his murderer was the Swede who left hotel with him and it being clearly established that he had not escaped on train, and that supposed murderer was a stranger just arrived, Insp. Piercy neglected to send a party down the trail to cut off his escape in that direction. Insp. Piercy having, including the detachments at St. Albert, North Edmonton and South Edmonton, at least ten men who could have been sent out South in various directions on this duty on the evening of the 11th, but nothing was done until next day.

If the Rabbit Hill party, under Serg't Dunning, had gone out promptly they could have got sufficient information from Telford to enable them to capture the murderer on the first night, or, at any rate to get ahead of him and cut off his retreat south. One Constable was not even sent out to warn the settlements South.

It is also apparent that Insp. Piercy in wiring to his Commanding Officer at 4.45 P.M. even then neglected to give all the information in his possession re nationality &c. nor did he mention the points to which he had wired, thus causing considerable delay in notifying Red-Deer, Calgary, and Regina (see telegrams 2 & 4) places Insp. Piercy should have notified at once, and wired his C.O. that he had done so.

The delay, until the afternoon of the 12th, in wiring Red Deer is particularly reprehensible. I consider that there is no excuse for Insp. Piercy for the above instances of neglect of duty, as that Officer has had large experience in Police duties, and I shall report the matter at once to the Department for their decision.

With regard to Sergeant Dunning's connection with the case, you will make a charge against that Non-Com-Officer, and try him for neglect of duty in not following the supposed murderer to Peace Hills, as his horses could have gone on just as well as return to Edmonton.

You will call ex-Constable Telford as a witness as Inspector Piercy's report—marked C—on the information given by that ex-Constable to Sergeant Dunning, does not agree with that Non-Com's statement.

You will also report to me at once all the circumstances connected with the offering of a reward as I am informed the Lieutenant Governor never authorized it.

Commissioner.

Ottawa, 7th June, 1893.

Memo on a letter from His Honour the Lieutenant Governor of the North West Territories, dated 18th May, 1893, in reply to a Despatch transmitting copy of a Report of a Committee of the Honourable the Privy Council, approved by His Excellency the Governor General in Council, on the 27th February, 1893, on the subject of the offering of a reward in November, 1892, for the arrest of the murderer of one Skaalent near Edmonton, N.W.T.

His Honour reiterates the charges which he preferred against Supt. Griesbach, as follows:

1. Taking upon himself to offer a public reward for the arrest of an ordinary murderer, without first communicating with the North West Executive, and submitting his reasons for advising the adoption of such a step.

The usurpation of one of the gravest functions of Government (that of the Administration of Justice) by a public official, and more particularly by one of the Commanding Officers of the Police Force, showing palpable evidence of an absolute lack of judgment.

2. By offering the reward in question, taking the very dangerous course of inciting a number of settlers to turn out with arms in pursuit of the murderer, to the imminent danger of the life of any isolated traveller, whose appearance might have borne some traits of resemblance to the murderer, as described in the notice.

3. Causing a very serious difficulty between a majority of the Legislature and the Lieutenant Governor last session, when an attempt was made to compel the latter to assent to an item placed in the Estimates for the payment of a liability incurred without Executive sanction or authority.

With regard to the first charge, the undersigned respectfully repeats his previously expressed opinion that Supt. Griesbach was not responsible for the adding of the money reward to the poster.

The instructions which that Officer telegraphed from Fort Saskatchewan to his subordinate, Inspector Piercy, at Edmonton, were as follows:—

"Get hand bills printed, if possible some in German, send down immediately full particulars, nationality, has he any friends this way. All information you can give. Have you notified any other Posts, if so, which. Who is man murdered. Wire reply."

The reward of $200.00 was inserted by Insp. Piercy with the concurrence, and on the authority, of the two Members representing the Edmonton District in the North West Legislature, who assured him that, if necessary, they would pay $100.00 each from their local grants.

Insp. Piercy when telegraphing Supt. Griesbach at Noon on the 12th November, enlarging his previous description of the murderer, added to the message, "North West has offered a reward of two hundred dollars for his arrest." He did not, however, state that the reward had been included in the descriptive poster issued over the name of Supt. Griesbach.

His Honour the Lieutenant Governor is of opinion that on Supt. Griesbach becoming aware of the reward having been added to the poster, his proper course would have been to disown at once the unauthorized action of his subordinate Officer, and, in support of his contention that Supt. Griesbach was responsible for the offering of the reward, he quotes from a telegram dated 25th November, 1892, and a letter dated 3rd December, 1892, expressions of that Officer to the effect that he considered the offering of the reward both expedient and necessary.

As a matter of fact the posters were printed and distributed on the morning of the 12th November, but Supt. Griesbach did not receive Insp. Piercy's telegram, nor a copy of the poster, until the evening of that day. As the case then presented itself it is questionable whether he would have been justified in immediately despatching men and telegrams all over the country discrediting or recalling the poster. In the opinion of the undersigned, the acknowledgment some time afterwards that he considered the reward both expedient and necessary, should not be accepted as evidence that he endorsed the manner in which it was actually offered.

With regard to the second charge of His Honour that the offering of the reward incited a number of settlers to turn out with arms in pursuit of the murderer, to the imminent danger of the life of any isolated traveller, whose appearance might have borne some traits of resemblance to the murderer, as described in the notice, the undersigned begs to remark that the reward of $200.00 was offered for *information that would lead to the arrest of* "Ole Mickleson", whose description was quoted in the poster; that fire arms were not resorted to by the pursuers until after the murderer had identified himself by offering money to be allowed to escape, and had fired on his pursuers; and that the fatal shot was fired only when "Ole Mickleson" was approaching a house in which there were defenceless women, and from which it might have been difficult to dislodge him without further loss of blood.

The circumstances connected with the shooting of the murderer were the subject of a Coroner's inquest which rendered an "acquittal" verdict. Proceedings were then instituted against the same person, on a charge of manslaughter when he was again acquitted.

With respect to the third complaint of His Honour, the undersigned assumes that it would not be proper for him to comment upon differences between the Lieutenant Governor and a majority of his Legislature.

Inspector Piercy was censured by the Hon. the Minister for lack of judgment and energy in connection with this case. Whether the censure preyed upon his mind or not, it is impossible to say, but the fact remains that he took his own life a few months afterwards.

Respectfully submitted.

(Sgnd) Fred White

Comptroller.

87. THE EDMONTON LAND OFFICE DISTURBANCES, 1892

PAC, RCMP Records, Section A-1, vol. 68, no. 492.

Received at 6.45 P.M.

Edmonton, 18th June, 1892.

To Supt. Griesbach,

Send up men at once to assist Piercy, mob collected and preventing me removing Office furniture. Have taken off nuts off wheels &c.

(sgd.) Thos. Anderson

Received at Ft. Saskatchewan 7.10 P.M.

Edmonton, June 18th, 1892.

To Supt. Griesbach,

Not necessary to send any men here, everything all right.

(sgd.) Wm Piercy.

Fort Saskatchewan,

Re disturbance at Edmonton.

Sir,

I have the honour to append hereto copies of two telegrams received by me on evening of 18th inst, one from the Edmonton Land Agent and one from Insp. Piercy, both received at the same time, also a report from Insp. Piercy received by me on evening of 19th.

I took no action on the telegrams, they not calling for any, but on receipt of the report, on 19th, I at once made arrangements to go to Edmonton with all available men.

The party left at 6 A.M. of 20th, I going on in advance.

On arriving at Edmonton, I decided to encamp my men at "Rat Creek", about a mile out of the Town, in order not to increase the excitement or bring them into collision with the mob.

Passing through the Town I saw the Mayor who also saw me but he did not ask me for assistance of any sort.

The position of affairs then was that the Mayor, Mr. M. McAuley, had telegraphed to different Ministers and Members of Parliament on the subject of the removal of the Land Office to the South side of the River, and were waiting replies thereto, the Land Office being in charge of the Police.

I telegraphed you and then waited the result of the telegrams sent by the citizens and also instructions from you.

About 11.30 A.M., I was walking up the street when I saw a notice written in chalk on a blackboard at the Town Clerk's Office, signed by one Colin Strang, a Town Councillor, ordering the "Home Guard" to parade at 1 P.M. armed. This they did to the number of 80 to 100 men and Ball Cartridge was served out.

Having now myself seen the state of affairs and not having been required by the Mayor or Council to intervene, I kept my men aloof.

At or about 6.30 P.M. the Mayor, Mr. McAuley, and Councillor Strang waited upon me (this being their first interview with me since the commencement of the disturbance) and had with them several telegrams from Cabinet Ministers, and others, the purport of these telegrams being that it was only the intention of the Government to open a branch office on the South side of the River and this they intended to do, but that the permanent Office would be built on the North side, and, further, that the Police would be instructed, and that Mr. Gordon, Inspector of Land Agencies, would be up.

They then asked me what steps I proposed to take in the matter, both saying that they had no wish to oppose the Government. My answer was that I had nothing to say to them under present circumstances, but that I would take no action until I had received instructions and conferred with Mr. Gordon.

The interview then ended.

On the morning of the 21st, I received a cipher telegram from Regina, instructing me to avoid Police interference if possible but, if necessary, to afford protection during removal of books and to guard the building, and also to see Mr. Gordon and take such steps as circumstances might demand.

On the morning of the 22nd, seeing that Mr. Gordon could not arrive till the night of the 23rd, I sent the greater part of my men back to Fort Saskatchewan, and went down myself to attend to my duties there.

Shortly after I left Edmonton, telegrams were received from the Hon. Mr. Dewdney by Mayor McAuley and Mr. Anderson, Land Agent, the substance of which was that the office should get to work, as great inconvenience was being caused to the incoming emigrants and to the business of the office generally.

These telegrams were shown to Insp. Piercy who, in my absence, carried out the wishes of the Minister with the knowledge of Mayor McAuley and Mr. Anderson, Land Agent.

A Police team went down, with Insp. Piercy in charge, and in presence of the Land Agent, Mr. McAuley and some of the Councillors, selected the books and papers necessary for the opening of a branch office and conveyed them to the South side.

As the team was leaving, the bells again rang out the alarm and a mob rapidly assembled, but too late to interfere. The team drove away to the Upper Ferry, which Insp. Piercy had secured and guarded, and crossed without incident. The books were safely put away on South side and placed under guard and still continue so.

Business was commenced next morning on both sides of the River.

The mob, on finding that the books had been taken away, made loud threats that they would bring them back or destroy them, but up to the time of writing no such attempt had been made.

On Thursday the 23rd, I proceeded again to Edmonton to meet Mr. Gordon who however did not arrive.

INCIDENTS

A system of alarm bells was organized to signal the mob to gather at the Land Office, and a watch was kept on the office day and night.

On one occasion, seeing that the Land Office books were likely to suffer damage from rain, they being packed in waggons and covered with sheets only, I directed Insp. Piercy to have them placed in the Office under cover. So soon as the small guard of Police on duty began the necessary work, the alarm bells commenced to ring and a mob of about 150 collected in a few minutes, they being under the impression we were going to remove the books, but on finding out the facts of the case, they dispersed looking foolish.

On the evening of the 18th, when the first attempt was made to remove the books, Mayor McAuley who addressed the gathering then assembled, is said to have used the following words:—"We have been too long dead, we don't want to be called rebels but it has come to this that we must fight for our rights and we *will* fight for them too."

Previous to the speech in which the words above are said to have been used, the crowd gathered was of a more or less orderly nature, but after the speech by the Mayor, it became a howling mob ready for anything.

Pitchforks were served out to be used in preventing teams from getting over the Ferry, and a pair of strong nippers specially made for cutting the wire rope should the teams get on board the scow, were said to be in readiness.

To account for the arms in possession of the mob, I have to report as follows:—30 stand were issued by order of the Minister of Militia for temporary use of the Edmonton Rifle Association receipt for which I hold from Mr. Colin Strang.

Besides these there are a number of Snider Rifles in the hands of different people which were not called in by the Militia authorities at the close of the Rebellion, and which were consequently never placed under my charge.

I consider the calling to arms of citizens in the excited state in which they were and with saloons in the close vicinity, a most dangerous and unwarrantable proceeding calculated to do untold harm, and to have a most pernicious effect on the mixed population of the District, comprising as it does Indians, Half-breeds and white men of nearly all Nationalities, and calculated to bring authority into contempt and to encourage the idea that mob law can prevail and be enforced with arms.

The concluding paragraph in the account published in the "Edmonton Bulletin" of 20th inst, shews clearly that the idea was to oppose armed force against the Police in the lawful execution of their duty, and this, backed by three Justices of the Peace, one of them being the Mayor of the Town.

And further, I have to recommend that the parties who have so grossly broken the law be prosecuted.

In connection with the matter I may say that two Government Officials paraded under arms, viz:—A. D. Osborne, Edmonton Post-Master, and John Looby, Inspector of Weights and Measures.

These men should, in my opinion, be immediately suspended pending investigation.

Also the Commissions, as Justices of the Peace, of those who were responsible for the assembling of armed citizens should be forthwith cancelled and each prosecuted.

Of course I take it for granted that Mr. Colin Strang, under whose command they paraded, and who signed the notice calling to arms, and the men who paraded, will also be prosecuted, and, in fact all persons concerned in the riot against whom evidence can be collected.

Since this affair occurred it has come to my knowledge that unless the Government vindicate their authority and support the Police, further trouble may arise. The Indians and Half-breeds at the present moment believe that the Government, as represented by the Police Force, has been "stood off", as they term it, by the white men, meaning the citizens of Edmonton. Consequently, I, as the Officer Commanding the District for a number of years past and being well acquainted with the Indian and Half-breed character, can readily understand their ideas of the affair, and the most of it will be made by disaffected persons.

In conclusion, I have the honour to recommend that I be authorized to call in all Militia Arms now in the possession of the citizens and others at once, and to use all lawful means to enforce the return of the same.

Trusting that decisive action will be taken in the matter

I have the honour to be,

Sir,

Your obedient servant,

(sgd.) A. H. Griesbach, Supt.

Commanding Ft. Saskatchewan District.

SPECIAL PROBLEMS: NATIVE PEOPLES, IMMIGRANTS, AND LABOUR

88. KEEPING AN EYE ON THE INDIANS, BATTLEFORD, 1888

PAC, RCMP Records, Section A-1, vol. 17, no. 192.

N.W.M.P.
Battleford
August 21st, 1888

Sir:

I have the honor to submit herewith my weekly report.

On the evening of the 17th inst. word was brought to me from the Indian office that a number of runners had been seen on Poundmaker's and Little Pine's Reserve. The story appearing to be well founded—being supported by an official report from Farm Instructor Gopsill. I immediately had a party paraded consisting of 25 non. com. officers and men and proceeded to the reserve taking with me Ass't Surgeon Aylen, Guides Laronde, Nash, Indian Scout John Thomas, another Indian sent in by Mr. Gopsill, who professed great anxiety to have these men captured. The weather being very hot, and it being advisable not to reach the reserve before dark, I camped during the heat of the day and reached Mr. Gopsill's house about 10 P.M. The Indian "Johnny", mentioned above as having been employed by Mr. Gopsill, searched the reserve but found no strangers in any of the tents. However he stated that he could guide me to where a party were camped; and about midnight I started on the trail of this party. After travelling about 12 miles day began to break, another Indian "Johnny" pointed out the plain trail of three ponies, the remains of several camp fires etc. The trail was followed for some distance further, but the country becoming so bad for travel, and the evident impossibility of overtaking these men, on account of the long start they had had, combined to decide me in returning to Battleford. This I did on the evening of the 20th.

The Indian Johnny's story, whatever it may be worth, is to the effect that a party, numbering some 20 odd men, all well armed, have been camped near the reserve for some days. They are said to be some "Crows", some "Gros Ventres" and the balance "Crees" who left this District at the time of the Rebellion. They are said to carry messages to certain Indians supposed to be looked up to by their fellows and also letters to certain of the Halfbreeds and the Bresaylor Settlement, among them being Charles Bremner, who is away from here at the present time. These alleged letters are said to have been written at the dictation of Gabriel Dumont by an American Officer (?) through the American Govt. interpreter at Fort Assiniboine, Louis Sayer, who is a halfbreed from this neighborhood and who decamped through fear of the consequences of his actions in the trouble of 1885. This is a very circumstantial story but it is only supported by the word of one other Indian—a squaw—and the trail of the three ponies in the bad lands. The Indian Johnny says that the remainder of the party have gone to Duck Lake, Onion Lake and other places—I have notified Sergt. Hall to keep a sharp lookout for strange Indians and ascertain fully the nature of the business of any such who may appear in his neighborhood. I may say that Mr. Gopsill expresses himself as being fully satisfied of the truth of the Indian Johnny's story, and Mr. Gopsill has proved himself to be a man not usually affected by the ordinary rumours of Indian movements. Father Cochiu priest on the reserve also stated that he had heard from the Indians of the presence of strange Indians in the neighborhood of the reserve. I will have all parties supposed or known to be disaffected in this district carefully watched, and will furnish you at once with any information I may gain.

Inspector Chalmers with one Constable from Regina arrived here on the morning of the 19th with the transport that had taken Inspector Starnes to Swift Current.

The delivery of hay on this year's contract commenced on the 20th inst. and if the present fine weather continues, the contract will be completed at an early date.

I am in receipt of your telegraphic instructions to report at Saskatoon on the 31st with all available men, and am making the necessary preparations to do so.

Sergt. Mahoney has just returned from Onion Lake where I sent him to put the detachment through a course of musketry instruction and target practice.

The returns show a good record and high average.

> I have the honour to be
> Sir
> Your Obedient Servant
> (Sgd.) Joseph Howe, Insp. C

89. MOUNTED POLICE VIEWS ON INDIAN ADMINISTRATION, 1889

PAC, RCMP Records, Section A-1, vol. 26, no. 28.

> North-West Mounted Police
> Head Quarters
> Regina, Jany. 3rd, 1889

Sir:

I have the honor to submit the following suggestions, for your consideration, in connection with the management of the Piegans, Bloods & Blackfeet.

Having been in your Department for some years, and having had considerable success in assisting Indians to help themselves, I think you will receive these suggestions as they are intended.

These Indians have never had a fair chance with cattle, the original Piegan herd having been badly managed, and I would suggest that a small number of cattle be distributed among those Indians who express a desire to have them; the increase to belong to the individual Indians as soon as they have returned to the Department the original number received by each, the cattle returned to be issued on the same terms to other Indians.

This system was introduced with the *Cattle Companies* approval among the Sioux during my agency and was very successful.

The S.W. Indians are in possession of a large number of good pony mares, and I would strongly urge upon you the advisability of encouraging them to castrate all their calfs at a year old, and all stallions not passed by the agent as being calculated to improve stock, as you are about to institute a stock book the present time is most opportune for a new departure. I would then recommend the purchase by the Indian Department of a number of first class Stallions, Small and chunky, the old style of Lower Canadian horse preferred. These ponies can still be bought in parts of Quebec. The mares from this stock, out of Indian mares would be fit to mate with larger horses and even the first cross would be very saleable.

To induce Indians not to ride their young colts handsome prizes should be offered for the best colts of all ages, and the same for the best cattle. All the stock business should be placed under the immediate control of the individual agents, who should be compelled to take an interest in the matter, and should know all the cattle and horses in the agencies.

There is on all your S.W. Reserves plenty of hay, and I would suggest that under the agents' supervision mowers and rakes be supplied, and that the Indians be encouraged to put up hay for sale. The encouragement has been given and works well with your Indians north of Regina, and with the Hon. Ministers consent I shall be extremely pleased to purchase a certain quantity of hay for cash at all Police posts where Indians can deliver. I have generally found that Indians will work when properly encouraged and when they can see the pecuniary advantage.

Sir
I have the honor to be your Obedient Servant
(sgd.) L. W. Herchmer
Commissioner

The Commissioner of Indian Affairs
Regina.

90. STAMPING OUT THE SUN DANCE, 1891

Extract from report from Supt. S. B. Steele, Commanding the Mounted Police at Fort Macleod, for the month of June, 1891.

N.W.M. Police,
District Office,
Fort Macleod, 23rd June, 1891.

The Commissioner,
N.W.M. Police,
Regina.
Sir,

I have the honour to inform you that a rumour having been reported to me that Chief Red Crow had visited the ration house at the Upper Reserve of the Blood Agency and seized a quantity of tongues without the Agent's permission. I have caused careful enquiry to be made and am informed that the tongues in question were issued by Mr. Packlington's orders in addition to the regular ration and that no friction has occurred between the Indians and their Agent.

I regret very much that permission has been granted to the Bloods and Piegans to hold a Sun Dance. It is a relic of barbarism that should be stamped out at once and forever. I am convinced that the present generation of Indians have outgrown the early faiths and have absorbed sufficient civilization and Christianity to render the ceremonies accompanying the Sun Dance a burlesque. It still, however, has power to excite the Indians and takes them away from their legitimate occupation of farming and inflames the young bucks with a desire for glory that can no longer be gratified, but finds vent in cattle killing and horse stealing. Rumours are current on the Reserve about the Sioux going to war and a contemplated visit from the Gros Ventres. I place little faith in these reports but will keep a close watch and report. There is undoubtedly a slight tendency to uneasiness in the camp and I am sure a series of Sun Dances will not tend to allay it.

I have the honour to be,
Sir,
Your obedient servant,
(Sgd.) S. B. Steele,
Supt. Commdg Dist.

91. WELFARE WORK WITH INDIANS AND MIXED-BLOODS, 1889

PAC, RCMP Records, Section A-1, vol. 33, no. 318.

N.W.M.P.
Battleford
March 19th, 1889

Sir:

I have the honour to submit herewith my report for the week ending this day.

From personal observation I am able to say that the Indians in this district are in a more contented condition than I ever saw them before.

There appears to be absolutely no disaffection among them, and, what is somewhat singular at this time of the year, no rumors even of such being the case.

I visited Moosomin's reserve on the Saskatchewan on the 16th instant, and found everything on that reserve in excellent order.

Mr. Applegarth the instructor, has instituted a novel system for dealing with the issue of the flour ground from the grain grown by the Indians.

Instead of the flour being placed in the Departmental storehouse, he placed in the hands of each Indian the flour ground from the grain he had grown.

Thus the men who worked hard all season and had good crops are reaping all the benefit derivable from their work; while those who did no work but simply amused themselves hunting and fishing all summer are now without flour of their own, and are compelled to obtain supplies from their neighbors. Mr. Applegarth who has exercised a careful supervision over this matter, tells me his system is working admirably.

The Indians who now have abundance of flour seem to realise to the fullest extent what it cost them to obtain their flour, and dole out small portions to their needy comrades without waste, and in many cases demanding an equivalent for it. All seem fully imbued with the idea of working hard during the coming season.

I attach herewith a return of all halfbreeds in this district carefully compiled by Guide H. H. Nash.

I have had to issue a further supply of rations to Mrs. Villebrun of Bresaylor, whom you will see from the return is a widow with a large family of small children of which she is the only support.

I have the honour to be
Sir
Your obt. Servant
Signed, Joseph Howe
Insp. Comdg.

North West Mounted Police
Battleford
March 25th 1889

Sir:

I have the honour to submit herewith my report for the week ending this day.

Nothing unusual has been noted in the actions of the Indians in this district. They are all remaining quietly on their different reserves, and busy with preparations for the spring work.

I have now issued orders on the different stores in town for the payment of 80 cords of wood.

This wood I have distributed in contracts of five cords each to Half-breeds whom I consider to be in such condition as to require help from the Government.

I have taken the greatest care to see that this help given by the Government has not been abused.

I have had applications for this work enough to put in over 500 cords of wood, but except in really necessitous cases I have refused to take advantage of the power vested in me.

I attach herewith a list of persons to whom rations has been issued in consequence of their destitute condition. I need hardly say that I have been most particular in making this issue. No help has been given in any case until I satisfied myself perfectly of the necessity of the applicants, and their inability to obtain food from other sources.

The weather proving so mild I have been holding parades, both foot and mounted, for drill nearly every day.

I have the honour to be
Sir
Your obedient servant
Sgd. Joseph Howe
Inspector Commanding

The Commissioner
N.W.M. Police
Regina

Rations are issued to

Lemire Franceis	9 rations	
Smith Alfred	5 rations	
Lemire J.	4 rations	

(All at work regularly around Post.)

Mrs. Sauve	4 rations	Husband ill
Mrs. Villebrun	7 rations	Husband dead
Mrs. Williams	2 rations	Husband deserted her
Mrs. Deslarmes	5 rations	Husband dead
W. Fisher	1 ration	Sick
P. Decham	3 rations	old & infirm, wife and child.

92. PROTECTING THE IMMIGRANT: GERMAN SETTLERS AT QU'APPELLE, 1894

PAC, RCMP Records, Section A-1, vol. 97, no. 587.

Starr's Point,
Qu'Appelle Station,
Assa: N.W.T., July 17th, 1894

The Hon: T. M. Daly,
Minister of the Interior,
Ottawa.
My dear Sir,

The past year or two this part of the Territories, have had quite a number of German Emigrants settled here, who have turned out to be the very worst and lowest class of people under the sun, and who are considered quite a nuisance, and ought to be banished from the country otherwise they will be the means of driving every respectable settler out of the place. They steal and plunder whatever they can lay their hands on, and now, they go about, under cover of the night, and cut and steal and carry away Hay wherever they can get it and are not at all particular to whom it belongs, and every settler is complaining about them. I have had upwards of twenty tons of hay cut and taken away by them, even close to my crop, and not more than one mile from my residence, all done during the night. My object in writing is to draw your attention to the facts, and to ascertain whether anything can be done to put a stop to such doings, or must the settlers submit to it. Possibly if the Police had authority to be on the look out and watch their movements by night and by day, and when caught to have them imprisoned, and made to pay damages, it may have the effect of stopping their game both as with regard to stealing wood as well as Hay. Something must be done, and that very soon.

Kindly favour me with a reply immediately.

Believe me,
Yours faithfully,
'Sd.' D. Henry Starr.

N.W.M. Police
Qu'Appelle, Aug. 14th 1894.

The Officer Commanding
B. Division
Regina.
Sir,—

I have the honor to report as follows, re the enclosed communication. I proceeded to Mr. D. Henry Starr's residence to-day and, in reply to my questions he informed me, that he had no reasons to suspect the German settlers of being "the very worst and lowest class of people under the sun" only from what he has heard about them, having had no dealings with them himself. He suspects them of taking his hay from what he has heard about them and states, that he was informed, that a German was offering a load of hay for sale in Qu'Appell Station which looked like what his hay would be when cut. In regards to his statement "they steal and plunder whatever they can lay their hands on," he is unable to prove it as he admits he never had anything stolen except hay which might just as likely be taken by any other class of settlers, as the hay crop being a failure this year, no one was particular where they obtained it. I visited a number of settlers in the vicinity, none of whom had any complaints regarding the conduct of those Germans beyond the fact that they suspected them of having taken hay where they had no right to it; but admitted that any other settler would do the same this year. The nearest German settler is about seven miles West of Mr. Starrs residence.

I might state, from my own experience with those Germans I am not prepared to say they are any worse than other class of settlers. A few cases have been brought against some of them for wood stealing and they have been punished.

I have the honor to be,

Sir,

Your obedient servant

D. Holmes, Corpl.

93. PROTECTING THE IMMIGRANT: CHINESE AT CALGARY, 1892

PAC, RCMP Records, Section A-1, vol. 68, no. 521 and vol. 69, no. 615.

N.W.M. Police,

Calgary, 1st, July, 1892.

Sir,

I have the honour to submit the following special report;—

Yesterday the Mayor Mr. Lucas informed me that a Chinaman at the Laundry on Stephen Ave., next to Hallidays confectionary shop, had been found to have the small pox. Steps were at once taken by the town authorities to isolate the case. All the Chinamen living in the house were sent to an empty shack across Nose Creek and I was asked to furnish a guard to see that they did not leave. The guard tent is pitched some distance from the shack and a sentry posted on a rise of ground in view of it.

Last night the laundry and all its contents was burnt by the town authorities, they having determined to take stringent measures to prevent a spread of the disease.

So far there is only the one case and this one came from the coast a few days ago. I will see Mr. Lucas tomorrow about utilizing one of the islands in the Bow River should any more cases disclose themselves, as the settlers in the vicinity of the present quarantine object to it. Should there be any vaccine at

Regina I would request to have some sent here for the purpose of vaccinating the members of the Division as a precaution in the event of a spread of the contagion.

I have the honour to be, etc. etc.

The Commissioner,   (Sgd.) A. Ross Cuthbert, Insp.
N.W.M.P.
Regina.

N.W.M. Police,
Calgary 3rd August 1892.

The Commissioner,
Regina.

Sir,

I have the honour to report the following circumstances:—

Yesterday evening the health Officer released the Chinamen who had been in quarantine. At about 11 p.m. much yelling etc. could be heard in town. In view of the Municipality having its own Police Officers I took no steps at that time beyond holding some men in readiness in case of need. Sometime later the disturbance seemingly increasing I sent Insp. T. Snyder to notify the Mayor that should our services be required a request for such was to be sent, the Mayor was absent from town and there seemed to be no one in authority. The streets were in possession of a drunken mob and the Chinese habitations being sacked at about the same time (about midnight) a chinaman came to me asking for protection and another was brought by a citizen. They were being ill used, some had run out in the Country and 6 had been sheltered by Mr. Dean the Methodist clergyman in the parsonage. Realizing that mob law could not be allowed to prevail in the N.W.T. even in a Municipality and that serious trouble might ensue I turned out some men and went up town with the intention of acting under the statutes if necessary. The Town authorities seemed completely demoralized and in the absence of the Mayor none of them (including the Actg Mayor) knew what to do. There was a town constable visible but he was quite powerless to check the lawlessness.

I was requested by several of the respectable citizens to take action and also by Mr. Cushing representing the Police committee of the town council. As the constituents of the mob were getting drunker and the lawlessness likely to increase I think I would have been justified in putting a stop to it in any case, even if not requested to do so.

Three arrests were made and the streets cleared. The effect was so instantaneous that some of the crowd who were mounted left their horses behind. 10 chinamen sought shelter in Barracks going away again this morning.

We kept streets clear till 4 a.m., but everything was quiet after our first appearance.

The origin of the disturbance which resulted in considerable damage to a few houses in town seems to have been a cricket match between two local clubs followed by a dinner at which some of the participants got drunk subsequently instigating the demonstration which possibly got beyond their control after starting.

The intention of the more sober minded is to hire a car and ship the chinamen quietly. The peaceful and respectable citizens would not object to that, but last night's demonstration was something very different and might have led to serious trouble if not checked.

The Mayor will return this evening when probably he will assure the chinamen protection.

I am alive to the advisability of our not acting in town unless requested to do so by the town authorities when the necessity is obvious, but it is difficult to determine in a case of this kind where a harmless demonstration will end and bodily injury commence.

I have the honour etc. etc.

(Sgd.) A. Ross Cuthbert, Insp.

N.W.M. Police,
Calgary, 4th August, 1892.

To the Commissioner,
Regina.
Sir,

Re. the Chinamen: Yesterday evening threats having been made to the Chinamen who left Barracks during the day, they commenced to gather at Barracks at dusk for protection. I waited on the Mayor who had just returned and represented to him that the situation was getting absurd when harmless citizens of the town had to seek shelter at night in barracks, and that I would send them back to their places and see they were protected if the town was powerless in that respect.

The Mayor called a meeting of the council and it was then decided the Chinamen were to be protected at any costs. Mr. Lucas subsequently waiting on me and requesting on the part of the council that I should stop any disturbance which the town authorities as organized for the purpose specially last night were unable to quell, and that I would be at once notified to that effect.

I kept some men in readiness, sent the Chinamen back to town under the protection of the Mayor. No disturbance took place and I don't think any is likely to occur in the future.

The chinamen have taken steps to recover damages from the town.

There are no new small-pox cases. Forty five persons were vaccinated in and about Sheppard by S/S Hayne.

It has been reported to me that one of the chinamen sent out of quarantine on 2nd inst is making his way down the C.P.R. in hopes of reaching Medicine Hat. Every one is afraid to go near him (tho' it is quite safe) he can get no food and is reported as being weak. I am trying to intercept him at Gleichen and looked after.

I have the honour etc. etc.

(Sgd.) A. Ross Cuthbert, Insp.

N.W.M.P.
Calgary, 5th August, 1892.

The Commissioner,
Regina.

Sir,

I attach a letter brought to me last night by the Chinamen, who were again sheltered in the Barracks, there was no disturbance. The situation is getting very complicated in town owing to the sympathy with the mob, of the Mayor & perhaps a majority of the council.

This afternoon I was asked to meet some gentlemen informally. Without knowing the object I did so. There were present Messrs Hurdmen, & Dean Clergymen—Braden, Thompson, J. B. Smith, Amos Rowe, Marsh, Cushing, & McBride, the two later councillors.

The situation was discussed and I was asked for protection in town etc. etc., I told the gentlemen that I would be acting within my rights in doing so in any case but as a matter of courtesy & custom, & as the consequence might be serious if the mob was persistent I would like such a request from the citizens through the Council their representatives. The matter was then discussed in all its aspects, the Chinamen were today formally warned (without knowing the individuals) that they must get out, even the domestic servants or be injured & their places burnt. Mr. Braden that the Tribune building would be burnt for sympathy with the chinamen. The people are thoroughly alarmed. After my views to the Meeting I came up to Barracks & immediately Messrs Cushing, Freeze (the members of town Police Committee) King, McBride, & Orr, representing the Mayor & a majority of town council waited on me & asked that the peace & safety of the citizens be maintained by the Mounted Police.

We will patrol the streets tonight, the remainder of the Division being kept in Barracks in readiness.

It is difficult to determine how it will all turn out, but many threats have been made and the mob seems determined. If cowmen are brought in from the Country and plied with whiskey there is sure to be bloodshed, & in this event I would represent the weakness of the Divn to deal with the mob on the streets, we have no swords & cobble stones are plentiful. Even as it is the strength is inadequate to be sure of success in the face of anything like a serious disturbance.

There are barrack guards & quarantine guard besides other duties & to-night I have between 20 & 30 men available all told, to deal with a determined mob of between 2 & 3 hundred & I need not dwell on the bad effects of getting worsted.

Besides the above reasons it will necessitate the Division practically being on duty night & day. If possible the Division should be temporarily strengthened until the excitement dies out.

I have etc. etc.,
(Sgd.) A. Ross Cuthbert, Insp.

N.W.M.P.
Calgary, 6th August 1892.

The Commissioner,
Regina.
Sir,

Up to the present there has been no attempt at a disturbance re. the China-men, but I understand it is said by the hot headed ones that they will gain their ends in spite of the Mounted Police, this however may be only idle talk.

There are no new cases of small-pox & sixteen persons are to be allowed out of quarantine this evening.

The chinaman who was allowed out from quarantine on the 2nd inst and who ran away during the riot was found by us at Langdon & brought in last night. At his own request he has been provided with a ticket & certificate of health by the Board of Health & leaves tonight for Vancouver.

The Mayor after his absence yesterday returned this a.m. and I presume will disappear again tonight.

The Council are ignoring him however & the respectable inhabitants speak of taking decided & vigorous measures in dealing with him.

All possible steps in so far as the strength of the Division will allow have been taken to deal with a disturbance.

I have etc. etc.,
(Sgd.) A. Ross Cuthbert, Insp.

N.W.M. Police,
Calgary, 19th August 1892.

The Commissioner,
Regina.
Sir,

The quarantine camp ceased to exist on the evening of the 16th Instant when Dr. George released the last of the quarantined, including himself. He offered to resume his work as Act. Asst Surgeon at once having taken all precautions in the way of disinfecting himself, but I thought best to wait till next Monday before he should commence altho. I am anxious that he should do so as Dr. Mackid has been most unsatisfactory.

Sergt Brooke who was Health Officer at Sheppard is returning today and the small-pox appears to be a thing of the past.

A man by the name of Locksley Lucas arrived here Wednesday to lecture (?) against the Chinese. He did not succeed in arousing much sympathy in his subject and in his attempt to form an Anti-Chinese league he only received Mr. Orr as member of a Provisional Committee and Mayor Lucas, who was also chairman of the entertainment. Being very down hearted at his treatment yesterday he attempted suicide at his hotel by taking opium, a Doctor was called in time to save his life and he was arrested and taken to the Town Police Station.

A woman of the town of the name of May Buchanan also attempted suicide yesterday.

There is little talk now of Chinese disturbances and I have discontinued a day patrol, but still keep a N.C.O. and 2 men on Town duty from 8 P.M. till after train time. The scheme which the rabble contemplated of which I was privately informed and which was to start an uproar in some distant part of the town to draw the Mounted Police while a few of the leaders could wreak their will on the Chinese undisturbed, has evidently been abandoned.

I attach one of Mr. Lockley Lucas' announcements.

I have etc. etc.,

(Sgd.) A. Ross Cuthbert, Insp.

94. LABOUR AND THE POLICE: RAILWAY CONSTRUCTION, 1897

PAC, RCMP Records, Section A-1, vol. 145, no. 56.

Extract from weekly report of Supt. Deane.
CROW'S NEST RAILWAY
The contracts for the second fifty miles of Railway were let on the 19th inst., and contractors are rapidly moving men and material into the Country. The works have not advanced to such a stage yet, as to require any particular Police protection.

All Patrols when passing near construction work have orders to go, out of their way if necessary, and look in upon working parties, enquiring of the foreman if there are any complaints.

As far as I have been able to learn, so far, the rate of wages does not exceed one dollar per day and rations. Some Contractors do not pay quite so much, and I should judge from the appearance of the men, that I have seen, that they will not care to squander their money when they get it.

I have asked Mr. Haney to request the Contractors to give us notice in advance of their pay days so that special attention may be paid to the various parties for the time being.

The horses are a very fine lot. We have no positive information yet about the alien labour law, which will hardly make as much difference as many people imagine.

The Galt Co'y's officials, for instance, go into Montana one day and on the next day, being already resident there, they receive an appointment which would not be allowed to hold if they went over for the purpose of receiving. Labourers therefore may engage, and be engaged here on the same terms.

Extract from report of the Police Officer on duty at Crow's Nest Pass for the week ended 18th September, 1897.

Construction work is going on satisfactorily on the whole, no trouble of any importance having occurred yet. This is due in great measure to good luck and the presence of the Police.

In this connection I beg to report what, if true, is a disgraceful way of employing men in the East. Some 100 men, chiefly French-Canadians and axe men have recently been employed and sent up by one Landry from Ottawa, acting as Agent of the CPR, and presumably on commission. All these, who had occasion to testify before me, swear to the fact that Landry engaged them as choppers for bush work: that they would have no blankets to pay for and, in some cases, no fares. Not one in ten can read English and do not know the text of the contract they signed. And it is safe to say that one in every five is physically unable to dump a scraper.

They have been placed to work with various contractors on the grade and very few have ever handled a pick, shovel and scraper. They naturally get into trouble and in a great many cases refuse to do work they did not engage to do and cannot do, and then we are called upon to compel them or send them to jail. They are completely discouraged and do not much care what happens to them.

Some have left families dependent upon what they can remit them, and they find themselves bound by a contract apparently signed under false pretences and a debt it will take them more than a month of uncongenial work to wipe out, whereas they would willingly work at their accustomed employment in the bush.

The matter should be enquired into by the CPR authorities, and the responsibility fixed. There are at present some half a dozen of these men in the Guard Room at Macleod undergoing sentence for desertion or refusal to work, and others at large.

For my part, as a Justice, I have intimated to the contractors who prosecuted the last batch of such cases that I will not deal with any more like cases, unless there is special reason, such as a new and well understood engagement.

Macleod, October 23rd, 1897.

The Commissioner,
Regina.
Sir,

RE LABOUR ON CROW'S NEST CONSTRUCTION

I have the honour to bring to your notice the condition of affairs in this District regarding labour on the construction of the Crow's Nest extension of the CPR.

Owing to the fact that all labourers are charged with their Railway fare from where they are hired to Macleod, and also in many instances, with their transport from Macleod to the particular camp at which they are to be employed, a great deal of dissatisfaction has arisen and much hardship experienced. This has been accentuated by the fact that the hiring Agents in the East, particularly about Hull and Ottawa, have misrepresented things and made promises to the men which the management of construction here refuse to ratify, they also send up men totally unfit for the work.

Inspt. Casey and myself have had these matters prominently brought before us in numerous actions for the recovery of wages which have been tried under the Masters and Servants Ordinance.

There is no doubt whatever that a great number of these men would never have come out here had they known they had to pay their fare, which from Ottawa here at a cent a mile is $22.49. These men have families in the East and when they discover that after working six weeks or two months there is not a cent coming to them or more probably they are in debt to the Contractors, that they have no money to send to their families, and that they have nothing themselves, they as a rule leave that particular employer and wander around destitute, without blankets or even boots in some cases, looking for other work, and people have had to supply them with food and in some instances I have had to do so, also give them a night's lodging.

There are numbers of men who are totally unfit for the work and what will become of them during the winter is hard to surmise.

Mr. McCreary, Immigration Agent, was here the other day and saw the way matters stood, whether he is in a position to do anything I cannot say, he expressed himself as anticipating trouble.

The position is this, that the CPR say, supplies a Contractor with 100 men from Ottawa, this costs the Contractor $2249.00 for Railway fare, which he deducts from the men together with $3.00 or $4.00 from each man for transport from Macleod to the scene of their labours. By this means the work of construction is cheapened.

Where the men have clearly understood their agreement in the East that they had to pay their Railway fare, we have endeavoured to make them stick to their Contract. But where they were evidently brought up under false pretenses, we have, as Magistrates, when the cases came before us, discharged them from their contracts.

No provision has been made by the Company for returning these men to their homes, winter is coming on and there is likelihood of much hardship and destitution.

In regard to class of men sent out from England and inducements offered I attach a report from Inspt. Casey with newspaper cutting. This report you will see was make [sic] some time ago but for some reason not brought to your notice.

Some pressure ought to be brought to bear for fairer treatment of the men.

I have the honour to be etc.

(sgd.) G. E. Saunders, Inspt.

The Commissioner,
Regina.
Sir,

North West Mounted Police,
Macleod, Oct. 30th, 1897.

RE LABOUR ON CROW'S NEST CONSTRUCTION

Referring to my former report of 23rd. inst. on this subject, I beg to further advise you as follows: —

Several of the men from Ottawa and Hull have brought action for the recovery of their wages, under the Masters and Servants Ordinance. Judgment was given in favour of these men, by the Magistrates, and the cases were then appealed to the Supreme Court. The Magistrates also discharged the men from their present contract. Owing to the appeal, the wages awarded the men were not paid over to them and they have to wait until the next sitting of the Supreme Court (November 11th).

They could not hang round without money so we got another Contractor, Mr. Buchanan, to employ them until Nov. 11th. The management of Construction however, intimated that these men would not be allowed to work and they were again discharged. This proceeding, after everything had been arranged amicably pending the Judge's decision, and after the decision of the Magistrate's Court, was, to say the least, certainly foolish on the part of the C.P.R. and practically meant interference with the course of Justice. The men they knew from their action, would not be able to stay here without money.

Mr. Haney being away, I remonstrated with Mr. Turnbull the Asst. Manager of Construction, and pointed out that if they pursued this policy it would only cause more embittered feelings on the part of the men, arouse public sympathy and make their relations with the men throughout the work, more strained. I explained to him also that we could not have men lying round here idle.

Mr. Turnbull saw the men this morning and offered them work pending the decision of the Court in their cases. The offer was not made in the most agreeable way and whether the men have accepted or not I cannot say. I warned them that if they remained around here idle they would be arrested as vagrants.

The Management of Construction have been given to understand that we recognize the difficulties they have to contend with in controlling such a large body of men, and the great necessity on their part to retain the upper hand, but at the same time, it has also been pointed out that any injustice or attempt to interfere with the due course of the law would be stopped.

There is no doubt at present, they are going to fight the question of the Railway fares to the end, and as long as this continues there will be hard feeling on the part of the men.

I have the honour to be,
Sir,
Your obedient servant,
(Sgd.) G. E. Saunders, Inspt.
For Supt. Steele off duty.

Extract from Inspector G. A. Sanders Report, December 21, 1897.

MEDICAL ATTENDANCE

In regard to medical attendance the doctors have so much ground to travel that they cannot accomplish their work. Men who are seriously ill are carted all the way to Macleod and Lethbridge—distances of between 100 and 150 miles. There is no accommodation for such men along the line of construction and to see men with rheumatic fever, broken limbs &c. jolting along the rough mountain roads in all kinds of weather seems, to say the least, inhuman. The men subscribe 50 cents per month for medical attendance and I understand this is not sufficient to pay for the medical service. I am under the impression that if there were places along the line where men could be attended by the doctors in charge of sections there would be a great saving of expense and better medical attendance for the men.

Canadian Pacific Railway,
Crow's Nest Branch,
Construction Department,
Macleod.
October 17th 1898.

S. W. Herchmer Esq.,
Commissioner N.W.M. Police,
Regina.

Dear Sir,

The necessity for the North West Mounted Police on the construction of the Crow's Nest Branch will probably cease soon, and in case I should over-look doing so later on, I take this opportunity of conveying you my apprecia-tion of the good work accomplished by the members of your force during the past year.

Inspector Sanders the officer in charge, has been most indefatigable in the discharge of his duties, which, owing to the country being unorganized, scarc-ity of local magistrates, and the long distance to be traversed, have been greatly increased to what they would have been had the country through which the road is being constructed been more thickly populated. By his tact and influence Insp. Sanders has, I believe, saved a lot of unnecessary trouble among a number of the men, who owing to outside influences, were led to imagine they had grounds for complaint. Considering that the majority of the laborers came on the work looking for grievances and with, therefore, an inclination to give trouble, and also taking into consideration that there has been no real trouble, no strikes or frictions of any importance between master and employee and that good order has prevailed to a much greater degree than is usual on works of this nature, I am disposed to the opinion that a good deal of the satisfactory condition of affairs is due to the action of Inspector Sanders and the Police under his command.

Assuring you again of my appreciation of the services rendered.

I am,
Yours truly,
(Sgd.) M. J. Haney,
Manager of Construction.

95. LABOUR AND THE POLICE: COAL MINERS, 1905

PAC, RCMP Records, Section A-1, vol. 300, no. 517.

Fernie, B.C.
June 9, 1905.

W. A. Galliher, Esq. M.P.
Ottawa.
Dear Sir:—

The President of District No. 18 of the U.M.W.A. has sent word to me that on the 6th inst. at Lille in Alberta, sixteen men at that time in the employ of the West Canadian Coal Co., and occupying houses belonging to that Company, were discharged by said Company. It was required that the men so discharged should immediately quit and deliver up possession of the premises occupied by them and should also leave the Village. I am instructed that this order was effectually carried through the instrumentality of the Royal Northwest Mounted Police who were called in for the purpose. Coming as my information does in a brief way, I am unable to state whether there are any facts which qualify the general statement thereof. Until further advised in the premises, I do not wish to commit myself to making any charge against either the Colliery Co. or Police. My instructions are to bring the matter to the attention of the proper department at Ottawa, requesting that an investigation be made touching what was done by the Police and their authority acting. I may add that the United Mine Workers of America, for which I am, as to District No. 18, general Solicitor, have at all times endeavored to keep themselves and every member of the organization, within the law, and I know that Mr. Sherman would hardly make a complaint if the facts did not justify such. You are well aware that in the several matters between that organization and employees throughout the Crow's Nest, the executive have signally succeeded in effecting settlements and coming to agreements which have assured for a long time to come the existing prosperity of this rich and growing section of the Dominion. It is not, I submit, asking too much to claim from the Government that protection which the law is supposed to give to the humblest subject working within the Dominion. Sometime ago, and even more than once, I brought to your attention the fact that in the section of the Country referred to, there is no Solicitor to whom the miners may turn for advice. Personally I dislike advising with reference to affairs in that Province, and only do so because there is no alternative. I intend to go to Lille tomorrow if I can get away. From there or upon my return here, I shall write you further on this subject. In the meantime, may I ask you if you will kindly submit this matter to the proper Department to take such action in the premises as the nature thereof may call for.

Yours faithfully,
(sd.) L. P. Eckstein

R.N.W.M. Police,
Frank, June 14th, 1905.

The Officer Commanding,
R.N.W.M. Police,
Macleod.

Sir,

Re your telegram received here to-day, re trouble at Lille, I have the honour to report as follows:—

On Tuesday the 6th June, at 8 A.M. I received a telephone message from Mr. Williams, Manager of the W.C.C. Co., at Lille, asking for two policemen to be sent up at once. I went up immediately with Const. Thunder, arriving at Lille at 9 A.M. I found Mr. Williams, and he informed me that he had discharged eleven Italians, who were Miners and Assistants, and he intended to pay them off at 9 A.M. and he feared trouble would arise over their dismissal, as the night before a shot had been fired in the direction of the office, and several of the Italian assistants had demanded the same as the miners were getting. There had also been several violent quarrels amongst these Italians and in one case a knife had been drawn. These men did not appear at the office at 9 A.M. to draw their time-checks, and as they all lived at No. 1 Camp, (about a mile) Mr. Williams asked us to accompany him whilst he made the payments, as he feared violence. He also stated that he intended to give them two hours to vacate their houses and leave the premises. I informed him very strongly that as far as the ejecting of these men was concerned, I would take no hand in it, but if any violence was used, he would have Police protection. Mr. Williams gave these men their cheques and told them to leave the place in two hours. As far as the Police are concerned I gave no orders whatever to these men to vacate their houses. We were merely there to prevent any breach of the Peace. There were no signs of trouble, and we returned to Frank at 11.30 A.M. Your telegram was received at 4.30 P.M. to-day, by Const. Thunder, who saw Mr. Williams immediately afterwards. He said that all these men were on the premises yet, and four of them had been re-engaged to work. I intend to see Mr. Williams myself to-morrow, and will get a full report from him in connection with this matter, which I will forward to you at once, and which, I think, will show that the Police gave no orders at all to these Italians to vacate their houses. I may say that there have been several quarrels recently amongst the Italians and English-speaking men, and in several cases the White men have been threatened, several of them saying they do not care to work in the mine, as they are scared of getting a pick in the back, when they were not looking.

I have the honour to be,
Sir,
Your obedient servant,
(Sgd.) S. J. Kembry, Corpl.

L. P. Eckstein,
Barrister-at-Law
Solicitor
Notary & C.

Offices:—Cuthbert Block, Victoria Ave.,
Fernie, British Columbia
June 24, 1905.

W. A. Galliher, Esq. M.P.
Ottawa,

Dear Sir:—

I am in receipt of a letter, under date 20th inst., addressed to you by the Comptroller of the Royal North West Mounted Police, with accompanying enclosures, all of which I am forwarding to Mr. Sherman. As I have already suggested, no reason exists for pursuing this matter any further. I may remark, and you will observe that it was to say the least somewhat unusual for a Mine Manager to travel, as he claims to have done, about one mile to meet the Italians for the purpose of handing them their time checks. It is only necessary to exercise one's common sense to be convinced of the absurdity of believing that Mr. Williams went so far out of his way as to call upon the Italians to hand them their time checks when they failed to call upon him therefor. To my mind the very answer made by Mr. Williams and by the Corporal is per se, sufficient to convince the ordinary mortal that there is some truth in the charge which was made by Mr. Sherman in behalf of the miners. The Police contend that they went there to prevent a quarrel. Why did Williams go there at all? It is plain that he wanted to do something more than hand them their checks and he used the Police as a shield against what might have been the results of an aggressive act. The Police concede that Williams wanted to eject these men. I suppose if the men had in the exercise of their lawful rights, refused to be thus ejected summarily by Williams, that the Police would have interfered. For my part, I know the record of the Police far too well to ever think that they would knowingly lend themselves to the commission of an act which was not lawful, and in this instance, I must advise my clients that the Police are wholly blameless insofar as intention to offend was concerned. I believe that they were called up to assist by their mere presence, in enabling Williams to eject the men without due process of law. I shall be pleased if you will submit this letter to the proper department.

Yours faithfully
L. P. Eckstein

Ottawa, 29th June, 1905.
Dear Mr. Galliher:—

I have your note with enclosure from Mr. Eckstein who, I think, takes a very fair view of the action of the Police in connection with the Lille miners.

One of the most delicate parts of Police duty in the North West, has been in deciding where their authority begins and ends. We have had many cases where efforts have been made to use the Police Force for the collection of debts recoverable by civil action. Also, as apparent in the Lille case, an effort to use men in uniform, with all the semblance of the authority of law, to awe those against whom preceedings have been taken. The Police, of course, have to respond to such calls, and even with the most perfect organization, errors of judgment occasionally occur and the Police get the blame.

Another point which has given a great deal of anxiety to the Police is when a man is justified in firing at an escaping prisoner. So far we have had thirty years of escape from any charge which has been sustained, but I feel that at any moment some of our men may get caught, and I shall be glad if you will kindly say to Mr. Eckstein that I appreciate his interpretation of Police action in the Lille case.

Yours very truly,

F. White

Comptroller

GUIDE TO FURTHER READING

The literature on the Mounted Police, though extensive, is not very consistent in quality and must be approached by the student with caution. The sources mentioned here are discussed roughly in order of credibility, from most authoritative to least.

The *Annual Report of the Commissioner of the North-West Mounted Police*, which was published from 1876 on in the Canadian Sessional Papers, is an excellent primary source. The reports are a very complete summary of the year's activities and contain a great deal of useful statistical material.

The best general introduction to the history of the Mounted Police is S. W. Horrall, *The Pictorial History of the Royal Canadian Mounted Police* (McGraw-Hill Ryerson, 1973). *Maintain the Right: The Early History of the North West Mounted Police* by Ronald Atkin (Macmillan, 1973) is readable and provides an excellent picture of the conditions under which the Force operated in this period. Hugh A. Dempsey, ed., *Men in Scarlet* (McClelland and Stewart, 1974) is a collection of thirteen papers presented at an RCMP centennial conference held at the University of Lethbridge. Two other articles, one by S. W. Horrall, 'Sir John A. Macdonald and the Mounted Police Force for the Northwest Territories' in *Canadian Historical Review*, 1972, and E. C. Morgan, 'The NWMP: Internal Problems and Public Criticism, 1874-1885' in *Saskatchewan History*, 1973, are indispensable for an understanding of the first decade of the Force.

A number of members of the Force wrote memoirs of their careers which provide interesting glimpses of the work of the Mounted Police. Most of these works were written many years after the events described and therefore must be checked carefully against other sources, but they help convey the flavour of the period. The best of these personal views include: Jean d'Artigue, *Six Years in the Canadian North-West* (Toronto, 1882), John G. Donkin, *Trooper and Redskin in the Far North-West: Recollections of Life in the North-West Mounted Police, Canada, 1884-1888* (London, 1899), R. Burton Deane, *Mounted Police Life in Canada: A Record of Thirty-One Years' Service* (London, 1916), and S. B. Steele, *Forty Years in Canada: Reminiscences of the Great North-West with Some Account of His Service in South Africa* (Toronto, 1915). Two periodicals, *Scarlet and Gold* and the *RCMP Quarterly*, also contain many personal reminiscences.

The final, and largest, category of works on the Force consists of books written without the benefit of extensive archival research. These books almost invariably were the work of admirers of the Mounted Police and tend to be uncritical. The best of the secondary works on the Force is John Peter Turner's massive two-volume study, *The North-West Mounted Police, 1873-1893* (Ottawa, 1950). Turner's book is a mine of detailed information on uniforms, equipment and regulations but the descriptions and interpretations of events are often suspect because Turner, who began to collect material for the book in 1910, relied heavily on second- and third-hand accounts from his friends in the Force. Ernest J. Chambers' *The Royal North-West Mounted Police: A Corps History* (Montreal, 1906), although it is the earliest history of the Force, is in many ways more accurate and entertaining than such later efforts as A. L. Haydon, *The Riders of the Plains* (London, 1910), R. G. Macbeth, *Policing the Plains* (London, 1922), R. C. Fetherstonhaugh, *The Royal Canadian Mounted Police* (New York, 1938), Cecil E. Denny, *The Law Marches West* (Toronto, 1939), or even Nora and William Kelly, *The Royal Canadian Mounted Police: A Century of History* (Edmonton, 1973). An exception to the rule that the history of the Mounted Police has been written by its admirers is *An Unauthorized History of the RCMP* (Toronto, 1973) by Lorne and Caroline Brown. A critical look at the history of the Force would have been welcome had it been based on substantial research but the historical portion of this book is so shoddy that it adds nothing to our knowledge of the subject.

IV The Ranching Frontier in Canada, 1875-1905

David H. Breen

INTRODUCTION

In the middle 1870s, as cattlemen were moving their herds into the Powder River country of northern Wyoming Territory and along the sheltered river valleys of central and eastern Montana, others were locating even further north in the Blackfoot country beyond the forty-ninth parallel. Traders from Fort Benton, Montana, and from Hudson's Bay Company posts to the north, who had frequented the area over the preceding decade, had long been conscious of the climatic and physiographic qualities that marked the region's grazing potential. The North West Mounted Police had hardly completed the construction of their new post at Fort Macleod in 1874 before a few of these ex-traders arrived in the vicinity with small herds.

The arrival of the police from the east at the time the American cattle kingdom was thrusting northwards towards the forty-ninth parallel proved to be of critical importance in determining the way in which the industry would develop on the Canadian side of the boundary. The police immediately provided the two essential prerequisites that the development of a stock-raising industry required—a market and security. Like the military posts scattered across the American plains, those of the Canadian police provided a limited local market about which a small indigenous cattle industry could develop. This, with the promise of expanded sales as soon as the government commenced the purchase of beef to assist the increasingly dependent Indians of the region in accordance with the obligations assumed in 1877 in Indian Treaty Number Seven, assured the industry's growth.

The intending cattleman's other concern—security—stemmed from the character of his industry. Since the bulk of his capital investment, namely his herd of cattle, was exposed and vulnerable as it wandered often unattended over the vast range, the rancher demanded a close day-to-day protection not sought by any other economic group in the west. In this context the treaty concluded with the much-feared Blackfoot Confederacy in 1877 was again of central importance. It meant that the nascent cattle industry could expand safely beyond the immediate environs of Fort Macleod, and that cattlemen pushing into the foothill valleys would not fight the Indians to gain possession, as was the frequent pattern in the cattle country to the south. The rapport that the police quickly established with the Indians assured the continuance of the predominant northern tradition of peaceful co-existence. On the Canadian side of the boundary ranchers moved on to ranges regularly patrolled by a federal police force that fully accepted the responsibility of protecting the rancher's property. Through their efficient execution of this task the police determined that the powerful cattlemen's associations functioned within the law, and that the vigilance committee was unnecessary and consequently unknown in the northern setting. The stability that the presence of the North West Mounted Police lent to the developing Canadian cattle kingdom proved such that ranchers were never able to envisage their region or the well-being of their industry without the Force. They long remained the influential champions of the police at any hint of their reduction or withdrawal.

While the physical presence of an effective law-enforcement body had this obvious effect upon the evolving character of the ranching frontier in Canada, the influence of the police had another less tangible but equally significant dimension in this phase of western development. Police recruits, particularly those from parts of Ontario and Quebec's Eastern Townships where stock-raising was an important activity, were quick to observe the success of the first few traders-turned-ranchers and to measure the opportunity at hand. When the first three-year enlistment contracts expired in 1876, a number of the men elected to remain in the west to ranch, thus initiating what can be observed as a yearly pattern till well after the turn of the century, as men and officers of the force continued to be absorbed into the ranching industry. As the core about which the early ranching industry developed, ex-policemen with their eastern and largely middle-class backgrounds contributed in an important way to the evolving social milieu. While ex-members of the Force figured prominently in the small pioneering group that povided a practical demonstration of the region's ranching potential, they were even more important as publicizers of ranching prospects in the western territory through their frequent trips back east to seek investment capital. Policemen returning to the west were often accompanied by relatives and former neighbours who had become enthused about stock-raising opportunities and were anxious to become direct participants in ranching ventures. Not surprisingly the newcomers for the most part were cut from essentially the same social fabric as the police. Thus, in the larger sense as well, the police-ranchers played a prominent role in building and defining the character of the region's new population base.

The interest in the Canadian ranch country awakened by the police in the late 1870s developed as part of a continent-wide phenomenon. As railroads began to penetrate the American west after the Civil War, cheaply grown western beef gained access to high-priced markets in the eastern United States and Great Britain. It was essentially this price difference, with its promise of vast and continued profit, that was the dynamic force behind the incredibly rapid expansion of the American cattle kingdom. The arithmetic of gain was blatantly straight-forward; a good calf, worth five dollars at birth in the west, could be fed on almost free grass and would bring its owner forty to sixty dol-

THE CANADIAN RANCHING FRONTIER, 1885

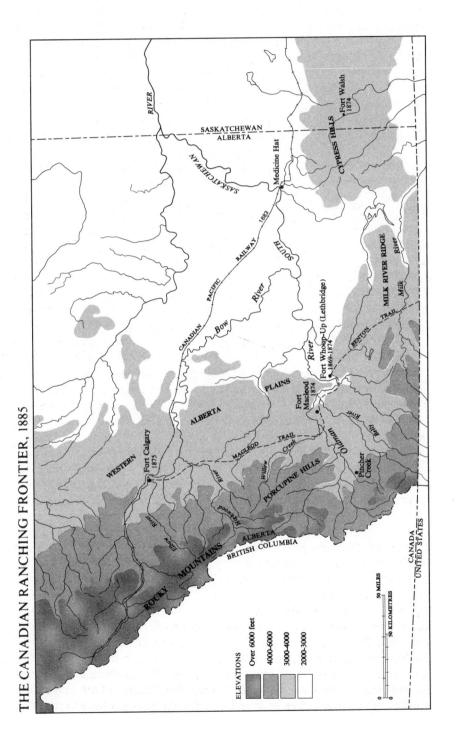

lars when marketed in the east three or four years later. Popular and financial journals alike were soon filled with reports from western ranching operations claiming profits of thirty to one hundred per cent per year. By 1879 the great cattle boom, the 'Beef Bonanza', was under way. Ranching fever developed simultaneously in Canada as Canadian capitalists discovered that a comparable grazing area, already proven by small stock-raisers, existed in their own west. The Canadian press joined that of the United States and Great Britain to proclaim this new 'Eldorado', and as construction of the new transcontinental railway across the Canadian prairies began, a host of hastily formed cattle companies jockeyed before federal ministers for preferred western lands.

The larger company ranches that were established in the western foothills by 1882 were capitalized at sums ranging upwards from $100,000, and their respective boards of directors read as a 'Who's Who' in the Canadian business and political world of the day. This, with the continued arrival in the west of well-to-do easterners along with numerous gentlemen and aristocrats from the British Isles embarking on private ventures, underlines the fact that the economic structure of the cattle industry itself went a long way in determining the class base from which the original population of the cattle country was drawn. To initiate his enterprise the prospective rancher first had to acquire a herd of cattle and this, in contrast to the initial costs faced by the intending farmer, required a substantial capital investment that tended to eliminate those of lesser means. Furthermore, the new rancher found that the operational structure of the cattle ranch was particularly conducive to the support of the English country-estate ethos, which so many in the ranch country found congenial. Cattle ranching permitted the retention of the manager-employee relationship as well as a leisured life style, and in this manner actually assisted in the perpetuation of an imported social system that helped to set the ranch community apart from the general social development of the agrarian frontier. Cereal agriculture, in contrast, was unable to support the rural establishment desired by the would-be gentlemen. Few persons wanted to take employment on another's farm or become tenant farmers in a country where they might easily acquire land of their own. Ranch labour on the other hand was seldom in short supply.

The cattlemen's emergent empire in the Canadian west rested firmly upon a particular form of land tenure. The system adopted was determined through negotiations during the winter of 1880-1 between Senator Matthew H. Cochrane, representing eastern investors anxious to ensure that land holdings acquired in the west would stand on a secure legal footing, and the Prime Minister, Sir John A. Macdonald, representing a government eager to attract investment to a region considered too dry for regular agricultural settlement. The terms eventually agreed upon and ultimately made public by Order-in-Council in December 1881 gave the government authority to grant leases of up to 100,000 acres for a term of twenty-one years at the rate of ten dollars per 1,000 acres—or one cent per acre per year. In light of later developments, perhaps the most significant feature of the new lease policy was the provision that excluded all except the lessee from the right of immediate homestead entry.

The lease system was the foundation upon which the ranching industry in Canada was built and it meant that the Canadian range developed in a manner significantly different from the American pattern. Grasslands in the western United States were theoretically open to the free use of all. In practice the traditional phenomenon of the American frontier—squatter sovereignty—determined what land could be used by whom. Such sovereignty was based upon the custom of priority; when a cattleman drove his herd into some promising valley and found cattle already present he continued elsewhere. Early legislation in the southern cattle country provided punishment for those who drove stock from their 'accustomed range'. Though designed against cattle rustling, such laws indirectly recognized the fact that by grazing his cattle in a certain area, the stock-owner gained a kind of prescriptive right to the range as opposed to one who might come later. Such a system worked well as long as there were new valleys into which the industry could expand, but as the range became more crowded such ill-defined range rights proved most difficult to defend by legal means. In contrast, in the Canadian west, through leasing the public domain rather than allowing it to be used as common pasture, the government maintained a much more direct control of land use, and by establishing a clear basis of legal ownership helped prevent the range wars that occasionally developed south of the border among ranchers disputing one another's rights to a particular range. The legal position of the Canadian leaseholder was explicitly defined by statute and this, with a federal police force at hand to uphold the provision of national laws, provided a security that the American rancher dependent upon 'range rights' did not possess. Those who squatted on the extensive leaseholds did so only at the sufferance of the leaseholder and more often than not were summarily evicted by the rancher and his cowhands or by the police.

Even more important than the obvious impact that this system of land tenure had upon the development of the ranch country was the general attitude or philosophy from which it stemmed. The adoption by the Canadian government of the principle that users of the range land should pay a rent is evidence, first, of the somewhat different Canadian attitude towards public lands—a difference perhaps further implied by the traditional Canadian term 'Crown' as opposed to 'public' lands. Second, and more important, one sees in the lease laws the hand of a government that was prepared from the outset to play an active and direct role in western development. The federal presence in the ranch country as manifest in the lease system with its concomitant ranch inspectors was characteristic of Ottawa's supervisory commitment towards the use and disposal of western lands in general.

In the western ranch country the lease policy fostered stability within the stock industry, and insofar as it tended to prevent over-grazing, contributed to the superior husbanding of the land's resources, but it also restricted greatly the activities of the small or beginning cattleman who could not afford to buy or lease land. Even those who could afford to lease often found that the desired range had been given to someone in the east who had important friends in parliament. The lease system in effect gave control of the region to the big operators, and in this way functioned as another important factor influencing the region's evolving social and economic pattern. The government's range policy consequently precipitated much ill-feeling among smaller stockmen and intending settlers who saw about them great tracts of seemingly little-used leased land upon which they could not legally locate. In short, though the system countered some of the difficulties characteristic of the American range, it initiated a struggle that was to plague the federal authorities for the next three decades.

From the outset the cattlemen maintained a posture of open hostility towards the intending farmer or, as he was less charitably known in the cattle country, 'sod-buster'. Canadian stockmen no less than their American counterparts were determined to resist the encroachment upon their large and profitable holdings of the agriculturalist with his ubiquitous barbed-wire fences. In the first years of this contest advantage lay with the ranchers. Their representation within the upper echelons of the metropolitan business community and the Conservative party provided the stockmen with a most effective and often decisive political voice. And while the regional hegemony that the large ranchers were able to exercise till the mid-nineties had much to do with the character of these extra-regional contacts, it was sustained further by the regional domination that they exercised over the stock-raising industry through their cattlemen's associations.

The very nature of the stockmen's organization reflects the basic difference of attitude that set the rancher apart from his farming neighbours. Unlike the western farmer, the stock-grower did not seek co-operative effort to remedy the wants growing out of isolation such as roads, schools, social amenities, and increased land values. His motivation towards organization came from the reverse reason, not because of isolation, but because his isolation was threatened and in this sense the cattlemen's organization was unique to the western experience. Settlement was a potential threat to the rancher's range and his rewards were potentially the greatest when his isolation was most complete.

Control of the stock associations permitted the larger ranchers more or less to dictate the manner in which the industry was administered locally, since these associations set and enforced local regulations concerning brands, branding, organization and times of roundups, control of bulls on the range, and the ownership of unbranded cattle or 'mavericks', as they were known to cattlemen. Such domination also provided the large stock-growers with a useful platform from which they could claim to speak to the world outside as the legitimate and official voice of the cattle industry.

The encompassing strength of the organized ranchers, or as they might be termed, the 'cattle compact', is manifest through the first two decades of their western presence in their ability to secure, among other things, desired quarantine legislation, stock-import restrictions, expanded police patrols, and the removal of the despised sheepmen from their region. But even more important than the local domination that they were able to achieve within the cattle country, and central to the defence of the ranchers' cause, was their ability to maintain at the national level, the 'special-region' argument. The essence of this argument was that the combination of light sandy soil and dry climate characteristic of much of the southwestern prairie, along with the high elevation and broken nature of the foothill country abutting the Rocky Mountains, made these lands largely unfit for cereal agriculture. This assessment rested comfortably on the earlier evaluations of the southwestern prairie made by the Palliser and Hind expeditions in the late 1850s, and it remained the pivotal point of the ranchers' defensive position. Cattlemen vigorously maintained that it was economically absurd and morally wrong to encourage farm settlement in a region that nature had determined to be grazing country when such a policy could only bring eventual ruin and hardship to unfortunately misguided settlers, and in the process destroy an established and profitable industry particularly suited to the dry country. The lease system stands as initial testimony to the Department of the Interior's acceptance of the rancher's view that the southwest had to be considered a distinct region within the western territory and administered accordingly. Until the mid 1890s this remained the predominant attitude among the technical experts within the department. To William Pearce, Superintendent of Mines and perhaps the most influential department official in the west, it was simply a question of efficient land use. If the dry plains and broken foothill country were to be used for the purpose for which they were best suited, or in short, most productively, then the cattlemen and their industry had to be sustained through appropriate legislation.

This conception of the southwest as ranch country was challenged almost from the beginning. Within several months of Ottawa's announcement of its lease policy about fifty settlers gathered in Calgary to protest it. In 1883 settlers who had located in the Porcupine Hills near Fort Macleod in the heart of the ranch country protested to the Department of the Interior that they had been encouraged to settle in the northwest by pamphlets published and distributed by the department, only to be informed after having erected houses and ploughed the land that the properties they claimed were under prior lease. The federal government however was not sympathetic and the 'trespassers' were forced off their claims. As the pressure of settlement and the consequent number of evictions in the hills increased through the following summer, the animosity between the ranchers and prospective settlers grew in proportion. The readiness with which ranchers were prepared to press their legal advantage through 1884 precipitated a crisis in the spring of 1885. On April 5th a large group of settlers responded to a word-of-mouth summons to meet at the farm of John Glenn on Fish Creek several miles south of Calgary. In a petition to the government they protested their inability to obtain legal title to their lands and threatened to join the Indians and Métis in rebellion if the government did not respond to their grievances.

It became apparent to the federal government and to the cattlemen by 1886 that the growing popular agitation against the lease system required some accommodation. To this end the Department of the Interior cancelled a number of the unstocked speculative leases in the Calgary area, opened some government reserve land, and announced that leases granted henceforth would no longer contain the offensive 'no-settlement' clause, thus permitting homestead entry. The ranchers, in agreeing to acquiesce to this change, were able however to convince the government of the need to establish a system of public water reservations from which settlement would be restricted. If the cattlemen's empire could not be maintained through a system of closed leases, it was clear to those familiar with the dry country that the same ends might be achieved even more effectively through control of the region's springs, streams, and river fronts. The change that had occurred in the ranch country as a result of settler protest was therefore more apparent than real. It was only on new leases that homesteading was to be sanctioned. Beyond this the 'special-region' philosophy, now bolstered by water-reserve legislation, remained ascendant.

The new lease policy and the cancellation of a few speculative leases not surprisingly brought only brief peace to the Canadian range. Tension between the two groups continued in the Bow River valley as the contending parties petitioned the Department of the Interior with threats and counterthreats. At the same time further south the large ranch companies continued rigorously to police their leaseholds. The British-owned Walrond Ranch Company pursued a particularly aggressive policy against would-be settlers and the stern ejection procedure followed by the manager of this company gained the attention of parliament in 1889 and 1892. The latter episode, stemming from a mid-winter eviction and an incendiary attack in reprisal on Walrond property, set the squatters and ranch companies on a collision course that threatened an all-out range war.

The ruling Conservative government found itself in a most difficult position. On the one hand public opinion, supported in parliament by the opposition Liberals, was actively hostile to the ranchers. On the other hand the Conservatives had little desire to antagonize a group so strongly based within the party. Bound to its powerful capitalist supporters in the east, the government felt compelled to help maintain their outpost in the west. But as the tide of public criticism advanced, and as the government was repeatedly called upon to account for the apparent disregard of its own longstanding commitment to western settlement, it became increasingly expedient to arrive at a compromise with the ranching interests. To this end the Minister of the Interior early in 1892 called upon the ranchers to send a deputation to Ottawa to discuss the lease situation. The consequent meeting was followed by the announcement that the cattlemen had been given notice that all the old 'closed' leases would be cancelled in four years. Before termination the leaseholders were given the option of purchasing one-tenth of their lease at $2.00 per acre, a price that the ranch lobby was later able to reduce to $1.25 per acre, or one-half the amount charged to homesteaders for pre-empted acres in the Macleod region. But the key factor, as in 1886 when the federal government negotiated lease changes with the 'cattle compact', was the unwritten promise of expanded water reserves for stock. It seems that the cattlemen subsequently divided themselves into regional committees to draw up lists of desired reservations in their respective localities. These lists were forwarded to the Superintendent of Mines, William Pearce, who inspected the properties in question and then sent his recommendations to the department in Ottawa. Since the selections made by the cattlemen were nearly all approved, by 1894 springs, creeks, and river bottoms were well protected throughout the southwest and especially in the foothill country. Once the water reserves were selected, the department, through Pearce's initiative and the ranchers' vigilance, vigorously prevented settlement on or even near the reserves. Squatter evictions therefore continued in the ranch country, but from this point they were from the water and shelter reservations rather than from the closed leases as in the past.

This dimension of the rancher-settler feud easily lends itself to presentation in very black-and-white terms, and if not explicitly drawn, the theme very often implied or called to mind is one of the 'weak' versus the 'strong', or the 'progressive yeoman farmer' facing a 'reactionary vested interest'. But a caution needs to be advanced. Quite apart from the basic question of land use, it must be recognized that among the so-called settlers were a sizeable minority who were not really legitimate settlers at all. Many were professional speculators who squatted on a choice part of a lease, usually on a spring or valley bottom, expecting to be 'bought off'. Others were not really interested in farming at all, but hoped to become cattlemen despite limited or no capital by stealing the beginnings of a herd of their own from among the numerous strays from the great herds on the open range. Against such individuals, as well as legitimate settlers whose fence around a spring or along a creek bottom might render hundreds of adjacent acres useless, William Pearce until 1896 efficiently co-ordinated the efforts of the cattlemen, his department, and the police in eviction proceedings.

The year 1896 marks something of a turning point in the history of the ranching country. Not only did the lease system upon which the cattlemen's empire had rested for a decade and a half come to a scheduled end, but there was also a change of power in Ottawa and the cattlemen were confronted with the party they had always regarded as the 'farmers' party. Over the next decade the political influence of the ranchers steadily declined. Though the first Liberal Minister of the Interior, Clifford Sifton, was prepared to view the southwest as a preferred grazing area and therefore to maintain the water-reserve system, many of the immigrants attracted to the northwest from the United States by his department's vigorous immigration campaign were impressed with the grazing country while traversing the region and decided therefore to terminate their northward trek and seek a spot to settle in the ranchers' preserve.

The arrival in force from the 1890s on of this new frontier figure, the American dry-land farmer, extended the former competition between rancher and farmer for the same habitat from the creek and river bottoms to the plains beyond. For a decade the weather conspired to lend credence to the drylanders' optimism. While the two settlements at either end of the hypotenuse of the ranching triangle, Calgary and Medicine Hat, very seldom enjoyed more than ten inches annual precipitation between 1885 and 1895, the average never dropped below fifteen inches from 1896 to 1903. The voice of caution from those inhabitants of the two previous decades, coming as it did mainly from the cattlemen, was dismissed as simply the anti-settlement propaganda of a die-hard vested interest. For the most part ranchers were unable to remove the label fixed upon them by the settlement press as being a landed and reactionary establishment standing in the way of settlement and 'progress'. The farmers on the other hand appealed to a morality that was much more in step with the buoyant enthusiasm of nation building that gripped the country during the first decade of the twentieth century. The tradition of small farm homes for poor men lived on among politicians who did not trouble themselves to learn that all prairie lands were not identical to the farm country of Ontario, of Manitoba, or of the Qu'Appelle Valley. 'Progress' and 'settlement' came to be synonymous terms. In this atmosphere the cattlemen who proposed restricted settlement, or predicted drought and spoke gloomily of eventual disaster, were entirely out of harmony with national feeling and therefore received little attention and even less understanding.

The growing strength of the anti-ranch sentiment was personified in Sifton's successor as Minister of the Interior in 1905. Frank Oliver, the Liberal editor of the Edmonton *Bulletin*, had long opposed the ranching interests in the southern half of his new province and once in office was determined to help those squatters who had sought his assistance in the past. Oliver spoke for those who were inclined to view the west in terms of what had come to be popularly known as the 'mixed farm' that, it was alleged, would produce both grain and cattle, and at the same time create a populous and independent citizenry that would comprise the matrix of a growing and progressive nation. In pursuit of this goal Oliver, within a few months of taking office, commenced the disposal by auction of the region's water reservations, thereby casting aside the 'special-region' argument and opening the southwest to general settlement.

In the end the ranchers' dire warnings proved true, as the drought-driven refugees of the early 1920s and the 1930s bear witness. Ironically however it was the faltering cattle kingdom that was first to suffer nature's wrath. The winter of 1906-7 turned out to be the worst ever experienced in the ranching country. This seemingly unending winter began with a heavy snow storm the third week in November and by December 8 temperatures had descended to between -30° and -35°C, where they hovered almost without respite for the next two months as the indispensable chinook failed to make its accustomed appearance. Northern cattle moved south by the thousand where, if they did not perish along fence lines, they collected in the sheltered valleys of southern rivers. When the final reckoning had been made many of the big ranches had losses in the thousands. It was claimed for example that the Two Bar Ranch near Gleichen lost 11,000 head from a total herd of 13,000. For many of the big ranchers and cattle companies that had managed to survive to this point this proved the final blow. The 'Carrion Spring' as Wallace Stegner has termed it in *Wolf Willow*, marked the end of the old order on the Canadian range.

The myth, stereotype, and fiction that surrounds this phase of western development greatly compounds the usual difficulties of historical assessment. To counter this problem, and to assist in placing the ranching frontier within the broad context of western Canadian development, the following collection of primary documents is offered for the reader's consideration. While the documents can be used more narrowly to focus on specific aspects of the ranching industry and western settlement, in their collectivity they also lend themselves to the assessment of certain broader comparative themes. There is, for example, an obvious continental perspective that must be acknowledged in any consideration of the ranching frontier in Canada. Indeed, given the geographic unity of the Canadian and American ranching frontiers, the industry's simultaneous development on either side of the border, and the common form of economic organization, one is led to wonder to what extent the forty-ninth parallel is relevant in an examination of this topic. Just how far can comparisons be drawn between the Canadian and American ranching frontiers, and are the apparent differences ones of substance or merely of degree?

In addition to questioning how the ranching frontier in Canada relates to the larger North American ranching scene, the ranching industry must also be considered in the national perspective. That is, how do the cattlemen and their industry fit into the opening and development of the Canadian west? In entertaining this question one might begin by recognizing that the ranch country comprises a distinct physiographic region. The all-too-common practice of viewing the Canadian prairie west as an homogeneous unit, while it might have some merit in the broad discussion of national history, has usually obscured the fact that there is significant diversity within the region. In this context it must be noted that the semi-arid environment ensured a separate evolution that set this area apart from the main pattern of western development. In other words, the environment in the long run tolerated only those enterprises that were able to adapt to its uncompromising demands. The cattlemen were the first to seek accommodation, and through their prolonged efforts a large and profitable industry particularly suited to the dry southwestern climate was pioneered. There were however, almost from the beginning, others who sought to use the land in different and competing ways. Very early the sheepmen sought grazing areas for their flocks, and more and more as the turn of the century drew near, the confident voice of the dry-land farmer was heard demanding lands on which to demonstrate his 'progressive' farming techniques. The long and sometimes bitter contest between rancher and farmer can therefore be better understood, by recognizing it as a struggle between two economic groups with competing forms of land use. To this end each group vigorously championed their chosen vocation and lobbied for legislative support to advance their enterprise at the expense of the other.

Intrinsic to the struggle and also to be considered are the conflicting land-use philosophies upon which either side ultimately rested its case. On the one hand is revealed the traditionally dominant *laissez faire* attitude that held that it was the right of the individual to determine not only where he would settle, but also how he would use the land once located. This disposition rested upon the optimistic and widely held conviction that the innovative North American spirit would ultimately triumph in any setting. Success was assumed, but if failure was the reward of a few individuals (and it must be stressed that defeat was rarely considered), the cost was judged trifling in support of the principle of individual freedom. The other view, always weaker in the new world, was that the government should control settlement so that the land's resources would be used to best advantage, and for this reason the rights of a few thousand would-be settlers could not be permitted to stand in the way of the larger national or public good.

THE LAND

96. A GRAZING COUNTRY PAR EXCELLENCE

G. M. Dawson, Fort MacLeod, N.W.T., October 17, 1881, in *The Gazette* (Montreal), November 17, 1881.

So much is written about the Northwest country at present, that the topic is perhaps likely to become tedious to those whose interests centre chiefly in other matters, yet there is none other of equal importance at this time to Canada. A few words as to its capabilities as a stock-raising region, of a character more general than would be proper in an official report, may be of interest to some of your readers.

The Northwest—meaning by that term a vast tract of country of rudely triangular form, having one angle at the little Province of Manitoba, a second about the 60th parallel on the MacKenzie, and the third at the intersection of the Rocky Mountains with the boundary line—is naturally divided into agricultural and stock raising regions. Each of these includes certain tracts which, for sufficient reasons, may be considered as permanently unproductive and barren, but these, fortunately, appear to be comparatively small. The agricultural region, beginning in Manitoba, stretches westward and northward, following the North Saskatchewan River and extending to the basin of the

Peace. This includes the border of the great northern forests and a belt of partly wooded country and plain of varying width. It has been euphuistically [sic] termed by some writer, who certainly deserves to be enshrined in future Canadian histories, the "Rainbow of the North." The abundance of timber in itself constitutes an important point in its favour as a farming country, but this is not so much a cause, as an effect of a difference of climate, more particularly an abundant rainfall which adapts the country for agriculture.

As regards climate the requirements of a stock-raising country, as understood in this western part of the continent, and those of a farming country are to a great degree antagonistic. The very dryness of climate which causes grasses to be produced which retain their nutritious properties during the winter and prevents the exuberant growth of wood, renders agriculture precarious or impossible except when irrigation can be resorted to with facility. In addition to this the elevation of much of the stock-raising lands is such that summer frosts not infrequently occur, rendering the growth of some crops uncertain.

The stock-raising country, proper, of the Northwest lies to the southwest of the great agricultural zone . . . and is drained chiefly by the South Saskatchewan and its branches, though the Milk River, a tributary of the Missouri [that] runs through a portion of its southern extent. Regarded broadly this region may be described as sloping gently eastward and north-eastward from the base of the Rocky Mountains, with an elevation of from 2,000 to 4,000 feet above the sea. In regard to pasturage, it may be divided into the "buffalo-grass" and the "bunch-grass" districts. The latter forms a belt along the base of the mountains, while the former includes the whole eastern portion of the region with the exception of a few barren sandy or "bad land" tracts. The bunch-grass district is that to which attention is at present most particularly drawn, but it may safely be predicted that the great plains of buffalo-grass will before long claim their proper place.

THE BUNCH-GRASS DISTRICT

. . . It would be difficult to imagine a more beautiful country in a state of nature than many parts of this region. The landscape is often quite parklike, with groves along the streams or filling the retired hollows among the hills, the upper parts of which are frequently crusted with rock and dotted with spruce or pine trees. The Rocky mountains in this latitude do not hold any true glaciers such as cause the milky opacity of some of the rivers flowing from those further to the north, and the innumerable small streams which course eastward are therefore clear and blue, deriving their supply from the melting snowfields of the higher peaks throughout the summer. . . .

The surface is everywhere covered with a luxuriant tufted growth of bunch-grass from a foot to eighteen inches in height, and in summer is gay with flowers for the most part of species strange to Eastern Canada. The combination of these features may be supposed to produce a beautiful country, but there is yet one dominant feature to which I have merely alluded,

THE ROCKY MOUNTAINS

themselves. These form the back-ground to most of the landscapes; their high wild summits patched throughout the summer with perennial snow, and in autumn and winter glittering in white scarcely lined with blue or purple, giving an element of grandeur to the whole. Varying as their outlines do it would be difficult to indicate the most striking or attractive localities, . . .

THE QUESTION OF CLIMATE

is an all-important one, and though we are as yet in possession of few scientifically accurate observations, it can fortunately, in so far as stock-raising is concerned, be answered practically in a highly satisfactory manner. The summer is characterized as a whole, by dry fine weather, though there is generally in May or June a short period of copious rains. The heat is seldom excessive, and the nights almost always cool. In the autumn, after the equinoctial storms, there is usually a long period of open fine weather. As compared with that of the older parts of Canada, the winter may be characterized as mild,—extremes of cold are occasionally experienced, with fine calm weather, but these are not generally of long duration, and may, at any time in a few hours be suddenly brought to an end by the advent of the mild "Chinook wind," . . .

. . . For the purposes of the stock-raisers it suffices to know that for a great part of the winter, much of the surface is free from snow, and that it seldom or never attains a depth sufficient to prevent animals from feeding. . . .

In the great bunch-grass region there are at present less than sixty actual settlers, and including those imported by Hon. Mr. Cochrane and others this summer, probably not more than six thousand head of cattle. The occupation and utilization of this country can, therefore, scarcely be said to have been well begun, but stock-raising is not like agriculture, requiring a long time for its development, and in less than ten years all will be changed, and the plains and hills over which one may now wander for days without meeting with either game or human inhabitant, will be covered with cattle and dotted with ranches.

THE CATTLE INDUSTRY

The Cattle Companies and the 'Beef Bonanza'

97. THE ARITHMETIC OF VAST PROFIT

Alexander Begg, 'Stock Raising in the Bow River District Compared with Montana' in J. Macoun, *Manitoba and the Great North-West* (Guelph, The World Publishing Co., 1882), pp. 273, 275-8, 281.

In reference to the best way of proceeding to stock a ranch in the North-West,

I cannot do better than quote from a lecture delivered by Professor W. Brown, of the Ontario Agricultural College, Guelph, before the Farmers' Club at Markham, Ontario, 6th December, 1881. Mr. Brown had given considerable attention to the subject, as parties had been in correspondence with him as to the character and standing of the entirely new line of cattle grazing opening in the North-West territory. . . .

The capital required for establishing a ranch and carrying it on for two years was . . . considered. It included all settling down, house building, fencing of cattle station, enclosing corrals, in addition to the necessary number and variety of live stock, household maintenance, and some implements for ordinary cultivation. After this two year period some revenue should be accruing, though not necessarily so much as the annual average to be afterwards expected; because in place of selling all heifers along with the steers, the greater number would be retained to increase the breeding stock. The following is his estimate:—

Personal expenses of one examining ground and securing lease . . . $	400
Price of four yearling bulls	1,600
Price of three thoroughbred heifers	900
Price of 250 cows and heifers at $25	6,250
Price of two yoke of oxen	300
Twelve saddle horses (natives)	600
Total for live stock	10,050
Cost of dwelling house, stables, and shed	600
Fencing 100 acres as cattle station, the home property	500
Enclosing two corrals	150
Agricultural implements, tools, saddles, &c	1,000
Unenumerated	300
Total for building, fencing, &c	2,550
Household maintenance and personal expenses of three	
principals during two years	750
Wages and keep of two lads two years	2,000
Incidental expenses	250
	3,000
Rent of 2,000 acres	40
Price of 100 acres cattle station	125
	165
Total capital required	15,765

In naming 2,000 acres as the size of the ranch, Mr. Brown said, "it will be evident we are calculating circumspectly *pro tem*, whatever the future may bring about. Until grazing locations become as regular as Ontario farms are to each other, our 2,000 acres may be 20,000 so long as neighbors don't push or out feed us in the number of stock".

But the most important part of this grazing question is the estimate of annual revenue after the first two years. In doing this we will assume the non-necessity of much winter keep to breeding stock, all required being an occasional bite of hay at more severe times,—the absence of any sweeping epidemic or extensive stealing, but allowing for ordinary proportion of deaths. Entering upon possession in, say early spring of 1881, the 250 breeding cows and heifers, less deaths and non-breeding, will have dropped 550 calves by August 1883, one half of which will be two and a half years old, and their disposal then best as stores, the other half being yearlings and calves to be retained for another season's culling. Of these 275 head twenty-five heifers would be kept for filling up blanks among breeders, and 250 to be sold. In taking stock, therefore, on 1st September 1883, there should be about—

250 breeding cows and heifers.
275 yearling calves, steers, and heifers.
250 two-year-olds for sale.

———

775 head in all.
Estimate of increased value at the end of two-and-a-half years:

First draft of two-year-old steers and heifers, averaging 950 lbs.; 250 head at $23, delivered at railway	$5,750
Value of 275 yearlings and calves retained, at $12	3,300
Value of seven additional thoroughbred bulls and heifers	1,500
Gross increase from live stock	$10,550
Depreciation in value of older breeding cows and bulls, none over five years old	$400
Depreciation in value of horses, oxen, implements &c .	300
Miscellaneous debits	300
	1,000
Net increase during 2½ years	$9,550

Professor Brown concluded his lecture by saying—"Does any one doubt the existence of a market for all the flesh that this continent can produce? Speaking for ourselves and on the supposition that we do our very best with these north-western grazings, even to fitting the animals for the butcher, the 50,000,000 acres of reliable area which we have should give us 5,000,000 head of cattle yearly, which is about four billion pounds of saleable dead beef. Why this would give every Briton only 100 pounds a piece per annum. With all her apparently enormous importations of food for her 35,000,000 of souls, the United Kingdom last year could only get $140,000,000 worth of flesh (alive, dead, fresh, and salted), which distributed gave the pittance of fifteen pounds a piece. You cannot possibly overstock that market for some time."

I have also before me another estimate of the cost of establishing a ranch commencing with 250 cows for two years. The estimated capital required is put at $13,150. Gross increase from live stock given at $15,160, and the net increase during two and a half years $9,625.

Another estimate for five years, taking as a basis the same number of cows, but only selling steers and retaining heifers for breeding purposes, shows that the proceeds of the sales of steers is sufficient to pay working expenses after the second year; pay rent and six per cent interest annually on the capital invested, and leave a handsome balance in hand the end of the fifth year, when the live stock, which at the commencement was worth only about $5,000, then represented $55,000 in value.

Larger ranches will undoubtedly yield a greater revenue in proportion to the stock invested. A Montana stock-man writes: If $250,000 were invested in ten ranches and ranges, placing 2,000 head on each range, by selling the beeves as fast as they mature and all the cows as soon as they are too old to breed well and investing the receipts in young cattle, at the end of five years there would be at least 45,000 head on the ten ranges, worth at least $18 per head or $810,000. . . .

The Canadian North-West from its situation and advantages, it is evident, is destined to become the chief stockraising country in America. In a few years it will be difficult to find a vacant range in Wyoming, Nebraska, or Montana suitable or capable of sustaining 5,000 head of cattle. The Dominion of Canada, on the other hand, has "limitless" ranges waiting to be taken up and occupied.

THE CATTLE COMPANIES, 1884

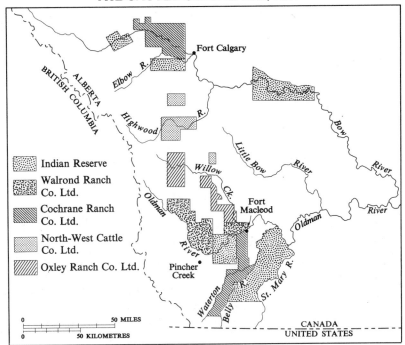

98. SENATOR COCHRANE'S PROPOSAL

PAC, Department of the Interior, Timber and Grazing Branch, vol. 10, 142709, pt 1. Subsequent documents selected from this source are cited according to the archival listing, RG15, B2a

Ottawa 17th Dec 1880

The Right Hon'ble Sir John A. MacDonald
Minister of the Interior

Sir

I have for some time past been making arrangements to establish a Stock Farm in the North West, with the view of affording emigrants settling in that part of the Dominion an opportunity of stocking their farms with improved breeds of Cattle and Horses, and also in the belief that a large foreign trade can be developed in the Export of stock from the Canadian North West.

At the present time settlers going into the new territory are compelled either to transport their stock from Ontario, at an expense usually in excess of their means, or they are forced to purchase inferior animals at high prices from the United States.

Owing to the limited number of domestic cattle in that country the government have in the past been obliged to purchase the cattle and beef supply for the police-force and for the Indians from Montana Territory. The amount thus paid to foreigners for food supplies has been very considerable.

Now as we have ample grazing grounds on the north side of the line, it is obviously in the interest of the Dominion to favour in every legitimate manner an industry that will enable the Government to purchase food supplies within its own border and allow settlers an opportunity of purchasing improved stock in the country.

In order to render the enterprise fairly remunerative and permit sales commencing within two or three years to be made, a large capital has to be invested, I propose starting with a herd of from two to three thousand animals including about seventy five thoroughbred bulls which must be imported from England. This will involve an expenditure of about $125,000.

To warrant so large an outlay, I should like to feel confident of obtaining the Lease of a sufficient area to enable me to increase the Herd to 10,000 animals and the right to purchase a sufficient acreage within the leased area for a farm on which to erect the necessary buildings for a certain amount of winter protection and forage—as I deem it prudent in testing what is largely an experiment to be provided with both food and stabling in case of an unusually severe winter.

The *thirty fifth* Section of "The Dominion Land act 1879" authorizes the Governor in Council to grant Leases of unoccupied Dominion lands for grazing purposes.

The section of country I have selected may be described as being bounded on *the east* by the 114 parallel, on *the south* by the southern branch of High River which flows east into Bow River, on *the west* by The Rocky Mountains, and on *the north* by a line twenty miles north of the 51st degree of latitude and parallel with it, shown within the red lines on the accompanying section of the North West plan. Excluding of course the land immediately around Calgary and also the Indian Reserve at Morleyville.

This area is 150 Miles from the Railway lines, and is unoccupied.

From the best information available I do not think that it has any special attractions for settlers who desire to farm as there are vast areas to the east of it that will for many years be more desirable for settlers whose object is to carry on general farming.

To enable me to commence operations during the coming spring it will be incumbent on me to make immediate arrangements. I should therefore feel obliged if you would favour me by an early reply to this application.

I have the honour
to be your obedient Servant
M. H. Cochrane

99. THE FRANTIC RUSH FOR GRAZING LEASES

PAC, RG15, B2a, vol. 20, 179180.

Windsor Hotel
Montreal
May 28th 1881

Col Dennis
Dep't Minister Interior
Ottawa

Sir

Referring to the interview I had with you yesterday, I have requested my associates in this enterprise to forward from Halifax an application for 100,000 acres of pasture lands in the N.W.T. for Ranche purpose [sic], and of course we shall expect to be placed upon the same terms [as those] who applied previous to the new regulations issued under date of May 25th and we are assured by Sir Charles [Tupper] which you were also kind enough to corroborate, that the Govt are most anxious to have the N.W. developed as fast as possible and wish to give every facility to those who are settling or investing Capital there. You inform me that it would lie with the Government to decide and they will certainly have no object in giving some half dozen gentlemen exceptional priveleges [sic] which they refuse to a half dozen others who applied a few weeks later. These later applicants would of course expect the same terms as the former, . . . We had an interview with Sir Charles Tupper on the 23 instant and upon the basis of that interview I left an active business and at considerable personal inconvenience for the North West to select a Ranche; you will see by the letter from Sir C. which I took to your department that he assured us we should be placed upon the same terms as those who had previously applied and there being no public notice nor intimation of any kind to the contrary we certainly think it would be doing us an injustice if we are not . . . [treated as the others].

Trusting that our request will be complied with and thanking you for your courtesy to me while in Ottawa

> I have the hon to be
> your Obedient servant
> J. E. Chipman

100. POLITICAL PREFERMENT AN ASSET

PAC, Macdonald Papers, A1 (d), vol. 389, 184507-510.

> 22 Simcoe St.
> Kingston

Private
November, 24, 1882

My dear Sir John

I am getting capital for my ranch company. I have $35,000 from officers in India. But a business concern cant be run entirely by soldiers and the majority of them in India—I must have one or two business men *in Canada* and I cant trust money entrusted to me to business men who have no stake or interest in the concern—Anyway you will see it is essential to have some Canadian Capitalists in a Canadian Company—Mr. Gunn M P—of Kingston offers to take stock in my Company. He is a good solid business man whatever he may be in politics [Liberal]—Business is one thing politics is another—I write to tell you believing *you* will have no sort of feeling in the matter. Rather the Contrary, [you] will feel your position strengthened when your political opponents take advantage of the measures you take for the prosperity and opening up of the Country as they are doing every day in the matter of protected manufactures. When they also benefit by the grazing lease system their mouths will be shut on that point. I thought it best to let you know frankly what I propose doing in the matter—

> Yours truly
> J. B. Strange

P.S. There is no need for you to answer this if you dont think it necessary. I will consider silence gives consent

101. THE ENVIRONMENT OF URGENCY AND EXPECTATION

Glenbow-Alberta Institute. 'Trip of Charles Edward Harris to the Canadian North West: 1882', ms. (Extract).

Halifax, N.S., March 1, 1892.
This little transcript is a short thing to write, but it took a long, tedious time in actual experience, and I must confess, in looking backward, it embraces too many hardships and anxieties, and too few recollections remaining pleasant, to make the writing interesting pastime; still there is sufficient interest about it for me, as will be seen, to induce me to go on.

In the year 1881, after the building of the Railway to Vancouver, B.C. from Winnipeg, had become a settled fact, and when the great possibilities of the Prairie Country, between Winnipeg and the Rockies, were being written up by paid agents, a few Halifax business men conceived the idea of being the first, or amongst the first to grasp, some one of the many chances then offering, at the very beginning, to reap a fortune, to say nothing of fame.

Well do I remember the sly, quiet gatherings that were held by this chosen few, in the back office of the firm, whose leading members were the promoting spirits in this scheme. The undertaking decided upon, after the most profound research and calculation, being a Cattle and Horse Ranche beneath the Rocky Mountains, where, according to written reports, the seasons were about like an Eastern summer and autumn all the year round. There was no question, at those little meetings, about the climate—that was a settled matter, and useless to discuss. It was merely a matter of taking hold promptly and with determination—the result was certain.

I was one of the select party. I was engaged in the Hardware & Ship Chandlery business, in the stone store, corner of Prince and Water Streets. The title of the firm was "Harris & Co." My business was a good appearing one, but the net profits very small. I was eager for gain and glory. This Cattle and Horse Ranche business was very enticing. I was offered the management of the business, the salary being $1200 per year, besides my living. The result was I closed my business and accepted the position. I was a partner in the undertaking also, having subscribed, and was then prepared to put in Three Thousand Dollars ($3000). I did put in this sum. My duties as then discussed were very attractive. I was to do the business, including correspondence; superintend the men; I was to have horses and men at my command, and it naturally got fixed in my mind, that I was going to have a most enviable, free sort of life: but oh! the horrible reality!

The Stockmen's Associations

102. A NEW STOCK ASSOCIATION

Macleod Gazette, April 20, 1886.

Large and Representative Meeting on Tuesday and Wednesday— The Constitution and By-laws Carefully Discussed, and Finally Adopted—The New Association Fairly Launched into Existence.

The meeting of the stockmen of Alberta for the purpose of forming a new Central Association, to take the place of the old South-western Stock Association, was called for Tuesday last at two-o'clock. At about that time a large number of stockmen assembled in the Macleod town hall. Among them were representatives from Calgary and High River. All the other districts were well represented. . . .

Mr. Garnett explained that this meeting was called by the stockmen of the country, and was the outcome of a meeting held on the 4th March, and was intended to discuss the advisability of forming a new head Association under a different constitution. He explained further concerning the object of the meeting, to the effect that the old Association had been found wanting and should lapse, and a new one be formed.

The printed constitution of the new Association was then handed around.

Mr. Garnett then moved that the meeting adjourn to seven o'clock in the evening, the old Association not to be discussed, but the formation of a new one. . . .

EVENING SESSION

The amended constitution of the new Association is published this week as a supplement to the *Gazette*, and it is not necessary, therefore, to refer to it at any length in this report. We shall simply speak of any clauses that excited important and interesting discussion. . . .

After considerable discussion, and a motion and several amendments, it was decided that the name of the new Association be the "Canadian Northwest Territories Stock Association" thus taking in a wider name than the word Alberta implied. The amendment which was moved by Mr. Pinhorne carried by only a small majority. . . .

Mr. Cottingham asked to be allowed to refer to the object of the Association, which was the protection of dealers etc. in livestock. He said there were few settlers who were not dealers in livestock. He had been told that a petition had been sent down by stockmen, asking the government to protect them against settlers. One cow entitled a man to become a member of the Association, and to the protection it afforded. He asked for the distinction between a stockman and a settler.

It was explained that the article on qualification would answer that question.

Discussion then followed as to the number of delegates which should be sent from each district to the annual meeting, and as to whether each district should send the same number of delegates, or in proportion to the cattle owned.

A motion was made to have two delegates from each district, to hold office for one year.

An amendment making it three was carried.

The question of electing delegates aroused much discussion. Mr. Pinhorne proposed that the district vote on delegates according to the number of cattle owned, in the same ratio as the old sliding scale.

Mr. Inderwick objected to this on the ground that this was the very thing that split up the old Association. This was simply a copy of the old Association laws, and was far removed from the idea of the meeting of the 4th of March. He thought what Mr. Pinhorne proposed was entirely different from the views expressed at the last meeting. He thought Mr. Pinhorne wanted to vote the small men down.

Mr. Frields thought that if members were assessed according to the number of cattle owned, they should vote according to the same.

Mr. Inderwick thought that, by the new rules the tax would be regulated by the districts. He contended that under the plan proposed the men who represented companies would have the pull over men who had their all invested. The representatives of large companies would run the country.

Mr. Lyndon thought the big companies would be able to elect their own men as delegates.

Mr. Cottingham could not see the use of the small men joining the Association if Mr. Pinhorne's motion carried. In such a case it would be better for the large owners to form an Association, and let the small owners run a show of their own.

Mr. McCaul asked to be allowed, as having had something to do with drawing up the constitution of the old Association, to refer to this matter. He contended that Mr. Pinhorne's suggestion was a thoroughly good one. It was a compromise basis, and one which the small men had before fallen in with. He said it was not the rock upon which the old S.W.S. Association had split, but the only tie that bound them together. He thought it was absurd to propose that the man with 5,000 cattle could be out voted by the man with 100 head. The question was how to arrange a compromise basis on which the two could meet. When the old Association was formed, delegates from the large and small men had met, and framed the clause which contained the sliding scale. . . .

Mr. Pace intimated that he was a Conservative to the backbone, but there was no use in getting up Conservative ideas. They must all have the same voice whether they owned ten cattle or 10,000. There was no good in two or three getting together and thinking that they were going to run the world. Why get up a paltry meeting like this—you can't do it—(cries of order).

The chairman explained that many of the old rules had been found beneficial to the stockmen of the country, and as far as possible the new constitution had been taken from the old one. The main alteration was the government by delegates, and this was to facilitate matters. . . .

Mr. Pinhorne's motion was then put, and carried by a considerable majority.

103. CONSTITUTION OF THE CANADIAN NORTHWEST TERRITORIES STOCK ASSOCIATION

Macleod Gazette, Supplement, April 20, 1886. (Extracts).

ARTICLE I—NAME

This Association shall be known as the Canadian Northwest Territories Stock Association with headquarters at Macleod.

ARTICLE II—OBJECT

The object of this Association shall be the advancement and protection of the interests of stockmen and dealers in live stock within the Northwest Territories. . . .

ARTICLE IV—OFFICERS AND THEIR DUTIES

(a) The affairs of this Association shall be controlled and managed by an executive committee consisting of twelve members, viz., three from each of the above districts, [Calgary, High River, Willow Creek, Pincher Creek] who shall be appointed for one year. The said committee shall elect their own officers, who shall consist of a president, two vice presidents and a secretary-treasurer. If the committee desire to appoint as secretary-treasurer any person not a member of the committee, the said person shall be eligible to serve but shall not have a vote at any meetings of the committee. . . .

ARTICLE V—MEETINGS
Annual Meetings

(a) The annual meeting of the Executive Committee shall be held at Macleod on such day as may be appointed by the President between the 15th day of April and the 15th day of May inclusive. Notice of such meeting shall be sent by the Secretary of the Association to the Secretary of each District at least six weeks before such meeting shall take place, and each District shall then proceed to elect members for the Committee. In voting at all district meetings each stock owner shall be entitled to vote in proportion to the number of stock he owns in accordance with the following scale:

One vote for 500 head and under.
Two votes for 500 to 1,000 head.
Three votes for   1,000 to   2,000 head.

Four votes for   3,000 to   4,000 head.
Five votes for   5,000 to   8,000 head.
Six votes for   8,000 to 12,000 head.
Seven votes for 12,000 to 17,000 head.

Qualifications
(a) Any person, or persons, *bona fide* engaged in the business of raising, breeding or dealing in horses or cattle in the Northwest Territories shall be eligible for membership. . . .

Proposal and Election of Candidates
(c) Any other person desiring to become a member of the Association must be proposed by a member from the district in which he resides at the annual meeting; notice in writing of such proposal having first been handed in to the Secretary-Treasurer. An open vote shall then be taken on such application. Two adverse votes shall reject.

Agreement of Members
(d) Every member shall, immediately on becoming a member of the Association, sign the roll of members, and an agreement on behalf of himself and his employees to keep and observe the by-laws and resolutions of the Association.

Membership to be Personal
(e) Membership shall be personal. No firm, as such, shall be admitted, but any number of partners, also the manager, or authorized agent of any ranche may become members by election. These shall only be entitled to cast collectively the number of votes to which the number of stock would entitle one owner according to the sliding scale adopted. . . .

Assessments
(a) The executive committee shall have power to levy an assessment as often as may be required, on members of the Association, in proportion to the number of live stock owned by its members. Such assessment shall be due forthwith after the committee shall have declared the same. The limit of assessment for any one year shall be two cents per head on the stock owned by each member of the Association.

Fines and Penalties
(b) The committee shall have power to affix such fine or penalty to the infringement of any of their by-laws or regulations as may be deemed expedient, and any member neglecting or refusing to pay such penalty before the

next annual meeting after the same shall have been declared, shall cease to be a member of the Association, but shall not, on this account only, be deemed ineligible for re-election. . . .

By-Laws
Prairie Fires

Article 1—That in case of a prairie fire it shall be incumbent upon every member of this Association, resident within a distance of fifteen miles from the starting point or place where the fire may be burning, or any member receiving notification that his assistance is required, to immediately turn out to such fire and shall also, with all possible haste, inform his nearest neighbors of the fact of the fire, and render all assistance in his power towards extinguishing it. Any member neglecting to observe the above provision shall be liable to a fine not exceeding ($50) fifty dollars, by and in the descretion [sic] of the committee, unless such member shall give satisfactory reasons to the committee for such neglect.

Rewards

Article 2—Any person giving such information as will lead to the conviction of anyone setting fire to the prairie, or killing or stealing cattle or horses, shall be entitled to a reward of $100, to be paid from the funds of the General Association.

List of Calves

Article 3—That the round up captain of each district do send to the secretary of the Association a list of all calves branded with brands and marks that do not belong to the district, and the Secretary shall advertise the same in four issues of a newspaper published at Macleod and Calgary. . . .

Mavericks

Article 5—All mavericks shall be sold by the foreman of the district in which they are found, and the proceeds shall be paid to the secretary of the district.

Use of Corrals

Article 6—No person shall be allowed to join the round-up or use any corrals belonging to any district of the Association except members of the Association and persons in their employ.

Driving Cattle

Article 7—Any member of the Association desiring to brand or drive cattle out of any district at any other time than during the Spring and Fall round-ups, shall give notification before starting out to two members of the Association in the vicinity of where such cattle are. . . .

104. THE ASSOCIATION AS THE POLITICAL ARM
OF THE CATTLEMEN

PAC, RG15, B2A, vol. 159, 141376, pt 1.

To the Hon.   Macleod, December 3rd, 1886.
The Minister of the Interior,
Ottawa,

At a specially convened meeting of the Canadian North-west Territories Stock Association, held at Macleod on the 27th of November, 1886, it was unanimously resolved that the following memorial be forwarded to the Hon. the Minister of the Interior:

1. That after five years experience of the Province of Alberta as a stock country, we are of opinion that unless immediate measures be taken for the protection of the country it will assuredly be rendered valueless within the next five years for that purpose, from the same causes that have destroyed the stock ranges of the adjoining American states with which we are familiar.

2. The cause of this deterioration of the southern ranges, and of the consequent removal of cattle has been the absence of all effectual control by the Government for regulating the proportion of stock to be placed on the different ranges. The capacity of the stock ranges of Alberta is limited only by the amount of stock which the winter range proper can safely carry without deterioration on the average of years. This area, from experience of the country at present stocked, does not probably amount to more than one third of the whole, which is further diminished by the large allowance which must be made for the destruction caused by prairie fires and we are of opinion that an Order in Council should forthwith be put in force, prohibiting any person or persons from driving in cattle unless possessed of a lease or other lands, and then only in the proportion of one animal to every thirty acres.

3. This Association begs to express its appreciation of and thanks for the protection to the stock-raising industry of Alberta, afforded by imposing the duty on cattle, and would respectfully petition that the same be not again removed. As our export trade to the European markets is seriously threatened by recent outbreak of disease in districts from which cattle may be driven to this country, we also respectfully suggest that the quarantine regulations recently put in force be continued so long as any danger exists. British Columbia and Ontario can now supply by the Canadian Pacific Railway healthy breeding stock in sufficient quantities.

4. We would also suggest that the time has arrived when the Government should take early action with regard to leaseholders. We are aware that leases have been obtained in districts entirely unsuited for stock ranges, with the object of driving large herds of cattle into the country, which cattle must necessarily, in order to survive the winter, find their way to ranges already leased to us. It is of immediate importance to us that we should know whether

the Government are prepared to confirm us in the peaceable possession of the privileges that they have granted us, or permit others to usurp the privileges for which they have not paid, and plead the authority of the Government in justification. The efforts of individuals to resist these unfair encroachments upon their legal rights have produced elsewhere encounters and consequences most prejudicial to the well-being of the community, and in the long run disastrous to the industry itself.

5. It is understood, though not distinctly enacted, that leaseholders should reside upon their own leases. We consider that it cannot be too soon officially announced that no man has a right to build his ranch on another man's lease, without his consent.

6. We desire again to call the attention of the Department to previous memorials against permitting sheep on the cattle ranges represented by this Association, as there is sufficient land in the country for both industries, without clashing.

7. A stringent enactment against any person, whether leaseholder or settler, securing to himself the exclusive right to any open water on the ranges should, in our opinion, be at once put in force. We would on this point, refer you to the admirable report on this subject by Mr. Pearce, on page 19, Part 1 of the Annual Report of 1885 to the Department of the Interior. The gradual enclosure of water is annually rendering valueless for stock purposes large tracts of country.

8. We desire to submit this memorial to the favorable consideration of the Government, and to request the honor of an early reply to the same.

Your memorialists represent all the practical stock owners of this country, men who have built up this important and growing industry, and whose practical knowledge and experience they are anxious to place at the disposal of the Government. They are conscious that, in so doing, they are contributing not only to the protection of an important industry, but are taking a material part in preserving to Canada the last and best stock range on the Continent, the loss of which would be recognized, when too late, as a national disaster.

All of which is respectfully submitted.

(sgd.) C. E. D. Wood,
Sec'y C.N.W.T. Stock Association.

105. THE ASSOCIATION AS REGIONAL ADMINISTRATOR OF THE CATTLE INDUSTRY

Glenbow-Alberta Institute, Western Stock Growers' Association Papers, Extracts from Minutes.

CONTROL OF DISEASE

Moved by Kettles—Seconded by Duthie

That the Secretary and Southern Managers draw up a circular and forward

it to all members informing them of the steps required by the Government to be taken this year for the eradification of mange. All animals showing the slightest suspicion of mange must be gathered and dipped under the supervision of a Government Inspector, being taken up on the Spring Round up. The District Association [should] instruct their Captains of Round-ups to gather every suspicious animal, irrespective of ownership, they find on the range. It is recommended that so far as possible all animals whether apparently affected or not be dipped at least once during the year.
Carried. [13 April 1900]

COMPENSATION FOR RANGE CATTLE KILLED BY PASSING TRAINS

Moved by Cochrane—Seconded by Wylie

That the C.P.R. be requested to amend the schedule of values of cattle upon which compensation is reckoned, to the following:

	Value	Com.
Steers, 4 years and up	50	25
Steers, 3 years and up	45	22.50
Steers, 2 years and up	30	15
Steers, 1 year and up	20	10
Cows 3 years and up	35	17.50
Cows 2 years and up	30	15
Cows 1 year and up	20	10

Carried. [13 April 1900]

Moved by A. P. McDonald—Seconded by C. Kettles

That Messrs Andrews and Springett be a committee to wait upon Mr. Whyte of the C.P.R., for the purpose of discussing the present unsatisfactory arrangements as regards the compensation paid by the Railway Company for cattle killed on the track. That the expenses of the deputation be paid together with $2.00 per diem while so engaged. And in the event of no satisfaction being secured from Mr. Whyte that the c'tee be authorized to place the whole matter in the hands of Messrs Oliver and Scott, M.P.'s and ask their assistance.
Carried. [9 January 1901]

HOMESTEAD APPLICATIONS

Moved by Jas. Hargrave—Seconded by R. D. Porter

That in the event of applications for Homestead or Purchase of land contained in any grazing lease, that notice of same be given to the Lessee with the option of purchase of said lands.
Carried. [11 April 1901]

LEASES

Moved by F. G. Forster—Seconded by R. C. Becker.

That the Western Stock Grower's Ass'n communicate with the Dep't of the

Interior asking that it be made compulsory to state in the official notices of applications for grazing lands posted up in Post Offices, . . . whether the lease applied for is for cattle, horses or sheep or for what actual grazing purposes. Carried. [11 April 1901]

MAVERICKS

Moved by G. Lane—Seconded by H. Harris.

That all badly blotched and unbranded cattle and horses [the ownership of] which are not proven be gathered and sold at public auction by the captains of the Roundup or Stock Inspector of each district, and the proceeds be turned into the Treasury of the Western Stock Grower's Ass'n. If ownership can be proven to the satisfaction of the Association the money, to be refunded. Carried. [11 April 1901]

STOCK FACILITIES

Moved by J. Hargrave—Seconded by A. Middleton.

That sufficient land for grazing and sufficient water for Stock Watering purposes be reserved in the immediate vicinity of Dunmore Junction and Walsh Stock Yards on the C.P.R.

Carried. [11 April 1901]

(The actual locality required to be reserved was instructed to be furnished [by] the Secretary)

WOLF BOUNTY

Moved by F.G. Forster—Seconded by A.R. Springett

That the Stock Ass'n memorialize the Dominion Government asking that a portion, say 25% of the amount of revenue raised through the rental of grazing leases in the Northwest, be annually returned to the ranchers through the Western Stock Grower's Ass'n for the purpose of expenditure in payment of wolf and coyote bounties.

Carried. [11 April 1901]

STOCK INSPECTION

The Committee appointed to consider desirable amendments to the Stock Inspection Ordinance reported as follows:—

We recommend that the Stock Inspection Ordinance be amended in the following particulars.

1st. That no butcher or his employee be eligible for employment as a Stock Inspector.

2nd. That the following section be inserted. Every person other than a butcher who slaughters any head of cattle for Beef shall exhibit the hide of such animal at the time and place the beef is offered for sale, and before such beef is offered for sale the hide shall be punched and a record of the brands, if any, thereon made by an Inspector of Stock.

The report was adopted on motion of J.H.G. Bray, seconded by A.B. Mc-Donald.
[11 April 1901].

Moved by F.W. Godsal—Moved by D. Warnock
That a memorial be sent to the Gov't. setting forth our appreciation of the services of the N.W.M.P. and their necessity in this country, and that they be maintained at their full strength.
Carried. [11 April 1901]

J.H.G. Bray—R. Duthie
That a vote of thanks be tendered the c.p.r. for the reduction granted to Delegates of this Ass'n while attending this meeting. Also for their courtesy in providing a Pass to the Ass'n Inspector.
Carried. [11 April 1901]

Problems of Collective Concern

106. ENCROACHMENT OF AMERICAN STOCKMEN

PAC, RG15, B2a, vol. 159.

Alberta N.W.T.
To the Hon'ble   Oct. 21st, 1886.
The Minister of the Interior,
Ottawa.
Sir,

At the annual "Round up" gathering of the Stockmen of Alberta just concluded, the following points were the subject of earnest discussion—and it was suggested that the responsible heads of the various Ranches in this district, should respectfully solicit your opinion on the matters which are likely to seriously affect in the immediate future the prosperity of the smaller stockowners (the majority) in this district.

It is well known that owing to overstocking and the absence of official Stock-laws the adjoining territories of Wyoming, Montana, and Oregon are now practically ruined, and the owners there are using every endeavor, to save themselves by driving their stock into our country. The value of beef cattle has fallen in the five years that this country has been stocked, from $80 to $40. In five years more this country too will be overstocked and ruined unless immediate precautions are taken. All the additional stock, both horses and cattle required for this country, can now be obtained by C.P.R. Railway in sufficient quantity and of superior quality from our own provinces of British Columbia and Ontario. We have always set our face against the American system of attempting to govern our stock country by force of irregular combinations, and rely implicitly on constitutional measures.

We therefore desire most respectfully to appeal to you in the interests of the weak against the strong of the small Canadian stockmen against the large American stockmen and suggest as a first practical measure an enactment by the Government as follows:—

1. That no more stock be allowed to be brought over the lines [sic] without
   1. a rigorous veterinary inspection
   2. a payment of duty at least equivalent to that by which the American[s] exclude us from the Chicago markets.
2. An enactment for the protection of the limited stock country that Canada possess. That no leaseholder be permitted to put on more than 1000 head of stock per township, provisionally to be increased hereafter when it is proved that the country can carry more.
3. That you will appoint an officer to confer with the Alberta Stock Association—comprising all the Canadian stockowners on matters of vital interest to the country, on which they alone can supply the necessary practical information.

I have the honor to remain,

Sir, Your humble servant,
William Ed. Cochrane.
Manager of The Little Bow Cattle Co.,
Mosquito Creek, Alberta.

107. MAVERICKS

PAC, Clifford Sifton Papers, MG27, II, D15.

Pincher Creek
Alberta NWT
May 10th 1897

F. Oliver Esq. M.P.
Sir,

I notice that at the last Annual Meeting of the Western Stock Growers Association that it was resolved to petition the Dominion Govt. asking that "the ownership of mavericks be vested in the Stock Growers Association" [with the revenue gained from their sale going into the association's coffers to be expended for the general benefit of all.] Undoubtedly the matter of mavericks [unbranded cattle whose ownership is uncertain] needs some regulations but this proposal, if carried out, will cause endless trouble and gross injustice. Settlers with small bunches of cattle and rangers who look after their cattle closely, do not belong to this Ass'n. and consequently, any calf missed by them or temporally [sic] separated from its cow, accidentally or otherwise, will be scooped up by this Association, many members of which are noted for a keen eye for mavericks. In the spring and fall round ups they drive their herd of range cattle thro' a bunch of gentle stock, picking up everything as they go along and if one does not look out sharply his calves are likely to become mavericks, and if he does not belong to this Association and this proposal becomes law, are hopelessly lost to him.

It is useless for us to expect you to look after these things unless we keep you posted on both sides of the question, hence this dispatch. As the Minister of the Interior will probably also receive the beforementioned petition kindly see that he is placed in possession of these facts also.

Yours very truly,
Arthur Edgar Cox

108. SHEEPMEN

Glenbow-Alberta Institute, Medicine Hat Stock Growers' Association, Microfilm Minutes, 'Copy of Memorial forwarded to the Minister of the Interior re: Foreign Sheep Questions', May 1897, pp. 51-60.

Medicine Hat
May 15/1897

To The Honourable The Minister of the Interior

Ottawa

Sir:

The Petition of the undersigned Members of the Stock Growers' Association of Medicine Hat, The Ranche Companies and Individual Ranchers the owners of cattle and Horses in this district of Western Assinaboia Representing in plant and stock a Capital of $900000 Dollars Humbly Sheweth.

That your petitioners having read in the Public Press and heard from other Sources, That it is the intention of Certain Sheep-Owners in the adjoining State of Montana U.S.A. to move their Flocks and Herds into this district at an early date, deem it expedient to represent to You the justice of their Action in view of the following facts.

That in this district of Western Assinaboia the-The [sic] Aforesaid amount of Capital has been invested in stock and plant and that the Cattle and Horses the property of the several Ranche Companies and Individual Ranchers are roaming at large over the Cattle Ranges in this district.

That your petitioners desire to express their firm Conviction that its [sic] derogatory to the interests of the business of Cattle Growing that Sheep should be permitted to range on or in the vicinity of the Cattle Ranges. That it is essential to the success of the Cattle business that Cattle should be allowed a Wide and free range. And that the introduction of Foreign Sheep into this stock District would be most disastrous to the Cattle Interests.

That Your petitioners represent all the practical Stock Owners of this district. Men who have built up an important and rapidly growing Industry. And whose practical knowledge and experience they are anxious to place at the disposal of the Govt. They are anxious that in so doing they are contributing not only to the protection of an important industry, but are taking a material part in preserving to Canada one of the best Stock Ranges on the Continent. The loss of which when too late would be recognized as a National disaster.

That it is the firm conviction of your petitioners that the influx of Montana Sheep into this district will prove very detrimental to the cattle industry in various ways. First it is known to your petitioners that the Sheep Men have already selected for Sheep Camps some of the finest Springs on these ranges within the boundaries of the district covered by the Medicine Hat Stock Growers' Association (A District set forth in the Ordinance of Incorporation of the Western Stock Growers' Association and of which aforesaid Association this District forms a Component part) That once these Watering Places are occupied by Sheep Men with their Herds, Corralls, Tents & Dogs, No cattle will approach them. And setting aside the close cropping and contamination of the Ranges, the loss of the water alone will prove disastrous to the now Extensive industry of Cattle Growing.

That your petitioners would try to call your Attention to the Many acts of "Lawlessness" and "Violence" that have taken place in the last few years, in the adjoining States of Montana and Wyoming in consequence of the encroachments of Sheep Men on the Cattle Ranges and would Respectfully represent that there is plenty of land in this Country for both Industries without Clashing.

And Your petitioners would therefore pray That all Sheep be prohibited from coming into the district within the Boundaries of the Stock Growers' Association of Medicine Hat.

By Order
J.H.G. Bray
Secretary S.G. Assn
Medicine Hat

THE RANGE-CATTLE INDUSTRY AND THE NORTH WEST MOUNTED POLICE

109. PATROLS AND OUTPOSTS

Canada, *Sessional Papers*, no. 15, Report of the Commissioner of the North West Mounted Police, 1894, Appendix J., Annual Report of Inspector Z.T. Wood, 'E' Division, Calgary, p. 146.

The district has been thoroughly patrolled during the past year. Not only is a flying patrol sent out from the division headquarters daily, but from each of the eleven detachments men start out every day to ride over the adjacent country and visit the settlers. Special patrols have also been sent out to the Rosebud and Red Deer Rivers.

In October last special patrols were asked for by the Indian Department to visit the Sarcee Reserve, and in accordance with instructions from you, the reserve is patrolled now at least three times each week.

In May last, owing to complaints about the number of Indians wandering about the neighbourhood, a constable was stationed at the Messrs. Ings' ranch, on the north fork of High River, 25 miles west of the Calgary and Edmonton Railway (Macleod branch); in October it became necessary to send an additional man to this point owing to complaints of cattle killing by the Indians. The latter gather in the vicinity to hunt, and when sport is poor, are given to killing a stray steer or two for food. Owing to the broken nature of the country, right in the foot hills of the Rockies, it is impossible to catch the guilty parties.

110. INDIANS KILLING CATTLE

Canada, *Sessional Papers*, no. 17, Report of the Commissioner of the North West Mounted Police, 1888, Appendix F, Annual Report of Superintendent R.B. Deane, 'K' Division, Lethbridge, pp. 64-5.

On the 15th October another complaint was made by the St. Louis and Cypress Cattle Companies' ranchmen that Indians had killed some of their cattle, and I sent out Sergeant Walsh and a party to arrest the offenders, if possible.

On his return Sergeant Walsh reported—

"I went with two men of the Cypress Cattle Company's ranch to where a cow had been killed, as they believed, by Indians. I saw the carcase of the animal, which was lying on the edge of the river. The hide had been stripped off and carried away, and the meat had been stripped off the bones, leaving nothing but the skeleton: part of the heart was stuck upon one of the horns.

The employees of the ranche returned home and I crossed the Belly River, and went in the direction where I supposed the Indians were camped. I followed the river bank for about two miles and could see if any Indians were camped by the river. I came to a big coulee which runs out from the river for about half a mile, and as we could not cross it I followed it up from the river and crossed at its head. I saw a waggon [sic] trail, which I directed two of the party to follow; and I and another man went in the direction of the river and looked in coulees and river bottoms, but could not see any trace of Indians. I came upon a place where they had been camped a few days previous, as I thought by the look of the camp. I did not find any traces of meat or any part of the hide round the camp. There were lots of traces of antelope meat, by the numerous heads which I saw lying on the prairie. I followed the Belly River for twenty-five miles down to the mouth of the Big Bow River, and searched all the coulees and river bottoms where I thought they would camp. I then camped for the night and proceeded in the direction of the Galt railroad next morning".

A patrol which, during the past few days has been round the above mentioned neighborhood and has made exhaustive enquiries, reports that no Indians have been seen there for a month.

The strength of my division did not permit of it this summer, but next year it would be advisable to station a small outpost at or near the mouth of the Little Bow, so as to intercept Indians moving off their reserve into the ranges occupied by the cattle in question.

111. CATTLE THEFT

Canada, *Sessional Papers*, no. 28, Report of the Commissioner of the North West Mounted Police, 1905, Appendix C, Report of Superintendent, P.C.H. Primrose, 'D' Division, Fort Macleod, p. 52.

John Knowles, a small rancher, on Willow Creek, west of Stavely, was charged on the information of his accomplice, Daniel Dixon, who had been his hired man, with stealing one calf, the property of W. R. Hull. This case developed the fact that this year Knowles' cows were most prolific, as 32 cows had 68 calves, but the great difficulty was to prove who owned the calves which had been stolen. Knowles was running a dairy farm near Greenwood, B.C., and moved to High River in the fall of 1901, and in the spring of 1902 removed to Willow Creek, not far from the headquarters of the Oxley ranch, and it does not speak well for the observing powers of the cow-men that they did not discover with what wonderful strides this man's bunch of cattle was increasing. Daniel Dixon pleaded guilty, and was sentenced to two years at Stony Mountain, and Knowles, upon conviction, was given ten years at the same place.

112. PRAIRIE FIRES

Canada, *Sessional Papers*, no. 15, Report of the Commissioner of the North West Mounted Police, 1892, Appendix E, Report of Superintendent, R.B. Deane, 'K' Division, Lethbridge, pp. 88-9.

We have suffered, as is always to be expected, from the ever-recurring epidemic of prairie fire, but the immediate neighbourhood of Lethbridge has been comparatively free. Most of the fires were started at a great distance from here, entailing long rides to reach them, and it was impossible to trace their origin.

On the 13th December, 1891, a large fire was started at the head of Middle Coulee, about 40 miles from here, and burnt over a large tract of country. A party was sent out from here, but the detachment from St. Mary's had before their arrival put it out on this side, and the Milk River Ridge detachment put it out on the other. The men from St. Mary's undoubtedly saved J. Pearce's ranche from destruction.

On the 22nd April, about mid-day, a prairie fire started on the other side of the Belly River about five or six miles from here, and Sergeant Duchesnay with a party was sent to put it out. Judging that they were not making sufficient headway, about 3.30 P.M. I took out another party and extinguished the fire in some coulees near the river where it had become well established in brush and long grass. About 6 P.M. Staff Sergeant Duchesnay, who had been working at the other end, reported that in consequence of the high wind he could not control the fire; so I sent Sergeant Major Macdonell with a third party to head it off and prevent its crossing the Macleod trail, the danger being that it might extend into the Little Bow country. This party succeeded in stopping the fire and returned to barracks about 10.30 P.M. This fire was due to the negligence of a farmer, whose hired man was prosecuted and fined $25 under the ordinance.

On the 21st July a prairie fire was started by the south-bound train, and a party from here suppressed it after about four hours' work.

At this time, owing to the long drought, the grass had become as dry as tinder, and on the 21st July a disastrous fire broke out and burnt furiously during the 22nd and 23rd over the country lying between the Little Bow and Big Bow rivers. It is supposed to have started in the neighbourhood of Blackfoot Crossing. The Little Bow detachment worked at it, but it was so far from here that we knew nothing about it until it was over.

Fortunately the round-up party was in the vicinity. Mr. Harris, manager of the Circle Ranche, slaughtered no less than fourteen beasts, cut them in halves and "snaked" the carcases along. He said that twenty-eight of his horses had had their feet badly burned—that the ground itself was literally on fire; it was so dry that the roots of the grass held the fire after the blade had been consumed and a breath of air would fan it into a flame, so that it was impossible to tell when the fire was out. A vast deal of extra trouble was caused in this manner, by the fire breaking out afresh in places where it had apparently been extinguished.

113. BOUNDARY PATROL

PAC, RG18, A1, vol. 261, F823. F. White, Comptroller to the Minister of the Interior.

Ottawa, 30th November, 1895.
Memo respecting the drifting of cattle across the boundary line in the N.W. Territories.

The boundary line is marked by mounds of stone which were placed by the International Boundary Commission more than 20 years ago. Many of them have become obliterated either by the stones having been scattered or by the grass having grown over them.

It is impossible to prevent Canadian cattle drifting south, or U.S. cattle drifting north. Until recent years no inconvenience resulted from this, the cattlemen of the two countries mutually interchanging the drifted cattle on the occasion of their periodical round-up.

The enforcement of quarantine on the Canadian side of the line created a new condition of affairs, as it necessitated not only the holding in quarantine for 90 days of U.S. cattle coming permanently into Canada, but also the preventing of U.S. cattle drifting north and becoming mixed with those in quarantine, or with those belonging to Canadian Ranches.

The Mounted Police have done their best to enforce the quarantine regulations, and to keep U.S. cattle south of the line, involving great wear and tear of horse flesh and unceasing efforts on the part of the men, but it has been found impossible to effectively perform this service. The difficulties have been much added to by an enormous increase in the number of U.S. cattle immediately south of the boundary line, the consequent eating off of the U.S. pasturage, and the natural tendency of the cattle to drift north where pasturage is better and water abundant. This tendency on the part of the cattle has undoubtedly been encouraged by U.S. Ranchers, who, while not actually driving them across the frontier, stand on American territory and see them drift over. The Police drive them back, but only to see them return again next day.

In the hope of establishing a legal precedent, proceedings were taken against certain men for illegally bringing cattle into Canadian territory. The case was tried by the late Judge Macleod, who gave his opinion that a man might drive cattle to within an inch of the boundary line provided he did not drive them over it. The effect of this decision has been that U.S. Ranchers watch their cattle crossing the line and then, if brought to time by the Police, plead that they were not driven, but strayed, into Canadian territory.

During the past season bands of U.S. cattle, some of them 50 miles within Canadian territory, have been rounded up and held subject to the decision of the Customs authorities, with the result that the owners have been allowed to take them south on paying the costs of rounding-up and herding.

I have no hesitation in saying that it is impossible, except at an expense which would be prohibitory, to prevent the thousands of U.S. cattle in Montana from drifting north, and that owing to the superior character of Canadian territory for ranching purposes the difficulties will increase from year to year.

The question of brands is also one which calls for consideration. One large Ranching Company which owns cattle on both sides of the boundary line has a common brand, and it is not possible for the Police patrols along the frontier to distinguish the cattle of this Company which belong to the Canadian from those which belong to the U.S. side. The attention of the Department of Agriculture was called to this some time ago.

Under the existing state of affairs there is also danger, if the Canadian laws and regulations are strictly enforced, of reprisals on the part of the U.S. Ranchers whose cattle are seized on Canadian territory, and the arousing of ill feeling between the cattlemen of the two countries.

Having pointed out the difficulties, it is necessary to submit suggestions for the remedy thereof.

It has been suggested that two Townships, viz:—12 miles deep, along this frontier should be declared neutral territory on which cattle shall not be allowed to pasture.

This I am afraid would not work satisfactorily. The existence of such a reserve, and the consequent preservation of the grass thereon, would cause a rush of cattle at certain seasons of the year which no force could keep back.

If a private individual owns or controls a valuable area of territory which he desires to preserve for his own use, he fences it in, and if the Canadian ranching country is to be preserved for Canadian cattle, and the Revenue of the country is to be protected by preventing the intrusion of live stock without the payment of duties, the only practical and efficient course would be to erect a substantial fence along about 250 miles of the boundary. Indirectly, this would pay for itself in a few years.

The Blood Indians have not made much progress in agricultural pursuits, but they have developed considerably as freighters and in getting out logs and timber for the erection of buildings on their Reserve, and I would suggest that they be employed to get out the fence posts and distribute them along the frontier, the construction of the fence being done, as far as possible, by Indian labour under the supervision of white men. Strong gates could be placed wherever the trails cross the boundary, and at such other places as might be deemed necessary. Merchandise and live stock coming from the United States would then be required to enter at one of these gates, and if found on the north side of the fence without proper entry having been made, would be subject to seizure. Police would patrol this boundary fence, one man doing the work of at least five under existing circumstances.

Respectfully submitted.
sgd. Fred. White
Comptroller.

114. A TESTIMONIAL FROM THE INDUSTRY

Glenbow-Alberta Institute, Western Stock Growers' Association Papers, Minutes, December 7, 1905.

Moved by A.J. MacLean—Seconded by A. Gordon

Be it resolved that this Association, by its Executive Committee, strongly urges upon the Dominion Government the vital necessity existing for the continuance of the R.N.W.M. Police in this country. We desire to point out that without the protection of this body of men, the ranching Industry would suffer in many ways. Amongst the many now settling in the North West are some of the worst criminals that the country has known, as the records of the Courts, for the past two or three years will show. Another phase of the matter is this: that the small farmers will persist in burning around their places and the fires frequently get out of control and burn large tracts of country, which is most ruinous to the stock growing Industry, and it is only through the vigilance of the Police that we can carry on our business. We realize more and more that without the Police the stock industry would be in a very critical condition. We therefore strongly urge upon your Government the necessity there is for the continuance, and if possible the increase of the R.N.W.M.P.

Carried.

SEMI-ARID LANDS: THE STRUGGLE FOR CONTROL

The Cattlemen

115. HARASSMENT FROM WOULD-BE SETTLERS

PAC, RG15, B2a, vol. 5, no. 137261, pt 1.

Thos. White   157 St. James Street,
Minister of the Interior,   Montreal, 26 May 1887
Ottawa.

In compliance with [the] desire expressed by you at the interview which I had with you yesterday, along with Senator Cochrane, relative to the encroachments by squatters upon the British American Ranche Compys. lease, I beg to annex extracts from [a] letter lately received from the Company's Manager, which fully explains the trouble which threatens the existence of this Company.

As things now appear, continued operations in the Horse & Sheep Ranching business will be rendered impossible, unless some guarantee is given of peaceable possession of a definite tract of land. They (the Compy) must feel that they will be undisturbed not only as to their buildings and grazing lands, but that their necessary water frontage, and hay lands, to which they trust for their winter feed will be secured to them. The company has already laid out large amounts upon improvements and more are required. Upon their Range they now have one thousand horses, and about ten thousand sheep.

I think I need hardly inform you, that a large portion of the two Townships lately relinquished by this Company at the request of the Government, and lying between their present lease and Calgary, are yet unsettled. There is therefore no excuse for *bona fide* settlers going out of their way to harass Ranchemen, and practically destroying that industry, by robbing them of the means of keeping their stock alive during winter—it being upon the hay lands they choose for squatting.—

Before incurring any further expenditure the Directors will anxiously await your reply, stating what protection this company may expect from the Govt. and for how long a time they may expect to occupy their lease undisturbed.

I am,
Sir,
Your Obedt. Servt.
J.M. Browning,
Sec. Treas.

Extracts from letter addressed to the Company from their *manager of the Ranche* dated 14, May 87.

"We are having a great deal of trouble with new settlers coming in on the lease where we absolutely cannot have them. I am serving notices upon all of them so that we can take legal action against them. Can you let me know what the exact rights of the Company are in regard to settlers? Should we put the case of any one refusing to go off, in the hands of our attorneys here, or evict the men forcibly ourselves—they are coming in and trying to put up buildings etc., quite close to the horse camp and all over our hay grounds there, which we cannot give up. We shall not be able to cut any hay for the horses if they are allowed to come in. . . .

Morrison was out among some of the settlers the other day, pretending to be looking for land—he asked one man if the B.A.R. Co'y would not turn him off if he settled on their lease and the fellow's answer was "Oh, just show them a box of matches and they will leave you alone" and then proceeded to tell how he was on one of the Townships lately thrown open, but if he had not gotten his way before long he would have done some burning. This shows what kind of fellows they are. I believe that many of them are not bona fide settlers at all, but are coming on just to make a row, or are being put up to it by someone"

Copy of notice served on squatters.

"I hereby give you notice that you are a trespasser on the lands leased by the British American Ranche Compy. Ltd.—and that you are notified to leave said lands without delay and that if you make any improvements on said lands, you do so at your own risk.

(Signed) E.B.C.

for B.A.R. Coy.

116. SQUATTERS ON THE LEASEHOLDS

PAC, RG15, B2a, vol. 5, no. 137261, pt 1.
The Bow River Horse Ranch Co.

Cochrane, Alta. March 15th 1889

To the Secretary of the Dept. of the Interior
Ottawa.
Sir,

Replying to your letter of the 4th inst. requesting our side of the question in re. Petition of Squatters settled on the above Lease I beg to point out.

1st That we bought the Lease on the express understanding that the Government would not recognise Squatting as per enclosed notice signed by Mr. Burgess [Deputy Minister of the Interior].

2nd That all Squatters were aware of the terms of our Lease restricting squatting and had the above notice served upon them *before they had made any improvements.*

3rd That of the 10 Squatters viz Micker, Edge, Fary, Wains, Odlin,

McKay, Butler, Shindler Bros and Healy—Odlin is a moneyed man and having a section adjoining the Lease squatted on our land in spite of the strongest advice to the contrary—Monroe lives in town and has put up a board shack about 12 ft. x 6 ft. without other improvements to claim land on the Lease. McKay has a "hay" shack open to weather and has ploughed half an acre but *does not live there*. Butler is building a house which he commenced *after the agitation* and against all we could say to him.

Shindler Bros. were notified as soon as we perceived them building in November and *when only the frame of the house was up*.

Healy has a cheese factory and house off the Range and is squatting during the Winter on the Range in order to claim land. Micker Edge Fary and Wains have made homes here but were *all served with the Government notice* before making any improvements.

4th The Squatters materially diminish our available supply of Hay and we had to buy from them last Fall.

6th They are doing much fencing and taking up water rights by which our stock, which used to Winter within 5 miles of the home corrals, are now driven for pasture and water 15 and 20 miles away—the open spring being too near the Squatters' homes for them to water there and the best hay cut—the result of this is very apparent this Spring in their unusual poverty in spite of a mild Winter.

7th That there are large quantities of land open for settlement that are not taken up and that scarcity of such land cannot be urged as an excuse for squatting on our Range.

8th That if squatting on the lease is not stopped *others will come* and in a short time all the best hay land will be taken up and the Range [will] become practically worthless as the majority of the land is too poor to produce Winter feed.

9th That some of the Squatters are running cattle on our Range "on shares" with outside parties and there is nothing to prevent them all doing the same thing.

10th That we are fully stocked having 1 head in 13 acres and are doing our best to fulfill all the conditions of our Lease which we entered into bona fide, that we are advertising the Country well in England and spending much money in improvements and importation of stock.

11th That the Government sanctioned the transfer of all the privileges of the British American Ranch Cos. Lease to our Company without which guarantee we should not have invested and we feel that such being the case and having such a large stake in the Country we should be *as fully protected in our rights* as any other. . . .

12th and lastly—the Squatters themselves acknowledge the justice of the action we have taken as being our only chance if we would get any good out of our Range but openly defy our power to maintain our rights by law.

I submit these facts for your consideration fully believing that you will protect the stock interests of Alberta and that we shall receive that justice at your hands for which you are well accredited by those who have the honour to know you.

I am Sir,
Yours faithfully,
Gilbert E. Goddard

117. THE THREAT OF VIOLENCE

PAC, RG15, B1a, vol. 184, 255938.

Montreal, 27th Jan. 1891

Fred White, Esq.,
Controller N.W.M. Police,
Ottawa.
Dear Sir,

As you may probably have had reported to you, a fire recently occured [sic] by which about 300 tons of hay was destroyed at our Cattle Ranch [on] Beaver Creek, which fire I have every reason to believe was incendiary in its origen [sic]. Threats have been made by a family named Dunbar, whom we are preventing from taking up the very best and an essential portion of our leases. Also by one D.I. Cochrane who however had left the district before the fire occured [sic], leaving however his squaw behind him, also I believe by one Jerrard Paisley, who was prevented from settling on the lease.

So far no direct clue has been discovered by our men. As this is the inauguration of a reign of terrorism and lawlessness which if not checked at the commencement will doubtless extend, and there is no saying what complications will arise. I hope therefore that you will instruct your officers to do all in their power to trace up the guilty parties. There being no Detective system in the country, it appears to me that in the public interest, and for the protection of life and property, for whoever would burn would also kill, you should have attached to your force some men who would act as detectives. . . .

It is my intention to offer a reward of $250 for the conviction of the party or parties but thought as it is generally thought here that the Department of the Interior ought to join us in offering a reward. May I take the liberty of asking you to see the Hon. Mr. Dewdney and to show him this letter and ask him if he will join in offering a reward or make some suggestion as to how it should be dealt with.

Hoping that you will be able to give this your immediate attention in the public interest.

Yours very truly,
D. McEachran.

118. RANGE WAR IMMINENT

Glenbow-Alberta Institute, Dewdney Papers, Walrond Ranche Correspondence.

Montreal, 13th Aug, 1891.

Hon. E. Dewdney,
Minister of Interior.

Dear Sir,

I herewith enclose a letter just received from our Local Manager by which you will see the spirit of lawlessness which we have to contend with on the Dunbar family I would again request that the Police or better still Detectives in the employment of the N.W.M. Police be utilized for the purpose of preventing what may result in a serious breach of the peace, as our men will prevent trespass.

It might perhaps be well if Mr. McMullen would see this letter of Lamar's and be informed that every such threat on their part but lessens their chances of a settlement by purchase.

As to opening the Hollis lease for settlement there could never be more than half a dozen settlers find locations between the Hills and the Pauperism of the Dunbars who have had every chance having stock and being Ontario farmers of experience, will show how successful farming there has been.

Surely the Government ought to give us some protection we have spent more money now than we can afford in protecting our rights, surely there must be some available means whereby this can be put a stop to we have spent $5000 on fencing alone on that lease, I have paid Cochrane $2700 for his so called improvements, besides his cattle $1600 worth of hay was maliciously, burned by settlers our law expenses about $500 more. All this I have paid in endeavouring to prevent ill feeling, but we cannot continue paying and it would be but fair for the law to be so amended as to give us protection.

My fear of a collision between them and our men prompts me to thus appeal to you.

Hoping that yourself or the Department of Justice will order such action at once as will relieve us of such trespass on our rights.

I have the honour to be,
Sir,
Your obedient servant,
D. McEachran.

COPY

Extract from a letter dated Cow Ranch 4th Aug, 1891, from J. Lamar to Dr. McEachran,

"Cochran promised me as I came through Macleod that he was coming right out after those things of his so I waited several days and he did not come and two of the boys and myself went over to pull the house down we met Dave on our way over we told him what we was going to do he forbid us doing it but we went ahead and pulled it down just the same the whole tribe of them are boiling over with wrath I hear Dunbars are saying that they are 6 or 8 of them are going to get together and put up a house some night and have Sam in it next morning I think this is only to make us uneasy at any rate we will only try to watch them the closer Baily is going around with a petition and getting settlers names to send to Ottawa for the purpose of getting the Hollis lease opened for Settlement."

The Settlers

119. DIVISION IN THE FOOTHILLS

PAC, Macdonald Papers, MG26, ALB vol. 409.

Reserves des Gens du Sang.
N.W.T.
18th November 1884.

To The Honorable Sir H. Langevin
Minister of Public Works
Ottawa
Sir,

I beg your indulgence for reading what follows; because I shall necessarily be lengthy; though pointing out only the principal questions. Please, next, if you think it necessary, trace a line of conduct to be followed; if I can be useful to our friends and to farmers, I am ready to give all the time I can dispose of, to help them.

Our population is divided into two well distinct clans: the Stock-Raisers who have the monopoly of the lands in this part of the country, and the *bona fide* farmers including the old squatters and the new Ranchers. The first of the last class have undeniable wrights [sic] acknowledged by the Government in a certain clause of the leases obtained from the Stock-Raisers. It is but justice for them and I congratulate the Government which has had the wisdom to provide for it. . . .

Since my arrival in this Country, over which I have travelled in all directions from Calgary to St. Mary River in the South, and from East to West for over hundred miles, I have everywhere met the same divisions; the two clans are engaged in a struggle and recently things have assumed a serious turn; each party claiming to be right.

Everywhere the will of the strongest is the law to which they have to submit. The Stock-Raisers claim this right, though they have no title to it, and proclaim loudly and in every way: "No farmers in this Country we have no need for them. The land is good but for pasture and nothing else; why, then, attempt, uselessly, to establish farms. Farmers coming here to establish themselves, choose the lands on the rivers. It is a nusance [sic] for us, because our cattle will soon be unable to reach water. Down with farming"!

Farmers, on the other hand, answer with the same energy and with more right: "If the land is good for pasture, do they add, it must necessarily yield a large quantity of grain. . . . Therefore if the land is good for one thing it must be good for the other. After all, what is it that creates prosperity in a Country, if not farming. "*No Farming, No Country*"! Everywhere farmers have caused the wealth of their Country".

Thence quarrels, law suits &c., &c. . . .

The difficulties arise from the monopoly exercised by lease-carriers (Stock-Raisers).

Certain farmers arrive with the avowed object of devoting themselves to agriculture. Before definitly [sic] settling they go searching the lots which offer them the best advantages. The moment they have made their choice they are immediately notified that these lands belong, by lease to such or such other Stock-Raiser. If they go elsewhere, the lands belong to another Stock-Raiser.

Our farmers astonished and surprised at such a state of things proceed to Mcleod [sic], if they have not already been there, to find the land office. They, then and there, get the following plain answer: There is no land office, and if you are determined to settle on a farm, do like this or this other one; build up a house and do not mind the notice.

Full of confidence and ardor, they return to their first choice and begin to work.

Some day or other they are sued with order to appear on a certain day.

Their defence entails attendances, costs and loss of precious time. And, still, if they were to succeed!

Providence, Fate or Fortune, as it may please you, has decided otherwise. After the usual proceedings, they are condemned to pay costs always onerous, and expelled without mercy. What has recently happened to some of them, will, no doubt, happen to the great number for some time to come. . . .

In my humble opinion, I believe, Honorable Sir, that it would be time, for us to be represented in the different Federal Houses by able and honest men, having at heart the progress and the advancement of the Country.

The whole submitted to the High Consideration of Your Honor.

I am Honorable Sir
Your most humble Servant
F.A. Girard
M.D.

120. MEETING AT JOHN GLENN'S

Calgary Herald, April 9, 1885.

The following is a report of the meeting of settlers held at John Glenn's of

Fish Creek on Sunday last; Mr. Livingston was elected chairman. In taking the chair he made a few opening remarks. He stated that he had been about twenty years in the country and had largely improved and cultivated land in the vicinity of Calgary; that he could not obtain not even an entry in the land office although he'd been on his place nine years and was long ago entitled to a patent for his lands. He stated that between government reserves, leases, school lands, Hudson's Bay lands, and a man was unable to find a spot to settle. If a man did settle he was sure to be chased by someone, either by the police, land agents, or government officials of some kind, and that a settler was worse off than a wild animal, as a wild animal had a closed season in which he could not be hunted but that the settler was chased at all seasons of the year. That as long as the lands were under leases, the country was no use for settlers as they might as well settle in the Pacific Ocean. That at the time the Cochrane Ranch was granted there were about 1100 head of cattle running on the Bow River belonging to himself and other settlers, and today there's not a hoof on the range, and that the range was now a sheep pasture. That when the lease was granted the settlers numbering 17 sold out and left the country.

"There was never any notice given as to land about Calgary being reserved as far as I know. When I settled in 1875 the police tried to prevent me cutting wood on my own claim, for my own use, and put up notices that they claimed all the wood and grass for ten miles around Calgary. I have known of my own personal knowledge some forty or fifty settlers being driven out of the country because they could not get land, and just now a number of young men from near Chicago have been searching to find land to settle on, and cannot as it is all taken up by settlers, leases or reserves of some kind. I had about a year ago a number of cattle on the Cochrane range. There was not an animal on the range belonging to the company and the manager drove my cattle off onto burnt ground. I compelled him to drive them back but lost 35 head of my cattle through the action of the company. Unless the country is opened up at once for settlement and patents granted to those entitled to them I would as soon as not burn up all my improvements and leave the country. For the present I defend my claim as my neighbours do, behind my Winchester. Unless the land is all opened up for homestead entry all must either fight for our rights or leave the country and if I am compelled to leave, I will leave marks on the trail behind me".

Mr. John Glenn was called on. He said, "I settled here about the same year as Mr. Livingston. Unless the country is all thrown open for settlement it is of no use for the settlers in it at present, and no use for settlers who may wish to come and settle. I have known a great many people go out of the country because they could not get land to settle on". He said he would hold his claim with a shotgun and the rest of the settlers would do the same. "When the land office was opened here I made application for entry to the agent here. The agent said my [grass?] was peculiar and that he would report on it to the government. It is so peculiar I have not heard a word of it since. Then I saw

Crozier's [NWMP Officer] notice as to grass and wood, I asked what he would do if I took any of either he said he would fine me. I asked him about the land; he said I could have it if I wanted it. I never saw any notice of land reserve about Calgary. It is useless for us to remain in the country unless we get our rights in every respect. If we do not get them, I will be compelled to burn my place and if I do I will not leave many ranches behind me". . . .

All present, to the number of fifty, formed themselves into the "Alberta Settlers Rights Association", and signed the roll of membership.

The following telegram, embodying the resolutions, was forwarded to Sir John MacDonald [sic] after the meeting.

Meeting of settlers of this district was held today at John Glenn's, about fifty present. The following resolution was passed unanimously; That wereas [sic] a number of townships about Calgary are not opened for settlement, which are now largely settled, and many of the settlers having resided on such lands over three years and have made more than sufficient improvements to entitle them to patents, and have made repeated demands at land office for entry, which have been refused! And Wereas leases cover a large tract of land near Calgary fit for settlement, and a number of settlers have settled on these leases;

And Wereas a number of leases have been granted and no cattle or sheep are put on them;

And Wereas it is absolutely necessary that this country be represented at Ottawa without delay, as we are now governed by agents who are interested in misgoverning this country;

And Wereas settlers cannot bring cattle in without paying duty, and lease holders can do so without;

Be It Resolved that in the opinion of this meeting it is necessary that all the townships about Calgary be immediately thrown open for homestead entry and settlement and that parties who have complied with the Dominion Lands Act as to residence and improvements have their patents granted immediately; And all leases, the terms and conditions of which have not been complied with be cancelled and land be thrown open for homestead entry;

And that all the lands suitable for agricultural purposes on leases now granted be thrown open for entry and settlement; Also that settlers importing cattle into the country be put on the same footing as lease holders; And also that this meeting regrets that the Bill introduced to give representation to the Northwest Territories in the Dominion Parliament has been defeated, and would thoroughly impress upon the government the absolute necessity of a government measure being introduced and passed this present session, having the object in view, as the only means of quieting the present discontent among settlers in the Territories, and of properly governing them; and that the government without taking a census has sufficient information to warrant a measure for representation, and this meeting would press immediate action in this regard to prevent a repetition of the trouble which now unhappily exists in these Territories;

And it is further Resolved, that the half breeds in these Territories are entitled to and should receive the same privileges as regards lands as have already been conceeded [sic] to their brethren in Manitoba.

I send this by request of meeting. A memorandum of grievances goes forward next mail with two hundred signatures. (Sgn.)

Sam Livingston
Chairman

121. CONFRONTATION IN THE BOW VALLEY

PAC, RG15, B2a, vol. 5, no. 137261, pt 1.

Calgary. Jun. 18th 1889
To the Honorable
E. Dewdney
Ottawa
Minister of interior

Dear Sir,

I feel it is my duty as a politicle frient and well wisher to inform you of the serious turn afares have taken here recently.

I refer to the suit entered in the courts of law by the Bow River horse ranch co. to force the settlers off the leace their are nine settlers living on the leace at present. Seven of the nine located in May. 87 and have lived on their farms continuesly up to this present time and have made good improvements in Buildings, Braking, & fencing and in doing this the spent their small captil the had when starting and if the are forced off now the are ruined financielly as I know to my own certain knowlage the have no means to defend the case in a court of law, in adition to the number mention above who have been on the lece since May 87. four more are comeing on and will be here in March. the have two houses erected last summer and ready for the family when the arive. now I have been perticuler in giving you the actual number living on the leace. because their is an atempt made by some party to create the imprssion that their are but two squetters on the leace, the communication I refer to will be found in the Calgary hereld Jan. 2nd

Dear Sir it is to fore warn you that I presume to adress you on this most important subject. for I fear a conflict may occur at any time between the contending parties. I am the more convinced of this as the are resolved to stand by each other and defend themselves with their wincheter rifles. a resulution to that effect have been already passed in case the are sherrifed off.

grate excitement prevales here in consequence of the action taken by the com. again the settlers as I am living close by the lease and know all the circumstances in connection with the above. and as a disinterested peson in the dispute refered to I feel the more at liberty to approach the Gov. on a question of such vast importence. it is not my intention to dictate to the Government what cours the shale pursue in this vexed question. not only in this locality but in other places. Ranch men have driven of settlers after being on their places for some time. a settler who located on the Stimson leace was driven off and his buildings distroyed, a petition is being signed by the calgary people and the farming community praying the government to proteck the settlers in what they deem to be their rights and will be forward to you immedietly, if the government can see their way constitutionly and clearly to protect the settler in this case it will be a very popular act on their part with the electorate thrughout the lenth and bredth of the N.W.T. But should the remain nutrel or decide in favor of the compeney and again the settler I venture to say it will be the most unpopuler act the government have committed for the last 15 years I may just here say that the settlers have decided by a resulution to give the oposition in the commons the full perticulars of the case, should the Government not come to the defence of the settlers. I am fully convinced the government will have to make some arangement with the ranch co. and cancil the leace as their is some verry choice land cover by the leace and settlers will go on and locate. it is convenient to calgary and also to timber good grass and an abundence of spring watter and now that war is wedged between the paries I think the government should step in and remove the bone of contention and allow peace and harmoney to dwell amongs us in the future Mrs. Cowan and the family joins me in wishing you and Lady Dewdney a happy new year.

Yours truly
John Cowan

Address
Calgary

122. THE RANGE HERD AS A PROTECTIVE SHIELD

PAC, RG15, B2a, vol. 171, 145330, pt 3.

High River, Alta.
February, 1897.

To Frank Oliver Esq. M.P.
Dear Sir,

We the signers of the enclosed petition settlers in the High River and Sheep Creek Districts urgently request you to bring the subject of this petition before the proper authorities at your earliest opportunity.

We may add that we look to you to uphold our rights, and we may say that we have the most thorough confidence that you will do the utmost in your power to have our grievances as enclosed herein redressed.

The object of this petition is to prevent Companies and parties who have ranches South of High River from driving their cattle to the North side of High River and holding them there.

In order to enlighten you as to what has been the practice of the cattle companies and large individual cattle owners living South of High River: that it has been their custom annually for the last ten years or more to gather their cattle, some 12000 head (this is a small estimate) and drive them from the South to North side of High River and to hold them there all summer by placing riders along High River to keep them from going South.

The result has been that year by year the country north of High River has been getting more and more eaten out and consequently our stock has been suffering correspondingly from lack of pasture and at the present time a large proportion of our stock are actually suffering from starvation and to get hay in this country unless fenced is now almost out of the question. We claim that we who live in this country and are improving it have the right to the grass in it. We are improving the country by cultivating the land and constructing irrigation ditches and other ways. Inducing other settlers to come in and thereby make this a prosperous country. But so long as large bands of cattle are allowed into this settlement the grass will not recover and thus settlers will be kept out and our cattle will suffer. We are continually harassed by large bands of range cattle coming around our fences and destroying them and in many cases our cattle follow them off and very often we never see them again. If they are unbranded and fall into the hands of the Stock Association Round Up they are sold by them the proceeds going to the Stock Association.

The pasture around many of us is now so much eaten off that we will have to move to a different part of the country unless there is a change.

Why should we be sacrificed and our homes broken up in order to enrich the pockets of large companies and rich men, few of whom live on their ranches, but live and spend the money they make away from them.

Therefore we appeal to you Mr. Oliver to make our wants known and to obtain protection for our cattle and our homes.

It may not be amiss to say a few more words concerning the Stock Association for it has been rather a ruling power in this country in the past but we trust that we may not have so much of it in the future. Many of us are unable to fence in all the land we own and our stock though on our own land are very often driven off by the Association Round Up, and though they have been the means of losing our cattle we have to pay them one dollar per head before we can get them back. Also we understand that the Stock Growers Association are desirous of having a law passed by which it becomes illegal for the settler to drive off range cattle. We strongly protest against this, but we would point out that if the cattle owned South of High River were kept there we would not require to drive them away.

We would further point out to you that there is ample pasture South of High River for the cattle owned South to be kept there all the year round but we have good reasons for believing that the reasons they are not kept there are, 1 That the cattle can be held North at a less cost than they could be held South.

II That the cattle keep the grass eaten down and this discourages new settlers from coming in and is calculated to drive present settlers out.

In conclusion we may say that we trust that you will take the necessary steps to bring the subject of this petition before the proper authorities at your earliest convenience. We do not doubt that you will see the urgent necessity of having range cattle kept south of High River from the present time for if allowed to be brought north of High River next Spring many of us will be forced to move away from our homes.

Robert Findlay et al.

The Government

123. THE PRIME MINISTER'S IRRITATION

PAC, Macdonald Papers, MG26, A1(e), vol. 525, pp. 165-6. J. A. Macdonald to A. Campbell, Minister of Justice regarding the ranching scheme proposed by the latter's brother, 'Charley'.

Ottawa June 23, 1883

Private

My dear Campbell

I should like to help Charley as much as possible but look at this application.

Some 8 or 9 Companies got Ranches on giving the assurance that they were both able and willing to stock them. It turns out that they all lied and merely got their leases for the purpose of selling them—other parties were prevented from getting and stocking these lands. A year or so has been lost and not a hoof or home put on any one Ranche.

These Speculators now club together to make one large Company with a [range] the size of a Province to speculate upon, and propose to hawk this round in England. Neither Charley nor Beatty nor Mills have capital—to work or stock these Ranches—and don't intend to do so.

Beatty may have some money—If he had intended to go into the grazing himself he would have taken one Ranche and been now buying cattle somewhere between Montana and Texas—he is not going to bring out his herd from England or Scotland. It is too transparent a job. It cannot be concealed and next session it would be aired in such a manner in the Commons as to work great [disadvantage?] to all concerned. . . .

Yours faithfully,
John A. Macdonald.

124. AN INFLUENTIAL VOICE WITHIN THE DEPARTMENT OF THE INTERIOR

PAC, RG15, B2a, vol. 5, no. 137261, pt 1.

Office of the Superintendent of Mines
Calgary, 28th March, 1889.

Confidential
To the Hon. E. Dewdney,
Minister of the Interior,
Ottawa, Ontario.
Sir:

In addition to the official report on the squatters on the Box River Horse Ranche Company lease, I would, for your information, report confidentially what Mr. Goddard, who is on the ranche, stated to me, and also some other matters: . . .

From the sketch you will see that if the squatters are granted what they want, and enclose by fencing, the [Bow River Horse Ranche Company] lease is nearly cut in twain, leaving their headquarters on the portion containing the least pasturage.

If the Government insist on these squatters obtaining the land claimed, there will not be in one month an even section in the lease desirable for settlement that will not be squatted upon, not only on this lease but on all others of the same nature. It will be observed that most of these squatters admit that they knew they were settling on lands not open for entry, but did so thinking that as Tp. 24 R. 2 and 3 had been opened for entry because squatted upon, any further lands squatted upon would be treated likewise; that they were encouraged to squat by their neighbors, and particularly by the people of Calgary, who seem to think that the Cochrane lease has been a great source of damage to Calgary's interests, forgetful of the fact that there are thousands of acres yet vacant, of as good land and as close to Calgary as any within the leasehold.

Therefore, in dealing with this particular case the general effect must be borne in mind. In this connection I would like to obtain the Hansard report of Sir John Macdonald's statement in I think 1882 or 1883, when attacked regarding his grazing lease policy I only saw the newspaper report, but if my memory serves me right he stated the Government had reserved the right to cancel on a two years' notice, if it were found the land was required for actual settlement, and the impression which rested on my mind was that so soon as there was a fair demand for land within any lease the two-years' notice would be good. It would, I think, be a great pity that just at present indiscriminate squatting should be permitted on these leases; a certain amount of settlement combined with stock-raising by these companies will be of advantage both to the settler and stock-man. The time is not far distant when stock raising in this country, to be most profitable, will be carried on in bands ranging from 100 to

500 head of either cattle or horses, and if the transition from the present to that is gradual, and not interfered with by indiscriminate squatting, the greater the resources of the country will be utilized, but if squatters are permitted to take up land where they please, the water and hay will be taken, and the rest left, and taken, too, by a class who have not the capital to utilize the domain to the capacity it should be. These remarks do not, however, apply to this leasehold, as water can be obtained readily almost anywhere, and the greater portion of the lease has areas in each case of such extent that where hay does not grow naturally, oats, cut green for hay, can be cheaply grown, but whatever action may be taken in the case will no doubt be cited as a precedent in all others considered.

If, however, an arrangement can be come to between the squatters, and the company, the Government will be relieved of taking any action in the matter and relieving themselves of possibly an awkward precedent. . . .

Respectfully submitted.
I have the honor to be,
Sir,
Your obedient servant,
Signed: William Pearce,
Superintendent.

125. PARLIAMENTARY DEBATE, 1891

House of Commons *Debates* (1891), XXIII, cols. 6153-62.

McMULLEN. I desire to add a few words to the remarks made by the hon. member for Yarmouth (Mr. Flint), with regard to the case submitted to this House connected with the Waldron Ranche Company of the North-West. . . .

I am not going to quote the figures which have been submitted by the hon. member for Yarmouth, but will simply state the facts briefly as they appear in the documents in my hands relating to this unfortunate case. Mr. Dunbar settled there in 1882, and took up a homestead and was permitted to retain his homestead; his sons lived with him for some time in order to secure first for their father and family a comfortable home by erecting a house, and so on, and then in 1883 they took up sections for themselves. After they had been on those locations in peaceable possession of them, and after they had received notice from the department that they would be permitted to homestead and obtain preemption entry for that particular section, very unexpectedly and to their extreme surprise they got notice from the Waldron Ranche Company that they were not to continue occupying the land, nor even to cut the hay on their own place. After that the company took an action to prevent their making further cultivation or even cutting the hay. . . .

. . . Dr. McEachran, on behalf of the Waldron Ranche Company, took action to eject those men from the land of which they had been in possession as squatters for a number of years, and for which they eventually got homestead entries in 1889. Those in the House who are acquainted with legal proceedings will easily understand that had the Government not come to the assistance of the Waldron Ranche Company by cancelling those entries it would have been impossible for that company to have succeeded in their action at law. But in order to assist Dr. McEachran and the company over which he presides in getting a decree against those men to evict them from the lands they had possessed virtually from 1883—for although, perhaps, they had not resided on them day and night, but had lived with their father in their immediate vicinity, they had made improvements on the land with the view of occupying it, had erected houses, put in a crop and took the necessary steps to secure its being closed in—the Government cancelled their entries. In the face of all that, it was cruel on the part of Government to cancel their entries, even supposing those entries had been inadvertently made. . . .

. . . Now, as I said before, a mistake may have been made in this case. The Government may have rented this land to Dr. McEachran without first learning the facts with regard to these settlers being in possession of it; but I hold that from the very moment they became aware that these men had gone in there and settled upon that land in good faith, having the assurance of the late First Minister, when he was Minister of the Interior, that squatters' rights would be acknowledged, and under the declared policy of the Minister of the Interior, that in every case the bulls must give away [sic] to the settlers who wanted to occupy the lands, I say, in face of all these declarations, it is seriously to be regretted that any settlers should be placed in such a position that they can be harassed and annoyed, instead of being allowed to go in there and make comfortable homes for themselves. I have in my possession letters concerning that section of the country, and I am glad to be able to say, and I state it on information that I can rely upon, that in that section of country this year they have reaped from 45 to 50 bushels of good wheat to the acre; they have reaped as much as 50 bushels of barley, and 50 to 60 bushels of oats. They have splendid crops, and some of these men say to me in their communications that they believe they are in the very centre of creation, that this is the best portion of the world they were ever in; that they have been in the old country, they have been in Ontario and in the United States, yet they never lived in any section that is more delightful, that yields better crops and is a more desirable country to live in, and in which to make comfortable homes. This is the testimony of men that are in possession of these lands, and in view of these facts I say it is in the highest degree in the interest of the people of that section, in the interest of the settlement and development of that country, that the lease should be at once cancelled, and that these people should be allowed to go in there and settle and make comfortable homes for themselves. I do not know what the rent is; it may be one cent, it may be two cents an acre. I fully endorse the sentiment expressed by the late First Minister, when he said that ranching should be a secondary consideration, and that the settlement of the country, and the privilege of the people to go in and make homes, should be the first and great consideration. . . .

In all my experience, which is not very extensive, I admit, in all the hardships that I ever read of, and the ejectments that have taken place in unfortunate Ireland, where the landlords rule with a rod of iron, I have read no case of hardship that exceeds the one I have now presented to the House, and the case that was presented by the member for Yarmouth (Mr. Flint) this afternoon. If you allow these things to be published in the newspapers of Europe or Canada it is enough to deter people from going in to settle those lands, when they find that settlers, after being there eight years, struggling with the difficulties and privations they have had to suffer, are subjected to all these additional hardships. . . .

Mr. DEWDNEY. This question is no doubt an important one, and it is one that will have to be dealt with in the very near future. The question of cattle ranches in Alberta is one of great importance, and one in which, probably a larger amount of capital is invested than in any other industry in the North-West Territories. The old policy of the Government, as the hon. gentleman knows, in 1880 and 1881, was to encourage the ranching industry in that western country. It was then reported that it was a magnificent cattle country; but it was uncertain, as no one had tested it, but capitalists were encouraged to go in there and take hold of those ranching lands and put cattle upon them. Consequently, in any dealings we have in this matter, in any change of policy we propose to adopt, we must take care that we do not do injury to those who came into the country, paid for their leases and put their cattle on the ground and carried out their part of the bargain in good faith with the Government. A great number of leases at the time were taken up, not only by capitalists, who were able to put cattle on the land, but by others as a speculation. Then from year to year, as the conditions were not fulfilled, as has been the case constantly, lands have been thrown open for settlement, and within the last month or two weeks the leases of two large ranches have been cancelled and the lands thrown open for settlement. . . .

In the particular district to which our attention has been called, where the Hollis and McEachran leases are situated, I may say that the Hollis lease was taken up in 1883. In 1888 Mr. Hollis indicated his wish to surrender that lease, and Dr. McEachran notified the Government that he was willing to take it and give up a lease adjoining it, close to Fort Macleod, and in regard to which a number of persons had applied to have thrown open for settlement. Consequently, when application was made by Dr. McEachran to take the Hollis lease, instead of the one he held near Fort Macleod, the Government were very glad to make the exchange. Then, Dr. McEachran's leased land was thrown open for settlement. It appears that on the Hollis lease the Dunbar family were settled. Shortly after Dr. McEachran's lease was given to him information reached the department that the Dunbar family claimed some portion of the land. Representations were made to us regarding other leases that parties were in the habit of making a business of settling on leased land, selecting the springs or other available water or other advantages offered, such as hayland, and causing complications with the object of being bought out. A number of people made it their business, and we had to be very careful to protect those who had invested their money and gone into the country in good faith. . . .

The hon. gentleman at the end of his speech I think was rather violent, and he spoke of the treatment these people received as being not unlike the treatment of the tenants in Ireland. Well, Mr. Speaker, considering the number of leases and the nature of the country there, I think it speaks well for the ranchers and for everyone concerned that we have not had more difficulties. I know that in a number of the ranches held under the old system, where it required two years' notice to cancel, some persons have gone in and settled with the permission of the ranchers and there has been no difficulty whatever.

126. THE RULE OF LAW

PAC North West Mounted Police, RG18, A1, vol 116, no. 72.

Superintendent of Mines
Calgary,
27th July 1893
[4]

R. Duthie, Esq.,
Manager "Alberta Ranche Company"
Pincher Creek, Alberta.
Sir;—

I find that it is necessary that the leaseholder himself should take steps to eject any squatters of his holding if such are objectionable to him. The modus operandi is as follows; you notify the officer in charge of the Mounted Police in your District to the effect that on a certain day you purpose forcibly ejecting certain squatters; on the day in question he will send a detachment to the place indicated to see that no breach of the peace occurs. You and your men then proceed to tear down the buildings doing no more damage than is absolutely necessary. I presume, however, you could restrain the squatter from removing the building material from the land; this probably you are not desirous of doing, though. I would, therefore, suggest that you give Messrs. Thiboutott, Gyr and others within your leasehold say three weeks notice to remove all their improvements etc., informing them what you intend doing; you may also add that you are doing it with the full sanction of the Department of the Interior. I would also suggest that you request Mr. Inspector Cuthbert of the Mounted Police to notify the parties of what you intend doing and also to tell them that he will have Policement [sic] on hand to see that no breach of the peace occurs, or rather to enable you to tear down their buildings.

I am, Sir,
Your obedient servant,
Sg. Lou Pearcep
Superintendent

127. GUARDIANS OF THE PEACE

PAC, North West Mounted Police Papers, RG18, A1, vol. 56, no. 695.

The Commissioner
N.W. Mounted Police
Regina.
Sir,

N.W. Mounted Police
District Office
Fort Macleod 17th October 1891.

I have the honour to report for your information that owing to rumours which have reached my ears of the dissatisfied state of the settlers on the leased lands and the possibility of some outrage being committed by way of reprisal, I sent Scout Denny round to visit all the settlers accopying [sic] farms on the Waldron Oxley, Winder, Victor and Glengarry leases. He reports a very irritated feeling existing on all sides but more particularly on the part of settlers on the Waldron Land who seem to entertain a personal hostility towards the Manager Mr. McEachran who they complain is continually threatening them and harrassing them, preventing them from cutting hay and refusing employment to any one who owns a hoof of stock in the country.

The settlers on all the leases were unanimous in declaring that the land reserved for the leases, particularly that in the Porcupine Hills is the only farming land in the District and that if driven off they would have to settle on the plains where on account of its being too dry they could not exist. They stated that two petitions had been forwarded to the Government, one through Mr. D. W. Davis, and one through Mr. Haultain, but that they had never been laid before the House.

They also complained that the occupiers of the leases do not fulfil the conditions required, not one of them having nearly the requisite number of stock. One and all assured Denny of their intention of abiding by the law but his opinion was that any more evictions would be followed by reprisals.

I have the honour to be
Sir
Your obedient Servant
Sgd. S.B. Steele Supt.
Commdg. Macleod District.

The Lease System

128. CANADA. DOMINION LANDS REGULATIONS

Order in Council No. 1710 of the 23rd day of December 1881.

PASTURAGE LANDS

Sec. 16. Under the authority of the Act 44 Vic., Cap. 16, leases of tracts for grazing purposes may be granted on the following conditions:

a. Such leases to be for a period of not exceeding twenty-one years, and no single lease shall cover a greater area than 100,000 acres.

b. In surveyed territory, the land embraced by the lease shall be described in townships and sections. In unsurveyed territory, the party to whom a lease may be promised shall, before the issue of the lease, cause a survey of the tract to be made, at his own expense, by a Dominion Lands Surveyor, under instructions from the Surveyor-General; and the plan and field notes of such survey shall be deposited on record in the Department of the Interior.

c. The lessee shall pay an annual rental at the rate of $10 for every 1,000 acres embraced by his lease, and shall within three years from the granting of the lease, place on the tract one head of cattle for every ten acres of land embraced by the lease, and shall during its term maintain cattle thereon in at least that proportion.

d. After placing the prescribed number of cattle upon the tract leased, the lessee may purchase land within his leasehold for a home farm and *corral*, paying therefor $2.00 per acre in cash.

e. Failure to fulfil any of the conditions of his lease shall subject the lessee to forfeiture thereof.

17. When two or more parties apply for a grazing lease of the same land, tenders shall be invited, and the lease shall be granted to the party offering the highest premium therefor in addition to the rental. The said premium to be paid before the issue of the lease.

129. THE ORIGINAL LEASE CONTRACT

Form of Lease based upon draught approved by Order in Council, No. 722, of 11th April 1882. Ref. 44,300, on T. & M. 2,319, with amendment to Clause 7—respecting Sheep—authorized by Order in Council, No. 892, of 11th May 1882.

These presents are made and issued subject to the following provisoes, terms and conditions, viz: —

7. That the lessee will not, during the said term, use or allow to be used any part of the lands and premises hereby demised for any purpose other than

grazing purposes within the true intent and meaning of the Dominion Lands Act and of these presents, and will not, during the said term, allow sheep to graze or to be kept upon any part of the said tract, without the consent in writing in that behalf of the Minister of the Interior, and will not, during the said term, cut or destroy, or allow to be cut or destroyed, any timber or timber trees without the consent in writing in that behalf of the Minister of the Interior, and then only in accordance with such terms, conditions and regulations as may be made or established in that behalf.

8. That should the Governor in Council at any time during the term hereby granted, think it to be in the public interests to open the lands hereby demised for settlement, or to terminate these presents for any reason, the Minister of the Interior of Canada may, on giving the lessee two years' notice, cancel these presents at any time during the time hereby demised.

10. That so soon as a survey of a township has been made and confirmed, such lands therein, as under the provisions of the said Dominion Lands Act are known and designated as the lands of the Hudson's Bay Company, and also such lands as under the provisions of the said Act are set apart as an endowment for purposes of education, shall thereupon become withdrawn from the operation of these presents, and the term hereby created shall thereupon cease and determine with respect thereto; . . .

11. That should any portion or portions of the land hereby demised be now occupied by any person or persons who may have settled thereon, such persons and those claiming through them shall not be disturbed in their possession by the lessee, unless with the consent in writing of the Minister of the Interior; and the Minister of the Interior may, if he thinks it expedient so to do, from time to time, give to the lessee written notice that the lands in possession of such persons respectively, and such adjoining lands as he may think proper (but not exceeding in the whole three hundred and twenty acres for each separate settler), are withdrawn from the operation of these presents, and thereupon such lands shall become withdrawn, . . .

12. That should any portions of the lands hereby demised be thought to contain gold, silver, copper, coal or other minerals, building-stone or marble, the Governor in Council may grant licenses to any person or corporation to explore and search for the same, subject to such conditions for the protection of the interests of the lessee as the Governor in Council may think proper. And should any portions of the lands hereby demised contain gold, silver, copper, coal or other minerals, building-stone or marble, or water power capable of being used to drive machinery, the Governor in Council may, from time to time, cause written notice to be given to the lessee that the same and such adjoining lands as he may think proper are withdrawn from the operation of these presents. . . .

14. That should the Canadian Pacific Railway Company become entitled to a grant from Her Majesty or Her successors of any portion of the lands hereby demised, whether as part of their land subsidy provided for by Chapter one of the Statutes of Canada, passed in the forty-fourth year of Her Majesty's reign

(A.D. 1881), or for the road-bed of the railway, or its branches, or for stations, station grounds, workshops, dock ground and water frontage on navigable waters, buildings, yards and other appurtenances required for the convenient and effectual construction and working of the railway and its branches, and should any other railway company, pursuant to any legal contract or statute in that behalf, become entitled to a grant from Her Majesty or her successors of any portion of the lands hereby demised, for road-bed and stations, and if Her Majesty or her successors grant the same, the land so granted shall thereupon become withdrawn from the operation of these presents. . . .

130. PRIVY COUNCIL REPORT, 1892

Order in Council, No. 2669 of the 12th day of October 1892.

On a Report dated 4th October, 1892, from the Minister of the Interior stating that, during the latter part of the month of December, 1891, and the early part of the month of January, 1892, he caused a circular to be addressed to the lessees of grazing ranches in the North-West Territories, of which a copy is hereto attached, suggesting that for the reasons set out in this circular it would be advisable that the lessees should meet at an early date, discuss the proposition outlined in the circular as to the cancellation of the existing leases and the substitution for them of leases on the new form, [open to homestead entry] and appoint a small deputation to visit Ottawa and talk the matter over with the Minister of the Interior.

The Minister further represents that at various times and on various occasions since the issue of the circular in question, he personally met and discussed with deputations of lease holders and individual lessees the whole question involved, and after mature consideration he (the Minister) has come to the conclusion that it would be in the public interest, and would tend to the settlement of this question in the speediest manner consistent with the interests involved to notify all holders of leases [granted] . . . by the Department of the Interior from the time the system was initiated up to the 17th day of September, 1889,—who are not in arrears for rent, have properly stocked their ranches, and have otherwise complied with the conditions of their leases, that the leases held by them will be terminated on and after the 31st day of December, 1896, that they will then or at any time during the interval, be permitted to purchase not in excess of ten per cent. of their leasehold at the rate of $2.00 per acre; [subsequently reduced to $1.25 per acre] and that from and after the said 31st day of December, 1896, it will be open to them if they see fit to accept leases for the unexpired portion of the term of twenty-one years, of such of the lands now held by them as may be agreed upon between them and the Government upon [what is] commonly known as the new form of lease.

The Minister considers that this would give such of the lease holders as may conclude that they cannot satisfactorily carry on their business under the new form of lease, ample opportunity of winding up their affairs.

The Minister recommends that he be authorized to communicate in this sense with all parties interested.

The Minister states that he is convinced that with the opportunity for consideration and reflection, which will thus be afforded them the majority of the Companies will conclude not to give up the business at the end of the four years, but will find that it can be successfully and profitably continued under the new form of lease, until the period when in the natural course of events the progress of settlement will have rendered the pursuit of the cattle business in its present form undesirable both from the point of view of the investor and the Government.

131. CIRCULAR: DEPARTMENT OF THE INTERIOR

Order in Council, No. 2669 of the 12th day of October 1892.

Ottawa, 21st December, 1891

Sir,

The demand for lands in Western Alberta for settlement, and to satisfy the land subsidies granted by Parliament to Railway Companies, makes it necessary in the public interest that some arrangement should be made with the lessees of ranches situated in that portion of the North-West Territories, whereby the Government would be in a position to meet this demand, and at the same time deal in a fair and equitable manner with those lessees who are in good standing by having paid up their rents, stocked their ranches, and otherwise complied with the requirements of their leases.

The Minister of the Interior, recognizing the fact that it could not be otherwise than prejudicial to the best interests of the country that so large and so important an industry as the grazing and breeding of cattle, as it at present exists in Alberta, should be unnecessarily disturbed, is of the opinion that a policy should be adopted which will not disarrange the business of the leaseholders, but on the contrary will justify the continued confidence of those who have invested their money in that business, and which will at the same time result in meeting the requirements of the settlers and the Railway Companies.

With this object in view, the Minister has submitted to his colleagues that it would be advisable to offer all those lessees who are not in arrear for rent, have properly stocked their ranches, and have otherwise complied with the requirements of their leases, the privilege of purchasing ten per cent. of the area of their leaseholds at $2 per acre, provided they accept for the residue of the term a lease of the lands now held by them on the new form, which provides for the withdrawal of lands from time to time as they are required for sale, settlement or railway purposes.

You are aware that the section of the Calgary and Edmonton Railway lying between Calgary and Fort Macleod is now graded to the Old Man River, and that it will in all probability be completed and running next season. This will doubtless bring into the country served by the road a considerable influx of people looking for land for purposes of actual settlement, whose demands for homesteads it is the duty of the Government to make every reasonable effort to meet, consistently with existing interests; and it will also be necessary to find in the vicinity of the line, by the time the railway is ready to be operated, as much as possible of the land to which the Company constructing it thereby become entitled.

The Minister thinks that it might be well that you and others similarly interested should meet at an early day, discuss the proposition outlined in this letter and the situation generally, and appoint a small deputation to visit Ottawa and talk the matter over with him.

In conclusion I am to say that it is hoped that this matter will receive as early attention as possible from all those interested, and the Minister will be glad to be informed of the steps being taken and the progress being made in the premises.

I have the honour to be,
Sir,
Your obedient servant,

132. CLOSED LEASES ESSENTIAL

University of Alberta, Pearce Papers, 14H6.

Honourable David Mills.   St. Thomas, Ont. Sept. 15th/1900.
Minister of Justice.
Ottawa.
My dear Sir-

Confirming my conversation on the train with you a few weeks ago, which you will no doubt remember. I have a grievance (not me alone but all the small stock raisers in the North West) which I wish to present for your consideration, and will make my case as plain as possible, and if mine is ruled it will fit all the other cases. I am in the stock raising business with my brother on a small scale; we commenced about three years ago, put up quite a good house, together with good stabling, or as good as we can at present afford. We are in this business to stay if the Government will assist us in the way of making the necessary changes in the law to give us some assurance that we will have some protection, or guarantee that every Foreigner cannot come along squat on the land we have leased from the Government; as the law reads, it would allow any scapegoat to come along and homestead on the land we have leased, using any part of it he saw fit.

We will buy this land as soon as we are able, but most all the cattlemen have gone in there with limited means and have to creep before they walk. Now if we could get any lease from the Government so that no one could interfere with us for a certain number of years, we could go right along and do business and know where we are at, or if the law was so changed that we would have the first chance to buy the land we lease, we could then tell what to depend on.

We do not want to monopolize the land; all we want is sufficient land to handle out [sic] cattle successfully, and I think if land [was] leased to us with the privilege of buying within a certain number of years, it would not hurt the land, and the stock business would soon be one of the greatest industries in Canada, as it is rapidly growing and getting better in every way. The land is principally hills and mountains and unfitted for anything but what it is used for. · However there is, and will be, as long as the law remains as it is, scape goats ready to squat on our land in order to make us buy them out; then there is the green Emigrant that comes out of the European Cities that know nothing about farming, and they will squat on the ranchers land and annoy them, while if we could be left alone for a while as the farmers are we would make this business a credit to ourselves, and the Government would be proud of the showing we make. We are almost all Canadians, while the people that are squatting are almost all Foreigners.

We do not believe the Government of which you are one of the leading representatives, are acquainted with the facts, as it was not passed by your Government, and we feel sure that when your Government will see the justice of our case it will be speedily adjusted.

We have another grievance we would like to draw your attention to viz, the land is, as already stated, rough and unfit for other than the business it is now used for, yet it is held at $3.00 per acre. We would before buying ask that an Inspector be sent out to value the same, as we claim it is not worth the price asked. While this has been done in some cases it has been refused us from your Inspector at Calgary. All we ask is a fair valuation and we are ready and willing to stand by the same. We ask for fair treatment in this matter and nothing more or less.

Anything you can see your way clear to do, to have this matter adjusted will be highly appreciated.

Yours &c
Sgd. J.G. Robb

133. REPORT ON THE GRAZING QUESTION, 1903

PAC, RG15, B2a, vol. 172, no. 145330 pt 4, 'Grazing Regulations' by R. H. Campbell, Department of Interior, Timber and Grazing Branch, to the Minister of the Interior, November 6, 1903.

The chief difficulties in administration [of grazing leases] have been caused by the differences between the homesteaders and smaller ranches and those wishing to control large leaseholds. Homesteads have been granted from time to time within ranches and the holders of such ranches complain that their business is being destroyed by the removal of these lands from their control. On the other hand, persons who have squatted or homesteaded prior to the applications for leases covering or surrounding the lands on which they are located, have made strong objection to the granting of such leases. . . .

The withdrawal of the [grazing lease] regulations [Sept. 1, 1903] leaves homestead entry as the only method of obtaining control of Dominion Lands and the suggestion has been made that all remaining lands should be left to be ranged over by stock in general, free or on payment of a tax of so much per head. Although this plan might have suited the conditions some years ago when there were comparatively few stock in the country, the time for it has gone by. The experience of the United States with the free range system has been very unsatisfactory as the following statements will show.

Professor R.H. Forbes, of the Arizona Agricultural Experimental Station says:— . . .

" . . . after the completion of the Southern Pacific Railroad in 1881, numerous small owners shipped in their herds from worn out districts in Texas and elsewhere, while still others, driving their cattle overland to California, and deterred by the terrors of the Colorado desert, stopped by the way".

The overstocking of the range caused the herbage to be eaten out, the wanderings of the herds in search of food wore pathways and the rains which came rushed down these ways gullying the lands and tearing out the grasses by the roots.

A striking instance of this process of ruin is offered by the San Simon Valley. This once beautiful district has been despoiled and hopelessly ruined within the short space of some fifteen years. . . . *The ruinous methods which seem inevitable upon a public range, which, being everybody's property, is nobody's care, have so destroyed its value, and have so changed the original condition of the country that in many cases, in spite of the present high prices of cattle, the ranges now carry but a tithe of what they once did.* In the San Simon Valley alone it is judged that within the past decade the number of cattle has fallen off from 75 to 90 per cent. This one district, at least twenty-five hundred square miles in extent, would at the extremely low rate of four animals to the square mile per year yield an annual revenue of $150,000 in a region where now it would take hard riding and a sharp eye to gather a single train load".

Professor Forbes would favor a system of leasing but for the opposition to it caused by the difficulties between the large and small ranchers, and the only further suggestion he has to make is for a system of grazing reserves to be controlled by the Government. . . .

This fairly establishes that either the Government must take control of the range or the individual must be given some such proprietary right in the land that it will be to his interest to see that it is kept in proper condition.

A homestead of 160 acres is not sufficient for a grazing ranch which is purely such. The form of grazing lease hitherto in use provides that the stock to be placed on the leasehold must equal one head for each twenty acres but not to exceed that number, and even if that number be doubled a homestead would still be too small for profitable operation.

Beside land, the other prime necessity is water. Provision for this has been made in a general way in the North West Territories by the setting apart of stock watering reserves for the use of the public. This will not, however, provide for every case and in any plan of administration the question of water supply must be kept in view.

134. LEASES TO CURB UNDESIRABLE SETTLEMENT

PAC, RG15, B2a, vol. 171, no. 145330, pt 3.

Russell House,
Ottawa, June 1st, 1904.

J.W. Greenway, Esq.
Commissioner of Dom. Lands,
Ottawa.

Dear Sir,

As one of the cattle men of Southern Alberta, I would like to call your attention to the very uncertain position we are in at the present time with our herds. For the past two seasons settlers were crowding into the country, and what used to be our summer range is practically all gone now and our cattle are confined to the hills and rough country along the eastern slope of the Rockies.

You can easily understand a man, who has some hundreds or some thousands of cattle, and who can neither lease nor purchase land for grazing, being in a very uneasy state of mind as to what the final outcome of his business will be if settlement still continues to crowd in upon him.

There may be good reasons for refusing to lease or sell large tracts of land for grazing purposes where it can reasonably be contended the land is fit for farming, but the same reasons cannot apply to the high, rough, broken country known as the foot-hills, and I would strongly urge that the Government reserve this latter country as a permanent grazing district. . . .

. . . This country is very rough and broken and stands at an altitude of 4,000 feet and upwards, and it is quite safe to say that in the average season it is subject to frost and snow ten months in the year.

The only arable land in this district is found in valleys lying between high hills and along river bottoms, and it would all be required for growing green feed for wintering cattle. Though settlers might wish to take up locations in the hills I think it would be undesirable to allow them to do so until the men who are now there with their cattle are allowed to acquire a reasonable amount of land, for over-crowding would mean scarcity of grass with the necessary result that every man's cattle would be thin, and poor and unfit for even the home beefmarket, to say nothing of the export trade which has hitherto been a very important business in that part of the country.

In the past cattle owned in the foot-hills, drifted out on the plains for the summer and the grass in the hills was thus saved for the winter months, but the large settlement along the Calgary and Edmonton Railway has cut off the summer range and the cattle are now practically confined to the hills all year round.

Further, homesteading in the hills, the only range that is now left, will simply mean the destruction of cattle ranching in that part of the country. . . .

It might be of interest to you to know that during the past two seasons nearly one third of all the beef produced in the Territories was grown in the district to which I refer.

Now, for the protection of this important industry I would suggest that a reservation from homestead entry or further settlement for the present time, be made along the east slope of the mountains in such a way as to include in the reservation all that portion of the country which I have described as rough and broken and unfit for farming purposes, . . . and that stockmen who are now bona fide settlers within that district be allowed to secure by closed lease, for a period of twenty-one years at a reasonable rental, a quantity of land proportionate to the number of cattle now owned by them.

In order to prevent the old cry of "The big man squeezing out the small man" I would suggest that small ranchers in this district be allowed to first select the land to which they may be entitled, such land to be taken as nearly as possible in the immediate vicinity of their present location, and that after this, the larger stockmen make their selection out of the remaining lands. If this principle be adopted I do not see how any hardships can be done to any one either in or out of the reserved district.

I hope the above proposition will meet with your early and favorable consideration.

Yours truly
Geo Lane

Stock-Watering Reservations

135. PRIVY COUNCIL REPORT, 1886

Order in Council, No. 2131 of the 13th day of December 1886.

To the Honorable
The Minister of the Interior.

On a Memorandum dated 23rd November 1886, from the Minister of the Interior, stating that in view of representations made to him by the Stock Association of the Provisional District of Alberta, that settlers were squatting upon lands along the river bottoms over which cattle were accustomed to go for water, it has been deemed advisable to have an investigation and a report made upon the matter by an Officer of the Department of the Interior, and that accordingly Mr. William Pearce, Superintendent of Mines, who has a thorough knowledge of the country was instructed to make and during the past season did make, the requisite inspection.

The Minister submits a Report from Mr. Pearce to the effect that the complaint of the Stock Association is well founded that squatters are taking up the water-frontages and watering places in certain Sections, and are excluding the cattle of the Stockmen therefrom, and with a view to prevent this difficulty from becoming a drawback to the Country, and in order to afford reasonable watering facilities it is suggested that the Sections and parts of Sections of land, colored pink on the annexed plan, be reserved for the purposes of watering and sheltering.

The Minister recommends that such of these lands as are at the disposal of the Government be reserved from sale and settlement, and that they be reserved as approaches to the water and as watering places for stock.

The Committee submit the above recommendation for Your Excellency's approval.

JOHN J. McGEE,
Clerk, Privy Council.

136. NOTICE TO VACATE

PAC, RG15, B2, vol. 159, 141376, pt 2.

Office of the
Superintendent of Mines,
Calgary,
13th April 1895

S. Carter Esq.
Macleod,
Sir;—

I am informed that you have commenced squatting on land within the lease of Mr. J.R. Craig, which is valuable for hay and watering purposes; if this information is correct it would be in your own interest to desist from this attempt. If within Mr. Craig's lease, he can eject you at any time and if the land is valuable for stock-watering purposes, the Government will certainly do so. A gentleman will probably start in a few days from here to locate certain springs for reservation in the Porcupine Hills as well as hay lands and shelter places and it is the policy of the Government to prevent squatting on such reservations even if forcible ejection is requisite. It is in the interest of the small stockman as well as the large one that such watering places should be provided and maintained and while no doubt such a one would seem particularly desirable to the squatter, the public interest and not that of the individual has to be consulted. The occupation of half a dozen spring [s] would in many localities render 20 to 50.000 acres valueless for grazing or at least depreciate its value by 50% and more. I have thought it well to write you fully, so that you may know what the policy of the Government is and the reason for same and that public opinion will sustain the Government in the rigid enforcement of it.

I am, Sir,
Your obedient servant,
WM PEARCE,
Superintendent.

137. STOCK-WATERING AND SHELTER RESERVATIONS

Canada, *Sessional Papers* (1897), no. 13, Department of the Interior, Report of the Superintendent of Mines.

The charge is frequently made that the area of these reservations is excessive and that there are many more of them than necessity calls for, also that many of them have no water at all. Of course, any one desiring to settle would naturally like to do so on a spring or open stream, and when a request is made it is invariably accompanied by the statement that there is no stockwatering at that point, or that, if he is allowed to settle there, he will take good care that there is plenty of access for stock to water. Regarding the first assertion, it is in 95 per cent of cases erroneous; but even if it were true, it would not necessarily follow that the reservation should not be maintained, for though the intending settler personally might not prevent stock travelling, grazing and watering as was desirable, he might be succeeded in a short time by one who would do so. It is anticipated that within the next decade there will be four times the number of stock that there is to-day, and these reservations have been made with that end in view, so that although there might be an excess of them at the present time such would not be the case a few years from now, so that if even the stockmen, large or small, in any neighbourhood petitioned to have the number or area of these reservations reduced, it might not be good policy to grant their petition. I find that the total area of the grazing district in Alberta, south of township 35, may be estimated to contain 17,438,210 acres, and the area now reserved is equal to 140,000 acres. It will thus be seen that these reservations only represent 4/5 of 1 per cent of the total area of the grazing district. Through the construction of irrigation works and the raising of winter fodder thereby, and realizing that the capacity of our ranges is only limited to the extent to which the winter fodder is available, he who predicts an increase of our ranch stock by four times its present number within the next ten years could not be called over sanguine. The second statement usually made, namely, that the applicant will see that free access is given stock to water on the land he desires, could not be entertained for a moment. It is not in human nature to stand by and see range cattle rubbing down your fences without taking measures to prevent it and that means chiefly running them off with dogs, and in one run of a mile or two more flesh is lost than can be put on in two weeks. Frequently cattle are absolutely ruined from the effects of dogging them. Of course if no fences were put up by these squatters and no dogs kept, no great injury might be done to the cattle by reason of a squatter residing near a spring.

Range cattle will not go near any place where dogs are kept and every settler keeps one or more. Another thing is, that during hot weather it may be observed that after drinking they invariably lie down, and as it is the habit of range stock to graze in considerable bands, from 100 up to several thousand, a very considerable area is required to allow cattle free access to the water; otherwise, the stronger animals will prevent the weaker ones from getting at it, and as they will not graze any considerable distance away from water during hot weather, the necessity for larger reservations becomes still more apparent, as a small area would soon be completely eaten off and the quality of the cattle would thus deteriorate instead of improve. The whole extent of what is known as the grazing district of the North-west territories would be valuable for cattle grazing were it not for the scarcity of water at any time. It is, therefore, the duty of the department to preserve as far as possible those watering places that are still available.

As to the charge that many of these reservations contain no water, this may be perfectly true in some cases, and still they may be extremely useful for the purpose of shelter and as furnishing access to valleys and bottoms where pasture and water is abundant. Such is absolutely essential unless the industry is to be completely annihilated. . . .

It may naturally be asked, why is the small stockman so objectionable to the larger one? The answer is this. The large man allows his stock to roam at large, therefore, he, in his own interest, must keep the range in such a condition, that cattle will have the freest possible access to all parts thereof. On the other hand the small man for the first few years, and until his band becomes of such size as to make it necessary to do the same as the former, lets them run in a narrow valley or around some fine spring or other open winter water where they are herded in proximity to his buildings, and in this manner often monopolises an excessive area of land absolutely vital for winter feed. It thus happens that while there is not much objections to the large operator settling there, the mode of settlement adopted by the smaller one is decidedly objectionable and injurious to the public interest. It has been asserted by those who probably best understand the situation that if settlement had been absolutely prohibited in all those portions valuable for winter pasture the country would have gained by such a policy. No one objects to settlement by men, large or small, in the cattle district, where all take equal chances; but when, from extreme selfishness or other motive, parties insist upon taking up locations choice in themselves, and if occupied very injurious to the stock industry and the public interest generally, it is only natural that hostility should be aroused. The cry is raised that the large stockmen are trying to crush the small ones. The larger stockmen have never objected to settlement, if the settler will only leave free access to all the winter grazing, shelter and water, for his stock, essential to their welfare, in fact, to the very existence of all. In many places a settler by squatting in a narrow valley, possibly only a quarter of a mile wide, may, by erecting a fence across the same, or even across a portion of the same and keeping dogs, prevent all access to the whole of the valley during the winter time when it is vital to prevent stock perishing. Those valleys contain from 500 up to 5,000 acres of invaluable pasture. As a matter of fact it is not even necessary for him to fence, as, by keeping one or two good dogs, the same end is attained. While such would be a very desirable state of affairs for the individual residing there, it is not in the public interest that it should be permitted. Instead of there being an excess of such points reserved, it would have been decidedly in the interest of the cattle industry and the public generally if more such places, which are now settled upon, had been reserved long ago. It was foreseen at the start that there would be considerable agitation against the reservation of these favoured points by individuals and the friends of those who desired to obtain the same; but it was hoped that through the ejection of a few squatters and a firm attitude on the part of the department in the matter of maintaining these reservations, the clamour against them would soon cease and every one would begin to realize that it is as much in the interest of the small stockman as in that of the larger one that measures of this nature should be adopted while the industry is yet in its infancy and while it is possible to protect vested interests in so doing, and it is asserted that if the squatters now in possession be ejected, the trouble will be ended; if not, the flood-gates for illegitimate settlement will be wide open and official encouragement will be given to a class of people whose ideas should at least not be encouraged. . . .

All of which is respectfully submitted.

I have the honour to be, sir,
Your obedient servant,
WM. PEARCE,
Superintendent of Mines

138. AN OPPOSING VIEW

PAC, Sifton Papers, MG27, II, D15, vol. 29.

Nanton Alberta Nov. 28th 1897

Frank Oliver M.P.
Ottawa, Ont.
Dear Sir: I take the liberty of addressing a few lines to you expressive of my

own, and all other small ranchers with whom I am acquainted, ideas regarding the land policy of the late government, and the action taken by the N.W. Stock Grower's Association in their recent meetings requesting the continuation of the so called Water reserve system that has served so well the purpose of preventing settlement in Southern Alberta. As you are well aware all the odd numbered sections in each Township are already reserved from home stead entry. Add to these the Hudson's Bay sections and there are twenty out of the thirty six sections in each Township practically reserved from settlement, so that without any further reserving five ninths of the public domain is out of the reach of the homesteader. It follows that five ninths of the water is already reserved, and will continue to be so until all the even numbered sections have been taken, and judging by the rate of settlement in this part of Alberta for the past ten years, it will be long after the much cherished "range business" has died a natural death before these even numbered sections are all taken.

The members of the Association above named have all availed themselves the privilege of selecting the best possible locations for ranches, keeping in mind the all important item to a ranch, of open water for their own use. They have also made fences for the protection of their winter ranges in such a manner as to secure "sheltered places and to stop up "run ways" so as to be able to hold what stock they wished to keep separate from the rangers. Hardly a rancher or ranching co. but has such fences and now these same people are petitioning this government to continue the "reserve" policy and have added the recommendation that "all run ways and places of shelter shall be kept open". In short this association seems to want to prevent a small settler doing what they have done, and if they are successful in inducing the government to continue this policy their [sic] will continue to be a lack of settlement and development in Southern Alberta.

That there may be instances where a water reserve is necessary I admit, but the present manner of reserving is utterly unjust and serves only to hinder settlement.

As an illustration I will give you a short history of my own experience in trying to secure a good location for a small ranch. I came with my family from Toronto to this Country in Nov. 1887. In February 1888 I sent a man to the Land Office in Calgary to find out whether a certain quarter sec in Tp. 16 R 29 E. could be taken as a homestead, it being an even numbered section. I received word that the quarter I wished to file upon was a "water reserve" as there was a good spring upon it. During the following spring this same quarter was fenced in by a man who owned a ranch alongside of it.

A few weeks after the fencing had been done Mr. Pearce of the land board stopped over night with me at Mosquito Creek, and I asked him if any one could fence in a water reserve. He promptly said no, and wanted to know if any one had done so. I related the factes [sic] in the case to him telling him the man who had done so was H.B. Alexander. This altered the case altogether, and he volunteered the information that in case of lease holders the government sometimes allowed water reserves to be fenced up. Five years ago last fall I came to this place, Tp. 14 R 1 W and have occupied it ever since. I chose it because there was a fine spring and good hay land near with excellent opportunity for irrigation. I also knew it was unsurveyed and therefore no water reserves, and no stock co had any lease in the Township. Under such circumstances I could not see how I could be interfered with by a government which professed to be anxious to have the country improved.

Last Dec. about the 10th I was in Calgary and called at the land officer to make sure that there were no reserves in the Tp. and found their [sic] had been some made or established, but was informed by Mr. Pearce that he would have to come out and investigate the locality before he could promise any assurance of my being able to hold my place. He wanted to know why all the small ranchers wanted open water, why we could not build Windmills to pump water for our stock or dig ditches, to run the water from the springs etc. etc. I suppose it really does seem strange to Mr. Pearce that a man with a small capital would want open water in his pasture and for that reason I think he is a very unfit person for the position he holds and should be granted a long leave of absence with a recommendation to go to Holland where he could study the windmill system to his hearts [sic] content.

I can assure you that I am not alone in my experiences with the land officials and I only cite it to illustrate what has been going on in Southern Alberta ever since I have lived here.

As a cure for this water reserve evil I would suggest that no water should be reserved in any Township without the consent by petition of at least two thirds of all the actual resident land holders of the Tp. and that all waters here to fore reserved shall be declared open so that if the resident owners or homesteaders in any Tp. wish to have any water reserved they can do so by legal petition. Such a regulation would take it out of the power of any association or Co to reserve or hold from settlement any land upon the mere pretext that it is wanted for the use of the public.

To cite my own case again I have no doubt that the Association or some members of it will try to have the water of this Tp. so reserved as to prevent further settlement and drive out those that are already here if possible. Not a member of that Association holds or owns a foot of land in the Tp or within ten miles of me and to have Mr. Pearce come out and look this locality over to see whether settlers who have lived here five or six years have any right to be here is what I call an outrage and a mockery of government supervision.

I have written the above hoping you will give it your consideration as I am confident that you aim to be the representative of *all* the people and are desirous of doing the greatest good to the greatest number.

Very respectfully yours,
D.V. Mott

139. A SETTLER'S CONCERN

PAC, RG15, B2a, vol. 171, 145330, pt 3.

High River, Nov 30th, 1897

Frank Oliver, M.P.
Edmonton, Alta.
Dear Sir:

You will remember a petition sent you last session by Robert Findlay from the settlers of this District asking that the Stock Association be not allowed to turn their cattle North of High River nor to hold them there. For some reason there was nothing done about it and now it is a common thing to hear some of the stockmen ask in a sneering way What has become of the "Findlay Bill" as well they try to make as much trouble as possible for those who signed the petition. This year there has been put on here between three and four thousand gentle steers and these with the range cattle were driven North of High River. The Stockmen say it is West of the settlement but how long does it take them to travel eight or ten miles where there is no effort made to keep them out. As a result of this as soon as cold weather comes on every settler in the place has a bunch of these dogies around his corrals and stacks. To-day I drove away from my own place over 150 head taking them six miles: when I got back there were as many as 50 more which had arrived from some other quarter. According to the Ordinance this is illegal and the stockmen are warning the settlers they will prosecute any one found driving their cattle. But what are they to do? As a Justice of the peace I have complaints from the stockmen about their cattle being driven and from the farmers asking what they are to do as no reasonable fence will keep the brutes out and every one of these settlers has cattle of their own some as many as 100 head which they try to keep close but with the range stock continually moving among them it is impossible and when they get away The Association may gather them at "Round Up" if they have not done anything against the stockmen. Last week I met the foreman of the Association a man I have known and been friendly with for 14 years and spoke to him on the matter and because I took the part of the settler I got nothing but abuse for my pains and told I might go the lower regions and said they would have laws passed that no one can handle any stock on the range except the Association men.

I then immediately wrote the Inspector of N.W.M.P. at Calgary also Mr. Haultain of the nuisance and that something should be done at once to prevent trouble. There is no need of this clashing if the stockmen would only have some regard for the rights of settlers and there is any amount of country south of High River and Little Bow another thing it is sure to do the country harm and is not to the benefit of either parties.

Then this meeting the Minister of the Interior at Calgary by the delegates of the Stock Association asking that more reserves of Springs be made and that they be given another slice of the earth, as if they have not got South Alberta now at their disposal so that no one else can get in if a man does get a chance to get a suitable place that is not reserved they make it so uncomfortable for him that he has to leave. It looks very much like "dog in the manger" for if you go to these ranchers places and not one of them but has built on Springs or good watering places and has as many enclosed in in their pastures as possible. As well most of them have large pastures built enclosing hundreds of acres of government land to which they have no right whatever. There no settler dare think of going.

This business of running stock at large is all right in its own place and where the country is not wanted for settlement but it is not right that large stockmen should be allowed to harass settlers at their pleasure and they are doing all in their power to prevent settlement. It would not take many settlers with their corrall [sic] bunches of cattle well taken care of to have more cattle for export than any of the large ranches and the country would be the better of them.

Then at last election you will remember how much these very men helped us. F. Stimson [manager of the North West Cattle Company] in particular —another of the delegates said he would *fire* every man he had that did not vote right.

You must not think that I want to be a general kicker as I wrote you last winter on another matter. (Timber inspection) but I have been asked by the people of this settlement to let you know how these things affect us so that you may lay them before the proper authorities.

I do not wish for the present that my name should be made public if this business can be made right without but if not I will take it up in the press and keep at it until it is.

Yours truly,
R.A. Wallace
High River,
Alta.

140. THE STOCKMENS' ASSOCIATION

Glenbow-Alberta Institute, Western Stock Growers' Association, Minutes, Fifth Annual Meeting, April 1901.

The Committee to consider the subject of Stock Watering Reserves reported recommending that the following telegram be sent Mr. F. Oliver M.P.

Many Settlers are this Spring injuring Territorial Interests by squatting on Stock Water Reserves. Western Stock Grower's Ass'n assembled in annual meeting request that immediate steps be taken to prevent this and to remove

such recent squatters. Instructions should be sent to all Land agents warning settlers against such trespass. . . .
The telegram was sent. . . .

Moved by F.W. Godsal.—Seconded by A.M. Morden

The W.S.G.A. desire to impress upon the Dominion Government the extreme importance of Reservations for Stock Watering purposes in Alberta and Assiniboia. They feel it their duty to do this, not in the interests of large stockowners only, but of every one who [has] a horse or a cow on the range, and in the interests of the settlers of this country.

It is well known that farmers with small bunches of stock become the strongest advocates of water reservations, as it is a serious matter to them when their stock have to wander far away in search of water. The outcry against water reservations is usually by new arrivals who have not the interests of the country at heart, but write to acquire these desireable [sic] locations as a free homestead, and in many cases they squat on these water Reserves, content to wait for the time, which they think will come sooner or later, when such reserves will be thrown open and they will get it for nothing.

Now this Ass'n does not advocate the throwing open of any existing reservations under any circumstances, but as the Government may consider this necessary in some cases now, and possibly in years to come, we would recommend that it be made one of the land regulations of the country that no land once reserved for Stock Watering purposes, or any portion of such land, whether there is water on it or not, shall be open to free entry, but shall only be disposed of by public auction, as in the case of school lands at an upset price of Five dollars per acre. This we believe will largely prevent the squatting on such lands at the present time, as men will know the hopelessness of ever obtaining a free entry and the possibility of being overbid at auction.

It will be also only common justice to law abiding settlers who have been building up this country for years, and who desired these water reserves, but had to locate on waterless lands adjoining, and whose time and labor have added to the value of these water Reserves: at auctions these old settlers will have an equal chance to acquire such lands, or at least they will know that the value of the land that was refused to them will go to help the revenue of their country. We believe that under existing land regulations land that owing to special circumstances has a value beyond the ordinary value of surrounding lands, or that is a cancelled homestead is thereby withdrawn from free settlement, and is disposed of by sale only: we feel therefore that our suggestion regarding water reserves is only in accordance with the spirit of the land laws. We would further urge upon the Government the importance of removing squatters who are now trespassing on Water Reserves, and to take steps to prevent such possible trespass in the future. We ask this in justice to surrounding settlers and stockmen who are thus prevented from using the water for their stock.
Carried.

A Grazing or a Farming Region

141. A VOICE FOR OPEN AND UNRESTRICTED SETTLEMENT

Calgary *Herald*, August 23, 1887.

Senator Cochrane has done more than probably any other man to discourage the development of the unrivalled resources of this district. He has decried the country on every possible occasion as useless for farming purposes. All this and more has he done to keep settlers out of the country so that he could hold for a long period of years an immense tract of land at a nominal rental of one cent an acre and practically without conditions. . . .

The lands on the Cochrane lease are worth from $5 to $10 an acre for farming, just as they are, and, once freed from the clutches of the leaseholder, will soon become one of the finest districts in the Territories. Senator Cochrane may tell the people in the east that the Calgary district is not favorable to agriculture, but he will not tell them that every acre of the two townships recently thrown open was entered for by actual settlers and farmers in two days. There are already a considerable number of squatters on other portions of the lease and it is against them that ejectment proceedings are now threatened. We trust the Government, or their agents, will not allow, much less assist, the company in any unjust action against the squatters.

142. A CATTLEMAN'S VIEW

PAC, RG15, B2a, vol. 171, 145330, pt 3.

Plume Creek,
Woolchester, Dec. 4, 1903.

The Minister of the Interior,
Dear Sir,

I am writing you to place my case before your notice. I am one of the pioneer ranchers of this district I homesteaded on my present location, also bought a section and a quarter and leased a little. I began with just a few head of cattle and horses and by steady perseverance now have about two hundred head of cattle and thirty two horses. [o] wing to settlers coming in thick round me, I have been obliged to sell to my next neighbor who also needs room to expand. I shall therefore be obliged to move out of the railroad belt as it is too thickly settled. . . .

What I wish to do is to go further back in order to expand if the government will allow me to purchase land. If I cannot do so I must sell and go to the Argentina where I can continue in the business for which I am best fitted. Farming I do not intend to try as this country is not fitted for it. There are years in which hot winds dry up all vegetation and bring nothing but vexation and debts to the inexperienced that try to farm on the strength of two or three wet seasons in succession,

Hoping to hear from you,

I remain
Yours truly,
Ernest Peachey.

143. THE LAST WORD

University of Alberta, Pearce Papers, 14H7.

Hon W.J. Roche,   Calgary, Alta. 4th December 1913
Minister of the Interior,
Ottawa, Ont.
Dear Sir:

Yours of the 17th ultimo enclosing copy of the Grazing Regulations reached here when I was absent and the delay in replying has been owing to such absence. The delay is regretted. . . .

You are probably aware that at one time I was or at least should have been, owing to the nature of my position, very familiar with the grazing conditions of the West. That was, however, prior to 1897. At that time most of the old leases were wound up and the administration of the grazing interests seemed to be devoted to demonstrating that the policy heretofore adopted was an erroneous one. The results have shown that the policy thus adopted was not the best. Probably a mean between the two policies would have more nearly furnished the best solution.

Though familiar with the topographical, meteorological and soil conditions of the grazing districts of Saskatchewan and Alberta since 1883, I must confess that my views regarding the best means of administering that territory have from time to time greatly changed, and no doubt in the future as conditions change any policy adopted should also. Ten years, however, is probably not too long a time to fix on any particular policy so as to give it a thorough testing out. . . .

. . . when I review closely the meteorological conditions which have existed during the past 30 years I can come to but one conclusion, that during the majority of those years for probably 40% of what is considered the grazing areas the conditions have for 75% of that period proved sufficiently favorable to furnish a fair return to the farmer in the way of grain and fodder cultivation providing of course the soil and topographical conditions were suitable. There are some districts which during that time have not had the meteorological conditions fitted to produce a crop 25% of the time. No Mixed farming settlement should be planted in any district except where at least fair crops can be obtained for at least two-thirds of the time. . . .

Yours truly
William Pearce

THE RANGE-CATTLE INDUSTRY IN DECLINE

144. THE CATTLE RANGE CONFINED

Glenbow-Alberta Institute, Cross Papers, B56, F442.

Jun 19 1901

Sandon, B.C.
Dear Cross,
I hear there are all kinds of settlers coming in on Mosquito Ck. I have just had a notice from the Land office saying they will cancel a homestead I applied for in Big Coulee in early days. I have been holding this in order to keep the coulee from being fenced up as it is the only pass left for cattle. I have written to the Agt. in Calgary saying that they ought to give me the chance to buy before letting it be taken up as a homestead by someone who will fence it. It would pay some of us who have cattle on Mosquito Ck. to buy it and hold it. It will be a very bad thing for stockmen if this Coulee is fenced up. It would be a good thing if you would write to the Dom. Land agt. in Calgary or to whoever you think has most influence and ask him to either make the half section (N. ½ Sec. 18 Tp. 16 R.29 W 4 M) a water reserve or offer it for sale.
. . .

Yrs. sincly.
H.B. Alexander

145. WESTERN STOCK GROWERS' ASSOCIATION, RESOLUTION, DECEMBER 1903

Glenbow-Alberta Institute, Western Stock Growers' Association Papers, Minutes, December 18, 1903.

Be it resolved at this meeting of the Western Stock Growers Ass'n. called for the purpose of discussing the serious outlook which at present confronts the Stock raising Industry of this country, that a memorial be addressed to the Dominion Gov't. setting forth the undoubted necessity that exists for some immediate Government intervention in the present land and other regulations if the Ranching industry is to be saved from extermination. We respectfully point out that a very large amount of capital has been invested in the ranching industry and that many of the investors have been engaged in the business for some considerable time and own a large amount of land which was bought purely for ranching purposes. Until within a year or so ago that condition that existed enabled the business to be conducted on the ranging system, but those engaged in it are now finding themselves confronted with an entirely different condition of affairs, owing to the rapid settlement which is now taking place throughout the country. We wish respectfully to point out that unless some privileges in the way of obtaining extra land or more satisfactory leases can be granted there seems an almost certain probability that many of those engaged in ranching and who have their whole capital invested in it, will have of necessity to close up their business and in such an abrupt manner that they must inevitably sustain heavy losses. If we cannot get some protection from the rapid closing in of our ranches and the disappearance of the open range by settlement, we must sacrifice our interests and get out of the business. It seems to us unfortunate both for us and for them that in many cases new settlers are located and are advised to settle on land and in Districts which are not suitable for farming, and yet where [their] advent is a threat to the ranching business.

146. PROGRESS OF SOUTHWESTERN SETTLEMENT DURING 1905: IMMIGRATION OFFICER'S REPORT

Canada, *Sessional Papers* (1905), no. 25, Department of the Interior, Annual Report, 1905, 108-10.

A point of considerable importance and greatly improving year by year, is Medicine Hat. Abundance of moisture has continued the desirable change of making what was considered a grazing district admirably suited for farming operations. At this point 244 new homesteads were entered for during the year. . . .

. . . the settlers between Calgary and Macleod were very much more numerous than in any previous year, and what was formerly known as a stock ranching country, with ranges from 5,000 to 15,000 acres, is now almost entirely divided into farms of from 160 to 640 acres, well fenced, and containing large fields of wheat, oats and barley, surrounding substantial farm houses. These settlers appear to be well content with their new homes. A decrease in the number of homestead entries in the Calgary district is noted, as land within easy distance of the railway has been largely taken up. . . .

The sub-agent of Dominion lands at Pincher Creek, reports that the change foreshadowed in previous annual reports has come to pass in his district, and large areas formerly used for the ranging of cattle are fenced and waving with a promising crop of fall wheat standing from three to six feet in height. Other crops are in equally favourable condition owing to the early spring and the amount of rainfall which has been ample for the purposes of present growth.

The large herds of cattle which formerly roamed over the land now under wheat have been removed nearer the mountains, and to unsurveyed lands, while the grower of fall wheat has still his bunch of stock which is improving in quality rather than growing in numbers, hence there are more cattle owned in small bunches. In consequence of closer settlement, homesteaders and purchasers have to seek land further from the centres of the district, and unsurveyed lands are being squatted on. The class of settler predominating in the district is of British and United States origin, and it is pleasing to note that the idea prevalent in some quarters of the Americanizing effect of settlers is without the least foundation, as no class appreciates Canadian laws and regulations more than does the settler from the United States.

147. SALE OF THE COCHRANE RANCH, 1906

Canada, *Sessional Papers* (1907), no. 25, Department of the Interior, Annual Report, 1907, 96-7.

One of the striking instances of the march of the settler is the sale of the Cochrane ranch, which comprises 66,000 acres, and will this year be very largely occupied by farmers. . . .

. . . Notwithstanding the general favour of irrigated lands, the great bulk of the new settlement is going on non-irrigable lands, and good crops are being obtained thereon from time to time. There appears to be a growing belief that 'dry farming' may make irrigation unnecessary altogether, and through widespread cultivation, not only retain but attract precipitation. The soil this spring is in excellent shape so far as moisture goes; the lakes and ponds are flooded and the mountains full of snow. One thousand four hundred and eighteen homestead entries were granted in the land office here [Lethbridge] as against 1,181 for the corresponding previous year.

THE RANCH ESTABLISHMENT AND THE SOCIAL MILIEU

148. CASTE AND CLASS IN THE FOOTHILLS

Glenbow-Alberta Institute, C. Inderwick, Diary and Personal Letters from North Fork Ranch.

The East Range Ranch
May 13, 1889.

Dearest,

. . . We have a cow-camp—a shack for the cowboys—and they have their own cook, so we only get an occasional one for meals if he happens to be riding nearer the house than the camp. They are a nice lot of men. I love their attempts to help me to appear civilized. Though they ride in flannel shirts, they never come to the table in shirt sleeves. There is a black alpaca (!) coat which hangs in the shack attached to the house for the cowboys' use—and each one struggles into it to live up to the new regime, which began with a bride at the ranche, and this is done so enthusiastically and with such good will that I have no qualms of conscience that I am a nuisance— . . .

. . . We are the grand owners of a dear ugly discriminating bull-terrier who does not allow an Indian near the place, but I have tried to make use of a squaw who is the nominal wife of a white man near us, to do the washing, but had to give her up, as she stolidly went on rubbing a table napkin all the time I was away from her side one morning and when I returned hoping to see a tubpile of washed clothes I found one table napkin in holes, the result of an hour's work. At scrubbing the floor she was equally hopeless as she sat in the middle and slopped all round her—aimlessly. Poor Shomacki—or some such name—and poor, poor John Fisher! Who was once I believe a missionary.

I gave up the task of training her—the odds were too much for my patience and courage and I now send my washing to a dignified coloured lady in Saint Francis [Pincher Creek] who boasts that she and the Police Commissioner's wife were the first white ladies to arrive in the country. Time is nothing to her, and if I were an ordinary woman and not a Bride with a good trousseau I shiver to think what might happen me when weeks go by and no laundry can be cajoled from our aristocratic Auntie's stately dwelling.

I must tell you about my first ball at Fort Lorne [Fort Macleod] at the Police Barracks. On our invitation was written the name of the people with whom we were to stay. We were new people and knew no one, so we were kindly taken in by a shop keeper & his sister, at least I was, for Geoffrey had some sort of a shake down in somebody's office. My maid also had an invitation to the same place & to the same ball. (I have since had to dismiss her as she got so discontented with her position.) It was the first ball to which the squaws were not allowed to go, but there were several half breeds. . . .

. . . There are so many English men here and a few English women—the latter of very different types but the men are almost all nice, though they nearly all have no tact in the way they speak of Canadians and Canada and the last straw to me is the way in which they say "but we do not look on you as a Canadian!". They mistake this for a compliment. It makes my Canadian blood boil. I answer that though I have married an Englishman I have not lost my identity—and that I am purely Canadian and am proud of it. They simply do not understand that I really mean it. However one day we had the Village Schoolmaster here; he is an Englishman but of a very different class to most of the men we know—he began to badger me about Canada and was surprised that I did not answer but took all he said as information. At last he said, "Why, I heard that you are very easily roused in defense of your country, and have a bad time being the only colonist among so many English!". Mr. Barret who was there, said, "you mistake—I am a colonist as you call it" and in a few words managed to show this very impossible man that he was overstepping the bounds of politeness. I was so surprised as Mr. Barret was ultra-English, but I found that he had been born at The Cape—His father was in the navy and was stationed there at that time. It strikes me very forcibly how inately [sic] different we are from the people of the British Isles. We are so adaptable—now in this way—people of this schoolmaster's type have a very fair education—have very good homes, more money than many of us Canadians and still they are far beneath us in every way—in *themselves* I mean—in a word they are not gentle people. I suppose the difference really is that our parents and grandparents *were* gentle men and women and in spite of the hardships of Canadian life in their generations, preserved the true spirit of gentle breeding.

I like Englishmen and yet at times I find the companionship of fresh Englishmen (there is no man so delightful as an Englishman who has been in Canada for a few years) very trying to my nerves. . . .

. . . [The Garnett's?] invited us to dine and sleep a couple of weeks ago and I did enjoy myself. There was a certain excitement about it which is lacking elsewhere for we had to dress for dinner, and one so very seldom wears a low dress that when one does, the occasion is a remarkable one. . . .

. . . [Miss Selton] has a very pretty drawing room—one great attraction being a small pretty English piano which insists upon going out of tune in this very dry climate, but is still a great pleasure as there are so very few in the country. Miss Selton sings in the most charming way. I think her singing voice delightful—and she is so good about it, she seems to love singing herself—I think she is a dear, but you should see her in Church! She wears always the same hat, a black chip English walking hat with a black veil, and a mannish coat, she looks very neat and you could mistake her for nothing but an English woman, and to her this is a very good way of paying her a direct compliment —She asks nothing better. There are a few other English women—of very different types. One lives with her husband on a small ranche near Saint Francis and is devoted to dogs. She invited me out to see a "real English home" so we rode over one lovely afternoon. . . .

149. THE HUNT CLUB

Macleod Gazette, November 17, 1892.

Last Thursday was Thanksgiving Day, and the Macleod Hunt Club took advantage of the occasion to turn out in strength. By a lucky coincidence Mr. W. Jordan came in from the Cochrane Ranche a couple of days before, bringing with him the pack of hounds belonging to that ranche, which have in their ranks several experienced and redoubtable warriors, and which in conjunction with the Club hounds, made a formidable array. The start was from the Macleod Hotel at 1 p.m., and sharp on time some fourteen horsemen pulled out, and their number was increased to nineteen by degrees. Almost before getting clear of the town a cayote was raised, but he managed to lose himself in a coulee before the hounds had got down to work. Working towards the Belly river, two more were soon viewed in the distance and with a rush the pack was away. A run ensued that was a stiff one and no mistake, and it was evident that the cayote was a rare old bird, . . .

150. A LADY'S LIFE ON A RANCHE

Moira O'Neill, 'A Lady's Life on a Ranche' in *Blackwood's Edinburgh Magazine*, 163 (January 1898), pp. 3-16.

. . . I cannot answer for all the English wives on all the ranches in Canada. I can only answer for one ranche which is flourishing, and for one small Irishwoman happily situated on it. There is perhaps a good deal of sympathy between Ireland and the North-West. In the old country we are accustomed to disregard appearances, to make all kinds of shifts and laugh at them, to neglect superfluities, mind our manners, follow after sport, and love horses. All that is good training for the North-West. . . .

As to the want of congenial society, . . . Here, besides our Canadian neighbours, who are unfailing in kindness and hospitality to new-comers, there live a fair number of Englishmen, ranchers and others; and some of the more adventurous have wives. What should hinder us from enjoying each other's society? It is true that we do not scatter cards upon each other or make many afternoon calls, for reasons connected with time and space and other large considerations. . . .

But when people who have like aims and occupations do happen to meet, the converse is particularly interesting, at least to themselves. Of course they talk shop. Nearly all the conversation worth listening to is shop of one kind or another. Prairie shop has a fascination of its own—cattle, hay and horses, timber, grass and calves, weather, Indians and wolves, fencing, freights and the English beef-market. Wherever Englishmen abound—and this is emphatically a Land of the Younger Son—there the talk is on out-of-door subjects, and there is sympathy with all that is doing in all the ends of the earth.

But to come home again, let us give heed to the household question,—that question which is with us all, and always with us. I have seen women in England nearly worn out with their servant-worries, their kitchen-ranges, and their complicated household arrangements. I would not change places with them for any consideration, even to have dinner in six courses every evening. Here we enjoy the luxury of one servant in the house, an able-bodied cook, and I never heard him complain that his cooking-stove had "gone back on him"; nor if he did, should I lie awake at night thinking about it. I made the usual mistake of bringing out a maid from home; but when in course of time the mistake rectified itself, and she went the way of all womankind in the West, I took to the broom and duster, and was surprised to find what a calmness descended on my spirit with release from the task of supervision. An average of two hours' housework a-day, and the trouble of mending one's own clothes, is not much to pay for all the joys of liberty. I keep up a conscientious endeavour to find some substitute for the vanished maid; and still every failure to secure one brings a secret relief, a sense that the days of liberty are lengthened. . . .

No doubt there is a certain difficulty about household service on a ranche. But then housekeeping is of a very simple kind. There are no elaborate meals, no superfluous furniture or plate to be cleaned; there is no attendance beyond what is necessary: in short, everything that may cause extra trouble is avoided. There is plenty of comfort on a ranche, but very little luxury; and every one must be ready to help himself, and to help others too, when the occasion arises. In case of sudden defection on the part of the cook, it is well to know how to prepare some simple things; though indeed almost any Western man can fill up the vacancy, so far as baking bread and cooking beef go. Then, in case of being weather-bound or otherwise cut off from a laundress, it is well to know a little of the gentle art of washing. No art is more useful, and none is easier to acquire, in a country like this, where "washboards", "wringers", and all kinds of conveniences minimise the labour.

When I first came here I did nothing at all, and enjoyed it very much. But now that I have a little—a very little—daily occupation, I enjoy it a great deal more. The fact is, that in a community where every one else is at work one does not feel quite at home in complete idleness—in riding over the prairie, gathering flowers, writing letters, and reading poetry-books all day long and every day. Abstraction is very pleasant; but it is pleasanter still to have a share in the general life, and by a very light experience of work, to gain some sympathy with those whose experience is of little else but work. . . .

But I want to make it plain that I am speaking of a lady's life on a ranche, without reference to those cases in which a pair of young people enter into matrimony with their bare hands and the labour thereof for sole support. Are there not plenty of people with small incomes, living busy lives and not desiring to live idle ones, yet released from drudgery or pressing anxiety, with health and leisure and capacity for enjoyment? These are the people who ought to be able to find happiness on a ranche in a good country; and if they cannot, they must be either strangely stupid or strangely unfortunate. I must be allowed to take it for granted that the ranche-owner is neither a duffer nor a "tender-foot", for the question of his methods and management does not enter into this article; yet a certain moderate amount of prosperity is necessary to happiness. Granted this, what is there to prevent a lady from enjoying her life on a ranche? In England, on a narrow income there is no such thing as freedom. You cannot go where you please, or live where you please, or have what you please; you cannot join in amusements that are really amusing, because every form of sport is expensive; you cannot accept pleasant invitations, because you cannot return them. And I think there would always be a wrangle with the cook, a railway journey, or a dinner-party lying heavy on your mind. But with the same income in a country like this, you can live on equal terms with your neighbours, and all your surroundings will be entirely in your favour; you have only to make the most of them. Shooting, fishing, and hunting, just the things which would bring you to the verge of bankruptcy at home, you can enjoy here practically for nothing. You can have all the horses you want to ride or drive. Your harness may show a certain dinginess for lack of the cleaning which no one has time to bestow on it; and the panels of your "democrat" will not be adorned with your worshipful crest and motto. But then—solacing thought!—neither will anybody else's be. . . .

. . . This is the country in which to find out exactly how deep one's own personal refinement goes, how many dainty habits and tastes will survive when all the trouble of them has devolved upon oneself. At home they are a form of unconscious self-indulgence; here they involve a principle, and an active one.

151. A VISIT TO THE COCHRANE RANCHE, 1902

Calgary Weekly Herald, October 9, 1902. The account of the visit is by the editor J.J. Young.

Though by far the largest, most important and possibly best situated cattle ranche in Alberta, the Cochrane ranche is as regards general details one of the least known; and the reason is its comparative isolation from the main lines of travel and the larger centres of population.

Think of seventy thousand acres of our choicest grass lands in a solid block, bounded on its two longest sides by rivers, stocked with fourteen or fifteen thousand head of well bred cattle, a ranche which brands nearly three thousand calves and sells a hundred thousand dollars worth of beef yearly and which has lost and made more money than any similar enterprise in Canada, and you have some idea of the big Cochrane ranche. When it was started the owners had the whole of Alberta to pick from. . . .

Nothing could be more charming than an autumn visit at such a ranche and such a house as this. Nothing could exceed the splendour of the view from the broad verandah of the Bungalow, a name by the way which gives no idea of the fine stone mansion it really is, with its green lawns, beautiful flower beds and vines and rose bushes, and furnished as it is with all the refinement that wealth and taste can suggest – with its fine reception hall, its open fire places, its pictures, its flowers, its trained servants from the Old Country, its pianola interpreting Chopin's music with the skill of a virtuoso and even a mocking bird in the conservatory.

The scene from the house, as already hinted, is matchless. Behind a broad meadow fringed at the river banks by trees clothed in the rich and changing colors of autumn rise the great bench lands of the Blood Reserve, and over them, crowning the picture the colossal jagged wall of the Rockies, half in Montana and half in Canada. . . .

One of the features of the visit was a drive with Mr. Cochrane to the "upper camp" of the ranche, the headquarters of ten or a dozen cowboys. It was a drive of fifteen miles over the company's splendid range, with the mountains facing us and through cattle all the way. And at the end of it there was still ten miles of the ranche not covered. About midway lie some lakes and toward these the cattle are attracted during the summer. From one point near the lakes we could see cattle grazing in every direction to the number of between four and five thousand. It is seldom, Mr. Cochrane informed us, that so many cattle are visible on the ranche except at a round-up.

It needed no expert to see that these cattle were a superior lot. For some years past the company has spared no efforts to improve the quality of the herd, especially by the introduction of new blood. Out of 230 bulls on the ranche, over two hundred are pedigreed Shorthorns and Galloways and the rest are being culled as fast as practicable. . . .

Now that the country is rapidly filling up with small settlers and land is reaching a value when it is perhaps more profitable to split it up into small holdings than preserve it for cattle ranges, the conditions are changing. Eight and ten dollar [an acre] land is too valuable for ranging cattle on under the old methods and either the big ranches must change their system or give place to the small holder. If the Cochrane company decide to close out it will make an important and significant chapter in the passing of the range. . . .

Life at the Bungalow, to a visitor at least, leaves nothing to be desired. Your comfort is attended to in a way that no expensive modern hotel could approach. No detail is overlooked. In your commodious bed room you find paper, envelopes, ink, pens, postcards and stamps. When you are called at 6 o'clock in the morning you find your boots polished, your "tub" ready for you in the bath room and everything systematically planned and arranged. Breakfast is ready at seven to the minute and you enjoy it as no town meal can be enjoyed, for there is Jersey cream, fresh eggs and other toothsome delicacies only to be found on a well regulated ranche—and indeed on few of these. The servants, too, are trained, noiseless and efficient. You are entertained with music and you are taken for rides behind fast teams or on the automobile, which gives you the exhilarating experience of gliding over smooth prairie trails at thirty miles an hour. The motor deserves a chapter to itself, but space forbids.

Then, too, there is such a garden as is not to be found even in Calgary. . . . In Mrs. Cochrane's garden and in the house there grow in splendid profusion the choicest flowers of England—Spanish, German and English irises, lilies of the valley, roses in abundance, tulips, the old-fashioned hollyhocks, carnations, peonies and many others, while climbing over the verandah and trelises [sic] and twining around the windows are such vines as the wild clematis, calistegia, nasturiums and Virginia creeper. Not a weed can be seen and the gravel walks and lawns are neatly kept.

GUIDE TO FURTHER READING

Published literature dealing with the ranching frontier in Canada is not extensive, and unfortunately some of the contemporary accounts that have been out of print for many years are available only in the larger libraries. The difficulty in assessing the Canadian cattlemen and their industry is complicated further by the fact that though the material published after the First World War is more abundant, with a few important exceptions it tends to be of a reminiscent and nonanalytical nature. To achieve some balance and to counter this deficiency, the reader's attention is also drawn to a number of recent articles.

CONTEMPORARY ACCOUNTS

Books

Craig, John R. *Ranching With Lords and Commons or Twenty Years on the Range* (Toronto, William Briggs, 1903). From his vantage point as an early ranch manager, Craig comments upon the cattle-company era and the problems of working with the British upper classes.

Deane, Captain Burton. *Mounted Police Life in Canada: A record of Thirty-One Years Service.* (London, Cassell, 1916). Deane, who spent most of his career in the cattle country, enjoyed a close rapport with the ranching fraternity. His book provides a sympathetic view of the cattlemen from the outside, as well as a contemporary view of life in the region from the 1885 rebellion onward.

Hill, Alexander Stavely. *From Home to Home: Autumn Wanderings in the years 1881, 1882, 1883, 1884.* (London, Sampson, Low, Marslow, Searle, and Rivington, 1885). Hill headed a group of titled British investors in a western ranch, and his discussion offers insight into the values and attitudes of this segment of the early ranching community.

Kelly, L.V. *The Range Men: the Story of the Ranchers and Indians of Alberta.* (Toronto, William Briggs, 1913). This is the first published history of the Canadian cattle kingdom. It is a detailed and 'colourful' account that should be used with caution.

Articles

O'Neill, Moira. 'A Lady's Life on a Ranch' in *Blackwood's Edinburgh Magazine*, CLII (January 1898), 1-16. This article reveals the social setting of the well-to-do in the grazing country at perhaps the height of the community's social and economic development.

Other Contemporary Published Sources

Fort Macleod Gazette (from 1882). Published in the heart of the foothill ranch country, this newspaper is an indispensable source for any assessment of the ranching frontier in Canada.

REMINISCENCES AND RECENT ACCOUNTS

Books

Bennett, J.W. *Northern Plainsmen: Adaptive Strategy and Agrarian Life.* (Chicago, Aldine Publishing Co., 1969). The adaptive response of the Indians, ranchers, homestead farmers, and the Hutterite Brethren to the Canadian great-plains environment is the focus of this study.

Long, P.S. *The Great Canadian Range.* (Vancouver, Cypress Publishing, 1970). This story of the author's youth on one of the oldest and largest ranches on the southern plains, in addition to its attractive personal quality, presents the range-cattle industry in its last years before the homesteaders completed their conquest.

Long, T.B. *Seventy Years a Cowboy: A Biography* (Regina, Western Printers Association, 1959). This is the personal account of a pioneer stockman whose ranching career began in Montana and continued on the Canadian side of the boundary in the Cypress Hills.

MacEwan, G. *Between the Red and the Rockies* (Toronto, University of Toronto Press, 1952). In this volume ranching is considered within the larger context of the growth and development of western agriculture.

MacInnes, C.M. *In the Shadow of the Rockies* (London, Rivingtons, 1930). Though dated, this study of the ranching region to 1905 remains the best available.

Murchie, R.W. *Agricultural Progress on the Prairie Frontier.* Vol. v of W. A. Mackintosh and W.L.G. Joerg, eds. *Canadian Frontiers of Settlement* (Toronto, Macmillan Company of Canada, 1936). The chapter on ranching in this volume is the best available survey of the range-cattle industry in the prairie west.

Patterson, R.M. *The Buffalo Head* (Toronto, Macmillan Company of Canada, 1961). Though relating to the period after the First World War, this autobiographical narrative offers an interesting look at ranch life in the Alberta foothills.

Sharp, P.F. *Whoop-Up Country: the Canadian-American West* (Minneapolis, University of Minnesota Press, 1955). The author's subject is Fort Benton, Montana and its economic hinterland, a region that, until the Canadian Pacific Railway reached Medicine Hat in 1883, included a vast part of the southwestern Canadian prairie.

Stegner, W.P. *Wolf Willow: A History, a Story, and a Memory of the Lost Plains Frontier* (New York, Viking Press, 1962). This distinguished author's history and reminiscence of his boyhood on the southern plains is perhaps the most readable of all books written about the ranch country.

Symons, R.D. *Where the Wagon Led: One Man's Memories of the Cowboy's Life in the Old West* (Toronto, Doubleday, 1973). This is a vivid personal account containing all the details of the old-time cowboy's craft and is effectively illustrated with the author's own pen-and-ink sketches.

Articles

Archer, J.H. 'History of the Saskatchewan Stock Growers' Association' in *Saskatchewan History*, Vol. xii, no. 2 (Spring 1959), 41-60. Stock associations date from the arrival of the first cattlemen, and this study of the political arm of the Saskatchewan ranchers focuses upon the efforts of stockmen to meet the problems inherent in the range-cattle industry.

Breen, David H. 'The Canadian Prairie West and the "Harmonious Settlement Interpretation" ', in *Agricultural History,* XLVII, No.1 (January 1973), 63-75. The broad question of settler-rancher relations in the Canadian west is examined in this study.

————. The Mounted Police and the Ranching Frontier' in Hugh A. Dempsey (ed.), *Men in Scarlet* (Calgary, McClelland and Stewart West, 1974). The special and intimate relationship between these first comers to southwestern prairie is the subject of this article.

————. 'Plain Talk from Plain Western Men: Cattle Baron v. Sodbuster, 1885' in *Alberta Historical Review,* XVIII, No. 3. (Summer 1970), 4-13. This article looks at one of the more serious incidents in the long contest between rancher and farmer for control of the foothill country along the eastern slope of the Rocky Mountains.

Lupton, A.A. 'Cattle Ranching in Alberta, 1874-1910: its evolution and migration' in *The Alberta Geographer,* 11 (April 1968). The changing geographic distribution and economic development of the stock-raising industry is examined.

Thomas, Lewis G. 'The Rancher and the City: Calgary and the Cattlemen, 1883-1914' in *Transactions of the Royal Society of Canada,* VI, Ser. IV (June 1968), 203-15. In this assessment the author examines the social milieu and the metropolitan character of the ranching community in the Alberta foothills.

Other

Canadian Cattlemen. This popular magazine has been widely read by stockmen for decades, and the issues through the 1930s and 1940s contain numerous reminiscences by 'old-time' cattlemen.

V The Development of Transportation and Communications, 1870-1905

John A. Eagle

INTRODUCTION

The completion of a rail link between St Paul and Winnipeg in 1879 marks the beginning of the railway era on the Canadian prairies. Until that time the most important modes of transport in the prairie west were the York boat, the Red River cart, and sternwheel riverboat.

After the union of the Hudson's Bay Company and the North West Company in 1821, boats were substituted for canoes throughout the Company's service. The York boat was the most common type; it was light enough to be pulled over rollers at portages, but seaworthy in the storms on Lake Winnipeg. It carried as much as several canoes and could hold machinery and other items that would upset or sink any lighter vessels. However by the 1860s it was being replaced by the Red River cart and the steamboat.

Beginning about 1860 the Red River cart became increasingly important for freighting goods between Fort Garry and St Paul, Minnesota. Much of the Hudson's Bay Company's trade goods and exports—furs and buffalo hides— were transported by this method rather than by York boat from York Factory on Hudson Bay. In 1869, 2,500 Red River carts made the journey between St Paul and Fort Garry. In 1868 the Company sent its first brigade of ox carts from Fort Garry to Fort Edmonton and inaugurated the era of overland freight and travel between Edmonton and the Red River settlement; the use of York boats on the North Saskatchewan River was discontinued at this time. It could take as long as three months for the carts to complete the lengthy journey from Fort Garry to Edmonton.

Although there were many prairie trails in the 1860s and 1870s, undoubtedly the most important was the Carlton Trail (also known as the Saskatchewan Trail) from Fort Garry to Fort Carlton on the North Saskatchewan River. The trail was about 500 miles (800 kilometres) in length, and Hudson's Bay Company servants and the Métis were not the only people who made use of it; private traders, missionaries, explorers, Mounted Policemen, government officials, and even tourists and sportsmen travelled it at one time or another; land surveyors and the early tide of ranchers and farmers who entered the fertile valley of the North Saskatchewan in the 1870s also used it.

In the 1870s the sternwheel steamboat was an important mode of transportation in the prairie west, especially on the Red and Saskatchewan Rivers. Steamboats could move large cargoes cheaply and fairly rapidly and some provided quite luxurious accommodation for passengers. However, low water levels often made steamboat navigation of such rivers as the Red and the Saskatchewan difficult and sometimes impossible. The steamboat was essentially a stopgap until the prairies obtained adequate railway facilities. The completion of the rail link between Winnipeg and St Paul in 1879 brought an end to steamboats on the Red and Assiniboine Rivers by 1881. However the CPR's decision not to build its main line along the North Saskatchewan prolonged the use of steamboats on that river. As late as 1887 there were three steamboats that plied the length of the river between Grand Rapids and Edmonton.

The Red River cart and the steamboat fostered the development of extensive contacts between the Red River settlement and the rapidly expanding state of Minnesota. The first Macdonald administration (1867-73) was determined to attach the northwest firmly to Canada and reduce drastically American political and economic influence in the newly acquired region. It was imperative that an all-Canadian transportation route be established in order to strengthen Canada's political and economic ties with the northwest, to bring large numbers of agricultural settlers into that territory, and to facilitate the despatch of a military force to preserve law and order there.

The Dawson route, begun in 1868, was to serve these three functions. The construction of the route was superintended by Simon J. Dawson, an engineer in the Department of Public Works (for location of the route, see map p. 327). By the spring of 1871 the route was in reasonably good condition so that horse teams could draw loads of up to 2,200 pounds (1,000 kilograms) on the corduroy roads from Thunder Bay to Shebandowan Lake, and loaded waggons could traverse the trail from Lake of the Woods to St Boniface on the east side of Red River opposite Fort Garry. In 1871 the men of the second Expeditionary Force traversed the route from Thunder Bay to Fort Garry in three weeks. In June of that year the Department of Public Works established a service for transporting immigrants to the northwest via the Dawson route.

Dawson's laudatory description of the route concealed its serious disadvantages for transporting goods and immigrants. It was in fact composed of a large number of independent pieces, and there could be frequent delays in transferring from one section to another. For immigrants, the length of the journey—ten to twelve days—and the necessity of bringing along large quantities of food were major drawbacks. One could reach the Canadian northwest much faster and more comfortably via the United States—by the Northern Pacific Railroad from Duluth on Lake Superior to Moorhead on the Red River (from 1872) and by steamboat or stagecoach to Fort Garry. But immigrants who took the American route might succumb to the salesmanship of U.S. immigration agents and settle in Minnesota rather than in the Canadian northwest.

The prospect of all-Canadian rail connection between central Canada and the northwest received a severe setback in 1873 when the Pacific Scandal discredited in the New York and London money markets Macdonald's project of a transcontinental railway to the Pacific. In 1874 the Mackenzie administration enacted legislation that provided for government construction of a rail line on the east side of the Red River from Selkirk through St Boniface (across the river from Winnipeg) to Pembina at the United States boundary. Construction began in 1875 but proceeded slowly until October 1877 when a railway locomotive was brought down the Red River by barge, pushed by the steamer 'Selkirk'. The steamboat had thus sealed its fate by inaugurating the railway age in the prairie west. This engine speeded up construction of the line, and by the end of 1878 the track was laid from Selkirk to Pembina, a distance of eighty-five miles (135 kilometres). On December 3, 1878 the first train steamed out of St Boniface for Pembina. In the meantime the Dawson route for immigrants had been abandoned in 1876.

The Pembina branch, as it came to be called, linked up at the United States border with the St Paul, Minneapolis and Manitoba Railroad (formerly the St Paul and Pacific), which extended to St Paul. Control of the latter railway had recently been acquired by a group of men who were soon to become the chief promoters of the CPR—George Stephen, Donald Smith, and James J. Hill.

The Macdonald government had committed itself in 1871 to the construction within ten years (by a private company) of a transcontinental railway from central Canada to the seaboard of British Columbia. Although the confidence of private investors in this project had been undermined by the Pacific Scandal of 1873, the route of the proposed railway was surveyed by government surveyors under the direction of Sandford Fleming. By 1877 the surveys of the route on the prairies were practically complete and a telegraph line had been laid for much of the distance. In general Fleming chose 'the fertile belt', that is the northern route by the valley of the Saskatchewan. His line at first ran from Selkirk on the Red River to cross Lake Manitoba high up at The Narrows, but this was changed in 1880 to one south of the lake. From Lake Manitoba his route curved northwest to Battleford, and kept south of the North Saskatchewan River to a point not far south of Edmonton. The route then extended west to the Yellowhead Pass, which had a favourable gradient for both the ascent and descent.

This route was at first adopted by the CPR, and it was written into its charter of incorporation approved by parliament in February 1881. However, later that year the CPR directors decided on a southerly route across the prairies, and this decision necessitated the abandonment of the Yellowhead Pass. In 1882 legislation was passed enabling the CPR to build through a pass other than the Yellowhead, provided it was not less than one hundred miles (160 kilometres) from the U.S. boundary. The company had already found a fairly satisfactory pass through the Rockies—the Kicking Horse (Bow River) Pass, although it had a much heavier grade than the easy ascent to the Yellowhead. But it was not until the summer of 1882 that Major Rogers, an American engineer in the company's service, discovered a pass through the Selkirk mountains, which has been named after him.

By the terms of the CPR contract of 1881, the Pembina branch was transferred to the CPR at no cost to the company. The CPR brought large quantities of construction materials and an army of labourers into Winnipeg from St Paul via the St Paul, Minneapolis and Manitoba Railroad and the Pembina branch. This arrangement greatly facilitated rapid construction of the CPR west of Winnipeg, so that by June 1883 track had been laid as far as the summit of the Rockies.

One of the most contentious provisions in the CPR's charter was the monopoly clause (clause 15), which was designed to give the company a monopoly of through traffic on the prairies and to prevent rival American railways such as the Northern Pacific from diverting some of that traffic to their own lines. From 1881 to 1887 the Macdonald government protected this monopoly by disallowing Manitoba legislation chartering railways extending to the American border. Initially these railways were chartered by the Conservative administration of John Norquay to provide badly needed branch-line facilities for settlers in southern Manitoba. Then in 1883 the CPR raised its freight rates very substantially. Immediately a groundswell of protest developed in Manitoba; farmers, merchants, and politicians of both parties began demanding that the provincial government establish competing lines in order to break the CPR monopoly and reduce the cost of transportation.

In 1888 the CPR finally surrendered the monopoly clause in return for a federal guarantee of the interest on a $15,000,000 bond issue and the federal government abandoned its policy of disallowance against Manitoba. Though the Northern Pacific built a number of lines in Manitoba, it did not conduct a rate war with the CPR but instead concluded an informal working arrangement to divide traffic. Thus Manitoba did not obtain effective railway competition until the arrival of the Canadian Northern in the period after 1896.

The project of a railway from the prairies to a suitable port on Hudson Bay attracted a great deal of interest and support in Manitoba and the Saskatchewan district of the North West Territories in the 1880s and 1890s. The apostles of the Bay route believed that it would offer competition to the CPR and induce that company to reduce its high freight rates. Such a line would also materially reduce the length of the haul to the world grain market at Liverpool, while the rail journey from Winnipeg to Hudson Bay would be much shorter than the one to Montreal. Thus the Hudson Bay railway would, its supporters claimed, substantially reduce the costs of transportation for prairie wheat exported to Great Britain.

Joseph Royal, a Conservative M.P. from Manitoba, raised the matter of a Hudson Bay line in the House of Commons in 1884. Sir John A. Macdonald endeavoured to appease Manitoba, where his government's policy of disallowance was extremely unpopular, by providing federal assistance for a railway to Hudson Bay. In 1884 the government enacted legislation that authorized a land grant of 6,400 acres per mile within Manitoba and 12,800 acres in the

Territories for the Winnipeg and Hudson Bay Railway and Steamship Company. Under the presidency of Hugh Sutherland, this company built only forty miles (65 kilometres) of line north from Winnipeg. Nothing further was done until 1896 when Mackenzie and Mann, the promoters of the Canadian Northern Railway, acquired Sutherland's charter with its land grant. The Canadian Northern did reach as far north as Hudson Bay Junction by 1900, but then turned westward to Prince Albert, leaving the Bay project still to be completed.

The CPR's decision in 1881 to build directly westward from Brandon and through the Kicking Horse Pass shifted settlement away from the valley of the Saskatchewan to the southern plains. It led the Macdonald government to move the Territorial capital from Battleford to Regina on the CPR main line in 1883. The CPR's adoption of a southerly route also left towns in the valley of the Saskatchewan such as Battleford, Prince Albert, and Edmonton without rail facilities for another decade, since the CPR was not active in constructing branch lines north of its main line in the 1880s.

The Macdonald government attempted to compensate for the CPR's inactivity by providing subsidies for companies that would undertake the construction of branch lines in the prairie west. In 1886 a group of promoters interested in the sale of western land secured a federal land subsidy of 6,400 acres per mile for the Qu'Appelle, Long Lake, and Saskatchewan Railway Company, which was to build a railway from Regina to Prince Albert via Saskatoon (see map p. 348). Three years later the company received additional federal assistance in the form of an annual cash subsidy of $80,000 in return for transporting mail and government officials at no charge. The main line reached Prince Albert in October 1890. The railway was operated by the CPR under a leasing arrangement. It was not a very valuable feeder line, since it was built ahead of immediate local requirements. In 1906 the Canadian Northern Railway acquired the line, which soon became the mainstay of that company's operations in Saskatchewan.

The Calgary and Edmonton Railway Company was incorporated in 1890 and received a cash subsidy from the federal government on the same terms as that given to the Qu'Appelle, Long Lake, and Saskatchewan Railway. Construction of the line north of Calgary began in July 1890 and proceeded very rapidly. Tracklaying was completed to Strathcona, on the south bank of the North Saskatchewan River opposite Edmonton, in July 1891. Edmonton did not receive rail connection until 1902 when the promoters of the Canadian Northern Railway built a short spur line from Edmonton to Strathcona. The line south of Calgary took longer to construct, and reached the north bank of the Oldman river opposite Fort Macleod in November 1892. The Calgary and Edmonton Railway served as a valuable feeder line for the CPR which operated it under a leasing arrangement until 1902 when the CPR concluded an agreement to purchase the line.

Although the CPR retained a *de facto* monopoly on through-rail traffic in the prairie west until the Canadian Northern Railway completed its line from

Winnipeg to the Lakehead in 1902, it did reduce freight rates in that region under the terms of the Crow's Nest Pass Agreement. The Crow's Nest Pass line is a branch of the CPR that extends from Lethbridge westerly through the Crow's Nest Pass to Nelson in southeastern British Columbia. In 1896 the CPR sought assistance from the federal government in constructing the line. The CPR and the Laurier government reached an agreement embodied in a bill that was passed in the 1897 session of Parliament and that subsequently became known as the Crow's Nest Pass Agreement. Frank Oliver, Liberal M.P. for the constituency of Alberta and publisher of the Edmonton *Bulletin*, took part in the Commons debate on the bill.

The terms of this complex agreement may be briefly described. The federal government gave the CPR a cash subsidy of $11,000 per mile up to a maximum amount of $3,630,000 to assist the company in building the line. In return for that aid the CPR agreed to make a reduction in rates of 10 per cent on a list of eleven commodities (such as binder twine, agricultural implements, household furniture) inbound into the prairie west, a reduction of 20 per cent upon coal oil, and of one-third on all green and fresh fruits inbound into the prairie west, and of 3 cents per hundredweight upon grain and flour outward bound to the Lakehead. The reduced rates came into full effect on 1 September 1899. These reductions constituted an important modification of clause twenty in the CPR contract of 1881, which exempted the company from government rate regulation until it earned a profit of 10 per cent on its capital stock. The Crow's Nest rates soon acquired the status of a sacred charter (Holy Crow) among prairie farmers. The Borden government's decision to suspend the rates in 1918 aroused a storm of protest in the prairie west and contributed to the rise of the Progressive party.

The Canadian Northern Railway was the creation of two enterprising Ontario-born railway contractors, William Mackenzie and Donald Mann. The two men gained experience in railway construction on the prairie in building sections of both the Qu'Appelle, Long Lake, and Saskatchewan Railway and the Calgary and Edmonton Railway. In 1895 Mackenzie and Mann acquired the charter of the Lake Manitoba Railway and Canal Company and, with the aid of a bond guarantee from the Manitoba government, constructed an urgently needed local railway in northwestern Manitoba from Gladstone to Dauphin. Running rights were negotiated with the Manitoba and North Western Railway, which enabled the new railway to make connections with both the CPR and the Northern Pacific. D. B. Hanna, an energetic Scot with extensive experience in many aspects of railway operations, served as the railway's first superintendent and continued in the same position when the Canadian Northern Railway was incorporated by federal statute in 1899.

In 1901 the Canadian Northern acquired 350 miles (560 kilometres) of Northern Pacific lines in Manitoba under a leasing agreement with the Conservative Roblin government of Manitoba. Under this agreement the Canadian Northern received bond guarantees that enabled the company to complete a line to the Lakehead by 1902. In return the company permitted general governmental control over all its rates. The Canadian Northern agreed to set a rate on wheat of 10 cents per hundredweight, a figure that compared very favourably with the 14-cent rate obtained by the federal government under the Crow's Nest Pass Agreement. In effect the Canadian Northern was providing real competition for the CPR in western Canada for the first time.

In 1904 the Canadian Northern was still largely a Manitoba railway, with 930 miles (1,500 kilometres) of railway in that province. But in the following year the company pressed energetically ahead on construction of the main line to Edmonton, which was opened for traffic in December. This line ran in a northwesterly direction from Dauphin, passed just north of Saskatoon, crossed the North Saskatchewan River at North Battleford and ran south of that river to Edmonton (see map p. 348). The Canadian Northern thus followed much of the original route of the CPR surveyed by Sandford Fleming in the 1870s. Together with the Grand Trunk Pacific Railway, it was instrumental in opening up the valley of the Saskatchewan to extensive agricultural settlement.

The Grand Trunk Pacific Railway was a subsidiary of the Grand Trunk Railway of Canada and was incorporated by federal statute in 1903. The company undertook to build a line from Winnipeg to Prince Rupert, British Columbia, via Edmonton and the Yellowhead Pass. The federal government assisted the construction of the line by guaranteeing principal and interest on a substantial amount of the company's bonds; unlike the CPR, the Grand Trunk Pacific received no cash or land subsidies. The Prime Minister, Sir Wilfrid Laurier, and western Liberal M.P.s such as T.O. Davis of Prince Albert strongly defended these terms during the House of Commons debate in 1903.

Construction of the Grand Trunk Pacific began in Manitoba in the summer of 1905. The main line from Winnipeg to Edmonton was opened for traffic in September 1909, while the remaining portion of the line to Prince Rupert was opened for traffic in September 1914.

In the period 1905-14 the governments of Manitoba, Saskatchewan, and Alberta actively encouraged the Canadian Northern and the Grand Trunk Pacific to construct an extensive network of branch lines on the prairies. In most cases this assistance took the form of guarantees of principal and interest on the bonds of the two companies. The CPR also undertook a major program of branch-line construction in the prairie west during this period. In the eight years between 1906 and 1914 total railway mileage in the three prairie provinces nearly doubled, rising from 5,965 to 11,708 miles (9,600 to 18,840 kilometres).

The federal government later took over the Canadian Northern (1917) and the Grand Trunk Pacific (1919), which together became the western section of the publicly owned national railway system, Canadian National Railways, formed in 1922.

The evolution of communications in the prairie west from 1870 to 1905 was intimately linked with developments in the field of transportation. In 1871 the system of postal communication between the Canadian northwest and the rest of Canada was heavily dependent on the co-operation of the U.S. postal authorities. This dependence was not overcome until 1884 when the CPR line from the Lakehead to Winnipeg was opened for traffic, permitting transportation of mail from Ontario by steamer and railway on an all-Canadian route. The completion of the CPR main line in 1885 improved the speed and certainty of mail delivery across the plains, and in the following year a daily mail service across Canada via the CPR was inaugurated. By the time Alberta and Saskatchewan were granted provincial status, the postal service on the prairies had expanded quite substantially. In 1870 there were only six post offices between the Lakehead and the Rockies; by 1905 there were 1,314 post offices in operation in the three prairie provinces.

The prairie west obtained telegraph facilities connecting it with the United States and central Canada well before the arrival of the railway. Under an agreement with the Dominion government, the North-Western Telegraph Company linked Fort Garry with the American telegraph system in 1871. The Dominion Telegraph, operated by the federal government, was started in 1874 and was built along the original route of the Canadian Pacific Railway on the prairies, a route located by government surveyors under the direction of Sandford Fleming. In 1882 the section of the Dominion Telegraph from Selkirk to Humboldt was abandoned and a line was constructed from Humboldt to Qu'Appelle on the CPR main line to connect with CPR Telegraphs.

The charter of the CPR gave it the power to carry on a commercial telegraph business along all its railway lines. Thus communities on the CPR main line obtained telegraph facilities by 1883. The federal government furnished telegraph service to communities that did not have rail connection with the CPR. For example, the government constructed telegraph lines from Calgary to Fort Macleod and Lethbridge in 1885. In a number of instances the CPR and the government pooled their resources. J.S. Macdonald, one of the first employees of the Government Telegraph Service, served as joint agent at Moose Jaw for the government telegraphs and CPR Telegraphs in the 1890s.

There was some competition in telegraph service, for the Great North Western Telegraph Company of Canada, incorporated in 1880, did build some lines in western Canada. In 1902 the Canadian Northern Telegraph Company was established to provide telegraph facilities to communities on the expanding Canadian Northern lines.

The telegraph and the railway served to break down the isolation of the prairie west from the rest of Canada and from the outside world in general. In 1885 the telegraph and the railway enabled the federal government to send a military force to the northwest from central Canada in a very short period and to quell the second Riel rebellion.

Until the turn of the century the telephone business developed quite slowly in the prairie west. The Bell Telephone Company of Canada, which received a Dominion charter in 1880, established exchanges in a number of communities such as Winnipeg, Brandon, and Calgary, and constructed long-distance lines. In smaller communities distant from the CPR main line, telephone exchanges were established by small local companies such as the Edmonton District

Telephone Company, formed by the Edmonton postmaster and two associates in 1893.

By 1905 there was a widespread sentiment in the prairie west in favour of public ownership of the telephone system. Many felt that Bell telephone rates were too high; the CPR's decision in 1904 to give the Bell exclusive rights to put telephones in CPR stations made the Bell company even more unpopular. People in rural districts wanted telephone facilities that the Bell was slow to provide. In the period 1906-9, the three prairie provinces each bought out the Bell's properties and equipment and established publicly owned systems in which the municipalities operated the local exchanges and the provincial governments built and operated the long-distance lines. The provincially owned systems extended telephone lines to many rural areas, thereby reducing their isolation and bringing them into closer contact with the larger towns and cities.

TRANSPORTATION

152. YORK BOAT

Joseph James Hargrave, *Red River* (Montreal, 1871), pp. 159-60.

The water carriage of the country is performed by means of what are called "inland boats." Each of these is worked by nine men, of whom eight are rowers and the other is steersman; it is capable of carrying about three-and-a-half tons of freight. Brigades composed of numbers varying from four to eight of these craft are kept plying in various directions, throughout the season of open water, on the inland lakes and rivers between those points to and from which goods have to be carried. The tripmen who man these boats are Indians or Half-breeds engaged at the place where the brigade is organized, and paid a stipulated sum for the performance of the trip. Between Red River Settlement and York Factory such brigades pass and re-pass throughout the whole season of open navigation. They are organized in the settlement, both by the Company and by such private settlers as have capital and inclination to invest it in that description of business. The cargoes sent to York are made up of furs and other country produce consigned thither by the Company for the purpose of shipment to England; the return freight from York to the settlement is partly composed of goods imported by private merchants and partly of those imported by the Company for use in its trading operations. These goods have all previously been shipped from England to York by the Company's annual vessel.

153. RED RIVER CART

Joseph James Hargrave, *Red River* (Montreal, 1871), pp. 58-9.

The carts composing the train were of uniform make, and of a species called "Red River carts." They are constructed entirely of wood, without any iron whatever, the axles and rims of the wheels forming no exception to the rule. Although this might at first sight appear a disadvantage, as denoting a want of strength, yet it is really the reverse, because, in the country traversed by these vehicles, wood is abundant, and always to be obtained in quantities sufficient to mend any breakages which might take place. The only tools necessary, not only to mend but to construct a cart, are an axe, a saw, a screw-auger and a draw-knife; with these the traveller is independent, so far as regards the integrity of his conveyance. Indeed, the cart may be described as a light box frame poised upon an axle connecting two strong wooden wheels. The price of such an article in the settlement is about two pounds sterling. The harness is very rude, and is made of dressed ox-hide. Each cart is drawn by an ox, and in cases where speed is an object a horse is substituted. . . .

The common rate of progress made by heavy freight carts is about twenty miles a day, of ten travelling hours, the load averaging about eight hundred pounds per cart. A train of great length is divided into brigades of ten carts each, three men being considered sufficient to work such a brigade; one of these three is invested with a certain minor authority over the other two, while an individual considerably more highly paid than any of the rest has charge of the entire train, and, moving about on horseback from one brigade to another, exercises a general supervision over the whole party throughout the journey.

154. DEFICIENCIES OF PRAIRIE TRAILS

Edmonton *Bulletin*, January 21, 1882.

ROADS

One of the greatest drawbacks to emigration to this part of the North-West is the difficulty of getting here caused by the length and badness of the road. Although there are four different trails by which to reach Edmonton from the east, during the latter part of the distance they are all so bad it is questionable which is the worst.

What was formerly the principal one, on the north side of the river from Carlton, has been almost abandoned of late years, on account of its numerous creeks and valleys. In wet seasons eight or ten creeks had to be rafted between here and Ft. Pitt, as there were no bridges, and in any season their deep valleys were a great hindrance to freighters. About sixty miles of the road, from Victoria to Sturgeon River was utterly execrable, although a large amount of money had been spent on it in making bridges across the smaller creeks, cutting out the roads through timber and grading on the hills. The bridges are now rotten and the trail is almost impassable.

The second trail opened up was the plain trail from Carlton, running by the Trampling Lake and Sounding Lake, crossing the Battle River near the Flag Hill and coming in by Hay Lakes, over the western part of the Beaver Hills. This road was used mostly by plains hunters in the days of the buffalo and although a good, dry and level road was not travelled much by freighters on account of scarcity of wood over a great part of the distance and in dry seasons a scarcity of water. Besides it was very lonesome, there not being a house the whole way, and at times the Battle River was not fordable.

When the telegraph line was built a trail was opened up along it from Battleford to Hay Lakes, from which place it followed the plain trail to Edmonton. It was a fairly good road with plenty of wood and water, no large creeks to cross, and with only one considerable valley—the Grizzly Bear. The last thirty-five miles of the road, from Hay Lakes in, however, was very bad, being hilly and through timber.

Four years ago a fourth trail was made, which turned off the telegraph line about eighty miles from Battleford, crossed the Vermillion river at its most southerly bend and followed the valley through the Moose Mountains, crossed the open plain south of Victoria and came in to Ft. Saskatchewan between the north-west slope of the Beaver Hills and the river. From Ft. Saskatchewan the road was good on either side of the river to Edmonton. This road avoided the Grizzly Bear valley and the Hay Lakes road, gave a direct route to Ft. Saskatchewan and was fully as short to Edmonton as any other road. It was established as the mail route, and for three seasons almost all the travel to and from the east came and went over it. Last summer, however, the season was so wet that the creeks on it were raised so as to make fording impossible, and rather than raft some and bridge others freighters and emigrants came by the Hay Lakes road. Of course a large amount of heavy freight coming over a narrow trail in a wet season does not improve it any, and consequently what was a bad road before is a great deal worse now.

A large emigration is expected here during the coming season and a great deal of freight must also be brought in, all of which will have to [be] brought over one or the other of these roads, and we think that it is not too much to ask that an appropriation be made for the improvement of them, by the Government of the North-West Territory, if they have any funds for the purpose, and if not, by the Dominion Government. A few hundred dollars would put either road in good shape, and Government money could never be spent to better advantage. The Hay Lakes road requires to be cut out wider through the timber, and a few small bridges to be made, while the Vermillion trail requires large bridges on the Vermillion and Beaver Rivers and small ones on six or seven little creeks. The expense in either case would not be heavy, and would be a great help to emigrants coming in, who have enough trouble at the best of times.

It is to be regretted that we have no representative to lay the matter before the North-West Council, but the members of it are fully cognizant of the facts, and it is to be hoped that they will in this matter consider the interests of the territory at large and not merely those of the part which they represent, or in which they happen to reside.

155. STEAMBOATS ON THE RED RIVER

John Macoun, *Manitoba and the Great North-West* (Guelph, 1882), pp. 579-80.

Up to the year 1859 no attempt had been made to put steamboats on Red River, and not a few in the colony derided the idea as preposterous, and maintained that the river was too shallow, too crooked, and too full of snags. One morning early in June of that year the colony was unexpectedly greeted with the whistle of the steamboat, and the "Anson Northrup" tied up at Fort Garry. This boat was brought at great expense by the proprietors from the St. Peter's River, and taking advantage of the spring floods reached the Fort. Its arrival was treated as a great event. The cannon of the fort thundered out a welcome, and bells pealed forth a merry chime as a signal of rejoicing.

The arrival of the "Anson Northrup" inaugurated a new era for the trade of the Red River Colony. When the Hudson's Bay Company saw the success of this venture they determined to try the river for their trade. With this object in view they acquired some property opposite River au Boeuf, 200 miles south of Fort Garry, and commenced a town which they named Georgetown, in honor of Sir George Simpson. Messrs. Burbank & Co. of St. Paul, established a stage line between Georgetown and St. Paul, and communication was opened with the outside world.

A few trips were made in 1860. During the next season the boat made regular trips between Georgetown and Fort Garry. The stages continued to run to St. Paul, so that the trip from Red River to Montreal could be made in twelve days.

In the spring of 1862 the "International" was launched at a cost of $20,000, and commenced to make regular trips. Owing to the Sioux massacre and various other causes, the navigation of the river was not a success, and little freight offering, her trips almost ceased. Trade languished until 1872, when the Northern Pacific Railway reached Moorehead from Duluth. As soon as the railway was opened the trade on the river took a fresh start, and Kittson at once took advantage of the new impulse given by the railway to perfect arrangements for regular traffic.

During the year 1872 immigrants began to pour into Manitoba, some going by the Dawson route, while others came by railway to Fargo and thence down the Red River to Winnipeg, which now began to be spoken of in connection with the west. In 1875 trade had increased to such an extent that Kittson, or the Red River Transportation Company, carried no less than 50,000 tons* of freight on Red River that year. I heard him make the remark that on the Red River, between Fargo and Winnipeg, more merchandise had been carried that season than on the Mississippi between St. Paul and St. Louis.

156. THE START OF STEAMBOAT NAVIGATION ON THE NORTH SASKATCHEWAN RIVER

The Standard (Winnipeg), August 28, 1875.

NAVIGATION OF THE SASKATCHEWAN

The Hudson's Bay steamers have made a successful round trip from the Stone Fort [Lower Fort Garry] to Edmonton, and demonstrated clearly that the [North Saskatchewan] river is navigable through its entire length for vessels of a large size. The steamer Northcote started from the Grand Rapids on the 30th of June, reaching Carlton on the 13th July, and Edmonton on the 22nd. Returning, she left Edmonton on the 25th July, reached Carlton on the 28th and Grand Forks on the 5th August, thus making the round trip in about five weeks. The Colville makes the trip at this end of the line from the Lower Fort to Grand Rapids in from three to four days.

The Captain of the Northcote reports a good stage of water all along the river; and the removal of a few boulders from Cole's Falls would render the navigation quite certain at all seasons.

The Northcote took a full load of freight both up and down.

During the debate on the Pacific Railway Bill in the House of Commons, Hon. Mr. Smith† declared that the Saskatchewan was navigable throughout its entire length, when the member for Lisgar [John C. Schultz] rose in his place and contradicted him. The accomplishment of this trip affords the fullest justification of Mr. Smith's statement, and sets at rest a question of vast importance in the development of the North-West. The Saskatchewan now takes its place among the navigable rivers of the continent; and we confidently look forward to the construction at an early day of other steamers to play [sic] upon its waters.

---

*[This is an overstatement. In the 1875 navigation season Red River steamboats carried a total of 76,078,680 pounds of freight (*Manitoba Free Press*, April 7, 1877).]

†[Donald S. Smith (later Lord Strathcona), at this time Conservative M.P. for Selkirk, Manitoba.]

157. STEAMBOATS ON THE NORTH SASKATCHEWAN RIVER

Edmonton *Bulletin*, November 5, 1881.

NAVIGATION

The wreck of the steamer City of Winnipeg, formerly the Manitoba, as she was being brought across Lake Winnipeg, is a great loss, not only to the owners, but to the people of the whole Saskatchewan country, as it will be impossible to put another boat in her place in time to be of much service next season. Each year the necessity for more and improved steamers on the river is more severely felt as the population increases and the country develops, and each year the difficulties of the roads between Winnipeg and here become greater. During the season now nearly over, it was no uncommon thing for carts to be three months on the way, while the distance could be made by steamer with all ease in twenty days. As the country opens up heavy goods, such as machinery, stoves and building hardware, are more needed. But the difficulty of bringing such articles in carts is so great as to almost prevent their being brought, and when they do get here the cost of freighting is so great as to put the price almost out of reach. The Saskatchewan is considered by some not to be fit for navigation to any extent, but it must be very bad indeed if it is not better than slow going oxen on a muddy road 1,000 miles long. . . .

. . . A good line of boats on the river would do nearly as much to open up the country as the railroad itself, and would, for all time to come, offer strong competition to the railroad, especially on eastern bound freight.

An advantage that a line of boats on the Saskatchewan would have over one on the Red or Assiniboine rivers is that full loads (coal and lumber) could be had for every return trip; in fact that is what is principally needed for the development of these two industries.

When the Lake Winnipeg & Hudson's Bay Railway is completed, as it will be ultimately, it, in connection with the navigation of the Saskatchewan, will form the shortest and most natural outlet for the surplus produce of this country on its way to the English market, putting Edmonton on nearly as good a footing for the shipping of grain as St. Paul is now.

158. THE PLEASURES OF STEAMBOAT TRAVEL

Winnipeg *Daily Times*, April 30, 1881.

THE STEAMER MINNESOTA

Many of our prominent citizens have been braving the storm and perseveringly fording their way through the tenacious mud to inspect the fine steamer Minnesota and admire her appearance in her greatly enlarged and improved state, and in every instance they have evidently considered themselves amply rewarded for their pains. . . .

The Minnesota presents quite an imposing appearance, as the results of her enlarged dimensions and numerous improvements. Seventy feet of her hull, cabin and deck have been constructed entirely new, thus making the steamer forty feet longer than before. The total length of the hull is now 170 feet, thus making the vessel altogether, including the wheel, 190 feet long. The addition gives a fine large forecastle and also ten more staterooms than before. The increased comfort of the passengers has been provided for by placing spring mattresses in all the staterooms. A large and convenient wash room and barber shop has been added, the water for which is supplied from a reservoir on the hurricane deck. The reservoir is filled by means of a force pump below, and there are pipes to carry away overboard the water which has been used. In the middle of the boat are gangways landing out upon the guards—a convenience which did not before exist. The guards are some two feet wider than before. Passengers will now find it very convenient to take a constitutional before breakfast. Some of the most important of all the improvements are noticeable in the storage. A strong railing four and a half feet high is placed along the outer edges on both sides from fore to aft, thus affording security against the drowning accidents which have been so numerous in former years on vessels navigating our north-western rivers. Steerage passengers will be made more comfortable than heretofore by means of berths, which are to be provided. Especial facilities are offered for the shipment of stock. One hundred horses can be taken without difficulty. The hold will be eighteen inches deeper in the forward part than before, making it 5½ feet deep. The vessel will draw eight inches less of water than before. The new smoke stacks are lofty and handsome. Derricks and spars, with guys and pulleys have been provided, which will greatly facilitate the process of landing.

159. A GOVERNMENT REPORT ON THE DAWSON ROUTE

Canada, *Sessional Papers* (1872), no. 4, General Report of the Minister of Public Works for the Fiscal Year Ending June 30, 1871.

RED RIVER ROAD

The total distance from Fort William to Fort Garry, as determined by the measurements, is 451 miles. . . .

EASTERLY SECTION

Immediately after the passage of the Red River expeditionary force in 1870, the works of permanent construction along the easterly section of the Red River route, lying between Thunder Bay and the Lake of the Woods, partly land and partly water carriage, were resumed and pushed on with vigour and system. At the close of the season the road was in excellent condition from Thunder Bay to Lake Shebandowan.

The land carriage on this section of the route is described as passing through a country where the soil consists of stiff red clay, necessitating a surface coating of gravel for the roadway and thorough drainage. These latter improvements were carried out during the past spring, and this section of the road now permits the passage of teams drawing from 1,800 to 2,200 lbs., which can make the round trip from Thunder Bay to Shebandowan Lake, going and returning, in three-and-a-half days.

WESTERLY SECTION

The works along the westerly section of the route, from Lake of the Woods to Fort Garry, 95 miles long, wholly land carriage, were begun in the month of July, 1870. To assist the passage of the expeditionary force, a bridle path was first cut, extending from the previously opened track to the north-west angle of the Lake of the Woods.

After the passage of the troops had been secured, notwithstanding the scarcity of laborers, caused by the disturbed condition of the territory, the works of permanent construction on this section of the route were at once taken up and continued throughout the summer, fall and winter seasons. At the opening of spring, 1871, the road was passable for loaded waggons over its entire length, excepting a few miles of swamp at the north-west angle which have since been finished.

Of this westerly section of the route the engineer reports that it is swampy from Lake of the Woods to White Mouth River, but intersected by parallel ridges of sand and gravel, which run longitudinally in the general direction of the line of route and have been made available in many places for the roadway. Where swamps had to be crossed the roadway has been laid upon timber and fascines. The engineer further reports that the general character of the route from Lake of the Woods to Fort Garry is a continuous level, abounding in the timber required for road or railway construction until it reaches the Red River prairie.

THE MILITARY EXPEDITION

As stated in my report of last year, during the military emergency that arose in 1869-70, the limited staff of engineers and assistants employed by this Department in the North-west was at once detached from the work of constructing the Thunder Bay section of the Red River road, and set to provide ways and means for transporting the expeditionary force from Fort William to Fort Garry.

This temporary diversion of the engineers and assistants employed on the Red River route caused some delay to the works of permanent construction, and entailed much additional outlay. On the other hand, by testing the work already done to its full capacity, and bringing into prominence both advantages and disadvantages, the emergency furnished prompt and reliable data respecting the security and convenience of the route and the solidity of the work.

The military journey from Lake Superior to Manitoba—including the boat navigation between Lake Shebandowan and Lake of the Woods, with the *portages*, and the temporary pathways which had to be cut beyond the finished road—in all a distance of about 400 miles, through an uninhabited and heretofore inaccessible territory, was made without accident, and was attended with far less discomfort than is usually incidental to such expeditions.

The easy and expeditious return, over the same route, of Her Majesty's regular troops, in the fall of 1870, afforded a second proof of the safety, convenience, and excellent condition of the route; while a third and still more conspicuous proof was recently had in the homeward march of the Canadian volunteers. Early in June, 1871, both the Quebec and Ontario Battalions left Fort Garry for Fort William, accomplishing the march without accident or delay, despite the swollen state of the rivers and lakes, and the severe action of the spring thaw upon the artificial causeways and bridges along the route. On both these occasions the employés of this Department were again detached to assist in providing for the safe conveyance of the troops.

The condition of the Red River road, in June, 1871, may be thus briefly stated: Besides the opening up of the whole land carriage (140 miles of roadway, exclusive of 12 portage paths), from Fort William to Fort Garry, the row-boats used in the military expedition have been put on Lakes Shebandowan, Kashaboiwe, Nequaquon and Lac des Mille Lacs, while two more are on their way to other lakes. Contracts have been signed for the building of two powerful steamboats to ply on Rainy Lake, 46 miles, and Rainy River and Lake of the Woods, 120 miles of unbroken navigation. These steamers are to be built at Fort Frances, so as to secure their easy passage to the respective reaches of navigation above and below the falls at that place. When completed they will enable the Government Transport Service to carry heavy and bulky freight, including cattle and horses, from Lake Superior to Red River.

EMIGRANT TRANSPORT SERVICE

Early in the spring of 1871, Your Excellency was pleased to approve an Order in Council, providing means and specifying rates and regulations for the conveyance of emigrants to the North-western settlements, *via* Lake Superior and Red River road. To give effect to this measure an Emigrant Transport Service was organized by the Department of Public Works, and a tariff of rules and regulations published, announcing that from the 15th day of June, 1871, emigrants would be forwarded to Fort Garry by the Red River route, at the following rates, viz.:—

Toronto to Fort William.—Adults, $5; children under 12 years, half price. 150 lbs. personal baggage free. Extra luggage 35 cents per 100 lbs.

Fort William to Fort Garry.—Adults, $25; children under 12 years, half price. 150 lbs. of personal baggage, free. Extra baggage, $1.50 per 100 lbs. No horses, oxen, waggons, or heavy farming implements to be taken.

Mode of Conveyance.—96 miles by railroad, from Toronto to Collingwood. 532 miles by steamer on Lake Superior, from Collingwood to Fort William. 45 miles by waggon, from Fort William to Shebandowan Lake. 310

miles broken navigation, in open boats and steam launches, from Shebando-wan Lake to north-west angle of the Lake of the Woods. 95 miles by cart or waggon, from north-west angle of the Lake of the Woods to Fort Garry.

It was also announced that though passengers were expected to furnish their own supplies for the journey, provisions would be given them at cost price from the Government depôts at Shebandowan, Fort Frances, and the north-west angle.

In addition to the row-boats and steam-launches, a large force of horses and waggons are now running over both the westerly and easterly sections of the route. Buildings for shelter have been put up on the Fort Garry road, in addition to those already built on the Thunder Bay Road during the march of the military expedition.

Many of the arrangements for this first year's transportation of emigrants are necessarily of a temporary character; when the road is fully built and equipped, and the steamers placed on the navigable stretches of the route, these arrangements will be succeeded by a more comprehensive and perma-nent system and tariff.

160. A CONTEMPORARY ASSESSMENT OF THE DAWSON ROUTE

George Monro Grant, *Ocean to Ocean: Sandford Fleming's Expedition Through Canada in 1872* (Toronto, 1873), pp. 64-5.

The road [Dawson route] has been proved already on two occasions to be a military necessity for the Dominion, until a railway is built farther back from the boundary line. If Canada is to open up her North-west to all the world for colonisation, there must be a road for troops, from the first: there are sufficient elements of disorder to make preparedness a necessity. As long as we have a road of our own, the United States would perhaps raise no objection to Cana-dian volunteers passing through Minnesota; were we absolutely dependent, it might be otherwise.

In speaking of this "Dawson road" it is only fair to give full credit for all that has been accomplished. Immense difficulties have been overcome, inso-much that, whereas it took Colonel Wolsley's force nearly three months, or from early in June to August 24th, to reach Fort Garry from Thunder Bay, a similar expedition could now do the journey in two or three weeks.

But, as a route for trade, for ordinary travel or for emigrants to go west, the Dawson road, as it now exists, is far from satisfactory. Only by building a hundred and fifty-five miles or so of railway at the beginning and the end, and by overcoming the intervening portages in such a way that bulk would not have to be broken, could it be made to compete even with the present route by Duluth and the railway thence to Pembina. The question, then, is simply whether or not it is wise to do this, at an expenditure of some millions on a road the greater part of which runs along the boundary line, after the Dominion has already decided to build a direct line of railway to the North-west. This year about seventy emigrants have gone by the road in the six weeks between June 20th and August 1st. The station-masters and other agents on the road, as a rule, do their utmost; they have been well selected, and are spirited and intelligent men; but the task given them to do is greater than the means given will permit. The road is composed of fifteen or twenty independent pieces; is it any wonder if these often do not fit, especially as there cannot be unity of understanding and of plan, for there is no telegraph along the route and it would be extremely difficult to construct one?

161. DIVERSION OF IMMIGRANTS TO THE AMERICAN WEST

James Trow, *A Trip to Manitoba* (Quebec, 1875), pp. 12-13.

Before leaving Prince Arthur's landing, like all travellers and immigrants, we were interviewed by paid American agents, who took a deep interest in our welfare, urging our party not to risk our precious lives on the Dawson Route; that it was morally committing suicide to attempt to go any other way than by Duluth and across the Northern Pacific; that not less than 400 poor half-famished immigrants were then at the North-West angle, and had been there for weeks; no teams, no provisions, perfect starvation prevailed, that if we persisted we might possibly get through before Christmas or New Year's* but in all probability our bones would be left to bleach on some portage or sunk beneath the waves; that if we wished for comfort in travelling, combined with speed, by all means take the American route; and providing we required land, the broad prairies were inviting us in Minnesota or Dakota. These smooth-tongued interlopers succeeded in poisoning the minds of several who intended to go through our own country. Agents of this kind are found in almost every city and town in the Dominion, seducing and influencing good settlers to cross the border and swell the great Republic.

162. IMMIGRATION VIA THE DAWSON ROUTE

Canada, *Sessional Papers* (1875), no. 37.

Ottawa, 15th February, 1875.

(Memorandum)

The number of emigrants conveyed over the route leading from Lake Superior to Manitoba, since the opening of the same in 1871, up to the end of October, 1873, and the approximate cost of their conveyance, were as follows:

Passengers conveyed from July, 1871 to October, 1873, 2,739 persons, of

---

*[Trow had arrived at the Lakehead about July 12.]

whom there were classed as emigrants 805, remaining permanently as settlers in Manitoba.

The estimated average cost of carrying emigrants was $25 per head, the actual charge in 1872 was $15 per head, and in 1873 $10 per head.

The line having been kept open for other purposes besides the conveyance of emigrants, such as the military occupation of the North-West Territories, and the carriage of workmen, materials and supplies, the organization for transportation was not exclusively chargeable to this service.

Previous to the opening of the line for emigrants, about 2,000 people, soldiers, workmen and others, passed over it to Manitoba, and of these about 400 remained in the country and became settlers.

Of the workmen employed subsequently, a considerable number have settled permanently in the country.

(Signed,) S.J. Dawson

MANITOBA'S CONNECTIONS WITH CANADA AND THE UNITED STATES, 1872

163. MANITOBA'S FIRST RAILWAY: THE PEMBINA BRANCH

Manitoba Free Press, December 5, 1878.

AT LAST!!
Rail Communication Established
Driving the Last Spike
The last rail is laid—the last spike driven! Manitoba, after many vexatious
delays which we now can afford to dismiss without a thought, is now con-
nected by

RAIL COMMUNICATION WITH THE OUTER WORLD.

This long-looked-for and anxiously-awaited event, of so much importance
to this northwestern land, has at length been consummated; and Manitoba
takes another stride in the

MARCH OF PROGRESS

which will result in her assuming a higher and more influential position in

THE SISTERHOOD OF THE CONFEDERATION.

With all the difficulties of communication of half-a-century ago, which
impeded the advancement of those then "western" countries; cut off from the
outer world almost entirely in the winter months; without the facilities for
freight and passenger traffic with which rival immigration fields were favored
—Manitoba, we say, encountering these obstacles, has kept pace with the ever
advancing stride of civilization, and largely diverted

"THE STAR OF EMPIRE,"

which, the poet tells us, "westward leads its sway", in a north-westerly direction. In the face of all the impediments to her advancement, the countless
advantages of her prolific soil, earning for her the appropriate title of "the
garden spot of the world," have induced a large immigration, and the isolated
and almost unknown community of a few years ago is strangely altered to a

PROSPEROUS PROVINCE

dotted over almost its entire length and breadth with happy and contented
settlements. We have truly heard—

—"the tread of pioneers of a nation yet to be;

The first low wash of waves where soon shall roll a human sea;"

—and that human sea is fast overflowing the land. A population liberally
estimated at ten thousand less than eight short years ago has increased to thirty
thousand; and with the facilities the Iron Horse will afford for bringing in

THE HOME-SEEKING MULTITUDE FROM THE EAST,

that number will be immensely augmented before Manitoba shall have been a
decade amongst the Provinces of Canada. The event celebrated the other day,
therefore, was an important one in the history of Manitoba, marking as it does
another of the

TRANSITIONS IN OUR MODE OF COMMUNICATION

with the world outside. From the York boat in summer, to and from Hudson's Bay, and the dog-sled in winter; the primitive Red River cart freighting long and tedious journeys a thousand miles to the south-east, then as the railways were extended through the Gopher [Minnesota] State, the trip reduced to five hundred miles; from the rudely constructed cart to the stage coach which yet faithfully performs its daily service, and the steamboat, at first running irregularly, but by the rapidly increasing volume of trade, expanding into a fleet of river boats; from these to

THE HAPPY CULMINATION—THE RAILWAY

—the precursor of a great and glorious future for the Bull's eye of the Dominion. . . .

164. FIRST SHIPMENT OF WHEAT BY RAIL FROM MANITOBA

Manitoba Free Press, December 6, 1878.

Telegraphic: Special Despatches to the Free Press
Emerson
The First Shipment
Emerson, December 6—The first car load of wheat from this Province was yesterday shipped by Barnes & Co. to Duluth. They have twenty thousand bushels here awaiting shipment.

165. A MANITOBA PREDICTION ON THE IMPACT OF RAILWAYS

Manitoba Free Press, December 9, 1878.

The departure of the first regular train to-day from St. Boniface station marks an era in the history of Winnipeg which will not soon be forgotten. The time will probably come—indeed, is not very far distant—when the Province will be seamed throughout its length and breadth with iron highways, and when the vast volume of railway business centering here will dwarf into insignificance the facilities we have just obtained, and of which we feel reasonably proud, but it will not dim the recollection of to-day, or lessen our appreciation of the importance of the stride we have just made. Distance, which isolated us in so great a degree from older settled communities, and made us feel almost alone in this great country, has been in a measure annihilated, and we are now enabled to take our stand on a basis of equality in many points, and superiority in others, with the older members of the family of Provinces which compose our great Dominion. Our trade will feel the impetus at once, and the railway will be the means of turning the stream of emigration towards us to an extent it has not yet reached. The field for an agricultural population is practically limitless, and our countless acres now lying waste only await the vivifying touch of the settler to transform them into fruitful and productive sources of wealth. Our work is as yet only begun. A great country lies to the west of us, which will soon be covered by multitudes of industrious people, and it behoves us to so devote our energies and apply our resources that they may be made a source of great wealth to us. The prospect is an inviting one, and only requires judicious co-operation and persistent effort to build up the country and make Winnipeg what nature seems to have destined her to be—the "Chicago of the North-West."

166. CANADIAN PACIFIC RAILWAY CHARTER

Statutes of Canada, 1881, 44 Victoria, c. 1.

AN ACT RESPECTING THE CANADIAN PACIFIC RAILWAY
(Assented to February 15, 1881)

Whereas by the terms and conditions of the admission of British Columbia into Union with the Dominion of Canada, the Government of the Dominion has assumed the obligation of causing a railway to be constructed, connecting the seaboard of British Columbia with the railway system of Canada;

And whereas the Parliament of Canada has repeatedly declared a preference for the construction and operation of such Railway by means of an incorporated Company aided by grants of money and land, rather than by the Government, and certain Statutes have been passed to enable that course to be followed, but the enactments therein contained have not been effectual for that purpose;

And whereas certain sections of the said railway have been constructed by the Government, and others are in course of construction, but the greater portion of the main line thereof has not yet been commenced or placed under contract, and it is necessary for the development of the North-West Territory and for the preservation of the good faith of the Government in the performance of its obligations, that immediate steps should be taken to complete and operate the whole of the said railway; . . .

Therefore Her Majesty, by and with the advice and consent of the Senate and House of Commons of Canada, enacts as follows:— . . .

3. Upon the organization of the said Company, and the deposit by them, with the Government, of one million dollars in cash, or securities approved by the Government, for the purpose in the said contract provided, and in consideration of the completion and perpetual and efficient operation of the railway by the said Company, as stipulated in the said contract, the Government may grant to the Company a subsidy of twenty-five million dollars in money, and twenty-five million acres of land, to be paid and conveyed to the Company in the manner and proportions, and upon the terms and conditions agreed upon in the said contract, and may also grant to the Company the land for right of

way, stations, and other purposes, and such other privileges as are provided for in the said contract. . . .

Schedule

This Contract and Agreement made between her Majesty the Queen, acting in respect of the Dominion of Canada and herein represented and acting by the Honourable Sir Charles Tupper, K.C.M.G., Minister of Railways and Canals and George Stephen and Duncan McIntyre, of Montreal, in Canada, John S. Kennedy of New York, in the State of New York, Richard B. Angus, and James J. Hill, of St. Paul, in the State of Minnesota, Morton, Rose & Co., of London, England, and Kohn, Reinach & Co., of Paris, France, Witnesses:

That the parties hereto have contracted and agreed with each other as follows, namely:—

1. For the better interpretation of this contract, it is hereby declared that the portion of railway hereinafter called the Eastern section, shall comprise that part of the Canadian Pacific Railway to be constructed, extending from the Western terminus of the Canada Central Railway, near the East end of Lake Nipissing, known as Callander Station, to a point of junction with that portion of the said Canadian Pacific Railway now in course of construction extending from Lake Superior to Selkirk on the East side of Red River; which latter portion is hereinafter called the Lake Superior section. That the portion of said railway, now partially in course of construction, extending from Selkirk to Kamloops, is hereinafter called the Central Section; . . .

4. The work of construction shall be commenced at the eastern extremity of the Eastern section not later than the first day of July next, and the work upon the Central section shall be commenced by the Company . . . at a date not later than the 1st May next. And the work upon the Eastern and Central sections shall be vigorously and continuously carried on at such rate of annual progress on each section as shall enable the Company to complete and equip the same and each of them, in running order, on or before the first day of May, 1891, by which date the Company hereby agree to complete and equip the said sections in conformity with this contract, unless prevented by the act of God, the Queen's enemies, intestine disturbances, epidemics, floods, or other causes beyond the control of the Company. . . .

9. In consideration of the premises, the Government agree to grant to the Company a subsidy in money of $25,000,000 and in land of 25,000,000 acres, for which subsidies the construction of the Canadian Pacific Railway shall be completed and the same shall be equipped, maintained and operated—the said subsidies respectively to be paid and granted as the work of construction shall proceed. . . .

11. The grant of land, hereby agreed to be made to the Company, shall be so made in alternate sections of 640 acres each, extending back 24 miles deep, on each side of the railway, from Winnipeg to Jasper House, in so far as such lands shall be vested in the Government—the Company receiving the sections bearing uneven numbers. But should any of such sections consist in a material

degree of land not fairly fit for settlement, the Company shall not be obliged to receive them as part of such grant; and the deficiency thereby caused and any further deficiency which may arise from the insufficient quantity of land along the said portion of railway, to complete the said 25,000,000 acres, or from the prevalence of lakes and water stretches in the sections granted (which lakes and water stretches shall not be computed in the acreage of such sections), shall be made up from other portions in the tract known as the fertile belt, that is to say, the land lying between parallels 49 and 57 degrees of north latitude, or elsewhere at the option of the Company, by the grant therein of similar alternate sections extending back 24 miles deep on each side of any branch line or lines of railway to be located by the Company, . . . —the conditions hereinbefore stated as to lands not fairly fit for settlement to be applicable to such additional grants. And the Company may, with the consent of the Government, select in the North-West Territories any tract or tracts of land not taken up as a means of supplying or partially supplying such deficiency. But such grants shall be made only from lands remaining vested in the Government.

12. The Government shall extinguish the Indian title affecting the lands herein appropriated, and to be hereafter granted in aid of the railway.

13. The Company shall have the right, subject to the approval of the Governor in Council, to lay out and locate the line of the railway hereby contracted for, as they may see fit, preserving the following terminal points, namely: from Callander station to the point of junction with the Lake Superior section; and from Selkirk to the junction with the Western section at Kamloops by way of the Yellow Head Pass.

14. The Company shall have the right from time to time to lay out, construct, equip, maintain and work branch lines of railway from any point or points along their main line of railway, to any point or points within the territory of the Dominion. Provided always, that before commencing any branch they shall first deposit a map and plan of such branch in the Department of Railways. . . .

15. For twenty years from the date hereof, no line of railway shall be authorized by the Dominion Parliament to be constructed South of the Canadian Pacific Railway, from any point at or near the Canadian Pacific Railway, except such line as shall run South West or to the Westward of South West; nor to within fifteen miles of Latitude 49. And in the establishment of any new Province in the North-West Territories, provision shall be made for continuing such prohibition after such establishment until the expiration of the same period.

16. The Canadian Pacific Railway, and all stations and station grounds, workshops, buildings, yards and other property, rolling stock and appurtenances required and used for the construction and working thereof, and the capital stock of the Company, shall be for ever free from taxation by the Dominion, or by any Province hereafter to be established, or by any Municipal Corporation therein; and the lands of the Company, in the North-West Territories, untl they are either sold or occupied, shall also be free from such

taxation for 20 years after the grant thereof from the Crown. . . .

SCHEDULE A, REFERRED TO IN THE FOREGOING CONTRACT

. . . 16. The Company may construct, maintain and work a continuous telegraph line and telephone lines throughout and along the whole line of the Canadian Pacific Railway, or any part thereof, and may also construct or acquire by purchase, lease or otherwise, any other line or lines of telegraph connecting with the line so to be constructed along the line of the said railway, and may undertake the transmission of messages for the public by any such line or lines of telegraph or telephone, and collect tolls for so doing; or may lease such line or lines of telegraph or telephone, or any portion thereof; . . .

20. The limit to the reduction of tolls by the Parliament of Canada provided for by the eleventh sub-section of the 17th section of "The Consolidated Railway Act, 1879," respecting TOLLS, is hereby extended, so that such reduction may be to such an extent that such tolls when reduced shall not produce less than ten per cent. per annum profit on the capital actually expended in the construction of the railway, instead of not less than fifteen per cent. per annum profit, as provided by the said sub-section; . . .

167. THE PRIME MINISTER DEFENDS THE CPR CHARTER

House of Commons *Debates* (January 17, 1881), 493-4.

Sir John A. Macdonald.

We desire, the country desires, that the road, when built, should be a Canadian road; the main channel for Canadian traffic for the carriage of the treasures and traffic of the west to the seaboard through Canada. So far as we can, we shall not allow it to be built for the benefit of the United States lines. . . . We believe it will carry freight as cheaply and satisfy the wants of the country as fairly as any American railway. But, Sir, we desire to have the trade kept on our own side—that not one of the trains that passes over the Canadian Pacific Railway will run into the United States if we can help it, but may, instead, pass through our own country, that we may build up Montreal, Quebec, Toronto, Halifax and St. John by means of one great Canadian line, carrying as much traffic as possible by the course of trade through our own country. I do not mean to say we can prevent cheaper channels being opened. There is nothing to prevent other railroads running across the continent through our own country. Our Dominion is as big as all Europe, and we might as well say that the railways running from Paris to Moscow might supply the wants of all Europe as that this railway might supply the wants of the whole North-West. There will be room for as many railways in that country by-and-bye as there are in Europe; and if there be any attempt—the attempt would be futile—on the part of the Canadian Pacific Railway to impose excessive prices and rates, it is folly that would soon be exposed by the construction of rival lines east and west, which would open up our country in all directions and prove amply sufficient to prevent the possibility of a monopoly which has been made such a bugbear of by hon. gentlemen opposite. . . . Sir, it was essentially as a matter of precaution, a matter of necessity, and a matter of self-defence, that we provided that this road should not be depleted of its traffic in the manner which I have mentioned. That road shall be allowed fair play for twenty years from now, and only ten years after construction; and that it should be protected from the chance of being robbed of all the profits, robbed of all the gain, the legitimate gain, which the Company expects to get from this enterprise, and the employment of their capital. This was done only to protect them for the first ten years of their infant traffic. We know perfectly well, it will take many years before that country is filled up with a large population, and the first ten years will be most unprofitable; we know perfectly well that it will require all the exertion, and all the skill, and all the management of the Company to make the eastern and western sections of this road fully compensate them, and fairly compensate them for their responsibility, and for their expenditure during these ten years. In order to give them a chance, we have provided that the Dominion Parliament—mind you the Dominion Parliament: we cannot check any other Parliament; we cannot check Ontario, we cannot check Manitoba—shall for the first ten years after the construction of the road, give their own road into which they are putting so much money and so much land, a fair chance of existence. . . .

168. THE LEADER OF THE OPPOSITION CONDEMNS THE CPR CHARTER

House of Commons *Debates* (January 18, 1881), 507-8, 511-13.

Mr. Blake. Now what does this railway monopoly mean? What does this freedom from competition for the through trade of the North-West really mean? I say that although this subject has been discussed at some length and from various points of view, the public mind and this House has not yet grasped the full significance of that part of the business. I regard it as by far the most serious question of all. I regard it as infinitely surpassing in seriousness all the other questions before us in connection with this matter. I have proved to you what the gentlemen to whom you are now about to entrust, if you do entrust them with the future of the North-West, to whom you are about to award this monopoly power, do with that monopoly which they now have. I have proved to you what they do with the single talent with which they are entrusted, and you may depend upon it they will make usury of the ten talents if you please to give it to them, and will be in that respect faithful servants, but not to you Sir, but to themselves. I have shown you that their rates on the St. Paul and Manitoba are monopoly rates; I have shown you that their rates for wheat are between five and six times the competitive rates charged on railways south of St. Paul, or at any rate on the series of railways between Montreal and St. Paul. I have shown you as to other goods—mixed goods, similar results; as with respect to agricultural implements upon which I gave freight quotations. I have proved to you that the way these gentlemen use their power on the 390 miles they have got, as an avenue or gateway to the North-West, is to charge between five and six times the rates of railways to the South. It is not unreasonable to say that a somewhat high rate may be allowed in respect to the smaller traffic, though I believe that that hardly applies to the traffic as extensive as that which even the St. Paul and Manitoba Railway has. But if you do allow extra for a smaller traffic, still the surplus, after making an allowance say of one-half the additional rate, is enormous. It amounts to paying them one-and-a-half rates, and afterwards for the transport of one bushel of wheat, paying them 25 cents per bushel extra beyond the rate and a half. Now what does this mean? That a toll shall be taken to the tune of 25 cents a bushel beyond an ample compensation for the transport of wheat....

... I am, therefore, entitled to say that the men to whom you are giving the power to keep closed the avenues of the North-West, who have at present control of those avenues, who are using that control as I have pointed out, will continue to use it in a manner in which they are now using it. But that is not all, because the people of the North-West must import as well as export, and they must pay freight on their imports as well as their exports. We know quite well that there are, among the imports which will come into that country, goods which are charged for at much higher rates by the railway companies. We know, also, from what I have informed the House as to agricultural implements, that somewhere about the same proportion of extra rates, of monopoly rates, of toll, tax, duty, imports, in addition to a fair charge for transportation, is levied by the St. Paul and Manitoba Railway, I say it is a moderate estimate to double what I have estimated as the rent for the wheat lands in ten years, as the toll, or rent, or charge, that they will put upon the imports of the North-West. I say it is a low calculation that the monopoly will be worth $10,000,000 a year to this Company in ten years, if the North West be one-half at that time what you now depict.... You give them the south-ward gate to Pembina, you give them the eastward gate to Thunder Bay, you give them control of both gates, and you allow them to put up the bars, and to charge such a toll as will just leave it worth a man's while to live in that country and to raise wheat and buy goods.... The views of hon. gentlemen opposite with reference to our North-West seem to me of the gloomiest character. They say, first of all, when you want to get an emigrant into that country, the only way you can do it is to practically blindfold him; because if you let him see or get within 100 miles of the American frontier he will be quite sure to go to the United States. After you have blindfolded him and settled him in the North West, what is the present phase of the Government policy? They say, if you intend to keep him in our country, you have got to fetter him, and if you wish to keep his trade you must also fetter his trade; if you build the railway close to the boundary both himself and his trade will go to Dakota and Minnesota and stay there too. If I thought that the future of the North-West depended on this drastic application, upon this compulsion, this forcing, upon this insisting upon particular measures, and lines and routes of railway, I should have very little hope in that future. My own belief is that if people do not want that country, they will not go there—that if they do not like it they will not stay there, and if they do not like the avenues of trade, they will seek a place where it is freer; and my own opinion is that you will accomplish nothing by the restriction and constructive process you propose to apply. . . . Then the contract provides that the land grant shall be exempt from taxation for twenty years, unless sold or occupied from the date of the grant. The money gain to the Company is enormous, there can be no doubt about that. There can be no doubt that the burdens which this Company are freed from are most serious. Hon. gentlemen opposite have said so. They have said they could not use this land grant otherwise, that nobody would buy if they supposed the Syndicate was to be subjected to the same taxes as the rest of the world. They get the choice of land and they are not to pay the same taxes as the rest of the community. Why should they not? Is it because they get a large profit? Because they are getting altogether four prices for building the prairie section, that therefore they are to be untaxed and free? Then the indirect loss is still greater by this mode of settlement, by the burdens it imposes on the adjoining settlers for the benefit of the railway company itself, by the imposition of double taxes on those who go in for the benefit of this great corporation. I do not know of anything that will more interfere with the development of the North-West than this clause of exemption from taxation. Will you free the lands, or will you make them subject to taxation? Will you give the Company the benefit of the exemption from taxation, or will you let the lands be subject to taxation, and let the progress of the North-West country be advanced by those lands, like other lands being subject to taxation? . . .

169. THE CPR ADOPTS THE SOUTHERN ROUTE

John Macoun, *The Autobiography of John Macoun, M.A. Canadian Explorer and Naturalist 1831-1920* (Ottawa, 1922), pp. 184-5.

In due course, I reached St. Paul and met the "Syndicate,"* with their engineer, who had charge of the railroad end. We sat in Mr. Hill's office at a round table with maps spread out and, amongst others, there were two gentlemen from Montreal, members of the "Syndicate". The maps that were spread on the table showed me that, at this time, the surveys had been extended beyond Moose Jaw and they had already located the road to that point, which was four hundred and four miles from Winnipeg. At this time, there was no

---

*[The promoters and directors of the CPR, which had just received its federal charter. This meeting took place in the late spring of 1881.]

decision made by them as to what pass the railroad should take. They were prepared to go to the north-west to the Yellow Head, or west, to the Bow River, as the "Syndicate" would decide. The engineer showed them that he had been stopped by the South Saskatchewan, because its banks were very high and they were of such nature that they were liable to crumble and wash away at any time. As we talked, I told them my experiences of the year before and told them of the easy road that could be made from Moose Jaw, west to Seven Persons Coulee (near Medicine Hat), and I told them of looking up the Bow River Pass two years before and seeing a wide open valley. I told them, also, that there were at least four hundred miles from Moose Jaw, where there were no trees and scarcely a shrub, and I was asked by the engineer where they could get the ties. I told him at once that was not my business, it was his. After some more discussion, Hill raised his hands and struck the table with great force and said: "Gentlemen, we will cross the prairie and go by the Bow Pass, [the Kicking Horse Pass], if we can get that way." He immediately gave his reasons for his assertion; he said: "I am engaged in the forwarding business and I find that there is money in it for all those who realize its value. If we build this road across the prairie, we will carry every pound of supplies that the settlers want and we will carry every pound of produce that the settlers wish to sell, so that we will have freight both ways." (Years after this, Mr. Fleming told me that for good or for evil, I had sent the road into the Bow River Pass.)

170. THE EFFECTS OF THE SOUTHERN ROUTE ON PRAIRIE SETTLEMENT

The Globe (Toronto), March 3, 1883.

A CONSEQUENCE OF THE DIVERSION OF THE C.P.R.

As already announced, the Canadian Pacific Company has declined to receive more than 5,000,000 acres out of the 11,000,000 in the odd-numbered sections in the forty mile belt between Winnipeg and Fort Calgary; and the fact of this declination has received all the publicity which a Government return can give it.

This is a most unfortunate occurrence for the country, and all the damage that will ensue from it is the direct consequence of the gross blunder made by the Dominion Government two years ago when the southern diversion of the main line was sanctioned.* Mr. Mackenzie's Government made a thorough exploration of the country. The result of years of careful investigation by the best engineering talent was that a route recommended by Sandford Fleming, north of the present main line, was adopted. This route traversed the greatest possible quantity of our most fertile land. For purposes which are only now

---

*[The change of route was sanctioned by legislation passed by Parliament in April 1882.]

unfolding themselves, the C.P. Company chose to throw away all the results of Mr. Fleming's laborious explorations. Instead of taking their line through the best of the Fertile Belt, they brought it as far south as they could. Instead of taking the Yellowhead Pass, they aimed for the Kicking Horse, through which it is absolutely certain no such first-class line as that projected by Mr. Fleming can be driven. The present Government, as if in duty bound, assented to this diversion—and what are the consequences?

The first of the consequences is to be recognized in the Company's refusing to accept one-half of the land in the railway belt. The next is, that in order to make up for the deficiency thus created the Company has gobbled up every odd-numbered section in the southern part of the old Province of Manitoba, and in the belt south of the railway and west of Manitoba. It has become inevitable that whatever other tract the Company asks for must be given to it. The object of the Company will of course be to locate as much of its land as possible in the eastern part of the North-West. From present appearances, nearly twenty millions of the twenty-five millions of acres will be thus located.

Worse than everything else is the fact that the Company's public refusal to take more than 5,000,000 acres along the main line goes forth to the world as a serious and unnecessary hindrance to all efforts for the promotion of settlement. Intending immigrants will surely put the worst construction possible on the matter. It will be impossible to explain to their satisfaction the objects of the Canadian Pacific Company in locating its main line through an inferior section instead of through the best land. They will certainly fail to recognize that the Canadian Pacific was extremely anxious to get its line far to the southward in order that no competitor could come between it and the frontier.

171. MANITOBA ASKS OTTAWA TO TERMINATE THE CPR MONOPOLY

Canada, Department of Justice, *Correspondence, Reports of the Minister of Justice and Orders in Council Upon the Subject of Dominion and Provincial Legislation 1867-1895* (Ottawa, 1896), pp. 860-1, 864-8.

Petition of Executive Council of Manitoba to Her Majesty the Queen To Her Most Excellent Majesty in Council [1887]: . . .

12. That after the passing of said Canadian Pacific Railway Act the legislature of the province did, according to its undoubted right (as hereinbefore referred to) by Acts of said legislature, charter divers railway companies for the purpose of constructing, maintaining and operating lines of railway wholly situate within the province as before defined, yet all of such Acts as chartered a line of railway to be constructed or operated to any point within fifteen miles of the international boundary line have been disallowed and vetoed by the Governor General of Canada in Council, and as the said Canadian Pacific

Railway was then incomplete, such disallowance was submitted to rather than in any way impede the completion and rendering permanent of the Canadian Pacific Railway, the same being a national highway.

13. That the said Canadian Pacific Railway has been completed for upwards of 18 months, and has become permanent and probably the strongest railway corporation on this continent.

14. That the province of Manitoba is separated from the markets of Eastern Canada by a distance of from 1,200 to 1,400 miles, and the province has only two outlets, namely, one north of the chain of lakes by way of the main line of the Canadian Pacific Railway, *via* Thunder Bay, and the other south of Lakes Superior and Huron, by way of branches of the Canadian Pacific Railway to Gretna and Emerson, and thence by the St. Paul, Minneapolis and Manitoba Railway, south and east, with which last mentioned railway the Canadian Pacific Railway is in close alliance, and consequently no relief can be expected therefrom.

15. That there is no railway competition in the province, the Canadian Pacific Railway Company having a monopoly of the carrying trade of this province.

16. That the depression and discontent arising from lack of railway competition have become so great throughout the entire province that the population almost unanimously demand that railway competition must be procured by the construction of an independent line of railway running from Winnipeg (the capital city of the province) to the southern limit of Manitoba within the province, as defined in "The Manitoba Act," where freight can be transferred to an independent line of railway and thus competition procured.

17. That through an interview had with the Honourable Thomas White, then and now Minister of the Interior, on the 4th of March, A.D. 1887, in the city of Winnipeg, which is reported in the *Daily Manitoban* of the 5th of March as follows:—

"A deputation of representative Conservative citizens waited on Hon. Thomas White, Minister of the Interior, at the Dominion Lands Office, yesterday afternoon, and had a conference with him on the question of disallowance. Among the gentlemen composing the deputation were, G.F. Galt, R.J. Whitla, F.B. Robertson, W.B. Scarth, M.P., E.P. Leacock, M.P.P., . . .

"Mr. Scarth introduced the deputation to Mr. White, and in doing so urged the discontinuance of the government's disallowance policy, and dwelt strongly on the fact that he had been elected on a pledge to vote against the government on this question.

"A desultory conversation then ensued, during which the sentiments of the deputation were expressed clearly to Mr. White. Mr. Whitla and Mr. Robertson were the principal spokesmen, and they pointed out how highly beneficial it would be to have competing lines of railway running in the country, that a more rapid development of the country would follow, that it would cause a confidence among the people, and give a renewed impetus to the various industries of the country.

"All present were agreed that the time had arrived for the abolishment of disallowance within the old boundaries of Manitoba." . . .

30. And that by reason of the said policy of disallowance of provincial railway charters, all classes of our people have suffered loss; distrust has been created where trust and confidence should have been inspired; trade and commerce have been mischievously unsettled and disturbed; immigration has been retarded; the progress of the province has been seriously checked, and our people feel that, in being deprived of their undoubted rights under the British North America Act, they have not the full freedom of British subjects.

Your memorialists would therefore respectfully pray: That they may be heard before your Majesty in Council through the Honourable John Norquay, First Minister and Provincial Secretary; the Honourable C.E. Hamilton, Attorney General of the province of Manitoba, and such Counsel as may be retained, to further explain the injurious effects of such interference with the legislative powers of the province, and that an early day be appointed for such hearing; and further, that the practice of disallowing acts clearly within the power of the local legislature may be discontinued; and that in the future the province may be allowed to exercise in this respect her constitutional rights.

And for such further or other relief as your memorialists may appear entitled to. And as in duty bound will ever pray.

Signed on behalf of the Executive Council of the province of Manitoba,

J. NORQUAY,
President of Executive Council.

172. FARMER SUPPORT FOR THE HUDSON BAY RAILWAY PROJECT

House of Commons *Debates* (February 11, 1884), 203-4.

Mr. ROYAL, in moving that a Select Committee be appointed . . . to take into consideration the question of the navigation of Hudson Bay; with power to send for persons, papers and reports, said: Every hon. member of this House is aware of the agitation that has been going on for some time in the Province of Manitoba with respect to the navigation of the Hudson Bay. This agitation arose in October last, when the farmers of Manitoba, after the frost of September, saw their grain run down in price by a combination of millers. After discussing many questions in connection with their grievances, or so-called grievances, it seemed to be the general opinion that the best way to escape what was called the monopoly of freights of the Canadian Pacific Railway would be to build a railway from Winnipeg to the Hudson Bay. This agitation led to a large meeting called lately in Winnipeg at which speeches were made and resolutions carried, embodying the strong opinion of all present in favour of the construction of this road.* The agitation also extended south of our own borders. The farmers of Dakota and Minnesota, as well as the farmers west of those States, had stronger grievances than ours, and at the Farmers' Convention held at Grand Fort a few weeks ago, which was attended by delegates from Manitoba, the project of constructing the Hudson Bay Railway was discussed. There was but one feeling on the subject, and that was a feeling of enthusiasm in favour of the project. I believe it was there said that if its feasibility was established not only would the Manitoba and South Western draw every bushel of wheat grown as far as three hundred miles south of Winnipeg, but would also bring into our border the wheat grown in some of the western States of the Union. This question should be ventilated by this House and an authoritative decision respecting it obtained through the formation of a Committee such as the one I propose. My object in having this Committee formed is to get from the most authentic sources all possible information respecting the navigation of the Hudson Bay. It is my object to bring before this Committee any persons who may have records of importance respecting the navigation of Hudson Bay. Of its navigability there is no question. The only question is during what period of the year it is navigable. Upon that question there is a great diversity of opinion: some say that the immense icebergs and the peculiarity of the tides will be a permanent obstacle to the establishment of any permanent communication by sea between ports in the Hudson Bay and the seaports in Europe. On the other hand, it is asserted that from 1610 . . . ships have navigated it every year according to reports furnished by the Hudson Bay Company employees. This would tend to establish that there is at least a period in the year during which the waters of the bay are just as safe for navigation as the waters of the Gulf of St. Lawrence. . . .

. . . the cause of the agitation that has been going on in the North-West with reference to this question is the fact that we are wheat producers; that we occupy the centre of North America; are therefore very far removed from the sea-board; and that we are obliged to seek the best outlet that will enable us to reach the market the most quickly and the most cheaply; and, if the navigation of the Hudson Bay, that is to say, if the period during which the waters of the Hudson Bay are open, is established to be three or four or perhaps five months, then the farmers in the North-West will benefit on the rates of freight on the whole distance so economized, as between the port of Churchill and Liverpool and between Liverpool and Montreal. Let me give you some figures, and I will conclude these few remarks. The distance between Winnipeg and Churchill is about 630 miles. By railway route it will very likely be some 710 miles. From Churchill to Hudson Straits is 650 miles, the Straits 450 miles; and from the Hudson Straits to Liverpool, 1,830 miles. The whole distance is then 2,930. From Montreal to Liverpool the distance is 2,765

---

*This is a reference to the convention of the Manitoba and North West Farmers' Protective Union, held in Winnipeg on December 19 and 20, 1883.

miles.... The exports of grain by Montreal last year were something like 10,498,265 bushels, that is to say 5,798,496 bushels of wheat, ... In 1881, the exports of grain reached the figure of nearly 15,000,000; in 1880, it was over 23,000,000, in 1879, 19,000,000; in 1878, 16,000,000. Now, to show how much, if the possibility of the project is once established, the farmer of the North-West will gain by the saving of such a distance, I will give you the rate of transport. A bushel of wheat from Winnipeg to Montreal, according to summer rates, costs 28 cents; according to winter rates, 49 cents; from Winnipeg to Liverpool *via* Montreal, a bushel of wheat by the summer rate 38 cents, and by the winter 59 cents. Now, Sir, according to the distances I have given, if the carriage of a bushel of wheat from Churchill to Liverpool will cost say—from Winnipeg to Churchill, about 15 cents, and from Churchill to Liverpool, 10 cents—in all 25 cents—you will see what a saving of money farmers in the North-West will be able to make by having such a route—if, of course, the feasibility of the project turns out to be assured. Now, Sir, the average price of wheat in Montreal, in 1882, was $1.33 per bushel. This price, of course, was governed by the price in Liverpool, and if we can save fifteen or twenty cents a bushel in the transportation to Liverpool through Hudson Bay, the farmer will, of course, obtain just that much more for his wheat....

173. FEDERAL AID FOR THE CALGARY AND EDMONTON RAILWAY

House of Commons *Debates* (May 5, 1890), 4419-21.

Sir John A. Macdonald moved that the House resolve itself into Committee on resolution ... respecting the proposed contract of the Calgary and Edmonton Railway Company.... This resolution is for the purpose of giving ... pecuniary aid ... [similar to that which was given to] the Qu'Appelle, Long Lake and Prince Albert Railway.... The other great line which the Government, and I hope Parliament, will see to be equally important is the line connecting Calgary and Edmonton. The House knows that is the great ranching country. It is at present one of the most favoured localities in the great North-West for immigration, and for the investment of capital in cattle-raising and other industries. The necessity of a railway in that region has long been admitted by Parliament, but that district has been singularly unfortunate in regard to securing railway accommodation.... When that country was almost in despair, the same parties who raised the money to build the Qu'Appelle and the Prince Albert roads, and the same contractors, agreed to build a road from Calgary to a point near Edmonton, and also to build from Calgary to the frontier. The $80,000 a year subsidy which we propose to give, is applicable only to the line between Calgary and Edmonton; that is the purely Canadian portion of it, and the company is to earn [it] for doing Government work, in the same way as the other roads. They propose to commence the road next year and to complete it in 1893. While they stipulate this period for commencement and completion, they intend to finish it much before that period, as they have done in the case of the Qu'Appelle road. . . . They have made arrangements, also, with the Canadian Pacific Railway, similar to those made between the Canadian Pacific Railway and the Qu'Appelle Railway, that is, the Canadian Pacific Railway undertakes to run the line, furnish the rolling stock, doing all the work of the railway, in fact, for six years from the time of the completion of the road, when it is handed over to them.

174. A CALGARY VIEW OF THE CALGARY AND EDMONTON RAILWAY

The Calgary *Herald*, July 22, 1890.

CALGARY

The building of the Calgary and Edmonton railway will make our town the most important railway centre, now existent, or that ever will be, in Canada west of Winnipeg. It will aid greatly in making Calgary the most important distributing and manufacturing point west of Toronto, bar none. This railway completed from the Athabasca country in the north to Montana in the south, Calgary will be in a position with the assistance of the necessary capital, to reach out east, west, north and south many hundreds of miles on every side and to carry its trade into every settlement and hamlet in prairie, mountain or woodland in all this vast territory,—a country larger than all Europe. The problem for our merchants and people now is how to bring about the early settlement of this tributary country, and every thought and act of theirs for years to come should be devoted to this question of questions.

175. AN EDMONTON VIEW OF THE CALGARY AND EDMONTON RAILWAY

Edmonton *Bulletin*, July 18, 1891.

THE TERMINUS

The survey of the town site at the terminus of the C. & E. line on the south side is in progress. . . .

Regarding the prospects of the railway town site and its probable effect upon the town of Edmonton, there is not any very great difference of opinion among people acquainted with the country. . . . Even if there were no town established on the north bank of the river, the fact that four-fifths of the settlement and nine-tenths of the trade of the district is on the north side would naturally tend to establish business on this side. But when there is an old and well established town on the north side, there is no good reason why it should not continue to grow and prosper even during the few years that are likely to elapse before the railway crosses the river in its future inevitable extensions northward and westward.

But no matter how great the confidence of the citizens of Edmonton in the standing of their town it would be altogether unwise for them to adopt a do-nothing policy. The influence of the C. & E. company will undoubtedly be used in favor of their own town site, and their influence—wealthy and astute business men as they are—may count for a great deal. There is no doubt that their interest lies in bringing as much of the business of the district as possible to their own town site to increase the value of their lots, and as little that they will use every means to this end, no matter how disastrous such a result might be to the people whose business and investments are in this town. On the other hand the interests of the citizens of Edmonton are not as opposed to the interests of the railway company. The nearness of the station is a great convenience, which has not cost the people of this town a cent. The building up of legitimate business on the south side means an addition of so much to the general wealth of the district and country, and assures all the more the permanence of this point as the trade centre of the vast regions to the north and west. The only point at which there is any necessary clashing of interests is, if the railway company attempts to use its private influence to secure undue advantages in the location of the public offices or the construction of public works of any kind that would better serve the public interests by being located on the north side. Outside this point the only jealousy that need be shown on the part of the citizens of Edmonton towards the new town site is the jealously [sic] to excel in everything that makes a town attractive as a place of business, a place of residence or a place of investment.

176. A PRAIRIE LIBERAL CRITICIZES THE CROW'S NEST PASS AGREEMENT

House of Commons *Debates* (June 18, 1897), 4558-9, 4564-5.

Mr. OLIVER. The building of this road was expected to mark a turning point in the affairs of the west. This was the principal inducement persistently held out by the newspaper advocates of material aid towards its construction.

A great deal has been promised, and therefore a great deal is expected; much more than would be under ordinary circumstances.

In the west, as in all Canada, and there probably more than anywhere else in Canada, the question of transportation is the great question. That question was popularly supposed to be solved when the Canadian Pacific Railway bargain was made for a line from ocean to ocean. Whether it has been solved, every farmer, every producer, every dealer in the Dominion must answer that it has not. The question of transportation is not in this day a question of railway against no railway: it is a question of one railway against other railways more or less favourably circumstanced, more or less ably managed, and handled more or less with an eye to the interests of one or other section of the community, or this or that region or country. There is no question of "railway or no railway" in this country now, wherever the circumstances will justify construction. The question is one solely of rates and management, and it is because the railway rates have been distinctly against the west in particular and in general from the first that Manitoba and the Territories have shown so much less rapid progress than was expected when the Canadian Pacific Railway was first aided. It is for the same reason that the trade of eastern Canada with the west has not increased as was hoped at the same time, partly because the trade is not there to be done, and partly because, owing to the more advantageous railroad situation of the United States manufacturing and commercial cities of Chicago, St. Paul and Spokane, a large proportion of the trade of the west is done from those cities. And as the duties are lowered a proportionately greater share of the trade will be done by them, unless the rates of transportation between eastern and western Canada can be reduced to a level very far below what they have yet been. A general and adequate cheapening of the rates from eastern and throughout western Canada would develop the west, and enable the east to reap the sole outside profit of that development. A failure to bring down the rates to the point of 'final' effective competition with the lines of the United States is to fall short of the mark; is to continue to retard the west, and to divide its trade between eastern Canada and the United States, to the increasing advantage of the latter. . . .

Taking the reduced rates and other concessions for what they are claimed to be worth, they do not sufficiently meet the case as it exists in the necessity for lower freight rates, while the agreement regarding them makes the new Government a party to the continuance of the monopoly established by their predecessors. The chance of further reductions is shut out, as far as it can be shut out, by the fact that the Government, on the one hand, has decided against a policy of railway competition in the west, either by aiding competing lines or by Government construction, and, on the other hand, having paid three and a half millions of dollars to get certain reductions of freight rates, they will be bound to argue that the reductions secured are sufficient. The Canadian Pacific Railway will use their success in this case as a precedent for demanding further bonuses when the demand for further reduction becomes so pressing that it must be conceded. Under this arrangement, the Northwest settler is to be the decoy of the Canadian Pacific Railway; that company is to squeeze him until he squeals loud enough to compel the Government to come to his assistance, and then the Canadian Pacific Railway will demand the price of relaxing the freight-rate screw, either in the purchase of its lands or in aid to additional branches to still further strengthen its monopoly. Is it to be expected that the Northwest will prosper under such a policy, or that the trade of eastern Canada will expand by reason of the progress of the west under such circumstances, or is it to be wondered at that a spirit of thankfulness does not diffuse itself, like a broad and happy smile over the face of the North-west because of this bargain? The people of the west will, I believe, when they understand the position, object to being placed in it. They do not wish to stand before the people of Canada, everlastingly clamouring against existing conditions, which require the payment of Government money to relieve them from. When it is only the action of the Government in insisting on the maintenance of monopoly, and in paying Government money to secure that monopoly, that makes the conditions as they are and perpetuates them.

There is no doubt that, had a policy of competition in railway transportation been adopted by the Government, either by the encouragement of the introduction of other railway systems under like or more favourable restrictions than have been agreed to by the Canadian Pacific Railway, or by the construction of the line as a Government work, there would have been a much greater immediate reduction of rates than that now promised, and reasonable grounds to hope that they would be followed by further reductions, as circumstances required, without further cost to the Canadian people. The fact that the Government had thereby announced that it was against monopoly, would have inspired the confidence both of capital and labour throughout and in respect of the North-west, and substantial progress according to the conditions of the country would have followed.

177. THE EARLY DEVELOPMENT OF THE CANADIAN NORTHERN RAILWAY

D.B. Hanna, *Trains of Recollection* (Toronto, Macmillan, 1924), pp. 131, 134-9, 143, 151-2. Reprinted by permission of The Macmillan Company of Canada Limited.

... in the spring of 1896, the Lake Manitoba Railway and Canal Company began construction from Gladstone, on the Manitoba North Western, thirty-six-miles from Portage, to Lake Winnipegosis. I was made the first superintendent of the infant, and on the fifteenth of December, 1896, we began operation, and issued our first time-table on January 1, 1897, a copy of which hangs in my office in the Dominion Bank Building, Toronto. It began for me, indeed, a long avoidance of calm repose. . . .

The time table over my desk shows we operated one mixed train each way twice a week. We had running rights over the Manitoba North Western from Portage to Gladstone. The first winter, though the road was graded and rails were laid from Gladstone to Sifton, sixteen miles beyond Dauphin, we only operated beyond Dauphin once a week. To Dauphin we ran 100 miles, over our own track, and 36 miles over the North Western. . . .

"Service" was our motto. We had more stopping places to the ten miles, I think, than any railway in the world. Only a few of them were on the time table. Over most of the route, where settlement was beginning, we put down and took up passengers and way freight to suit our patrons' pleasure. . . .

Fundamentally the Lake Manitoba was a colonization road. During the first summer of its construction the general election brought the Laurier Government to power. A month before we began regular service Attorney-General Sifton of Manitoba became Minister of the Interior, and responsible for immigration. In 1897 the work was done which resulted in the first considerable settlement of Galicians in the prairie country—they came into the territory northwesterly of Lake Manitoba.

Except the settlements of Mennonites between Winnipeg and the boundary, Manitoba had been almost entirely settled by Ontario and Old Country people, with the French-speaking Canadians numerous around St. Boniface, and in the Provencher district, east of Winnipeg. The advent of large numbers of people from southeast Europe was viewed with alarm by many excellent citizens; and there was much grumbling among the elect as the Galicians hove in sight.

I accompanied the first party which was destinated for Dauphin. They camped outside the town—not a very fashionable looking crowd, it is true. The women with handkerchiefs over their heads, their footwear made entirely for enduring ease, and their waistlines uncontrolled, deceived some onlookers as to their suitability for rearing Canadian citizens.

Pretty soon a deputation of townsmen waited upon Superintendent Hanna, with strong, straight intimation that by this unsolicited invasion a grave error in judgment had been committed, and a menace to the peace, order and good government of the realm introduced among a people who deserved a better fate. This threatened tide must be rolled back. And so on and so forth.

Superintendent Hanna reasoned with the deputation as well as he could, pointing out that these people had been attached to the soil for centuries; that they were accustomed to work, and not afraid of it; that their poverty was the best incentive to them to make good in a land where they would be free from some of the afflictions of their former country—compulsory military service, for instance.

The deputation went away as little satisfied with the prospects of this intrusion as they were when they came. The superintendent turned to more customary duties.

A couple of hours later the chiefs of the deputation returned to retract their objections to the Galicians. From shirts, and from stockings above the unfeminine-looking footgear, there had been brought forth enough cash to buy two thousand dollars' worth of supplies from Dauphin merchants; and faith and charity had begun to work up to lively hope among the stores that this was a mere shadow of things to come. The might of economics in social life never received a more vivid vindication than was furnished the superintendent on that day. . . .

So it came about that, in the session of 1901 the Manitoba Legislature passed an Act which transmogrified the Northern Pacific Manitoba feeders into Canadian Northern lines. In less than five years . . . we were hauling wheat from Swan River and Grand View, and from Brandon and Hartney, over our own lines into our own terminals at Winnipeg, and to Emerson, whence the Northern Pacific carried it to Duluth.

We could not deliver wheat to Port Arthur in 1901, but we did take part of that year's crop over our own lines to that port, for on January 1st, 1902, connection was completed at Bear Pass, a few miles east of Rainy Lake, and Manitoba had a juncture with Eastern Canada independent of the C.P.R. If the C.P.R. could have prevented it, Port Arthur never would have renewed its youth through the advent of the Canadian Northern. A fight was on, which never sacrificed official and personal courtesies, and never relaxed the vigilance of the senior, or restricted the pertinacity of the junior road.

The Canadian Northern, with a thousand miles of track through the best sections of Manitoba, and with immigration beginning to reach the West in a volume not approached since the feverish period of the foolish land boom, had passed almost unobserved by the public, from a local to an interprovincial proposition as to territory; and to an international factor as to finance.

THE PRAIRIE WEST, 1905

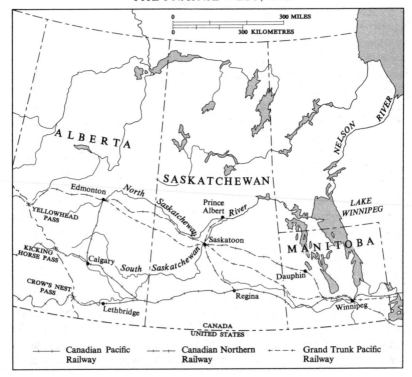

178. THE CANADIAN NORTHERN RAILWAY REACHES
EDMONTON

Edmonton *Bulletin*, November 25, 1905.

In the presence of thousands of citizens of Edmonton, and visitors from all parts of central Alberta, Hon. G.H.V. Bulyea, first Lieutenant-Governor of the Province of Alberta, at 2.15 yesterday afternoon, drove home with unerring blow the silver spike which held in place the first rail of the Canadian Northern Railway to reach the station in Edmonton. . . .

Mr. Bulyea said he had great pleasure in congratulating the officials of the C.N.R. upon their enterprise and industry. . . . The entrance of the C.N.R. would more closely connect Edmonton with the commercial centres of the east. A good many could recall the old days of the Red River cart, in which the trip from Winnipeg to Edmonton took some three months to make. The trip was now made over the C.N.R. in twenty-eight hours. One railway, even two railways were not enough to supply the needs and demands of this growing western country. Until there was a network of railways throughout the west there would always be room for enterprises such as Messrs. McKenzie and Mann had just completed. He hoped that this railway would prove as profitable to the company as it would for this section of the country. . . .

. . . His Worship then called for Hon. Frank Oliver, Minister of the Interior. . . . Mr. Oliver said they were all extremely glad to see the Canadian Northern enter the city today, after having waited so long for it, and he would like to call for three cheers for Dan Mann and Wm. McKenzie, the promoters of this great enterprise. The cheers were heartily given. This was a time, Mr. Oliver continued, for deeds, not words. The railway was a Canadian railway, and the company that built it a Canadian company. The land which would be developed by the C.N.R. was the richest agricultural country still unsettled in the world. The railway would benefit not only the company, but every citizen of Alberta, although the company no doubt had an eye to No. 1 in the building of it. The people were all proud of the railway and the company, and wished them luck. The speaker was glad to see that prominent citizens were present from various towns between Calgary and Edmonton. The railway would benefit every part of the Territories. This ceremony, however, meant something more than the mere building of a railroad. It meant the policy of this country was railroad competition and development. Workmen in every sphere of labor would reap benefits from this railway. . . .

The last speaker was Daniel D. Mann, Vice-President of the Canadian Northern Railway, and the man of the hour. Following is his address . . .

Other railways will come and, no doubt you will welcome them as you have welcomed us, but it is a great satisfaction to us that we are the pioneer road. Twenty-six years ago I was present at the celebration in Winnipeg when the first engine crossed the Red River on the ice bridge. I was also present at the beginning and finish of nearly all the railways in this Western country, but the completion of this road into Edmonton today is the most important event in my railway career. We are just as proud and glad to be here as you are to have the road to Edmonton. . . .

This address concluded the formalities of the occasion. The steel gang resumed work and hundreds of spectators during the afternoon followed their movements with a feeling not alone of curiosity but of interest.

179. THE PRIME MINISTER ENDORSES THE GRAND TRUNK PACIFIC PROJECT

House of Commons *Debates* (July 30, 1903), 7559-60.

Sir Wilfrid Laurier.

Exception has been taken to the immediate necessity of building such a road, exception has been taken to the policy which we have to suggest for the immediate construction of such a road; but as to the idea itself I have never heard a word of opposition, nor do I believe that such a word will be heard in the debate. The first of these objections, that is to the immediate construction of such a road, can be disposed of, I believe, with a single observation. To those who urge upon us the policy of to-morrow, and to-morrow, and to-morrow; to those who tell us, Wait, wait, wait; to those who advise us to pause, to consider, to reflect, to calculate and to inquire, our answer is: No, this is not a time for deliberation, this is a time for action. The flood of tide is upon us that leads on to fortune; if we let it pass it may never recur again. If we let it pass, the voyage of our national life, bright as it is to-day, will be bound in shallows. We cannot wait, because time does not wait; we cannot wait because, in these days of wonderful development, time lost is doubly lost; we cannot wait, because at this moment there is a transformation going on in the conditions of our national life which it would be folly to ignore and a crime to overlook; we cannot wait, because the prairies of the North-west, which for countless ages have been roamed over by the wild herds of the bison, or by the scarcely less wild tribes of red man, are now invaded from all sides by the white race. They came last year 100,000, and still they come in still greater numbers. Already they are at work opening the long dormant soil; already they are at work sowing, harvesting and reaping. We say that to-day it is the duty of the Canadian government, it is the duty of the Canadian parliament, it is the duty of all those who have a mandate from the people to attend to the needs and requirements of this fast growing country, to give heed to that condition of things. We consider that it is the duty of all those who sit within these walls by the will of the people, to provide immediate means whereby the products of those new settlers may find an exit to the ocean at the least possible cost, and whereby, likewise, a market may be found in this new region for those who toil in the forests, in the fields, in the mines, in the shops of the older provinces. Such is our duty; it is immediate and imperative. . . .

180. A PRAIRIE LIBERAL DEFENDS THE GRAND TRUNK PACIFIC PROJECT

House of Commons *Debates* (August 28, 1903), 10023, 10029.

Mr. Davis (Saskatchewan)

Now, as to the necessity of this road, as I said before, I do not think it needs any argument whatever. The people of that country have farmed on shares, so to speak, with the Canadian Pacific Railway Company for twenty-three years. Those hon. gentlemen who make speeches in this House on this question allude to the grand scheme that was put through by the Conservative party, and the hon. member for Marquette [W.J. Roche, Conservative] alluded to it as the pioneer of progress in that country. Pioneer of progress! Why, Sir, that scheme has had the effect of keeping that country back for twenty-three years, and I say here without fear of contradiction that if the advice of the Liberal party, when that scheme was put through this House, had been taken, and the road had been laid out as proposed by the Liberal party through the northern portion of that country, and built where this road is going at the present time, in place of the 300,000 people in that country, we would now have two or three millions; I say that without fear of contradiction. When this bargain was going through that these gentlemen talk so much about, the Liberal party then, as they are to-day, were well seized of the people's needs; and if their advice had been followed we would have seen a different state of things in the North-west, and there would not have been such a crying necessity for this road as there is at the present time. . . .

I have pointed out that we pay freight rates twice or three times as high as the freight rates that are paid in the east. Now we are getting people into that country and hon. gentlemen opposite are trying to take credit for it; they say that thanks to the policy of the Conservative party immigration is coming into the country. Think of it. For eighteen years, until 1896, the people there were on the verge of starvation and when we brought a few people into the country by one railway they dodged out by another. . . . And to-day they will tell you that they brought about prosperity that now prevails there. The hon. member for Marquette (Mr. Roche), for instance, in an eloquent peroration referred to the buffalo and the red men that once roamed on the western plains. If these gentlemen had been kept in power another seven years we would have had the red men back on the plains—the buffalo are extinct practically and could not be got on the plains but the red men would have possession. The other settlers would have been starved out. The idea of these gentlemen talking about their having assisted to bring about the prosperity we enjoy at the present time in western Canada. They had as much to do with it as they had in creating the universe. . . .

COMMUNICATIONS

181. POSTAL SERVICE IN MANITOBA IN 1870

Canada, *Sessional Papers* (1871), no. 20.

POSTAL ARRANGEMENTS

(No. 8)   Fort Garry, September 29th, 1870.
Sir,—I have the honor to report to you the state of Postal matters in this Province, and to request that you will take an early opportunity of bringing the same to the notice of the Postmaster General.

The entire Postal communication of the Province consists of a Mail from Pembina, down the Red River to Winnipeg, a distance of 65 miles; a Mail from Winnipeg further down the river to St. Andrews, about 14 miles; and a Mail from Winnipeg up the Assiniboine to Portage La Prairie, about 60 miles.

The two first named Mails are carried twice a week—the latter once. The total weekly travel is therefore four hundred and thirty-six miles, for which the weekly payment is about twenty-four dollars, or 5½ cents per mile.

There are four Postmasters, of whom two only are paid. . . .

The postage charged on each letter, is 1 d. sterling, per ½ oz.; on each newspaper, ½ d.

This fee is collected by the Postmasters and credited to the Provincial funds.

The carriage of the Mails was originally a private enterprise, the adventurer undertaking to carry the letters to Pembina for a fixed sum, each, in addition to the American postage.

The Government of Assiniboia afterwards assumed the duty, charging the postages above named.

Practically the business of the Department here is to carry the letters to Pembina and mail them there.

The party despatching letters that he wishes prepaid, not only pays here the 1d. Provincial Postage, but procures from the Postmaster here, American stamps, which are put upon the letters here, and thus when they are delivered at Pembina they are in a condition to pass through the American offices.

In this way, therefore, we pay double postage, our own and the American as well.

The Mails from this place are all sorted at Pembina.

That frontier town is the haunt of a number of disorderly persons, including some of those that were in arms here last winter. On the arrival of the Mails coming either way, the office is crowded with these people and the letters are open to their inspection.

The Postmaster is believed here to have repeatedly tampered with letters last winter, and seems to have taken an active part in the plots here.

A letter from him to Mr. Riel, of a very compromising character, was found among the papers left behind by the Provisional Government, and was, I think, transmitted to Ottawa. You can readily suppose, therefore, there is great doubt here as to the security of mail matter passing through the hands of this official.

The Mails arrive at Pembina at 7 o'clock p.m., on Tuesdays, but do not reach here till the evening of Thursday. They arrive at Pembina at 7 p.m., on Saturdays, but do not reach here till the evening of Monday, being thus forty-eight hours on the road from Pembina here, performing the sixty-five miles at the rate of about 1¼ miles an hour.

You can readily understand that such a state of Postal affairs could only exist in the primitive condition of things here, till lately, and cannot be tolerated now.

It seems to me that no time should be lost in having the whole matter put on a better footing.

In addition to the old population, we have now here seven hundred volunteers, a large number of whom receive letters and papers by mail.

In the month of August there were transmitted through the Winnipeg Office:—

	Letters	Newspapers
Per outgoing Mail	1,018	196
Per incoming Mail	960	1,375

In the first fortnight of September, from the 3rd to the 17th:—

	Letters	Newspapers
Per outgoing Mail	1,524	233
Per incoming Mail	1,050	1,536

This very large amount of Mail matter is entitled to better arrangements.

We should have the Mail from Canada for Red River made up and carried as a close mail, so as to save the delay of sorting at Pembina and the danger arising from the letters being open to examination by the people who crowd the office at Pembina.

We should have the same arrangements between Manitoba and the Post Office of the United States that exist in the other Provinces, so that a letter may be prepaid by a Canadian postage stamp, instead of having to pay our own postage and also that of the United States.

The postage prepaid in Canada or in the United States should exempt the letter from postage here. The arrangements for transmitting the Mail should be improved, and the time reduced from forty-eight hours to thirteen or fourteen.

As regards the transmission of the Mail at a higher rate of speed, that can easily be effected by allowing an increased rate of pay, and as it is of the highest importance that this should be done at once, I shall venture to take it on myself to act in anticipation of the arrival of an officer, and make arrangements for a few weeks at an advanced rate so as to insure the delivery within a more reasonable period.

I shall feel obliged if you will urge on the Postmaster General to give his early attention to these matters.

I have, &c.,

(Signed), Adams G. Archibald.

182. TELEGRAPH CONNECTION BETWEEN MANITOBA AND EASTERN CANADA

Canada, *Sessional Papers* (1872), no. 4, General Report of the Minister of Public Works for the Fiscal Year Ending June 30, 1871.

TELEGRAPH LINE

Under the authority of Orders in Council, approved by Your Excellency, in August, 1870, and May, 1871, an agreement was made with the North-Western Telegraph Company for the extension of their line, from the State of Minnesota to the capital of the Province of Manitoba. This work is proceeding rapidly, and before the present season has closed Fort Garry will be in telegraphic connexion with Ottawa.

The following are the conditions agreed upon to enable the Company to carry out the undertaking:—

1.—The North-Western Telegraph Company to build a one-wire line by September 1st, 1871, or before, if possible, connecting Fort Garry with the Company's present telegraph lines.

2.—The Company to maintain the line so constructed at its own cost for a period of three years from the date of the opening of the same.

3.—The Company to transmit official messages of the Dominion Government at a rebate of twenty-five per cent., on the regular tariff in force on the Company's lines in Minnesota, in cases where the messages contain not exceeding 100 words, and at a rebate of seventy-five per cent where messages exceed 100 words, said rebate applying also to all their lines.

4.—The Canadian Government to secure to the Company the right of property of line between Pembina and Fort Garry, and the right of doing business upon it free and without taxation. . . .

183. SURVEYING THE ROUTE OF THE DOMINION TELEGRAPH

Sandford Fleming, *Report on Surveys and Preliminary Operations on the Canadian Pacific Railway up to January 1877* (Ottawa, 1877), pp. 78-9.

Passing from the Mountain to the Prairie Region, the difficulties of route have been fortunately surmounted. From the eastern boundary of British Columbia to Red River, a distance of 1,043 miles, the line is practically established. On 787 miles the telegraph has been erected.

It was suggested, at an early period, that telegraphic communication should be secured along the entire line of railway. Apart from the advantages resulting from direct communication between British Columbia and other Provinces of the Dominion, it was held that the telegraph running continuously along the line of railway, would not only facilitate its construction, but favourably affect its cost, and at the same time largely assist in the settlement of the country. Accordingly, contracts were entered into for the erection of the telegraph as soon as the location of the line was established.

In addition to recommending that the telegraph should be the forerunner of the railway, the writer felt it his duty to point out;—that it was desirable to determine the sites for stations at intervals along the line; that the station sites could best be selected in advance of settlement, before municipal or private interests were created to interfere with the choice, and when engineering principles alone need be consulted. . . .

A correspondence took place setting forth the advantages to be derived from this policy, and recommending that, in laying out the land for occupation, a comprehensive system embracing these precautions should be carried out, in advance of settlement, as the present opportunity would never again occur.

These views were concurred in, and directions were given to act in accordance with them. Consequently, a reservation of land, one mile in width on each side of the railway, throughout the entire length, has been made, and sites for stations have been selected throughout the whole extent of the Prairie Region. These sites have been designated by names. Town plots will, as circumstances require, be laid out in their neighbourhood. The telegraph is already far advanced; and the railway will in due time follow. Each point will thus become a nucleus for population, as the work of construction progresses and as settlements advance. There will then be established at suitable intervals, and under circumstances the most favourable, a succession of villages, some of which, in time, will become cities, whose population will sustain the railway by the travel and traffic it will create.

184. THE CONSTRUCTION OF THE DOMINION TELEGRAPH

J.S. Macdonald, *The Dominion Telegraph* (Battleford, 1930), pp. 15-16, 19, 22-4, 34-5.

In July, 1874, the Government despatched a force of 500 mounted men westward from Dufferin, Manitoba, where they had been assembled, with the object of policing the North-West Territories—at that time a wide area in which strife between rum-selling "Whites" and horse-stealing Indians was a grave menace. In order to keep in touch with this force a telegraph line was a necessity. Apart from that it had been long felt desirable to link up the British

Settlements on the Pacific Coast with those in the East by telegraph and road. . . .

. . . In 1871 the Government had linked up Fort Garry with the American Telegraph System to give immediate connection with the West while the line from Fort William to Selkirk and Winnipeg was being built. In 1874 contracts were entered into to build various sections of a line from the Great Lakes to connect with the Telegraph System of British Columbia. The contracts included the clearance of a line 132 feet wide for the railway, and the formation of a trail or road for mules or horses the same to be made as soon as the location of the line was fixed. Accordingly, in 1874 a contract was entered into with Sifton, Glass & Fleming, of Winnipeg, to construct a telegraph line from Selkirk via the Narrows of Lake Manitoba—the route of the proposed railway—to Livingston, where the headquarters of the North West Mounted Police were to be placed, as it was thought, and where the first Government of the Territories were to be temporarily established. Livingston, or Swan River as it was generally known, was 36 miles north of the present town of Kamsack, twelve miles beyond Fort Pelly, the Hudson's Bay Company's post. . . . The telegraph office was called Pelly, after the Hudson's Bay Company's post. . . . The Sifton contract to build to Livingston was completed, and the line in operation by July 22nd, 1876. The average amount paid by the Government was $492.00 per mile for woodland areas and $189.00 for the prairies. $16.00 per mile per annum was given for maintenance and operation, together with the profits of the line. . . .

The contract for the second section of the line was awarded to Richard Fuller, of Hamilton, Ont., and extended from Swan River via Humboldt, at the junction of the Prince Albert and Battleford trails, crossing the South Saskatchewan at a point later known as Clark's Crossing, about 18 miles below where Saskatoon now stands, thence to Battleford and on to a point near where the Town of Leduc is built. To its terminus, the line followed the original survey of the Canadian Pacific Railway, which, keeping south of the Saskatchewan River, passed Edmonton by. At a later date the Canadian Northern Railway was built over practically the same route, but with Winnipeg as a starting point instead of Selkirk, and crossing the river to enter Edmonton. This western section of the Telegraph line was completed in November, 1876. . . .

No use was made of that portion of the line west of Battleford until 1877, when Mr. Fuller entered into a contract with James McKernan to maintain the line from a point 30 miles west of Battleford to its western terminus.* Mr. McKernan associated with him in this work his brother, Robert McKernan, who selected Grizzly Bear Coulee, about midway between Edmonton and Battleford, as his headquarters, while James McKernan settled at Hay Lakes, about 30 miles east of the western terminus of the line. No office was opened, but Mr. McKernan, being an operator, frequently sent and received messages,

---

*[Near the present city of Leduc, 15 miles (24 kilometres) south of Edmonton.]

chiefly for Government officials passing through the country, as also for the North-West Mounted Police, whose headquarters were Fort Saskatchewan. The first message transmitted was sent by Major Jarvis, Fort Saskatchewan, to Col. Walker, commanding at Battleford, November 20th, 1877. . . .

Edmonton was at that time little more than a Hudson's Bay Post with the addition of a number of free traders, but in 1878 the people of the village, feeling the need of telegraph connection, petitioned the Government to extend the line from its terminus to Edmonton, offering to defray the cost of extension if the Department would establish an office. The contractor, Mr. Fuller, offered to supply the necessary wire and other material free of charge. The offer was accepted, and, under the supervision of Mr. McKernan, the extension was made, the Hudson's Bay Company contributing the poles, and most of the labor. The line was completed on January 18th, 1879, and an office opened in a building opposite the Fort owned by Walters & Irvine, Mr. Taylor being the first operator. . . .

Upon completion of the line to Edmonton, the tariff was fixed by the contractors on the basis of $3.00 for ten words Edmonton to Winnipeg; $2.00 Battleford to Winnipeg, and $1.00 Edmonton to Battleford. The Press rate was half a cent per word, the Herald and later the Bulletin using the wire freely. . . .

In March, 1885, came the Rebellion, the causes of which have been dealt with by others and need not be gone into here. But it was the Rebellion which proved the incalculable value of the telegraph line and abundantly justified its construction. Without it the trouble could not possibly have been brought to an end during that year. Had there been no telegraph, I am satisfied that many additional bands of Indians would have joined those of their kinsmen who had gone on the warpath: For the Indians had the "Moccasin Telegraph", swift runners and horsemen, knowing every foot of the country, who carried the alarm from one reserve to another, always with boastful lies of great victories gained over the Whites. Without the wire, the condition of affairs throughout the whole northern country would have been absolutely unknown outside, for the Police were too few and too much occupied to establish a patrol to the newly-built railway to the south. Indeed, under the conditions, such an arrangement would have been impossible, and a chaotic state of affairs must have resulted. Police officers, Indian agents and missionaries did splendid work in pacifying and persuading the Indians of many reserves from rising, but lacking the information they received by way of the telegraph, their efforts would have availed but little. A knowledge of the fact that troops were on their way did more to keep the Indians on their reserves than all other influences combined. Indeed, had the rebels possessed a capable leader, the results might have been disastrous, in any case, for it would have been a comparatively easy matter to have cut and carried away sections of the wire, which would have put it out of operation until repaired—a work hazardous in the extreme. The wire was cut on a few occasions, leaving it on the ground, but these were ordinary breaks which were easily repaired by linemen who, however, took great chances of being ambushed. The Rebellion cost the country about 7 millions of dollars, but without the telegraph, it would have cost many times that sum, while the loss of life would have been infinitely greater. From a fairly complete knowledge of the conditions existing at the time, I am convinced that only individual Indians kept the peace from unselfish motives. And, considering the difficulties of the elders in restraining their young braves, for whom war spelt glory and the glittering promises of the rebel leaders, this is scarcely to be wondered at.

185. THE BELL TELEPHONE COMPANY IN MANITOBA

Manitoba Free Press, January 1, 1908.

The figures of the Bell Telephone Company in Manitoba form an interesting story of the growth of that company and also of the growth of the west. In 1900, after nineteen years of operation, there were 1850 subscribers in the province and 220 miles of long distance and rural lines; in 1905 there were 6,224 subscribers and 892 miles of long distance and rural lines. To-day [1908] there are more than 14,000 subscribers in the province and more than 2,500 miles of pole lines. . . . There are 100 local exchanges and large toll offices are maintained. There are 1,500 farmers connected with small exchanges whereby they can speak to any subscriber in any part of the province.

In Winnipeg there are 250 girls employed by the Bell company on the local and long distance exchanges and as accountants. . . .

The rates charged annually for the Bell telephones vary according to the size of the exchange with which the subscribers are connected. In Winnipeg the business rates are $50 and the residence $30; in Brandon the rates are $35 and $25; . . . and in such places as Carman, Carberry and Morden where there are from 50 to 100 subscribers on the local exchange and an equal number of rural subscribers the rates are $24 and $18. With the exception of the vicinity of Brandon and Portage la Prairie all the farmers in the province pay $24 for business telephones. The higher rates in these districts is charged because of the large exchanges to which the telephones are connected giving subscribers the use of the entire city exchange.

GUIDE TO FURTHER READING

In the general field of transportation history, the student should first consult the excellent comprehensive survey by G.P. de T. Glazebrook, *A History of Transportation in Canada*, 2nd ed. (Toronto, McClelland and Stewart, 1964). This study, first published in 1938, has been reprinted in a two-volume paperback edition; the second volume deals with the post-Confederation period.

The main transportation developments in the prairie west in the 1870s are discussed quite adequately in Pierre Berton, *The National Dream* (Toronto, McClelland and Stewart, 1970). For specific subjects the following works may be consulted. On the Dawson route see Lyn Harrington, 'The Dawson route' in *Canadian Geographical Journal*, September 1951, pp. 136-43. R.C. Russell, *The Carlton Trail*, 2nd ed. (Saskatoon, Prairie Books Service, 1971) is a thorough and informative account of the history of the Carlton Trail, with excerpts from contemporary observers. There is a good discussion of the Whoop-Up Trail (Fort Benton, Montana to Fort Macleod, North West Territories) in Paul F. Sharp, *Whoop-Up Country*, 2nd ed. (Norman, Oklahoma, University of Oklahoma Press, 1973). On the Red River cart consult Olive Knox, 'Red River Cart' in *The Beaver*, March 1942, pp. 39-43. For the York boat see R. Glover, 'York Boats' in *The Beaver*, March 1949, pp. 19-23. The beginnings of steamboat navigation on the Red River are discussed by Molly McFadden, 'Steamboats on the Red' in *The Beaver*, June 1950, pp. 31-3; September 1950, pp. 25-9. Bruce Peel, *Steamboats on the Saskatchewan* (Saskatoon, Prairie Books Service, 1971) is a comprehensive account of the development of steamboat navigation on the Saskatchewan River. There is a good discussion of the building of the Pembina branch in Heather Gilbert's biography of Lord Mount Stephen, *Awakening Continent* (Aberdeen, Aberdeen University Press, 1965). L.B. Irwin, *Pacific Railways and Nationalism in the Canadian-American Northwest, 1845-1873*, 2nd ed. (New York, Greenwood Publishers, 1968) has some material on the extension of the Northern Pacific Railroad to the Red River and its implications for railway development in the Canadian northwest.

There is a vast amount of secondary literature dealing with the CPR, much of it of limited value. The standard account of the company is still H.A. Innis, *A History of the Canadian Pacific Railway*, 2nd ed. (Toronto, University of Toronto Press, 1971). This is a thoroughly researched scholarly study that covers in detail all aspects of CPR construction and operation to 1921. A recent work that is quite useful is J.L. McDougall, *Canadian Pacific* (Montreal, McGill University Press, 1968). Although McDougall is often too sympathetic to the company's viewpoint, he does provide a succinct general account of the CPR from its inception to 1966. The most comprehensive treatment of the building of the CPR is the recent well-written study by Pierre Berton, *The Last Spike* (Toronto, McClelland and Stewart, 1971). The complex question of the reasons for the CPR's decision to change its route on the prairies in 1881 is examined in F.G. Roe, 'An Unsolved Problem of Canadian History' in *Canadian Historical Association Annual Report*, 1936, pp. 65-77. The explorations for a pass through the Selkirk range are discussed in Charles A. Shaw, *Tales of a Pioneer Surveyor* (Don Mills, Longmans Canada, 1970) and Thomas E. Wilson, *Trail Blazer of the Canadian Rockies* (Calgary, Glenbow-Alberta Institute, 1972). For a discussion of the agitation in Manitoba against the federal disallowance of provincial railway charters see W.L. Morton, *Manitoba: A History*, 2nd ed. (Toronto, University of Toronto Press, 1967). The two basic works on the federal government's railway land-subsidy policy are James B. Hedges, *The Federal Railway Land Subsidy Policy of Canada* (Cambridge, Massachusetts, Harvard University Press, 1934) and Chester Martin, *'Dominion Lands' Policy*, 2nd ed. edited by Lewis H. Thomas (Toronto, McClelland and Stewart, 1973). Hedges provides a thorough analysis of CPR land and colonization policies in *Building the Canadian West* (New York, Macmillan, 1938). For a discussion of the Crow's Nest Pass Agreement see McDougall, *Canadian Pacific* and A.W. Currie, 'Freight Rates on Grain in Western Canada' in *Canadian Historical Review*, vol. XXI (1940), pp. 40-55.

For information on railways other than the CPR in the period after 1885, the student should first consult G.R. Stevens, *Canadian National Railways*, vol. 2 (Toronto, Clarke, Irwin, 1962). For specific subjects the following works may then be consulted. There is a good account of the Hudson Bay Railway project in H.A. Fleming, *Canada's Arctic Outlet* (Berkeley, University of California Press, 1957). The more popular account by Grant MacEwan, *The Battle for the Bay* (Saskatoon, Western Producer Book Service, 1975) is also quite useful. The memoirs of D.B. Hanna, *Trains of Recollection* (Toronto, Macmillan, 1924) provide some interesting insights into the development of the Canadian Northern Railway; the author was the operating head of the company from its beginnings in 1896. For an excellent critical analysis of the Canadian Northern, see T.D. Regehr, 'The Canadian Northern Railway: The West's Own Product' in *Canadian Historical Review*, vol. LI (1970), pp. 177-87, and the same author's forthcoming book on this subject. On the Grand Trunk Pacific project, see A.W. Currie, *The Grand Trunk Railway of Canada* (Toronto, University of Toronto Press, 1957).

There is no general study that deals with the history of communications in Canada. However there are a few works that deal with certain aspects of this subject. William Smith, *The History of the Post Office in British North America 1639-1870* (Cambridge, Cambridge University Press, 1920) discusses the postal system in the northwest under Hudson's Bay Company rule, and gives a brief account of postal developments in Manitoba and the North West Territories from 1870 to 1914. On the telegraph consult J.S. Macdonald, *The Dominion Telegraph* (Canadian North-West Historical Society Publications, vol. I, no. VI, 1930). There is a good discussion of the development of the telephone in Alberta in the territorial period and the movement for public ownership of telephones in Tony Cashman, *Singing Wires* (Edmonton, The Alberta Government Telephones Commission, 1972). The development of the telephone in Manitoba is examined in Gilbert A. Muir, 'A History of the Telephone in Manitoba' in *Transactions of the Historical and Scientific Society of Manitoba*, Series III, no. 21 (1964-5), pp. 69-82.